Changing the Dinosaur's Spots

Changing the Dinosaur's Spots

The Battle to Reform UK Defence Acquisition

Bill Kincaid

With cartoons by Jim Potts

Foreword by Lord Robertson of Port Ellen

The Royal United Services Institute for Defence and Security Studies

RUSI Books

First Published in 2008

Published by RUSI Books
**The Royal United Services Institute for
Defence and Security Studies (RUSI)**
Whitehall, London, SW1A 2ET United Kingdom

www.rusi.org

**Changing the Dinosaur's Spots:
The Battle to Reform UK Defence Acquisition**

ISBN 0-85516-138-8

Edited by Rebecca Morgan and Adrian Johnson

Printed in Great Britain by Stephen Austin & Sons Ltd.

RUSI is a Registered Charity (No. 210639)

Acknowledgements

My previous *Dinosaur* books have been widely read and the last one – *Dinosaur in Permafrost* – has been in use at the Defence Academy for some years. It is now somewhat dated (it was published in 2002) and many people have been asking when I was going to write another. My stock reply was that I would consider doing so when there was something to write about. Lord Drayson's Defence Industrial Strategy, launched in December 2005, was that something, but it was not so much the Strategy but the implementation of it that had to be the subject. So time needed to pass before implementation could be initially assessed.

Much effort has gone into this implementation in many parts of MoD and industry, but how effective has it been? We can now see the direction it is taking and, despite the heroic efforts of many people, the MoD dinosaur's immune 'system' appears to be fighting back. The signs are that all is not well. If I can illustrate that with one example, it is the abandonment of the excellent aim to halve the over-long procurement cycle: only this month has this 50% aim been reduced to 'significantly shorter'. Who took fright?

The problem at this juncture for an author of a book, rather than a magazine article, is that so many people in MoD and industry are doing so much work that things can change relatively quickly (but often don't) making the choice of a publication date fraught with difficulty. Get it wrong and one or more of the author's arguments can appear out of date. The key is to keep abreast of what is happening. No easy task.

That task has been immeasurably eased by the many people who have advised and helped me over the last few months. First and foremost I must thank several members of the RUSI Acquisition Focus and, in particular, Sir Jeremy Blackham, John Weston, Tim Banfield, Bill Robins, Bob Barton, John Dowdy and Graham Jordan, who picked up many errors and weaknesses in the draft text and put me right. David Kirkpatrick was another who gave me so much of his time, not only with his specialist knowledge of costs, but in his logical examination of my arguments.

I am also extremely grateful to so many contributors to *RUSI Defence Systems* who have over the last three or four years built up a most impressive body of work on acquisition, and from whom I have taken so many snippets to illustrate my points.

Thanks, too, to my excellent editor, Rebecca Morgan, and to the RUSI Editorial staff, particularly Terence McNamee and Adrian Johnson, and to RUSI itself for agreeing to publish my thoughts.

Bill Kincaid
October 2008

Contents

Foreword

By Rt Hon Lord Robertson of Port Ellen KT GCMG honFRSE PC

When Labour was returned to power in 1997, I was proud to be appointed Secretary of State for Defence, one of the great offices of State. Although I was relatively new to defence having mainly specialised in foreign affairs, this was in many ways an advantage – I was an outsider with a clear mind. Right from the start, I was outraged to find that in many cases we were dealing with the same equipment problems that Labour defence ministers had been dealing with when they were last in power eighteen years before. Moreover, there appeared to be no one to blame.

The new government immediately called for a Strategic Defence Review, which I insisted would include a ruthless examination of how we could eliminate the huge cost overruns and delays that were all too common in the 1990s, and to improve value-for-money in defence procurement. We aimed to procure cheaper, faster, better. Of course, there was opposition to change – there always is – and I was asked if I really wanted to do this. But I was not going to be put off and insisted that we would do it, and do it properly.

So Smart Procurement was born. It was to be a comprehensive initiative. I was only interested in the results, not the process, as we had to get better at providing the right equipment at the right time in the right place. There had to be someone in charge from the beginning to the end of a project.

We made some early genuine progress with reorganisation, new procedures and cultural change, but then I left to take up the post of Secretary General of NATO. There I continued to crusade for the right capabilities at the right price – this time across the nineteen countries in the Alliance. Back in the UK, Lord Drayson later took the next step with his outstanding Defence Industrial Strategy in 2005, but a plan is just a plan and is useless without implementation. And implementation is exactly what is needed now.

Defence acquisition is a critical subject, not just because it takes a high proportion of the defence budget, but also because it must provide equipment that, in the necessary quantity and quality, gives the servicemen the best protection possible. We have to remember that lives are at stake. But let us be quite clear: there is unlikely to be more money for defence, so we will have to be absolutely definite about our priorities and spend our acquisition funds wisely, effectively and efficiently.

What should our priorities be? How do we make our funds go further? How do we safeguard our spending of public funds while getting first-rate equipment into the field much faster than we have traditionally done? These are difficult questions to answer, but we have to do so. This book is a valuable contribution to the ongoing debate that we must continue to engage in. Putting the difficulties into the 'too difficult' tray is not the answer.

21 October 2008

Chapter One

Acquisition Performance: Good or Bad?

Much has been written about defence equipment acquisition in the UK over the last two or three decades. Some of those words have been turned into action and some useful progress has been made, but many would say that, while some steps forward have undoubtedly been taken, they have been matched by almost as many steps backwards. Consider the following.

> *Despite the emphasis on realistic cost and timescale forecasting in the Smart Acquisition initiative of July 1998 and in the Enabling Acquisition Change report of June 2006 (and indeed in many earlier studies), the MoD still appears to be unable to generate either unbiased forecasts of project costs and timescales, or confidence limits on those forecasts which adequately reflect the risks involved.[1]*

> *Shortages of equipment were blamed yesterday for the deaths of British soldiers in Iraq and Afghanistan as two coroners in separate inquests made withering attacks on the Ministry of Defence ... Both inquests showed that an acute lack of equipment had played a part in the deaths ...[2]*

> *We need to enable a culture which is not merely tolerant of innovation but actively embraces it.[3]*

> *We haven't been as rigorous as we should have been with our equipment programmes to meet the strategic framework. There are things in that programme that we no longer need.[4]*

> *MoD has admitted that almost half of Britain's forces are unfit to be sent on operations because of equipment shortages.[5]*

The above are just a very small sample of the very many critical statements made over the last year or so that show poor acquisition

---

[1] Professor David Kirkpatrick, 'More spurious savings by the MoD', *Newsbrief*, (Volume 28, No. 1, RUSI, January 2008), page 4.
[2] Michael Evans, 'Coroners blame soldiers' deaths on an acute lack of equipment', *The Times*, 16 February 2008.
[3] Richard Maudslay, Chairman Dstl, 'UK Defence Research and Technology', UK Defence Forum, CP 64, March 2007.
[4] Sylvia Pfeiffer, Alex Barker, Stephen Fidler, 'Contracts at risk in crisis over budget', *Financial Times*, 28 April 2008.
[5] *The Times*, www.timesonline.co.uk, 18 November 2007.

management, the wrong culture, inadequate government funding and equipment shortages. Other statements are critical of time delays, uncaring politicians, cost overruns, 'flying coffins' and helicopters that cannot fly.

Sadly, the stories all have a basis of truth. Of course, not all acquisition is a disaster and there is much good news that, for goodness knows what reasons, MoD does not publicise, concentrating instead on spinning figures to make them look less bad and muzzling defence civilians and military officers. This last speaks volumes – if you are doing well, you do not need to stop people talking. The inescapable conclusion is that acquisition performance is poor. And that was the opinion of the MoD's Chief of Defence Procurement in May 2004 – that poor performance was 'endemic'.[6]

> The inescapable conclusion is that acquisition performance is poor

Does it matter? Yes. How important is it? It is important for two reasons. The first is that servicemen are putting their lives at risk in doing the bidding of politicians; in return those servicemen are entitled to the best possible care from those politicians. The second is that the nation spends around £35Bn per year on defence, of which something approaching 40% goes on equipment acquisition and support.

Examination of the first is outside the scope of this book, although it must be borne in mind throughout any discussion of costs, delays and obsolescence. The second, however, is central to any examination of acquisition. Recently there have been many calls for increased spending on defence but this is unlikely to materialise, at least in the necessary magnitude, in the foreseeable future. The Government likes to trumpet about recent increases in the defence budget, but the most recent – 1.5% each year for the next three years – actually represents a reduction because defence inflation continues to run at more than double the rate of national inflation. We need an increase in real-real terms – not a decrease.

---

[6] Sir Peter Spencer, Chief of Defence Procurement, Evidence to the House of Commons Defence Committee, 11 May 2004.

A Matter of Waste

But isn't £35Bn enough to do what the Services are asked to do? Many insiders and outsiders query what we are actually getting for our money. Lewis Page is one of them:

> *Much of the money supplied for the fighting people's support – that, for instance, used to purchase their equipment – tends to be squandered outright. The priority is not to obtain good equipment, or even to get value-for-money. It is, always, to provide well-paid civilian jobs … Many existing units are set up and equipped to fight enemies which do not and will not exist, or which could be dealt with by other means.*

There are two separate issues here but, if Lewis is correct, both waste a significant proportion of precious defence funds.

In the margins of a recent conference, I was talking to a senior military man in an important post in the MoD. We discussed the likely outcome of the recent planning round (PR 08) and he became more and more agitated about both the fixation on large, expensive programmes and the extreme overmanning in MoD. The first represents just an opinion – many others would see aircraft carriers and high-performance jets as essential. But the second is just one symptom of waste and MoD has now belatedly recognised this.

If we are to persuade politicians and the Treasury that the Armed Forces need more money, then it stands to reason that we need to reduce – better still eliminate – any waste in the defence budget. Where better to start than in procurement, with its cost overruns and delays? However, we should not start by doing what MoD does repeatedly when faced by an initiative that seeks improvement in acquisition output – overlaying yet more process and reorganisation on a system that already groans with them.

Of course it is not just in the UK that we waste acquisition funds. The US does too and Australian Defence Secretary Nick Warner has recently stated that excessive bureaucracy in procurement is leading to massive waste and that A$10Bn in savings will be sought.[7]

But citing weaknesses of other nations is not a valid reason for excusing our waste.

---

[7] *Sydney Morning Herald*, 10 June 2008.

Organisation, Process and Culture

While there was some good progress made in the implementation over the first two years of the 1998 Smart Procurement Initiative, it was not long before I repeatedly heard off-the-record remarks from Directors of Equipment Capability (DECs) and Integrated Project Team (IPT) leaders to the effect that they were 'drowning in process'. Over the last four years or so, such remarks dried up – not I suspect because 'process' had become less overweening, but because those at the sharp end of acquisition just got on with it and made the process-heavy system work as well as they could. Ominously, in the wake of new procedures introduced by the Defence Industrial Strategy (DIS), I am beginning to hear the same sort of remarks from those who have to make acquisition work.

> No two programmes are the same, nor are the processes by which each is best managed

No two programmes are the same, nor are the processes by which each is best managed. Yet, time and again, MoD fiddles with the processes and mandates a 'one size fits all' approach which has proved to be a serious hindrance to those in charge. Now those overmanned departments are at it again.

Let's stop flooding the practitioners with process and let them get on with the real work. If they are any good, they will work out their own answers. If they are not, they should be given the boot. We should allow leadership and initiative to thrive.

Why is leadership in MoD so noticeable by its absence? The answer is because middle managers are not able to exercise it. Why can't they exercise it? Because MoD culture is antipathetic to true accountability – the combination of responsibility and authority – and what is known as 'Mission Command'. There is very little power that IPT leaders can wield; they drown in process as their decisions are constantly neutered by others in the system, often by those without any responsibility for the outcome.

Changes to organisations and processes can be beneficial but in themselves may not improve delivery. A good leader will make any process or organisation work; a poor one will not make any work, while the mediocre one needs both organisation and processes to help him towards his goal.

It is culture that will make the real difference to delivery. You doubt that? Yet it has been demonstrated vividly in recent years by the rapid delivery of Urgent Operational Requirements (UORs) by MoD and industrial teams working closely together to deliver equipment to the front line in a timescale that continues to astound, given that such delivery continues year on year. Moreover, the two Pathfinder projects initiated by the DIS showed that a new culture could be achieved in a very short space of time and would have huge benefits. Other partnering arrangements flowing out of the DIS are also showing the benefits of changing culture. This is, of course, a change for both MoD and industry, and both benefit. But will this culture change become embedded right across the acquisition system? Not, I suspect, any time soon.

> Will this culture change become embedded right across the acquisition system?

Cost, Time and Agility

The National Audit Office (NAO) reports on MoD major projects have repeatedly shown huge cost overruns and long delays on many programmes. One reason for cost overruns is the so-called Conspiracy of Optimism[8] in which procurement costs are initially underestimated (often deliberately) thereby making it easier to get the programme into the Equipment Programme. Inevitably the costs rise substantially during the procurement cycle as reality is established.

But cost is also driven upwards by delays. In the world of Treasury accounting, it is held that delay makes the programme cheaper, which may be true in terms of the funding provided in the 10-year Equipment Plan, but in reality it is the opposite: partly because the higher defence inflation pushes up costs in 'real' terms, and partly because delay adds uncertainty and undermines commitment, thus adding more delay and yet more cost increases. Delay therefore makes programmes more expensive. Some years ago a US study looking at weapon systems procurement concluded that for every $1 deferred on an acquisition programme, costs in later years increased by approximately $2 (save $1

---

[8] The RUSI Acquisition Focus paper on the 'Conspiracy of Optimism' was first published in *RUSI Defence Systems* and is reproduced at Appendix 7–4.

now, spend $2 later). The MoD has begun to recognise this, but this gives rise to a strange anomaly: if deferral costs big money, why do we continue to delay projects to 'save' money?

This is relevant to the UK's 30-year effort to deliver the Future Rapid Effect System (FRES), the replacement for the FV430 and CVR(T) armoured vehicles – if we had not repeatedly deferred them, they would have come so much cheaper in the early 1990s, when we had three thriving armoured vehicle manufacturers in UK, and they would have been available for deployment in Iraq and Afghanistan with no need for the buys of interim vehicles.

Time is the more important. Most business people would agree that 'time is money'. Whitehall, however, acts as if time is of less importance than getting the process right – the reason cited being the need to safeguard the spending of public funds. While the latter is undoubtedly important, those charged with responsibility for this aspect do not seem to take into consideration the cost of delay. The financial civil servant may think that postponement of a decision where there is marginal doubt is a potential saving in expenditure, whereas the delay caused may well lead to huge cost increases.

Time cycles are also important if we are to become more agile in our procurement. In current Counter-Insurgency operations, the enemy often makes technology change work for them more quickly than we can take counter-measures. Technology is changing more and more rapidly and a procurement system that takes a decade or more to deliver is near useless in these conditions, with the result that we have to rely more and more heavily on UORs with all their imperfections.

> The delivery of UORs into the field is the one truly bright spot in acquisition performance

Despite these imperfections, the delivery of UORs into the field is the one truly bright spot in acquisition performance. This is just as well, for without the UORs, many of which are to take the place of delayed programmes (e.g. armoured vehicles), British Forces would be even harder pressed to do their job on operations.

UOR delivery shows what can be done by both MoD and industry. The culture is not only 'can do' but 'can do very quickly'. Industrial and MoD UOR culture is all about urgency, innovation, determination and supporting the servicemen in the field. MoD/industrial relationships are close and mutually supporting. Processes and scrutiny are sensibly reduced. The acquisition community, industry and the end-user are all on the same side and all are winners.

Of course, UOR processes cannot be used to develop, manufacture and support an aircraft carrier with its lengthy procurement timescale, its long in-service life and its major demands on non-equipment Defence Lines of Development (DLoDs). But cannot 'normal' acquisition embrace much of the culture and processes of UOR acquisition? Of course it can. We bought armoured vehicles in a hurry, as did the Dutch who wrote a requirement, held a competition, selected a winner, made the necessary national changes, got them to Afghanistan and trained the operators – from completion of the requirement to field deployment it took just over two months.[9]

The US now uses a fast-track approach for most of its operational requirements.

> *Going through the normal process, the Stryker, a brand-new vehicle, took about two years from an idea to a production model, and from an idea to a deployed fighting brigade in northern Iraq, four years. It normally takes ten years just to build the basic vehicle. In 110 attacks – IEDs, suicide bombers, RPGs – six soldiers have been injured and all have returned to duty; no one in that vehicle has been killed or seriously injured.[10]*

For very large systems, such as the Future Combat System, the US 'spins out' technology which is then developed quickly and fielded to give a new capability very early.

These examples, and there are others, show that much 'normal' acquisition can with great advantage incorporate much of the way UORs are managed.

Greater agility in procurement is vital and time cycles need to be reduced drastically – as the DIS states. MoD needs to study those aspects of the UOR process and culture that can be incorporated into 'normal' procurement and then implement the findings.

---

[9] Lieutenant Colonel Pedro Jooren, Royal Netherlands Staff, 'Fast-Track Fielding of the Bushmaster', *RUSI Defence Systems* (Volume 11, No. 1, June 2008), page 76.

[10] The Honourable Claude Bolton, US Assistant Secretary of the Army (Acquisition, Logistics and Technology), Interview, *RUSI Defence Systems*, (Volume 10, No. 2, October 2007), page 8.

The Defence Industrial Strategy

The implementation of the Smart Procurement Initiative ran out of steam in 2000, just two years after the Initiative had been launched. Some progress had been made, but over the next three or four years much of this progress was reversed. In May 2004, the then Chief of Defence Procurement told the House of Commons Defence Committee that poor performance in the Defence Procurement Agency was "endemic".

> The implementation of the Smart Procurement Initiative ran out of steam in 2000

In 2005 Lord Drayson, with a strong commercial background, was appointed Minister for Defence Procurement. He set a fast pace immediately and in December that year produced the DIS which was aimed at providing:

> *Greater transparency of our future defence requirements and, for the first time, setting out those industrial capabilities we need in the UK to ensure that we can continue to operate our equipment in the way we choose.* [11]

Although primarily about the future of the defence industry and sustainment strategies, it also laid down Defence Values for Acquisition and ways in which acquisition performance was to be improved. It was incomplete because it was produced so quickly, and the costs of sustaining industrial expertise as orders dropped were neither estimated nor provided for. But Drayson had planned a follow-on – DIS 2 – in which costs were to be addressed.

Under Drayson the pace was hot. Progress was being made. There was a feeling that acquisition was at last going to get the treatment that it needed. But it needed continuous commitment at the top over several years if DIS and acquisition change were to be successfully implemented. There was concern for the future if Drayson did not remain for a considerable period.

Implementation of MoD initiatives requires energetic and single-minded drive from the top. For a short while Drayson provided that drive. He has now gone. Will his achievements be confined to the rubbish heap

---

[11] *The Defence Industrial Strategy White Paper*, Cm 6697, The Stationery Office, London, December 2005.

and will MoD revert to 'business as usual' as if DIS never happened?

We will have to wait and see, but the omens are not good. The vital planning round of last winter (PR 08), which was deemed to be the last chance to bring coherence to the defence equipment programme, was undermined when Prime Minister Gordon Brown decreed that no major programmes were to be cancelled, so we were back to the 'salami-slicing' and delays, which while comfortable can no longer produce an affordable, coherent programme. The Services are now so over committed and short of resources that there is talk of the Army facing breakdown. Process, not delivery, rules again.

Is there a way out of these difficulties? Maybe, and this book will endeavour to examine in detail what has happened, what is happening and what progress has been made since 1997, before recommending the action that must be taken immediately.

PART ONE

WHERE HAVE WE COME FROM?

Chapter Two

The Historical Background

In 1958, Ministry of Supply studies found that, on average, actual costs of defence equipment were 2.8 times those forecast.[12] The main causes were said to have been changes to operational requirements, inadequate understanding of the scope of work, and 'cost-plus' contracts. In 1965, the TSR-2 aircraft was cancelled partly because of rising costs:

> *The cost of producing the first 150 TSR-2 planes had soared from the original*
> *£500 million to over £1000 million, and possibly as high as £2000 million.*[13]

More than 40 years later, after repeated initiatives to cut out cost increases, there is more than a whiff of déjà vu about such problems. True, cost overruns have been reduced, although they are still high, and, true, 'cost-plus' contracts have become very much the exception rather than the rule. Nevertheless, the situation today is distressingly similar to that which existed then. I will be returning to the subject of cost overruns in a later chapter.

It must be stated quite clearly that development of military equipment is a most complex business, as can be seen from the diagram (Figure 2–1) that I drew in 1994.[14] Of course it was much more complex than this, but I found it too difficult to include the sea, air and C4ISTAR environments on the same sheet of A4 paper; and more could be made of the other DLoDs, despite the inclusion of manpower and training. Nevertheless, I think it does show the complexity of the process.

But the development of much non-military equipment is also complex and yet its development is much quicker, driven as it is by the short time-to-market imperative. While time-to-market has never been given much priority in the MoD (except during wartime), military equipment acquisition has to cope with such factors as the uncertainties

---

[12] House of Commons Defence Committee, Eighth Report 97/8, *The Strategic Defence Review*, Volume 1, Paragraph 305.

[13] Franklyn A. Johnson, *Defence by Ministry*, Duckworth, page 133.

[14] I am told by many insiders that, although many of the titles and acronyms have changed, it is still a useful presentation of the complexities of military acquisition.

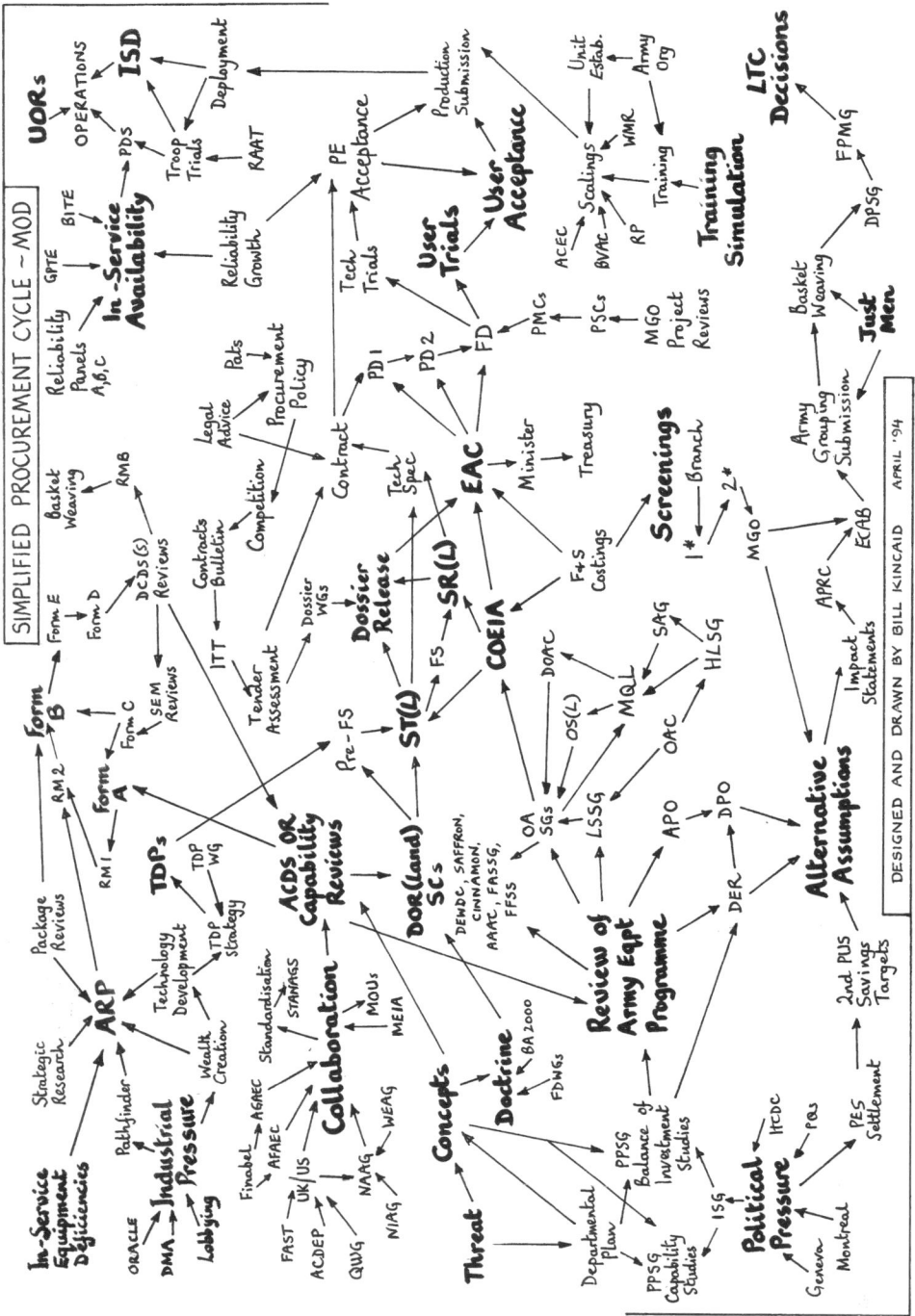

Figure 2–1: A Portrayal of Part of the Complex Ministry of Defence Acquisition Process in 1994

about the form of future warfare, failure being measured in human lives rather than share values, and the need to demonstrate value-for-money (however that may be measured) in the expenditure of public funds. Military procurement is without doubt very complicated, but is the management of the process, as practised by MoD and constrained by the Treasury, as cost-effective as it should be?

A good question.

The Cold War Years

Gibb-Zuckerman

In 1961, the Gibb-Zuckerman report[15] answered growing parliamentary concern, fed by the press, about escalating research and weapon costs in the 1950s.

> *The record from the early 'fifties was not good … the rising costs of military equipment in Britain was staggering, much of it traceable to poor initial estimates … aircraft carriers were slated to be built and were cancelled; missiles such as Blue Water, Blue Streak, Blue Steel and Skybolt were never produced in quantity; and aircraft such as the F-111, P-1154 and HS 681 remained only bad memories. The R&D costs alone for some aircraft rose 100 per cent.*

Sound familiar? We still authorise the start of programmes with poor initial estimates (the Conspiracy of Optimism is discussed in Chapter Seven); we still overrun on research and development (R&D) costs even in the early stages of a project (the costs of the assessment phases of three major projects today – the future aircraft carrier, UKCEC and the future tanker aircraft[16] – have all more than doubled); and, although we no longer cancel many programmes once large sums of public money have been spent on them, we strangle them by delaying with abandon while spending yet more public money on them to get them right, and/or eventually letting them die in obsolescence.

The Gibb-Zuckerman report established an improved procurement process whereby every major project would include:

---

[15] Office of the Minister for Science, *Report on the Committee on the Management and Control of Research and Development.*

[16] National Audit Office, *Ministry of Defence: Major Projects Report 2007*, HC 98-1 2007-2008, The Stationery Office, London, 30 November 2007.

- A formal Staff Target to define the capability required.
- A Feasibility Study to identify the main technical risks.
- A Staff Requirement defining key performance parameters.
- A Project Study to resolve risks, define development and forecast costs and timescales.
- Full Development leading to Production.

This has remained the basis for the procurement of military equipment over the last 47 years, although the details and terms have changed. This suggests that the new process was a good one. However, costs continued to rise. For example:

Seaslug, developed from a very modest naval anti-kamikase missile of the 'forties, was first estimated to cost £1 million to £1.5 million, and actually soared in the end to £70 million at the very least. By 1966, after cruisers had been adapted as bases from which to fire it, the entire complex was pronounced obsolete and abandoned.[17]

> **We continue to drown our acquisition practitioners in process and process change**

The new process might have been a great improvement, but it seems to have had only a small effect, suggesting that process changes are not the best way to improve output – yet we continue to drown our acquisition practitioners in process and process change.

Downey

By the late 1960s, it was perceived that the Gibb-Zuckerman reforms had not gone far enough and William Downey chaired a Steering Group on Development Cost Estimates which reported in 1968. This report[18] established the 'Downey Cycle' which governed all significant projects for the next 30 years. It built on the Gibb-Zuckerman project milestones, but replaced the Project Study stage by a more detailed Project Definition stage, which for complex projects was to be divided into two parts.

More importantly, Downey recommended that each phase must be fully completed before the next phase began, and that *"sufficient technical work should be done in the early Feasibility Study and Project Definition phases*

---

[17] Franklyn A. Johnson, *Defence by Ministry*, Duckworth, page 87.

[18] *Report of the Steering Group on Development Cost Estimating*, Ministry of Technology, 1968.

(ideally absorbing about 15 per cent of the total development cost) so that Full Development could be launched with confidence that projects would meet performance cost and timescale targets".[19]

Note this recommendation, for we shall see how it has been reiterated, and ignored, time and again since then.

The Downey cycle was, in itself, a useful framework but failed to take into account that every project is different and, ideally, requires different procedures to achieve optimal results. It was too slow and stately for small or less complex projects and it was not difficult to find good reasons (military, political, industrial) to depart from it and move on to the next stage before the previous one had been satisfactorily completed.

This was one reason why cost overruns and delays continued to be a problem. In 1975, the House of Commons Expenditure Committee, in examining the Statements on the Defence Estimates, expressed concern about the cost of some equipment projects, including the Tornado aircraft, and delays in introducing new equipment into service.[20]

Much of the problem lay in the failure to implement the Downey recommendation to spend around 15% of the total development budget during the early stages of a project, thus making it impossible to define the technical risks and establish ways of managing them before major expenditure began.

> We continue to make the same mistakes

We continue to make the same mistakes – notably the failure to reduce technical risks early in the project cycle and the insistence on a 'one-size-fits-all' approach.

Formation of the Procurement Executive

In the 1950s and 1960s, military procurement was split between the three Service Ministries, the Ministry of Supply, the Aviation Ministry and, latterly, the Ministry of Technology. In 1971, the Rayner Report[21] recommended the establishment of a Procurement Executive as a sub-

---

[19] House of Commons Defence Committee, 8th Report, *Strategic Defence Review*, Volume 1, paragraph 307.
[20] Second Report from the Expenditure Committee, 1974-75, The Defence Review Proposals, HC 259, paragraph 28.
[21] *Government Organisation for Defence Procurement and Civil Aerospace*, Cmnd 4641, 1971.

department of the Ministry of Defence to pursue improved value-for-money in defence procurement. A close but clear customer/supplier relationship between the Services and the Procurement Executive was to be established, as was an equally clear customer/supplier relationship between the Procurement Executive and industry. At the same time, the high-level equipment committee structure in the Ministry of Defence was overhauled and a new structure was designed *"to prevent unwanted projects slipping through. It has been authoritatively stated that 'the TSR-2 could not happen now'."*

Levene

The establishment of the Procurement Executive was revolutionary in the changes that it made to the organisation and management practices of procurement, but major changes to procurement methods had to await the arrival in 1985 of Peter Levene[22] as Chief of Defence Procurement. Concerned by the 'cosy' relationship between the Ministry of Defence and defence companies, which together with cost-plus contracts and requirement creep led to the view that industry was 'ripping off' the Government, he instigated a more commercial approach which included:

- Competition, involving foreign as well as UK contractors, for almost all defence contracts.
- Replacement of cost-plus contracts with fixed-price contracts, with stage payments linked to specific milestones.
- Appointment of industrial prime contractors.

The Ministry of Defence has estimated that competition has saved it £1Bn per year[23] in procurement costs and was a major factor in improving the competitiveness of the British defence industry.

> The Ministry of Defence has estimated that competition has saved it £1Bn per year

We were now at the furthest remove from the close but robust relationship between serving officers, civil servants and industry that had

---

[22] Now Lord Levene of Portsoken.
[23] National Audit Office, *Defence Procurement in the 1990s*, HC 390 1993-1994, The Stationery Office, London.

existed and worked so well during The Second World War, when demonstrating cost-effectiveness was rather less important than producing the equipment to defeat the enemy.

Jordan, Lee, Cawsey

TSR-2 could not happen now – but only because it had been scrapped years before. The costly demise of the Nimrod Airborne Early Warning (AEW) aircraft blew that self-congratulatory view out of the sky. In its wake, a Ministry of Defence Working Party was set up in 1987 to examine the management of major defence programmes. It recommended that[24]:

- In all major projects one should proceed step by step, demonstrate the technology and only commit to full development when clear performance goals and acceptance criteria can be established and made binding on the contractor.
- Each major project requires a single professional project manager who has effective control of all relevant resources, including specialist technical support.

The Working Party added: *"Previous reports, including the Downey Report of 1966 and [the] Rayner [report] in 1971, have identified much the same issues and reached similar conclusions"*.

The implementation of the Working Party's recommendations required, among other things:

- The creation … of the means by which agreed measures can be implemented and their effect monitored. The aim must be to ensure that the [MoD] corporately learns from experience.
- Greater emphasis on exercising control through 'criteria for success' in procurement, particularly at key decision points, and less central concern with adherence to procedures.
- The manager of a major development project should have a clear charter of responsibility, authority and accountability, and fewer layers between him and top management.
- MoD should commit to full development of an equipment only when initial demonstration of hardware (or software) and its integration has produced evidence that the equipment can be developed to the required level within the time and cost proposed.

---

[24] Jordan, Lee, Cawsey, *Learning form Experience: A Report on the Arrangements for Managing Major Projects in the Procurement Executive*, Ministry of Defence, 1987.

On this last point, the Working Party produced a range of evidence, including that of the Downey and Rayner reports, that 15–25% of total development cost would need to be spent before starting full development – the 'point of no return' in terms of MoD commitment to a project.

In 1988, the House of Commons Defence Committee reviewed a range of major equipment projects and noted delays and cost overruns on a number of them, although it did welcome improvement brought about by competition and incentive pricing.[25] However, it noted that only 8% of a project's total development cost had on average been spent on the Feasibility Study and the Project Definition phases, compared with the repeatedly recommended 15%.

The Nineties

Options for Change

In the wake of the disintegration of Communism in Eastern Europe and the dissolution of the Warsaw Pact, the Options for Change exercise was initiated to determine the future shape of the UK's Armed Forces in the light of a defence budget drastically shorn of a huge and immediate 'Peace Dividend'. However, neither this nor the 1994 Defence Costs Study (DCS) nor the subsequent Front Line First study produced much in the way of procurement change, except for the reduction in numbers of some equipments, and the confirmation of the move of the Procurement Executive from its large number of disparate locations in London to a purpose-built complex at Abbey Wood in the outskirts of Bristol.

1990s: Cost Overruns and Delays

Although the DCS failed to focus on procurement cost overruns and delays, the NAO reports on MoD major projects steadily increased general awareness of the scale of cost overruns and delays in procurement projects. These reports were introduced at the request of the Committee of Public Accounts in their 9th report of 1981–1982. Each year these reports examine approximately 20 projects which have the largest spend over the following ten years. The 1998 report[26] shows that,

---

[25] House of Commons Defence Committee, Fifth Report, *The Procurement of Major Defence Equipment*, HC 431 1997-1998.
[26] National Audit Office, *Ministry of Defence: Major Projects Report 1998*, HC 519, 30 June 1999, The Stationery Office, London.

for the ten projects common to both the 1993 and 1998 reports, cost overruns increased from an average of 3.2% in 1993 to an average of 13.7% in 1998 (see Figure 2–2), and that delays grew from an average of 32 months in 1993 to an average of 43 months in 1998 (see Figure 2–3).

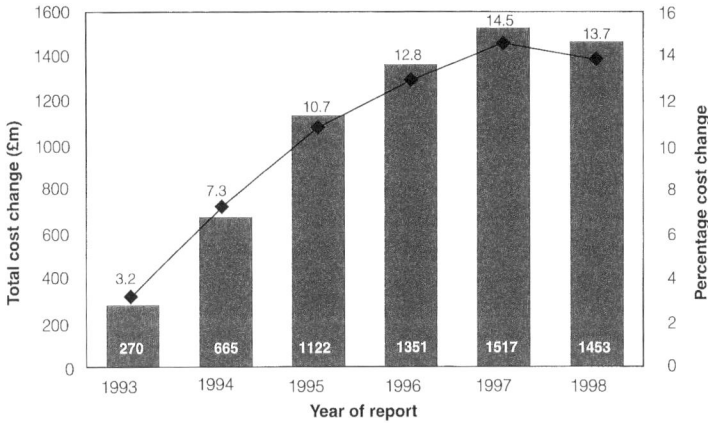

Figure 2–2: Cost Changes in the Ten Projects Common to the 1993 and 1998 Reports
(Excluding Eurofighter)
Source: National Audit Office, Major Projects Report 1998, Figure 11

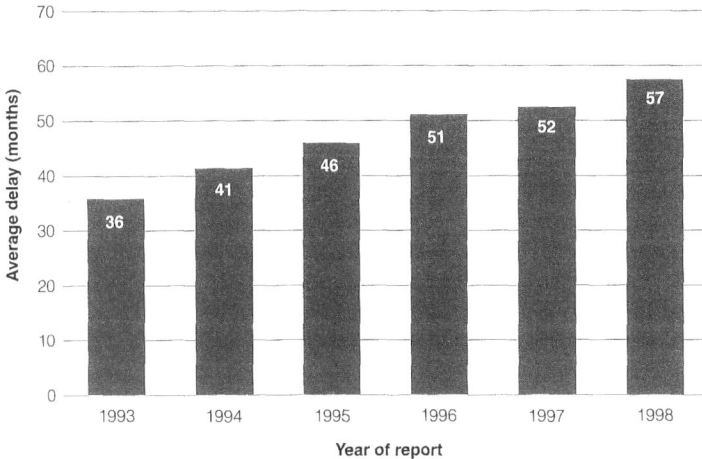

Figure 2–3: Average In-Service Date Delays for the Ten Projects Common to the 1993 and 1998 Reports
Source: National Audit Office, Major Projects Report 1998, Table 14

Despite the threat that inflexibly applied competition and smaller production runs for the smaller Armed Forces posed to the future viability of the UK defence industry, it was this worsening time and cost performance that captured headlines and thence the attention of the Labour Party's Shadow Defence Team. Its 1995 report[27] attacked the 'Ministry of Waste' and, quoting NAO reports, said it was:

> A national disgrace that the Ministry of Defence should be throwing away billions of pounds of taxpayers' money on vital projects which are hampered by lack of foresight and proper management control.

It promised that, when elected, Labour would carry out a Strategic Defence Review, initiate a partnership with industry and address the decline in research and development spending. How all this was to be done was not stated.

It was not only opposition politicians who saw the Ministry in this way. An MoD industry consultation study in 1994 described the views of defence suppliers as follows:

> MoD is perceived as a bureaucratic dinosaur ... mountains of documentations ... endless committees ... difficulties in establishing where the buck stops ... slow decision making ... not organised for effective management.[28]

It has a familiar ring to it.

The Whitehall Dinosaur

According to the NAO[29] the main reasons for cost variance and In-Service Date (ISD) delay were as follows:

Causes of Cost Variance	Causes of ISD Delay
Programme changes	Project definition
Inflation adjustment	Technical difficulties
Specification changes	Collaborative processes

---

[27] The Labour Party, *Strategy for a Secure Future, Labour's Approach to the Defence Industry*, October 1995.
[28] MoD, *SIP Industry Consultation Study*, March 1994.
[29] National Audit Office, *Ministry of Defence; Major Projects Report 1998*, 30 Part 2, June 1999.

But this was only part of the story. The reasons for the problems within procurement were spelled out in *A Dinosaur in Whitehall* in 1997.[30] I listed the main weaknesses as:

> ## THE MAIN PROBLEMS IN 1997
>
> - A lack of personal accountability, with responsibility and authority badly matched.
> - A lack of professionalism.
> - A consensus committee culture, leading to weak decision-making.
> - Convoluted procedures.
> - Stifling but ineffective scrutiny.

This analysis brought harsh condemnation from many Civil Servants and, while many military officers were largely supportive, they felt that there was as much chance of introducing realistic solutions as there was of breeding flying pigs. One senior official went so far as to say that he did not agree with one word of what I had written. That seemed a little over the top.

The key seemed to me then to be personal accountability: from that everything else could flow; without it, nothing very useful could be achieved. This was recognised by the Government's Efficiency Unit in its report Improving Management in Government: The Next Steps:

> *At present the freedom of an individual manager to manage effectively and responsibly in the Civil Service is severely circumscribed. There are controls not only on resources and objectives, as there should be in any effective system, but also on the way in which resources can be managed ... the rules are seen as a constraint rather than as a support; and in no sense as a pressure on managers to manage effectively. Moreover, the task of changing rules is often seen as too great for one unit or one manager or indeed one department and is therefore deemed to be impossible.*

By 1997, the perceived impossibility of changing the rules had become the main stumbling block to improved procurement. The faults in the

---

[30] Bill Kincaid, *A Dinosaur in Whitehall* (Brassey's, London, September 1997).

system were widely perceived and many knew what the solutions were. But, to both internal and external eyes, the Ministry of Defence had become about as stagnant as the Soviet Union in the Brezhnev era. But that system had thrown up Gorbachev and evolved – where was our catalyst for change to come from if the Whitehall Dinosaur was to be exterminated, or at least metamorphosed?

It came with a change of government.

Chapter Three

Smart Acquisition: Change At Last

By the time of the General Election in May 1997, it was widely recognised that procurement of defence equipment was in a mess. Project costs escalated wildly, project schedules slipped significantly, more than 80% of ISDs were missed and many key performance parameters were not met. Above all, large projects were taking on average some two decades in the procurement process before they were fielded. Although the 9/11 terrorist attacks were yet to come, the world had quite clearly said goodbye to the certainties of the Cold War and we needed to be able to react with rather more agility than in the 1980s.

The Smart Procurement Initiative

The new Labour Government immediately announced a strategic defence review which was to include:

> *A ruthless examination of how value-for-money in defence procurement, one of the most important aspects of the Review, can be improved … we are looking for 'smart procurement'.* [31]

Smart Procurement was born and it was to be 'faster, cheaper, better'.

In November 1997, the new government called in the consultancy firm, McKinsey & Co., who determined the major procurement problems. These included the following:

- Early stages of the procurement cycle were ineffective, unproductive and under-resourced.
- The procurement system was monolithic and inflexible.
- The process was too reliant on technical specifications.
- There was too much reliance on rigid competitive tendering.
- Project management was weak.
- There was too little delegation.
- Key people spent too short a period in post.

---

[31] House of Commons Defence Committee, Eighth Report 1997-1998, *Strategic Defence Review*, Volume 1, Paragraph 333.

- There was a lack of clear accountability.
- The oversight and approvals process was cumbersome and ineffective.
- MoD's 'carrots' and 'sticks' for dealing with contractors were too small.
- Technology management was ineffective.

These findings bore a striking resemblance to those discussed in *A Dinosaur in Whitehall*, which had been published a couple of months before and which had caused so much angst. But they should have come as no surprise as the problems were clearly understood, at least at the working and middle management levels. They were, in fact, common ground amongst those who had to work at the coalface.

Further work identified more problems, chief of which were that within MoD there was no clear, single customer for equipment and that a number of processes were managed separately, making an effective whole-life approach impossible.

The Recommended Changes

Diagnosing the problems was one thing; identifying adequate solutions was much more difficult. However, in July 1998 – a year after the Strategic Defence Review (SDR) had been launched – the Ministry of Defence announced the following changes:[32]

- Creation of a clear MoD internal Customer/Supplier relationship by reorganisation of the Operational Requirements staff, the Procurement Executive and the single-Services logistics organisations.
- Streamlined procedures including changes to the Downey cycle.
- Incremental acquisition to allow fielding of equipment of a less ambitious capability, which would then be upgraded in several lower-risk stages.
- A through-life concept to ensure that decisions would be taken on a broader view of the equipment's life cycle, making trade-offs between military requirements, costs and timescales.
- Partnering to involve industry more closely in the development of operational requirements and equipment designs.

---

[32] MoD, *Strategic Defence Review Report*, Supporting Essay Ten, Paragraph 8, July 1998.

- Personal accountability to improve time and cost estimating.
- IPTs consisting of all stakeholders and scientific staffs, as well as industry when competition allows, with a clear leader having authority to make trade-off decisions and who would retain responsibility for equipment after it had entered service.

A Smart Procurement Implementation Team (SPIT – an unfortunate acronym which was later changed to SPRINT) was formed in September 1998 and was driven hard by the then Secretary of State for Defence, George Robertson, strongly supported by the then Under-Secretary of State, John Spellar, who had

> The importance of this strong political leadership should not be underestimated

been given responsibility for Smart Procurement. The importance of this strong political leadership should not be underestimated because, without it, Smart Procurement would have been strangled at birth by senior figures in the Ministry who were uneasy about the changes that were required.

Organisational Change

A great deal of effort, which generated considerable heat at times, was initially focused on organisational change within the Ministry. The key changes set in motion were:

- The creation of a central MoD customer, by merging the Systems and Programme areas to create the Equipment Capability Customer (ECC).
- The conversion of the Procurement Executive (PE) into an Agency – the Defence Procurement Agency (DPA).
- The integration of the three single-Service logistics organisations into the purple Defence Logistics Organisation (DLO).
- The privatisation of the Defence Evaluation and Research Agency (DERA).

The Equipment Capability Customer

Perhaps the most significant of these was the formation of ECC. There was now a clear central MoD customer for acquisition of equipment, a role that the former Operational Requirements (OR) division could not discharge because its chief had no authority over the Equipment Plan

(EP), the responsibility for which lay with a different 3-star official. The change meant that the new 3-star Deputy Chief of the Defence Staff (Equipment Capability) – DCDS(EC) – now had both responsibility and authority as the MoD equipment customer and was henceforth accountable; he was 'empowered'.

ECC was now to think 'capability' rather than projects. Not what type of vehicle we needed to replace that in-service vehicle, not what manned aircraft we needed to replace this in-service manned aircraft, but what **capability** we needed. Should a manned aircraft be replaced by another manned aircraft or an unmanned one or a mix – or could it be done by something other than an aircraft? This made perfect sense and was enthusiastically adopted by ECC.

> ECC was now to think 'capability' rather than projects

Not without problems, however. The DPA was also looking more closely at the future and began to spawn future project IPTs well in advance of what the customer was considering or could afford. It took much effort to get such IPTs disbanded.

Another problem was more intractable. The EP was made up of a number of project lines. 'Wedges' and 'contingencies' were dirty words in the Treasury, so projects could only be started when a project (not a capability) funding line was included in the EP. That, of course, was well in advance of the start of the Concept phase which should have been examining capability. And, arguably, it is impossible to cost capability until some sort of equipment decision has been made.

The Defence Procurement Agency

While the change to agency status for the DPA brought with it the advantage of the freer way of doing financial business, the move of the PE in the late 1990s from various buildings in London to the purpose-built site near Bristol meant that the new ECC and the new DPA would have to work together with a geographical separation of around 100 miles. With modern IT this wasn't seen as a problem by senior management in Whitehall.

The core of the new DPA was a number of IPTs, the leaders of which were 'empowered' to make more decisions than the former project managers in the PE. This was clearly a step in the right direction.

However, the internal organisations of the ECC and DPA were not harmonised – the ECC was organised along 'capability' lines and was largely Joint, while the DPA's organisation was arranged around groups of similar projects – not similar in the equipment or capability sense but in the procurement stage which they had reached. So, each IPT leader had to deal with several different DECs, who in turn had to deal with many different 1-star directors in the DPA. As each DEC and IPT leader was 'empowered' this was clearly a recipe for difficulties.

Committees and Management

Equipment Committees were reorganised. Despite the clear thrust of Smart Procurement towards a strong central customer holding the money and deciding what was required, top equipment committees were now dominated by suppliers rather than the MoD customer. Both the DPA Chief Executive – the Chief of Defence Procurement (CDP) – and the new chief of the DLO – the Chief of Defence Logistics

> As each DEC and IPT leader was 'empowered' this was clearly a recipe for difficulties

(CDL) – sat on the top equipment committee, the Equipment Approvals Committee (EAC), but MoD's central customer did not. The customer was represented by the Vice-Chief of the Defence Staff, but his span of responsibility was so wide that he could not be expected to argue successfully against the suppliers whose responsibilities were so much narrower.

There was much uncertainty over the new management chains and, although the 2-star posts were retained in both EC and DPA, these experienced people did not seem to have a clear responsibility for any part of core business, so that much valuable experience went largely untapped. Nor was this remedied because of the fear that empowerment of DECs and IPT leaders would be undermined.

Stovepiping and Coherence

The empowerment of these key individuals was, without doubt, a major step forward, improving efficiency and effectiveness within a single IPT or DEC area. However, it was not long before an unwanted consequence became apparent – stovepiping. Decisions made by one IPT leader might have a detrimental effect on the cost, schedule or performance of another programme in another IPT, but there was now no effective means of monitoring or modifying such decisions to overall benefit without risking a backward step in empowerment.

The consequences were:

- A loss of coherence in procurement output.
- Greater difficulty in driving capability across these stovepipes.
- Greater difficulty in implementing the through-life concept.
- A decline in commonality of components across defence.

There was a wider stovepiping problem. While amalgamating the three Service logistics organisations into the single Joint DLO was clearly going to pay dividends in the future, the divide between the project procurement stages run by the DPA and the support stage managed by the DLO was now clearer and deeper. The 'throw-it-over-the-wall' approach at ISD was not at all helpful to the whole-life approach to acquisition, and allowed both to blame the other for shortcomings once in service. But this issue quickly became an out-of-bounds topic.

The DPA and DLO mega-stovepipes were exacerbated by the divide between the ten-year EP, which included only equipment procurement costs, initial support costs and upgrades, and the three-year Short Term Plan (STP) which funded the manpower, training, spares, running costs and infrastructure. Each Plan came under a different 3-star official.

There were yet more stovepipes. The three Services, increasingly Joint in operations and in capability terms, were anything but in procurement or support, each jealously guarding its own turf and each convinced that another Service could never understand its needs. Industry was stovepiped, some closely involved with one Service, others with another; there was little read-across from one industrial division to another. There were the three MoD 'tribes' – military, mandarins and boffins – who each looked askance at the others and certainly did not trust them.

> There were the three MoD 'tribes' – military, mandarins and boffins

In each case, there was no one in overall charge to limit the adverse consequences of these stovepipes. Perhaps no one in MoD really understood them all.

Research and Technology

Although McKinsey's had pointed to ineffective technology management, the Strategic Defence Review largely ignored research and technology (R&T). It stated that:

> *We will harness the opportunities offered by Public Private Partnership to strengthen DERA's [Defence Evaluation and Research Agency] ability to provide world class scientific research well into the next century.*[33]

And not a lot else.

At the time I argued against such a change[34] on several grounds but particularly because, as a commercial organisation, the privatised company may find important MoD research not profitable enough, and also because the attraction of US contracts could move its focus from MoD to DOD. This seems to be happening:

> *QinetiQ, the defence contractor spun out of the Ministry of Defence, is considering acquisitions in the United States ... About 40% of its business comes from the US, up from 30% last year. It aims to increase this figure to 50% within two years.*[35]

MoD holds a 19% stake in QinetiQ's business, and has the power to block any move to relocate its headquarters to another country. However, its Chief Executive said that MoD would sell its stake "at some stage".

Privatisation of DERA apart, Smart Procurement had little to say about R&T, leaving a clear impression that its importance was not understood and that any weaknesses would be deliberately allowed to remain.

I listed the main weaknesses as follows:[36]

- Insufficient MoD investment.
- Insufficient industrial investment.
- Ineffective use of that small investment through duplication of effort between MoD and industry.
- Inefficient technology transfer from MoD to industry.

---

[33] MoD, *Strategic Defence Review*, Supporting Essay 11, page 11–8, July 1998.
[34] Bill Kincaid, *Dancing with the Dinosaur*, Chapter Seven, UK Defence Forum, 1999.
[35] Catherine Boyle, Steve Hawkes, 'QinetiQ eyes up a US buying offensive', *The Times*, 29 May 2008.
[36] Bill Kincaid, *Dancing with the Dinosaur*, page 138, UK Defence Forum, 1999.

- Minimal success in pulling through the results of MoD research into winning projects.

Has anything changed much?

Forward and Back

So, despite the clear steps forward in empowerment and accountability, and despite the creation of the ECC providing a clear MoD customer with both responsibility and the financial authority, there were many problems that were either not addressed or were thrown up by the reorganisation.

> there were many problems that were not addressed

Process and Procedures

While so much effort was going into organisational change, it was perhaps inevitable that the more difficult task of streamlining procurement procedures – one of the main planks of the Smart Procurement Initiative – was largely put to one side and buried beneath a surface mulch of hype and spin.

However, the objectives were good and, if implemented, might well have contributed strongly to improved acquisition performance. They were:

- The Downey Cycle to be replaced by a new CADMID Cycle[37] with a reduced number of submissions[38] to the Equipment Approvals Committee[39] during the development stages.
- Financial delegation to be increased.
- Funding for the first two stages of the new procurement cycle (Concept and Assessment) to be increased to about 15% of total development funding.
- Annuality to be a thing of the past.
- Incremental Acquisition to be the norm.
- A through-life concept to be applied to all projects.

---

[37] Concept, Assessment, Demonstration, Manufacture, In-Service, Disposal.
[38] Two only – Initial Gate and Main Gate.
[39] The senior acquisition committee at that time and replaced in due course by the Investment Appraisals Board.

The CADMID Cycle

Not one of these was properly implemented. The CADMID Cycle was indeed adopted but the main difference – the reduced number of submissions – quickly disappeared. Little, if any, saving in time and effort was apparent. And, surprise surprise, the number of submissions began to climb.

The first CADMID submission, Initial Gate, was due at the end of the Concept stage and was to be a relatively low hurdle to release funding for the major Assessment stage, while Main Gate, after Assessment was complete, was to be a rigorous examination of the risks remaining. It was stated that some programmes could be expected to fail at Main Gate. This never happened. In addition, Initial Gate quickly became a major submission, making the Concept phase longer and more detailed than originally envisaged, and squeezing the time and funding available for the weightier Assessment phase.

Another concern was expressed a few years later:

> *A key aim of Smart Acquisition was to address a long running criticism that the process for acquiring defence equipment was too long and was too complex. A change introduced under Smart Acquisition was to rationalise the equipment approvals process. The number of points at which a major equipment programme was approved for continuance was cut from four to two. This concept of Smart Acquisition fits every procurement into a contractual straitjacket. A more flexible system might lead to better results in some cases.*[40]

Funding of Early Stages

We have already seen that previous studies (Downey and Jordan, Lee, Cawsey) had recommended that the early stages should be funded to the tune of about 15% of total development funding, but this had never been implemented. Smart Procurement reiterated that call but once again nothing happened.

> A more flexible system might lead to better results

> *There is no doubt that time and money spent at this stage in detailed planning and de-risking a project is extremely well spent, and the penalties for not doing so can be severe. One of the reasons that this has not been done over the last few*

---

[40] House of Commons Defence Committee, *Defence Procurement*, Volume 1, HC 572–1 2003–04, page 15, 28 July 2004.

years is the problems associated with integrating this approach with full blooded competition. It is highly unlikely that a contractor would be prepared to make this kind of investment as part of the bidding phase of the programme, where he is likely to be one of five or six bidders. In the event of his bid being unsuccessful he would have a very large write-off. Without spending this money the programme is loaded with significant risk; although this risk on fixed price contracts appears to be laid at the door of the contractor, in practice MoD also shares a proportion of the risk.[41]

The stumbling block was the need to find more money upfront, so it was easier to ignore the recommendation and let the consequences appear much later. The early funding levels that continued to be provided (at best around 5% to 6%) could only buy paper studies; for anything more worthwhile something greater than about 12% was needed – hence the call for 15%.

Type of Project	Project	Assessment Phase Spend	Result
Legacy	Brimstone	2.4%	Cost overrun, huge delay
	ASTOR	1.3%	Delay
	Astute	0.8%	Large cost and time overruns
	Typhoon	0.4%	Large cost and time overruns
	Nimrod MR4	0.1%	Large cost and time overrun
Smart	A400M	0.1%	Large cost and time overruns
	BVRAAM	1.5%	Cost and time overruns
	Type 45	3.8%	Cost overrun and long delay
	Skynet 5	4.2%	Cost and time overruns
	NLAW	4.6%	Few problems
	JCA	5.3%	Large cost and time overruns
	Sonar 2087	12.1%	Few problems

Table 3–1: Assessment Phase Spend on Current Projects
Source: NAO, MoD Major Projects Reports

---

[41] John Weston, email to the author, September 2008.

Table 3–1 shows two things. First, although in general terms the newer 'Smart' projects received a higher allocation for the Assessment Phase, the percentages were still far too low and in some cases still below those allocated to some legacy projects.

Secondly, in only one project (Sonar 2087) did the early spend approach the recommended level and this project had few problems. It is true that NLAW had few problems after an Assessment Phase spend of 4.6%, but this was a modified off-the-shelf procurement so there was less to assess.

Incremental Acquisition

Incremental acquisition quite rightly was a key part of Smart Procurement and was defined by MoD as follows:

> *Incremental Acquisition provides for a capability to be upgraded in a planned way, from the initial delivery of a specified baseline capability to eventual achievement of a higher full capability.*[42]

This definition is flawed as it makes no mention of time. Who would want a 70% solution in a similar timescale to the 100% solution? Incremental Acquisition (or spiral development or technology insertion) only makes sense if the lower baseline capability can be fielded within, say, half the time of the 100% non-incremental solution.

There had been numerous examples of Incremental Acquisition before Smart Procurement,[43] but Smart Procurement did not increase the number of incremental projects. In fact, it seemed to decrease them sharply. Why? The MoD view was that:

> *Incremental Acquisition may have disadvantages such as a lack of competitive pressure for later increments.*[44]

Yes, but partnering may bring benefit. There is a more intractable obstacle: top-level committees will find it challenging to authorise expenditure on the baseline capability when the cost and technical risks

---

[42] MoD, *The Acquisition Handbook*, Edition 1, page 20, April 1999.
[43] In the artillery and ground-based areas alone, they included Rapier, Javelin, ADCIS, Bates, MLRS, AS90 and Phoenix – although in the cases of ADCIS and Phoenix the later stages of each were cut in later planning rounds.
[44] MoD, *The Acquisition Handbook*, Edition 1, page 20, April 1999.

of the planned upgrade path are still unknown. But surely this is how the 'Great Men' should be earning their salaries – by making difficult decisions and balancing the advantages against the disadvantages, rather than considering only the difficulties.

Surprisingly, the MoD acknowledged that the advantages of incremental acquisition include:

> *A reduction of the risk inherent in introducing large improvements in capability through a single major technological step.*[45]

This was still the position spelled out in the Smart Acquisition Handbook in 2005. So, why did Incremental Acquisition never become more than a footnote to implementation? The answer lies in two words – competition and culture.

The Through-Life Concept

The through-life concept, another central theme, was also never implemented, although for different reasons. It was difficult to do so when the DPA, with its 'throw-it-over-the-wall' culture, was separate from the DLO, each with funding from different pots of money. But there was a greater problem – whole-life costing (WLC). If decisions during the development stages were to be made on a whole-life basis, then WLC had to be reasonably accurate. But WLC was not accurate. How could it be when costs 30 to 40 years ahead depended on a design that was still immature and an upgrade plan which was no more than a few words on paper? Huge and frequent cost overruns in development illustrate just how difficult costing is even a few years ahead, let alone decades.

> But there was a greater problem – whole-life costing

Figures have to be produced for the forward budgets, and can best be done on a historical basis by independent experts, but even this will not be accurate enough to make procurement decisions in many cases. The problems were overcome by ignoring the whole-life concept.

Annuality

One process change was trumpeted above all others: annuality would be

---

[45] MoD, *The Acquisition Handbook*, Edition 1, page 20, April 1999.

a thing of the past. How naïve! Maybe this was possible for the first couple of years because the new Government had stated that it would stick to Conservative spending plans. But after that, defence budget changes would be less predictable. In any case, to stay within the annual budget while defence inflation was outstripping national inflation and large cost overruns in equipment projects remained the rule rather than the exception, the EP would have to be costed each year and savings found. The increased stability that was proclaimed was only ever a chimera. But people wanted to believe, so they did – for a short while.

Defence Lines of Development

I have already referred to the chasm between the EP and the STP – both in terms of who was responsible and the period each covered – and the advance in empowerment only made the chasm wider. It made no sense for the STP to cover only three years when the EP planned ten years ahead and needed to be sure that the manpower, training and infrastructure funding would be in place once a system came into service. This might have been resolved through further structural reorganisation, but it wasn't. Instead it took some time (four to five years) for the problem to be addressed, when the DLoDs were defined and a Senior Responsible Owner (SRO) was appointed for major capability areas.

> In other words, the process problem was patched over

In other words, the process problem was patched over.

Drowning in Process

Process had now been elevated to the status of an ancient Greek oracle, at times somewhat Delphic, but at all times to be followed. A well-defined process is important but it should not have to be slavishly followed by experienced and empowered individuals. Many statements by acquisition officials of the time showed the frustrations quite clearly:[46]

The tick in the box is alive and well.

Process is more important than delivery.

---

[46] Bill Kincaid, *Dinosaur in Permafrost*, pages 35/36, (TheSauras Ltd, 2002). off-the-record remarks from MoD and industrial staff during a wide-rangin exercise.

We are all drowning in process.

Process undermines project delivery. Is it all necessary?

It's all process – we have lost sight of what we are trying to do.

This is not a criticism of Smart Procurement, but of its implementation. The process geeks had taken the objectives and had a ball. Unfortunately, no one understood what they were doing until it was too late. Delivery had been torpedoed by process.

Culture and Smart People

In June 1999, John Spellar, who then had Ministerial responsibility for Smart Procurement, summed up the importance of culture change[47] in MoD when he wrote:

> *The [Smart Procurement] initiative will not succeed unless we change the culture and our people respond to the circumstances we create for them … we need to become more flexible, responsive and receptive to new ideas. We need to depend less on rulebooks or precedent and more on judgement and experience.*

And:

> *We shouldn't be afraid to take risks, even if that means risking failure. If we fail, we should learn from our mistakes. Because if we never make mistakes we'll never change anything. My idea of the ideal public servant is not someone who never fails, but someone who always tries to make a difference.*

> Depend less on rulebooks? Risk failure? That would never do!

Anyone who has ever worked in Whitehall will understand the magnitude of the culture change that Spellar was proposing. Depend less on rulebooks? Risk failure? That would never do!

Culture change takes time and the bigger the change, the longer it takes. Spellar thought it might take more than five years; others thought longer.

---

[47] John Spellar, Under-Secretary of State for Defence, *RUSI Journal*, (Volume 144, No. 3, June 1999).

Empowerment

We have already seen that the reorganisations to form the ECC and the DPA allowed some empowerment of individuals – particularly DECs and IPT Leaders. But we have also seen that the organisations brought problems as well, not least the marginalisation of 2-star officials in the flattened management structures, and more importantly, stovepiping. Once these problems had been clearly identified, the organisations needed to be tweaked to resolve the problems without giving up the advantages of empowerment. This was difficult. To start with, perhaps unsurprisingly, the problems were ignored, at least in the DPA.

> Empowerment, one of the few early 'wins', withered

But as the adverse consequences of stovepiping were seen to increase costs, action was taken – but, alas, at the expense of empowerment. IPT leaders were increasingly hemmed in by restrictions, while management structures and procedures became more Byzantine. Empowerment, one of the few early 'wins', withered.

Smart People

It was clearly understood that the skills, training and experience of the acquisition community were, on average, not good enough. Much effort went into acquisition training but with only limited success – many did courses but not all applied the learning to their jobs when they returned.

Implementing the change in culture meant shifting people out of their comfort zones, but with little or no immediate personal reward on offer there was little to motivate any but the best. An increase in pay and rewards was impractical if it meant breaking away from Civil Service-wide norms (0.2% to 0.4% of salary at best); promotion was not likely to come any quicker; and risks were higher.

The Acquisition Handbook, in its paragraph entitled "What's in it for Me?" was only able to suggest[48] that individuals would now be more directly accountable for delivery, would have clearer roles and would be expected to use a range of best-practice techniques. Hardly motivation for anyone except the best – in fact the opposite. Not surprisingly, this paragraph disappeared from later editions.

---

[48] MoD, *The Acquisition Handbook*, Edition 1, page 32, April 1999.

People do not implement changes of their own volition without reward. It has to be driven hard from the top. And it became increasingly clear that not all the top men in MoD were enamoured of the changes. Sit tight, keep your head down and continue in your comfort zone for as long as possible was the attitude in many departments.

Moreover, the history of MoD initiatives tended to promote the view that there would be another one along soon and this one would be forgotten – so why bother?

Any failure to change culture would be seen as a victory for the reactionaries. In view of the much higher rewards that industry could offer to the best, this no-risk, no-reward MoD culture would be unlikely to encourage the recruitment of highly able scientific and engineering graduates, who were in any case becoming a much rarer breed, or retain the best once recruited. The best would leave, and the mediocre and the inadequate would remain. Not the recipe for the stated move to Smart People.

> The best would leave, and the mediocre and the inadequate would remain

If the standard of employees could be raised significantly and the percentage of the mediocre and inadequate reduced, it would be possible to reduce the manpower numbers because highly capable people can work that much more quickly and get much more right first time. Manpower savings translate into cost savings. In addition, with a more capable workforce, it should be possible to reduce the frequency with which specialist advisors or industrial companies are brought in to evaluate bids and devise and implement procurement strategies. Again, money can be saved. These savings could be used to pay MoD staff more, if a way could be found to do so within Civil Service and military structures.

Target Culture

Recent governments have embraced the target culture with fervour. Inherently, targets are a good thing, but the difficulties with setting them and the ease with which they can be 'spun' make them hit-and-miss with a propensity for upsetting coherent delivery.

As everyone knows, objectives should always be SMART – specific, measurable, achievable, realistic (given the resources) and time-defined. But SMART –

especially the achievable bit – is not always that smart because all too often objectives are driven by a higher political agenda, and the views of the front-line worker are ignored.[49]

To that can be added that those achieving one set of targets in one stovepipe can too often make the achievement of another set in another stovepipe more difficult. Moreover, the effort to achieve some targets may well upset the logical priorities of the team or department if they have not been set absolutely correctly.

Although a target culture was not specifically part of the Smart Procurement Initiative, implementation inevitably involved the setting of targets. This drove initial implementation strongly, but it did mean that emerging problems were ignored.

> Emerging problems were ignored

Where the target culture really fell down in the DPA (and still does) was in the setting of targets governing cost, time and performance of programme delivery. While it is important to minimise cost and time overruns during procurement, it is the overall cost and timescale that is more important. Not surprisingly, this is ignored.

The cost, time and performance targets have a mesmerising effect on many IPTs. They must be achieved – or seen to be achieved. Cost overruns and delays are easily spotted, so when they threaten to break out of the box, something else has to give. And that something is performance, where reduction is often less easy to identify. A 5% decrease in mobility in certain types of terrain, or a 3% cut in radar output power may not be easily translated into a shortfall in the performance specified in the target. More often, of course, numbers are cut or ISDs redefined, and the result is classified as a requirement change rather than reducing cost overrun.

Decision-Making

The Smart Procurement's "Faster, Cheaper, Better" was a fine aim, but just how much faster, cheaper and better? An early, if unofficial, catchphrase was "On time, in half the time at 30% less cost", but this was quickly shelved when it was thought that the Treasury might take 30%

---

[49] Melanie Reid, 'The Dangerous Nonsense of Performance Targets', *The Times*, February 2008.

out of the equipment budget there and then.

Nevertheless, it had been recognised that we had to do things much more quickly. It was not shortening the length of time that industry needed to do the design and development, but the MoD procedures – particularly the decision-making – that took much longer than they should. This took us straight back into Whitehall culture.

Decision-making by military officers in the field and by management in industry is as quick as it has to be if action is to be discharged effectively, either to defeat the enemy or to get to market. Whitehall does not see the need to meet any particular timescale, but time is money and ISDs can mean the difference between life and death.

That decisions can be made quickly and generally cost-effectively is borne out by the delivery of UORs. While this method of getting equipment into the field suffers from weaknesses (lack of support downstream, reduced coherence across fleets etc.), unforeseen requirements are met very quickly in weeks or sometimes days, as has been proved time and again for Northern Ireland, the Falklands, the Gulf War, Iraq and Afghanistan. So, a speedier decision-making culture does exist, but is not allowed to be extended into normal procurement. If the best aspects of UOR procurement were to be taken into normal procurement, decisions would be taken much more quickly and the whole process would be speeded up.

> Regrettably, Smart Procurement was unable to change the culture

Culture Change

Regrettably, Smart Procurement was unable to change the culture. 'Faster' was allowed to slip away, as were the huge potential cost savings.

Partnering Industry

The SDR called for:

> *A new relationship between the Ministry of Defence and its suppliers in which both sides can operate to their strengths, under formal partnering arrangements where appropriate, and which provides industry with the greatest incentive to perform.*[50]

---

[50] MoD, *Strategic Defence Review* (Cmnd 3999), Supporting Essay Ten, page 10–3, July 1998.

MoD and industry had been locked in an adversarial relationship for more than a decade, with competition and fixed-price contracts as MoD's sticks to beat industry into submission. This was claimed by MoD to be saving £1Bn per year[51] and, in the Cold War period, this competitive, adversarial relationship was sustainable. However, after the collapse of Communism and the 'peace dividends', shrinking orders left industry in a much harsher environment. The desperate need to win competitions depressed profit margins still further and defence companies had to win large export orders in the teeth of US, French and, often, Russian salesmanship. Many companies, particularly small ones, were either going out of business or moving out of the defence sector altogether.

> After the collapse of Communism shrinking orders left industry in a much harsher environment

A change was indeed necessary.

Shortly after the launch of Smart procurement, the relationship with industry showed signs of improvement, with one senior industrialist referring to a 'sea change' in their relationship with the Equipment Capability staff. Other industrialists mentioned greater trust and transparency, more lateral thinking and a greater willingness to recognise the other side's constraints, in their dealings with the DPA.

In the DLO, there was some support for partnering, primarily in long-term support contracts, and there were many examples of mutually beneficial partnering, notably with Vickers on Challenger 2 spares and repair and Rolls-Royce on Pegasus engines for RAF Harriers. Partnering, too, was the basis for PPP/PFI[52] projects, but the success of those was more difficult to determine so early in their lives.

Against that, many industrialists referred to a 'DPA culture problem' with its fundamental distrust, and a view that innovation was a threat. It became increasingly apparent that the DPA saw partnering as an exception, while 'competition, competition, competition' remained the rule. The Treasury, too, appeared to favour competition.

While modest progress was undoubtedly being made, it was slow and very patchy.

---

[51] Has this ever been proved?

[52] Public-Private Partnership/Private Finance Initiative.

Progress and Stagnation

There is no doubt that the Smart Procurement Initiative was absolutely right both in its overall direction and in the detailed proposals. It required

> This amount of progress was due to strong political leadership

a major change in organisation, processes and culture, and there were many who were unconvinced that this was the route that should be followed, and many others who were loath to move out of their comfort zone.

Initial Progress

Nevertheless, the changes implemented in the first two years went further than most people thought likely. This amount of progress – made in the teeth of considerable opposition – was due to the strong political leadership of George Robertson and John Spellar and included:

- Creation and empowerment of DCDS(EC).
- Empowerment of DECs, IPT Leaders and others.
- Changes to the relationship with industry, particularly in the ECC and some areas of the DLO.
- Improved acquisition training.

Stagnation

But against this limited and patchy progress, must be set a rather longer list of areas where no progress was made at all. These included:

- The through-life concept.
- Incremental acquisition.
- Low levels of funding of early project stages.
- Annuality.
- Transition from capability to project.
- Low levels of skills and personal qualities.
- Inadequate pay and rewards.
- Target setting
- Pervasive competition.
- Adversarial relationships with industry in many areas.
- No change in industrial culture
- No change in overall MoD/Whitehall culture.

New Problems

Any major change is likely to throw up unforeseen problems. The Smart Procurement Initiative was no exception and threw up several significant problems, including:

- Stovepiping of projects and capabilities.
- Undefined roles of 2-star officials in DPA and ECC.
- Increasing gap between the EP and STP.
- Primacy of process rather than delivery.

They needed addressing without delay. This did not happen.

Change Leadership

John Spellar had said that change would probably take five years or more to implement, and it was generally acknowledged that implementation would require strong leadership throughout this period if change was to be embedded. Implementation began in September 1998 but, in October 1999, George Robertson quit as Secretary of State for Defence to take over as Secretary General of NATO. Then, in July 2001, John Spellar was appointed Minister for Transport.

Their successors had other priorities, not least 9/11 and then Iraq and Afghanistan. The political pressure on implementing Smart Procurement was removed and the forces of reaction breathed more easily. Ticks were placed in boxes, Smart Procurement was supposedly done and dusted, congratulations all round.

> The forces of reaction breathed more easily

Well, not quite all round. The workers at the coalface now laboured in a confused world – bits of Smart Acquisition had been implemented, most had not; problems thrown up by the changes were left unsolved. Competition or partnering? Adversarial or not? Empowerment or stovepiping? Incremental acquisition or big bang? Through-life or throw-it-over-the-wall?

From mid-2001 to mid-2005, there was a procurement change vacuum. Of course changes continued, but mostly they fiddled at the edge of importance. Smart Procurement became Smart Acquisition, supposedly to emphasise that the overall initiative included in-service support, but in reality to give a veneer of progress.

By mid-2005, much of the initial gain achieved in the first two years had been reversed or allowed to wither away. In May 2004, the new Chief of Defence Procurement, Admiral Spencer, told the House of Commons Defence Committee that, "poor performance was endemic" in the DPA and that, of the seven fundamental aspects of the Smart Procurement Initiative, only one – the ECC – had been properly implemented. The surprise was not that performance was poor, but that it had been said in public: it was a clear indictment of the way Smart Procurement/Acquisition had been implemented. Later that month, the Minister (Defence Procurement) told the same committee that Smart Acquisition had shown "some signs of success". From a man who was presumably trying to talk up Government achievement, this was pretty minimal.

THE MAIN PROBLEMS IN 2005

- Empowerment and accountability was very patchy.
- Incremental acquisition was seen as risky.
- The through-life approach attracted lip-service only.
- The capability approach was difficult to implement
- Annuality still undermined commitment and investment.
- Early project stages were inadequately funded.
- Stovepiping and loss of coherence in procurement.
- High-level committees were led by Suppliers rather than Customers.
- MoD continued to use competition rather than partnering as the favoured procurement option.
- The relationship between MoD and industry remained adversarial in many procurement projects.
- Little culture change was evident in either Whitehall or industry.
- Technical innovation was regarded by MoD as importing risk.
- Personal skills and expertise remained inadequate.
- Pay and rewards remained too low.
- Target culture was pervasive and too often misplaced.

Implementation Stalled

It is fair to conclude that Smart Procurement / Smart Acquisition was an excellent initiative, but that implementation stalled (and was later reversed) once the political pressure was removed. The forces of reaction had won again.

It needed a really strong leader if the MoD was to return successfully to the problems of cost-effective acquisition.

SUMMARY: SMART ACQUISITION

The Initiative
- Faster, cheaper, better.
- A clearer internal customer/supplier relationship in MoD.
- Centrality of incremental acquisition and a through-life approach.
- Partnering with industry.
- Personal accountability.
- Creation of Integrated Project Teams (IPTs).

Progress
- Creation and empowerment of the Equipment Capability Customer (ECC).
- Empowerment of Directors of Equipment Capability (DECs), IPT Leaders and others.
- Changes to the relationship with industry, particularly in the ECC and some areas of the Defence Logistics Organisation (DLO).
- Improved acquisition training.

Stagnation
- The through-life concept not implemented.
- Incremental acquisition not implemented.
- Low levels of funding of early project stages continue.
- Annuality remains.
- Transition from capability to project not achieved.
- Levels of skills and personal qualities remain low.
- Inadequate pay and rewards.
- Target setting continues to be counter-productive.
- Competition remains the prime strategy for procurement.
- Adversarial relationships with industry remain in many areas.
- No change in industrial culture.
- No change in overall Whitehall culture.

New Concerns
- Stovepiping of projects and capabilities.
- Undefined roles of 2-star officials in Defence Procurement Agency (DPA) and ECC.
- Increasing gap between the Equipment Plan (EP) and the Short Term Plan (STP).
- Primacy of process rather than delivery.

PART TWO

THE DEFENCE INDUSTRIAL STRATEGY

Chapter Four

The Defence Industrial Strategy

The failure to implement most of the Smart Procurement programme left UK acquisition in a continuing downward spiral. Something had to be done, not only to solve the problems listed at the close of the last chapter, but also in response to several overlapping crises:[53]

- The rapid and persistent rise in the unit cost of successive equipment generations, and the much slower growth of the UK defence budget.
- The lack of constructive relationships between MoD and its industrial suppliers, many of whom saw the MoD's continuous commitment to competition as wasteful and damaging.
- The increasing dominance of the US customer for defence equipment, which led UK companies to seek contracts from the Pentagon, often through US-based subsidiaries.
- The increasing disparity between the annual US expenditure on R&T and that of the UK and other nations.

In May 2005, Lord Drayson took over from Lord Bach as Minister Defence Procurement. With his commercial background *"he was appointed by Tony Blair to use his experience in business to overhaul MoD procurement and to improve the prickly relationship between the Ministry and the arms industry. 'I come at the job knowing what it's like to be on the other side of the table. I know what it's like to be accountable to shareholders. So I can say some pretty direct, clear things to industry. They can't bullshit me'."*[54]

His commercial background was important, and it soon became apparent that here was a man who was going to drive change at a pace that the MoD would find challenging to say the least. He demanded that a Defence Industrial Strategy (DIS) be produced before Christmas. Predictably, he was told it could not be done so quickly; equally predictably, he ordered that it would be done. It was.

---

[53] David Kirkpatrick, *RUSI Defence Systems* (Volume 9, No. 1, June 2006) page 17.
[54] Danny Fortson, *The Independent*, 5 November 2006

Drayson's Strategy

There existed a Defence Industrial Policy, but it was a wishy-washy affair without teeth. The Defence Industrial Strategy was to provide a much clearer way ahead – with teeth. The starting point was the future of the British defence industry and its relationship with MoD.

> *In this strategy, we consider carefully which industrial capabilities we need to retain in the UK to ensure that we can continue to operate our equipment in the way we choose, to maintain our appropriate sovereignty and thereby protect our national security. The Strategy sets these out, and explains clearly for the first time which industrial capabilities we require to be sustained onshore, noting that – as now – there are many that we can continue to seek to satisfy through open international competition.*[55]

The need for such a strategy, ever since the fall of Communism and the 'Peace Dividend' had led to a significant reduction in the scale and frequency of orders for industry over the previous decade or more, was evident, but this was the first time that a real attempt had been made to tackle this subject. Perhaps the real driver was the position of the maritime industry which was facing a huge ship building programme over the following decade but the prospect of a dearth of orders in the decade after that. How could the expertise in design and development be retained onshore?

> How could the expertise in design and development be retained onshore?

So 'appropriate sovereignty' was the main driver, but the DIS went on to say:

> *To implement this strategy will require changes on behalf of both industry and Government. Industry will need to adjust to sustain the capabilities we need once procurement peaks are passed. The Government, too, needs to drive forward improvements in the way we acquire, support and upgrade our equipment.*[56]

Guiding Principles

The framework for DIS was given as six Guiding Principles:
- Appropriate sovereignty.

---

[55] MoD, *Defence Industrial Strategy*, Cm 6697, Foreword, page 2, The Stationery Office, London, December 2005
[56] Ibid.

- Through-life capability management.
- Maintaining key industrial capabilities and skills.
- Intelligent customers and suppliers and the importance of systems engineering.
- Value for defence.
- Change on both sides.

The DIS was signed by John Reid (Defence Secretary), Alan Johnson (Trade and Industry Secretary), Des Browne (Chief Secretary to the Treasury – later Defence Secretary) and Alun Michael (Minister of State for Industry and the Regions). This was encouraging, but had the Treasury really bought into it?

As suggested by the two extracts from the Foreword above, there were two distinct parts to the DIS document – appropriate sovereignty and acquisition change. The first was covered in much greater thoroughness and persuasiveness than the second, which was lumped in with implementation and was far from convincing. Change, as ever, was not a favourite subject in MoD. Was this a foretaste of what was to come?

> There were two distinct parts – appropriate sovereignty and acquisition change

Appropriate Sovereignty

After a Strategic Overview of the defence market, the UK business environment, innovation, exports and 'wider factors' – including security of supply – the DIS examined the requirements for retention within the UK industrial base in each industrial sector, as shown in Figure 4-1.

Appropriate sovereignty is defined by DIS as follows:

We must maintain the appropriate degree of sovereignty over industrial skills, capacities, capabilities and technology to ensure operational independence against the range of operations that we wish to be able to conduct. This is not 'procurement independence', or total reliance on national supply of all elements, and will differ across technologies and projects. It covers not only being assured of delivery of ongoing contracts, but also the ability to respond to Urgent Operational Requirements (UORs).

As an example, only a handful of countries in the world have the capacity to build nuclear submarines:

If Government and industry fail to fulfil their roles in pursuit of a viable industrial base, the cost of re-establishing the [base] at a later date would most likely be prohibitive and the country would lose a key strategic industry and defence capability.[57]

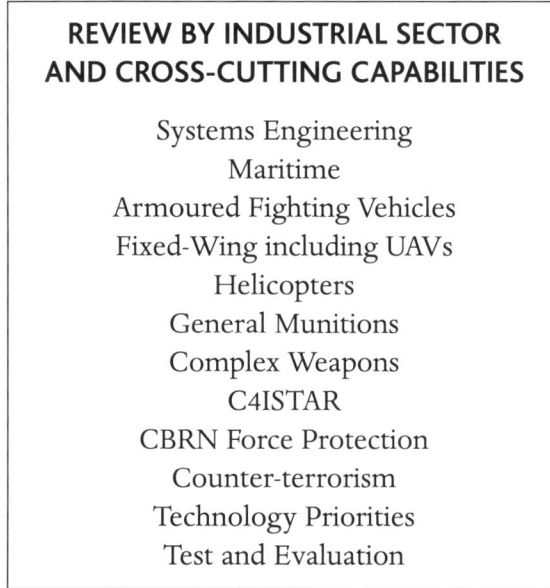

REVIEW BY INDUSTRIAL SECTOR AND CROSS-CUTTING CAPABILITIES

Systems Engineering
Maritime
Armoured Fighting Vehicles
Fixed-Wing including UAVs
Helicopters
General Munitions
Complex Weapons
C4ISTAR
CBRN Force Protection
Counter-terrorism
Technology Priorities
Test and Evaluation

Figure 4–1: Sectors considered by the DIS

Sustainment Strategies

To maintain appropriate sovereignty, UK needs to ensure that some or all of the skills to achieve the following (dependent on sector) are retained in UK:

- Requirement definition, modelling and analysis.
- Architecture, system-of-systems and system design.
- Assembly, integration, outfitting.
- Test and acceptance.
- In-service support.
- Through-life capability management.
- Upgrades, technology insertion.
- UOR delivery.
- Intelligent customer capability for non-UK designed systems.

---

[57] Gavin Ireland, 'Beyond Artful: Government and Industry Roles in Britain's Future Submarine Design, Build and Support', *RUSI Whitehall Report* 3-07, page 26, 2007.

The requirement will vary from sector to sector as can be seen at Appendix 4–1. For example, it was concluded that in the maritime sector, all of the above would be needed, although not all future ships would be built in the UK. In the air sector, the DIS did not envisage any significant investment in production facilities.

As a result, the sustainment strategies for each sector vary considerably. In the armoured fighting vehicle sector, the fixed-wing aircraft sector and the general munitions sector, strategic partnering arrangements were to be sought with BAE Systems, while in the rotary-wing sector, a strategic partnering arrangement was to be concluded with AgustaWestland. The maritime sector posed more of a problem as an industrial restructuring was necessary before any strategic partnering agreement could be entered into.

In contrast, both the C4ISTAR and the CBRN sectors were deemed to be 'buoyant' and not to need any sustainment strategy.

Strategic Partnering

This shift from the former adversarial, competitive relationship to strategic partnering had been part of the Smart Procurement Initiative, but then there was no real appetite for such a change in many areas of MoD and industry, particularly in the DPA and the Treasury, and once it became apparent that change would involve staff moving out of their comfort zones, this lack of motivation made this shift impossible. Now, eight years on, the move was rather more obviously urgent and it was being spelled out in much clearer language. Would it go ahead? And if it did, would it work?

I will explore how such partnering would work – or not – in the next chapter. For now, it is enough to say that partnering is not an easy thing to do. Competition is a far easier procurement strategy, and almost everyone in industry and MoD had built their careers in such an environment. This change is a considerable challenge.

To many observers, this strategic partnering sounded like a capitulation to the big boys. BAE Systems was to have a strategic partnering arrangement with MoD in many sectors. Lewis Page, not one of BAE's admirers, had this to say:

Really, then, we have received no benefits at all for the vast sums we have poured into BAE over the decades … And still BAE is heavily involved in all the big projects currently under way. Why?[58]

Why? Because it is the only large British prime contractor. The alternative is to buy foreign off-the-shelf, which is hardly the solution wanted by the DIS, or to award a strategic partnership to a foreign prime, which may also not be the answer to appropriate sovereignty further down the supply chain. We are where we are. Perhaps we should have addressed this issue when we still had three different armoured vehicle manufacturers in the UK. But we didn't; we fiddled about in Europe with the Multi-Role Armoured Vehicle (MRAV) instead.

Acquisition Change

DIS set out its approach to acquisition change, which would be built around the objective of achieving:

- Primacy of through-life considerations.
- Coherence of defence spend across research, procurement and support.
- Successful management of acquisition at the departmental level.

It was to address challenges remaining from the non-implementation of Smart Acquisition, particularly embedding a through-life systems approach, achieving a better and more transparent relationship with industry, improving risk and performance management, and tailoring the procurement approach to the needs of individual acquisition programmes.

Interestingly it didn't specifically include changing culture. It did, however, list the Defence Values for Acquisition (Figure 4–2) which the MoD had announced two months before:

---

[58] Lewis Page, *Lions, Donkeys and Dinosaurs* (William Heinemann, London, 2006), page 253.

MoD's DEFENCE VALUES FOR ACQUISITION

- Recognise that people are the key to our success.
- Recognise that the best can be the enemy of the very good.
- Identify trade-offs between performance, cost and time.
- Never assume that additional resources will be available.
- Think incrementally and seek out agile solutions.
- Quantify risk and reduce it by placing it where it can be managed most effectively.
- Recognise and respect the contribution made by industry.
- Value openness and transparency; share future plans and priorities.
- Embed a through-life culture.
- Value objectivity based on clear evidence rather than advocacy.
- Realise that success and failure matter.

Figure 4–2: The Defence Values for Acquisition as laid down in the Defence Industrial Strategy

It then went on to lay down the business environment that was sought. It was to be less adversarial, based on mutual understanding of where the motivations and interests of each party lay, with a willingness to share information and an ethos that encouraged potential problems to be brought to light early. All this, of course, could only be achieved by trust and transparency – not a characteristic of Whitehall.

The operations in Iraq, and later Afghanistan, reinforced the need for procurement agility, and the DIS acknowledged that there was much to learn from UOR procurement and that incremental acquisition was better suited to these challenges. The importance of innovation, the need to remain alive to developments in the commercial market, and a greater emphasis on the development of demonstrators were also stressed.

Enabling Acquisition Change

The DIS was relatively light on acquisition change and this was rectified in the ensuing Enabling Acquisition Change (EAC) study. It was admitted that this study concentrated on structures, organisation and processes, but *"this is not to understate the paramount importance of skills, training, culture and behaviour"*. Of course, that is exactly what it did.

Main EAC Recommendations. EAC did, however, recommend a list of changes that should be made. These included:

- A ten-year plan to be constructed for all equipment costs including those in non-equipment DLoDs.
- An increased emphasis on realism as opposed to a 'conspiracy of optimism'.
- Maintenance of an unallocated contingency in the ten-year plan.
- Appointment of an SRO for all major programmes.
- Merger of the DPA and DLO.
- Involvement of the Defence Management Board (DMB) for the highest value decisions.
- A single coherent acquisition reform programme led at Board level.

EAC Disappointments. These recommendations were all to the good. But overall it was a little disappointing. Many issues were not really addressed, and these included:

- The balance between IPT empowerment and stovepiping.
- Innovation and risk.
- Tenures of posts.
- Culture change.
- Leadership.
- Blame culture.
- Personal standards, although it did cover skills briefly.
- Motivation, pay and rewards.
- Target culture.
- Learning from experience and corporate memory.

Admittedly, most of these fell into the culture category which the MoD, wrongly, had decided not to cover in the EAC study, despite its acknowledgement that it is of paramount importance

Defence Acquisition Change Programme

The Defence Acquisition Change Programme (DACP) was then set in hand to implement the recommendations of the EAC.

The overriding objective of the DACP is to bring about a step change improvement in acquisition performance – i.e. in the delivery of capability to the front line and value-for-money for the taxpayer –

through creating a more agile acquisition system and managing capability through life.

Delivery Skills

It was recognised in Smart Procurement, and later by the then CDP, that professional delivery skills were just not good enough. This was reinforced by DIS:

> *We must ensure that the appropriate training, development and professional standards are in place for all those involved in acquisition, and that staff receive the reward and recognition for their competence and for their achievements in project delivery.*

The DIS's emphasis lay in improved training with the Acquisition Leadership Development Scheme, the new MSc in Defence Acquisition Management at the Defence Academy, and a Business Graduate Scheme.

> Professional delivery skills were just not good enough

Challenge to Industry

The DIS was primarily concerned with MoD's relationship with industry and MoD acquisition change. There was, however, one short section entitled 'The Challenge to Industry', in which it said that MoD is committed to driving the change agenda and that it was looking for parallel commitment from industry to:

- Plan more effectively and jointly for the long term, embracing through-life capability management.
- Invest in a systems engineering capability.
- Support greater interaction and collaboration between defence, industry and the universities to stimulate innovation.
- Emb⸺ ⸺ he use of open systems architectural and incremental ⸺ ⸺hroughout the supply chain.
- ⸺ r understanding of each other's objectives and ⸺ ⸺ices.
- ⸺ ⸺ering behaviours at all levels.

Implementation of DIS

Producing a comprehensive initiative is one thing – implementing it is quite another. The DIS had been put together in about six months by a relatively small group of people, but it could be expected to take five years or more to be implemented across industry and MoD. Section C of the DIS is entitled 'Getting Down to Work – Putting the DIS into Action'. Section C2 starts with this message:

> *The Defence Industrial Strategy sets out a comprehensive agenda for change, both in how we approach and interact with the market place in several areas and in how we and industry behave and are organised. Much effort has been expended – within the MoD, across Government and in industry – in putting it together. But all this will be for nothing unless Government and industry are prepared to work together to address the real challenges that we face.[59]*

MoD has a strong record on producing initiatives, many of which (but not all) are exactly what is needed. However, its record on implementing them is extremely poor – Smart Procurement being a good example. Often incomplete implementation is worse than no implementation at all, because problems that get thrown up during the initial execution are never resolved and remain a thorn to the real practitioners.

There are several reasons why implementation is so poor. Politicians are fond of initiatives as they give the impression of progress; they are also fond of 'quick wins', but these often have the least effect on delivery; and once an initiative is under way they are quick to dream up another. To politicians, initiatives are good, but implementation is boring and best left to others. But are politicians solely to blame? By no means. The officials are guilty of picking out the straightforward elements, which are relatively quick to introduce and most conspicuous, so as to impress their political bosses, but avoiding the more difficult and lengthy changes while expecting another initiative along shortly to get them off the hook. The 'tick-in-the-box' mentality then takes over. Human nature?

But there is another human failing at work – inertia. Change is difficult to introduce and requires staff at all levels to move out of their

---

[59] DIS, page 141.

comfort zones. Most people are happy doing what they are used to doing. Strong, consistent leadership of the 'Do-as-I-do', rather than 'Do-as-I-say' sort is required from the top over a long period (probably greater than five years for any major change). Leadership, not just management, is the key. This, of course, is difficult if some at the top levels are not convinced that the changes are required, and impossible if there is any opposition.

Guy Griffiths, then Chief Operating Officer of MBDA, had this to say on the importance of leadership from the top:

> *We're looking at a range of methods to change culture. One is leadership from the top – nothing is going to work unless people within our respective organisation see the people at the top behaving in this new way; and if there is any breaking of ranks at the top level, the whole thing will come tumbling down.*[60]

It is difficult to know just how much opposition there is to any one initiative. But the record of introducing many of the acquisition changes that have been recommended over the last 40 years suggests a lot. Take the recommendation, first made by Downey in 1968 and since repeated many times, that we should spend much more (15%) on the early stages of a project in order to reduce risks later in the procurement cycle. Spending more upfront is obviously a good thing to do, although the amount spent on each project will vary according to what you are trying to deliver, the risks associated with it and the operational urgency to get it into service: 15% should not be seen as a template, but might very well be an overall average. In the long run, spending more on the early stages will save money. Is it difficult to do? No. Although moving money forward is

> So, why hasn't this been implemented? Incompetence? Inertia? Opposition?

always difficult, meeting 15% could easily be done by a one-off round of delays to some project ISDs, not all of which it is essential to meet. And we are talking about relatively small amounts of money. So, why hasn't this been implemented? Incompetence? Inertia? Opposition?

---

[60] Guy Griffiths, then Chief Operating Officer MBDA, *RUSI Defence Systems* (Volume 10, No 1, June 2007), page 13.

Major Challenges

Clearly implementation will not be easy: there are several major challenges to the defence community to be overcome. An industry view:[61]

- Establishing the right level of investment in defence research and technology and organising ourselves to exploit it as effectively as possible.
- Embedding the right behaviours and the right techniques to introduce long-term partnering between MoD and industry, whilst retaining competition in, and innovation from, the supply chain.
- Planning procurement in a manner that eschews over-optimistic projection and encourages teamwork in reducing and managing risk.
- Working together to show to all stakeholders – front-line customers, taxpayers and shareholders – that efficient outcomes are being achieved while taking their interests into account.
- Demonstrating to our international partners that the UK remains committed to fair and free trade and cooperation, whilst achieving its national security goals through the DIS.

This is well put. The danger is that MoD action might well be hijacked by the changes that take the eye, such as the formation of the Defence Equipment and Support (DE&S) organisation, which obscure the most important challenges. Reorganisation and process change are almost entirely enablers – on their own they will do little to improve acquisition. The real benefit comes from culture change and improvement of staff qualities. The challenge here is to concentrate on that culture change while still devoting much effort to everything else.

> The real benefit comes from culture change and improvement of staff qualities

Lord Drayson was clear that DIS would be implemented:

'Can we implement?' was the dominant question that emerged from the last issue of RUSI Defence Systems *which focused on the Defence Industrial Strategy (DIS). My response to this is simple – we are. However, DIS set both industry and MoD a challenge. Ten months on, I continue to drive MoD and industry to maintain the pace of transformation.*[62]

---

[61] Derek Marshall, *RUSI Defence Systems* (Volume 9, No. 1, June 2006), page 34.
[62] Lord Drayson, *RUSI Defence Systems* (Volume 9, No. 2, October 2006), page 20.

And so he was. But this threw up another concern. Full implementation was going to take many years – four, five, six or more. Drive from the top would be required throughout this implementation period, but how long would Drayson remain to provide that necessary stimulus? If he was to move on, would his successor show the same commitment? Or would he or she have other priorities and allow DIS to run into the sand just as the successors to Robertson and Spellar did with Smart Acquisition?

Or would it be different this time? The Permanent Under-Secretary took responsibility as follows:

> When it comes to internal change, I am in no doubt that it is up to the permanent leadership of the Department to make this stick.[63]

But is the permanent leadership completely sold on DIS?

> Lord Drayson's legacy should be that he streamlined defence procurement, made partnerships work and cut through the 'process bollocks' beloved by some factions of the Civil Service. The question is whether he has the support to take on the Civil Service and win the process battle.[64]

Much of DIS follows on from Smart Acquisition – particularly the acquisition change programme. Smart Acquisition was never properly implemented. It is vital that DIS implementation does not fail too.

> It is vital that DIS implementation does not fail too

> Implementation is key. It needs to change the fundamentals, particularly culture and behaviours in both industry and MoD.[65]

Terminology

There was a further challenge to all those who were attempting to implement DIS: terminology. Many of the terms used daily by numbers of people in MoD and industry were not clearly defined and they were used with different meanings by different people. For example, in the Defence Values for Acquisition, exactly what do agile solutions, openness

---

[63] Bill Jeffrey, 'Implementing the Defence Industrial Strategy', *RUSI Defence Systems* (Volume 9, No. 2, October 2006), page 23.
[64] Paul Beaver, 'Is the Systems Ready for the Defence Industrial Strategy?', *RUSI Defence Systems* (Volume 9, No. 1, June 2006), page 17.
[65] RUSI Acquisition Focus, 'Implementation of the Defence Industrial Strategy', *RUSI Defence Systems* (Volume 9, No. 2, October 2006), page 78, (see Appendix 4–3).

and transparency, through-life culture and objectivity really mean? The answer is that they mean to individuals what each of those individuals expect them to mean within their narrow perspectives – and each will have a slightly different definition. The clearest example of this is Through-Life Capability Management (TLCM) – everyone interprets it differently. Value-for-money is another good example.

What Will DIS Cost?

Although DIS on the whole was generally, and quite rightly, welcomed, there were two glaring inadequacies. The first was the poor coverage of R&T, which I am leaving to Chapter Nine, but the other was far more critical. There was no mention of cost or how that cost would be met. The RUSI Acquisition Focus was clear on the importance of this omission:

> We question whether the worthy aims of 'good value to the taxpayer **and** good returns to shareholders' are achievable without substantial extra investment by the Government. Unless this is clearly addressed, the Strategy may fail before it really gets off the ground.[66]

It is self-evident that maintaining skills onshore when orders are inadequate to turn an industrial profit must cost money. Over the last decade or more, many industrial firms, particularly small ones, have gone out of business or moved out of defence altogether. Some of those could not be mourned, but others led to a reduction in the onshore expertise that DIS calls for. In the adversarial, competitive years, MoD was generally not interested in the fate of defence companies, but did in some cases enter into agreements that cost the taxpayer large sums of money to keep development and production expertise and facilities. DIS is now proposing that we do this on a much larger scale on a much wider basis.

> DIS is now proposing that we do this on a much larger scale

Lord Drayson believed that the costs could be contained:

> A number of commentators have questioned whether the implementation of DIS can deliver enhanced profitability for industry, better value for the taxpayer and improved capability for the front line. I believe it can – my experience in industry

---

[66] RUSI Acquisition Focus, *RUSI Defence Systems* (Volume 9, No. 1, June 2006), page 22, (see Appendix 4–2).

is that when customer and supplier engage in a robust programme of business transformation, a win-win result can be achieved.[67]

Some in industry were less convinced:

> You are not going to retain capability for the sake of retaining capability. Platforms manufactured in the UK are very good value compared to their equivalents in the US, for example. So you could argue that it will save money. There is, of course, the problem of peaks and troughs in new orders, and obviously a feast-to-famine situation is not going to cost you less.[68]

Other areas of likely cost increases include:[69]

- Reduced competition in those equipment sectors covered by long-term strategic partnerships between the MoD and chosen UK-based contractors [competition has allegedly saved large sums of money in the past].
- Diseconomies of scale in national maintenance, repair and upgrade of equipment procured from foreign suppliers.
- Measures to sustain, in particular equipment sectors, UK-based design, development and production capabilities in the intervals between military requirements for new projects in those sectors.

> DIS is an unbelievably bad deal for British taxpayers and servicemen

But to other people, including Lewis Page, the answer to how much it will all cost is lots:

> It's often said that British industry likes the Government's Defence Industrial Strategy (DIS) but doesn't believe it will really happen. The Government, injured, asks why. The true answer is that the DIS is an unbelievably bad deal for British taxpayers and servicemen, and industry fears that they will one day realise this. Buy British–Italian–American Lynxes at £14M each when you could get bigger, better American Seahawks for £6M? It's quite hard to believe we did that to begin with, let alone that we'll keep on doing similar things for the foreseeable future – which is what the DIS says.[70]

There will be many who see this the same way – that taxpayers are

[67] Lord Drayson, *RUSI Defence Systems* (Volume 9, No. 2, October 2006), page 22.
[68] Ian King, Interview, *RUSI Defence Systems* (Volume 9 No 1, June 2006), page 13.
[69] David Kirkpatrick, 'More Spurious Savings by the MoD', Newsbrief (Volume 28 No 1, January 2008), page 4, Royal United services Institute.
[70] Lewis Page, 'Under-investment and Waste', *RUSI Defence Systems* (Volume 10, No 1, June 2007), page 20.

subsidising uncompetitive British industry so that jobs in MPs' constituencies are not lost. Page suggests that we should buy cheaper, better US equipment and there is a case that can be made for that strategy. But DIS makes the case for a strong onshore industry that will give the UK 'operational independence' to carry out future operations. Whether equipment made or upgraded onshore by US companies or by British companies using US or other foreign subsystems is more operationally independent is a moot point.

But the clinching argument to my mind is our reliance on UOR procurement – we cannot, or perhaps will not, afford to do otherwise. Effective UOR procurement is very much dependent on three things: an expert MoD acquisition staff, an agile and innovative R&T community and a strong onshore defence industrial base – all three across most of the board. All three have been run down to a dangerously low level in recent decades, but can still function adequately as the UOR deliveries to Iraq and Afghanistan demonstrate. But they cannot decline much further. This is recognised by DIS with its insistence on improving MoD delivery skills, strong (if rather naïve) encouragement of R&T and, above all, by the heart of DIS, the protection of 'appropriate sovereignty'.

Who will pay? Not industrial shareholders. Not the Department of Trade and Industry (DTI). The Treasury? Was the lack of costings in DIS Treasury-imposed? They did sign up to DIS, but the signatory has moved on. I doubt if they will provide the extra money. That leaves the defence budget, which is desperately overheated.

> So, extra costs will be large but there is no provision to meet them

So, extra costs will be large at some stage in the future, but there is no provision to meet them. Can it be done by cutting costs in both MoD and industry, by eliminating waste through improved acquisition, by innovation and gainshare? Possibly, but that will only happen if DIS is fully and enthusiastically embraced by both MoD and industry.

Place your bets.

Strengths and Weaknesses

As with all major initiatives, DIS has both strengths and weaknesses. There was a variety of opinion, but in general the DIS was warmly welcomed by most of the acquisition community.

Vision

Lord Drayson needs to be congratulated on his vision of the future relationship between MoD and industry in the UK. As Dr Ronald Sugar, CEO of Northrop Grumman, put it:

> *Clearly, [the DIS] is looking not just to modernise, but to 'futurise'. The DIS has looked down the road a long way and made a shrewd assessment of where defence transformation is headed ... Clearly, the UK intends to capitalise on these trends to the benefit of the nation's autonomy and freedom of action. One can also infer a desire for the valuable, high-quality jobs that characterise intellectual capital and cutting-edge technology. For example, the document emphasises systems engineering, open architectures and the accumulation and retention of scientific and engineering talent. I see wisdom here.*[71]

Lord Drayson needs to be congratulated on his vision

Another view from industry:

> *I'm not sure that Smart Acquisition really addressed the through-life aspect. I think that's the major change – not focusing just on the initial procurement phase. There needs to be more emphasis on the in-service part of the CADMID cycle from the start.*[72]

Primes and SMEs

Many people saw the DIS as a benefit for platform primes, with little in it for non-platform companies or SMEs.

> *The only concern is from the 'little guys' – those enterprises that do not have direct access to the ministerial office, lead major trade associations or employ thousands, and who ask: 'Who looks after the little man – the SMEs?' They are often, in the words of the Minister himself, key to innovation and security of supply.*[73]

Most of the White Paper concentrated on partnering arrangements with platform primes – AgustaWestland and BAE Systems to the front with arrangements on helicopters, armoured vehicles and munitions. This

---

[71] Dr Ronald Sugar, 'Trends and Opportunities: UK/US Defence Co-operation', *RUSI Defence Systems* (Volume 9, No. 1, June 2006), page 25.

[72] Ian King, Interview, *RUSI Defence Systems* (Volume 9, No. 1, June 2006), page 11.

[73] Paul Beaver, 'Is the System Ready for the Defence Industrial Strategy?', *RUSI Defence Systems* (Volume 9, No. 1, June 2006), page 16.

drew criticism that it was a platform-prime benefit, with little helpful analysis of non-platform-producing companies or the supply chain in general.

Research and Technology

There was also some concern, although not as much as there should have been, about R&T.

> *Defence research is the key to the success of the DIS across all sectors. If we are to continue to provide our Armed Forces with world-class equipment we must remain at the cutting edge of defence technology ... Spending on defence research has halved since this Government came to power, from £900M to £450M today. The DIS has much sound rhetoric on research but, sadly, little substance.*[74]

Perception of the Aim

The DIS stated that its aim was to *"provide good value to the taxpayer and good returns to shareholders"*. This will be difficult, of course, but not impossible. However, the phrases 'good value to the taxpayer' and 'good returns to shareholders' are open to different interpretations. How would success be measured?

> **How would success be measured?**

> *This is not at all clear. The main reason for this is that the perception of the overall objective of the DIS may differ from one constituency to another. Is it to provide better equipment for the Armed Forces? Or to achieve better value-for-money for the taxpayer – or for UK plc? Or is it to ensure the preservation of industrial capabilities onshore – or just to make the defence industry feel good? Maybe it is all of these, so measurement of success is complex.*[75]

Cost

As already discussed at length, the potential cost of DIS, and how it might be funded, was not mentioned. This is perhaps the greatest weakness of DIS.

---

[74] Gerald Howarth, 'Taking the Temperature of the DIS: Drayson's Scorecard', *RUSI Defence Systems* (Volume 9, No. 2, October 2006), page 17.
[75] RUSI Acquisition Focus, 'Implementation of the Defence Industrial Strategy', *RUSI Defence Systems* (Volume 9, No. 2, October 2006), page 78.

SUMMARY: THE DEFENCE INDUSTRIAL STRATEGY

Main Strengths:
- Provides a clear approach, sector by sector, to retaining a strong onshore defence industry.
- Signals a clear move from adversarial competition to strategic partnering.
- Lays out definitive Defence Values for Acquisition.
- Emphasises the importance of a through-life approach.
- Highlights the need for innovation, agility and flexibility.
- Restates the importance of Research and Technology (R&T).
- States clearly that MoD will, with immediate effect, deliver on its revised policy of providing industry with a better and longer-term understanding of its future plans.

Main Concerns:
- Scope for different perceptions of the Defence Industrial Strategy (DIS) aim(s).
- Perceived as a platform-prime benefit.
- Little comfort for Small- and Medium-sized Enterprises (SMEs).
- Warm words but little substance on R&T.
- The lack of emphasis on culture change in the follow-on work of Enabling Acquisition Change (EAC).
- MoD acquisition skills level could undermine implementation of strategic partnering.
- The difficulty of implementation given the embedded MoD culture, its 'immune system' and the possible short time that architects are likely to be in place.
- Overall cost, which was not mentioned at all.

Appendix 4–1

THE DEFENCE INDUSTRIAL STRATEGY

APPROPRIATE SOVEREIGNTY: REVIEW BY INDUSTRIAL SECTOR

The Maritime Sector
Not surprisingly, perhaps, it was the maritime sector – the initial driver – that was given more detailed treatment than the rest. There was much discussion on the forward UK maritime programmes and the international industrial context. But it then set out a Sustainment Strategy, which included the following statements:

- To maintain the key capabilities, a vibrant onshore forward programme is required, focusing on high-value activities.
- Industry restructuring is a priority.
- Procurement strategies should deliver three key objectives: a sustainable enterprise, better performance for MoD and attractive rates of return for industry.
- We will take specific measures to ensure the sustainability of significant capabilities in 2nd- and 3rd-tier suppliers where these are at risk.
- The Maritime Industrial Strategy will be at the heart of developing a sustainable relationship between the MoD and industry.

There were others, but the above are perhaps the most significant.

Armoured Fighting Vehicles
The armoured fighting vehicles (AFV) section looked at two aspects – the future support and upgrade of the in-service AFV fleet and the procurement and support of the Future Rapid Effect System (FRES). The Sustainment Strategy for AFV included a statement of the Way Ahead:

> We will need to work hard with BAE Systems Land Systems, building on the discussions we have already set in train, and the agreement reached in December 2005, to give effect to the long-term partnering agreement required to improve the reliability, availability and effectiveness through life of our existing fleets ... We intend to establish a joint partnering team within the early part of 2006 and to establish a business transformation plan underpinned by a robust milestone and performance regime ... We are particularly keen to see a build-up in the UK of expertise in the systems

integration of complex land systems. If successful in their evolution, BAE Systems will be well placed for the forthcoming FRES programme.

Fixed Wing

This sector includes fast jets (no new systems envisaged after Typhoon and the Joint Strike Fighter (JSF)), large and training aircraft (for which there is a large international market), mission systems (where there is considerable onshore expertise, but under threat), propulsion (where Rolls-Royce is a world-leader) and UAVs (where there is little UK expertise).

The Way Ahead section states that:

> *We need to develop the dialogue in which we have been engaged by commencing negotiations with BAE Systems in earnest on the terms of a business rationalisation and transformation agreement required to facilitate the effective sustainment of the industrial skills, capability and technologies … to operate, support and upgrade our fast jet combat aircraft through life.*

The Way Ahead fails to mention anything other than fast jets, which seems to be a failing amongst airmen. But in the Sustainment Strategy and elsewhere it does state the following:

- We will continue to invest in propulsion technologies.
- There is no sovereign requirement to sustain an indigenous capability [for large and training aircraft]. We will continue to need, however, the systems engineering and design skills and access to intellectual property rights for the integration of new mission systems.

Although it is acknowledged that the strong UK-based capability in mission systems is now threatened, the Sustainment Strategy does not cover them.

As for UAVs and UCAVs, the Sustainment Strategy provides for investment in a substantial Technology Demonstrator Programme (TDP) *"Designed to give us and industry a better understanding of key technologies of relevance to UAVs and UCAVs more broadly"*. This is somewhat of a surprise. Having dragged its feet on UAVs for a couple of decades, and then been forced to buy abroad under UOR procedures, MoD is now providing investment for BAE Systems to play catch-up. It would seem that either the investment will be inadequate to do so, or it will be at the expense of areas of existing expertise which are threatened. The Strategy notes that the benefit for UK industry is the opportunity to develop a competitive edge in a potentially lucrative military and civil market.

Helicopters

The requirement for retention onshore includes the skills for the through-life support of current aircraft, systems engineering skills for upgrades and technology insertion. The Way Ahead states:

> We need to drive forward with AgustaWestland the implementation of the business transformation partnering arrangement.

General Munitions

The term 'general munitions' includes artillery, naval gun, armoured vehicle and infantry munitions (with the exception of precision types) and mines, explosives and pyrotechnics. BAE Systems provides 80% of them. A Framework Partnering Agreement (FPA), a long-term arrangement, was signed with BAE Systems in 1999 and this ensures a sustainable and secure onshore industrial capability. A partnering principles document was signed by MoD and BAE in September 2005.

Project MASS (Munitions Acquisition – the Supply Solution) is aimed at building upon the existing FPA to secure an agreement that delivers, in the long term, best value-for-money and a sustainable future for industry.

The Way Ahead includes two objectives: to 'take forward' Project MASS and to 'actively pursue' partnering arrangements with suppliers of the non-BAE 20%.

Complex Weapons

Complex Weapons include air-to-air, air-to-surface, surface-to-surface and surface-to-air guided missiles. Directed energy weapons (DEW) also fall into this category, but MoD "is assessing the potential military utility of DEW technology through a number of research programmes".

To maintain appropriate sovereignty, the UK needs to be able to use, maintain and upgrade specific capabilities, independent of other nations. The DIS states that:

> We need to establish a multi-disciplinary team charged with working with the onshore industry to establish how we might together seek to sustain the critical guided weapons technologies and through-life support capabilities ... Given the transnational nature of the industrial players, this dialogue will need also to engage our allies and partners, particularly in Europe.

C4ISTAR

The DIS concludes that the UK C4ISTAR industry is in good health and that defence can benefit from the weight of investment in the civil sector. It produces a C4ISTAR strategy that will achieve better cross-government coordination of demand for cryptology, to encourage civil industry to explore the opportunities for defence, to provide industry with visibility of MoD's forward plans and to encourage the use of open systems architectures and COTS.

All in all, the DIS does not see the need for any significant new action.

CBRN

For Chemical, Biological, Radiological and Nuclear (CBRN) protection, the DIS concludes that the UK commercial sector is "buoyant" and that the MoD will explore innovative partnering opportunities, and work with the Home Office and the Department of Health to maximise economies of scale.

Counter-terrorism.

The DIS concludes that no sustainability issues are currently evident.

Sustainment Strategies

To maintain appropriate sovereignty, UK needs to ensure that some or all (varying between sectors) of the skills to achieve the following are retained in the UK:

- Requirement definition, modelling and analysis.
- Architecture, system-of-systems and system design.
- Assembly, integration, outfitting.
- Test and acceptance.
- In-service support.
- Through-life capability management.
- Upgrades, technology insertion.
- UOR delivery.

Appendix 4–2

RUSI ACQUISITION FOCUS[76]

THE DEFENCE INDUSTRIAL STRATEGY: AN OBJECTIVE VIEW

The RUSI Acquisition Focus was formed in March 2006 to provide an expert objective view on aspects of defence equipment acquisition. At their first meeting on 20 March, the subject for discussion was the recently published UK Government White Paper, Defence Industrial Strategy. The members of the Focus are John Weston (Chairman, Spirent), Tim Banfield (National Audit Office), Bob Barton (co-chair of the MoD/industry Equipment Capability Group), Vice Admiral (retd) Jeremy Blackham (recently EADS UK President), Professor Christopher Elliott (GD UK), Air Marshal Lord Garden (House of Lords), Graham Jordan (formerly DG R&T, MoD), Major General (retd) Bill Robins (formerly DGICS MoD), Bill Kincaid (author of the Dinosaur books on acquisition).[77]

The Defence Industrial Strategy (DIS) was published in December last year after a remarkably short period of preparation. It is rather more of a 'stepping stone' to a strategy than the finished strategy itself. The newly formed RUSI Acquisition Focus met to discuss the major issues arising from it.

We agree that it is a most worthy document, tackling many of the key issues that have been left in the pending tray for far too long and that it should be welcomed. Indeed, it is a commendable attempt to change a long period of deterioration, even though there are inconsistencies in the fullness of its treatment of different sections.

But, as with any positioning document, significant questions arise and we are concerned as to how many of them are to be tackled. There are too many of these issues to cover in one meeting and our plan is to discuss most of them in future meetings. At our first meeting, we discussed four topics.

Partnering

The first concern we discussed was partnering. The DIS signals a major shift in emphasis from competition to partnering, but it is not at all

---

[76] RUSI Acquisition Focus, 'The Defence Industrial Strategy: An Objective View', *RUSI Defence Systems* (Volume 9, No. 1, Summer 2006), page 22.
[77] Names and posts of the members have in some case changed but were correct when this paper was published.

clear how this will be made to work to 'provide good value to the taxpayer **and** good returns to shareholders', as the DIS aims to do.

The word partnering appears to mean all things to all men and we think it doubtful that there is a common understanding of the term within MoD, let alone across the government–industry interface. Unless we are mistaken, it would seem crucial that the term be clearly defined throughout the acquisition community, so that the responsibilities of partnering are understood by all. Partnering will not succeed in improving acquisition unless those responsibilities of both MoD and industry are clearly defined, recognised and consistently put into practice.

The strategy is based heavily on partnering, except in a few capability areas. However, MoD has for many years been reliant on competition to push down prices in an attempt to achieve value-for-money (VFM). Competition has been applied as a 'blunt instrument' and we have a concern that, as a result, MoD no longer has the expertise to correctly assess VFM in the absence of competition. Indeed, it may be argued that the approaches MoD used pre-competition are not suitable for the path adopted by DIS.

One major concern is the criteria against which MoD chooses its partners. To do so on price, rather than on other issues such as track record, culture and alignment of interests, may be counter-productive, but it is by no means obvious that MoD has the skills to do this effectively. Genuine VFM evaluation is difficult and we doubt whether MoD has the right skills to achieve VFM in such an environment. Our concerns seem to be echoed in Part C of the document by the emphasis on improving professional skills. Partnering will not succeed unless this is driven through. And if partnering does not deliver VFM, the strategy will be fatally undermined.

Implementation

Our next major concern is implementation. The Smart Procurement Initiative of 1998 largely failed, not because it was mistaken, but because it was never properly implemented. MoD has become a difficult environment in which to make change, for the strength of its 'immune system' is such that very strong and continuous sponsorship is imperative. After implementation of Smart Procurement was begun, Lord Robertson quickly departed and implementation ground to a halt. We cannot afford for this to happen with DIS, which represents a greater implementation challenge than Smart Acquisition, particularly in the change of culture that is needed; and change of culture takes time and strong, consistent leadership from the top. Lord Drayson has provided that leadership to date, but we feel that he will need to provide it for some years yet, and that his successors will need to be equally committed, or there is a distinct possibility that implementation will not be satisfactorily achieved.

The implementation section, with a few exceptions, describes the huge amount of activity that is now being undertaken. However, it is far from clear on how this activity will be carried forward, particularly those parts that involve industry. Is there a common prize at the end? We feel that unless some common goals, measures and clear prizes for both sides become a reality, then true partnering will fail to materialise.

So, what are the prizes? Industry welcomes the acceptance in the Strategy that industry needs to make a profit if the relationship is to work, and there has to be a return for the risks industry undertakes. The transfer of high risk to industry can be self-defeating if the risks result in highly unprofitable contracts. The Americans discovered this in the early 1990s with large cost overruns on fixed-price development contracts such as the A12 and the P7 programmes, and Astute and Nimrod are recent examples in the UK.

This principle does, however, imply that the costs to MoD will overall be higher. How are these to be afforded? It is not at all clear that the only answer is to cut costs. There is potential here, but the DIS does not tackle other options, which include returns for both sides from a renewed emphasis on 'gainshare'; drastic reduction in procurement cycle time to cut out the 'dead time' during MoD decision-making; more commitment from MoD once a programme starts in order to avoid nugatory expenditure by industry; and a greater drive for adoption of suitable innovation. But even if all this was achieved, there is still the question of how much it will cost to retain onshore those industrial capabilities identified. MoD aspirations simply do not match the budget available and no amount of 'cosmetic surgery' can disguise this.

We are therefore concerned about the overall cost of the DIS and how it will be met, while 'providing good value to the taxpayer **and** good returns to shareholders'. If the MoD (and the other departments who have signed up to this) has not produced a ball-park figure and thought through options to foot this particular bill, it surely should do so without delay. Without this, many people will see the whole strategy of partnering and retention of industrial capability onshore as 'just talk'. Others will see it as a clear signal that the end-user will suffer reduced quality and quantity of equipment.

Role of the End-User

The end-user will not, of course, see such reduction as value for his money, particularly if he can see the possibility of more lives being lost on operations as a result. The end-user (or Customer 2 as Smart Acquisition dubbed him) was supposed to have been integrated into the acquisition process but, although some movement has occurred, the end-user has neither the time nor the expertise to look ten, fifteen or twenty years ahead, while grappling with today's issues. His future interests are too often given a back seat.

The procurement process is focused on the Defence Procurement Agency (DPA), which plays a dominant role, often to the detriment of imperatives of military capability. The DPA is not measured on how well it achieves military capability – surely a glaring inconsistency? Cost and time targets concentrate its thinking and it is performance or equipment numbers that are repeatedly cut throughout the concept and development phases. Clearly, this is not in the best interests of Customer 2.

The back seat given to Customer 2 is illustrated by the DIS: while it considers many industrial capabilities from ships to aircraft to C4ISTAR, it does not include infantry equipment as a separate area, even though this is arguably more important today than are many of the others. This is an area that had a low priority during the Cold War, and nothing seems to have changed. We believe not only that it must be accorded at least as high a priority as those capabilities considered, but that the end-user must be brought much more closely into the acquisition cycle.

Value-for-money

We returned to VFM. The DIS is signed by ministers from four Government departments, so this suggests that VFM is defined on a rather wider basis than how much defence equipment is bought for how many pounds, particularly as one of the aims is better value for the taxpayer. But if this is so, then other departments should be shouldering some of the bill. Are they?

On the wider definition of VFM, the DIS should have included a reasoned argument about the value to the nation of the onshore defence industry. Quantities of, and gestation times between, orders have led to supply-base reduction and consolidation. In simple economic terms, retaining UK supply is not a big enough driver; buying from the US or Europe would be cheaper, at least in the short term, than propping up failing industries, but there are other considerations. Is an onshore industry essential for implementing Urgent Operational Requirements (UORs)? How would politicians and unions be persuaded to allow the cutting of jobs particularly in depressed areas and marginal constituencies? Is it likely that the US will allow unrestricted technology transfer, absolute sovereignty and manufacture outside the US of spare parts and upgrade equipment? It is this last point that may be the overriding factor.

All this points to the need for retention of an onshore defence industry. But how extensive should the onshore capability be? During the Cold War, the list of key capabilities for on-shore retention was very short, but the DIS list is far more extensive. Do we really need all that it says we do? Or should it have been chosen more selectively, perhaps in the highest technology fields alone?

Another question: should the defence budget foot any bill arising from the DIS, particularly if it is sizeable? If it does, the taxpayer will not be getting as much VFM, in the narrower sense of buying defence kit, as he does now. So, VFM is not a precise term and it can be argued either way that the DIS does or does not improve VFM, depending on the definition adopted.

We suggest that the nation gets better value for the money spent on defence equipment when we go to war and implement UORs, throwing the normal acquisition rules out of the window: industry and MoD work in close partnership and kit is produced very quickly. While this approach cannot be adopted wholesale for procurement, it proves that pace and quick results can be delivered. We believe that elements of this approach need to become the norm in the acquisition process to arrive at a halfway house between today's slow and cumbersome process and the agile UOR approach.

The Bottom Line

Overall, we firmly believe that the DIS is a welcome initiative, which attempts to tackle many of the problems that have lain for too long in the MoD's pending tray. However, we question whether the worthy aims of 'good value to the taxpayer **and** good returns to shareholders' are achievable without substantial extra investment by the Government. Unless this is clearly addressed, the Strategy may fail before it really gets off the ground.

Implementation is key. It needs to change the fundamentals, particularly culture and behaviours in both industry and MoD, but, however worthy the aims of the initiative, it will fail, as the promising Smart Acquisition initiative failed, unless there is strong commitment and leadership from the top over an extended period . We wonder how strong that commitment is in MoD. And we wonder whether it is strong enough within commercial enterprises if they are to change their existing practices ahead of demonstrable change within MoD.

Implementation will not be easy. But that is no reason to allow it to fail.

Appendix 4–3

RUSI ACQUISITION FOCUS[78]

IMPLEMENTATION OF THE DEFENCE INDUSTIAL STRATEGY

The RUSI Acquisition Focus was formed in March 2006 with the aim of providing an expert objective view on aspects of defence equipment acquisition. Its first paper, which examined the UK's Defence Industrial Strategy, was published in the Summer edition of RUSI Defence Systems. This, its second paper, looks at factors affecting the implementation of the Strategy.

The members of the focus are: John Weston (Chairman, Spirent), Tim Banfield (NAO), Bob Barton (co-chair of the MoD/Industry Equipment Capability Group), Vice Admiral (retd) Jeremy Blackham (recently EADS UK President), John Dowdy (Director, McKinsey), Professor Christopher Elliott (GD UK), Air Marshal Lord Garden (House of Lords), Graham Jordan (formerly DG R&T, MoD), Major General (retd) Bill Robins (formerly DGICS, MoD), Andrew White (Chief Executive, Serco), Bill Kincaid (Editor RUSI Defence Systems)[79]

The Defence Industrial Strategy (DIS) included a section on implementation and this was divided into two parts:

- Taking Forward the DIS – the Challenges for Change.
- Getting Down to Work – Putting the DIS into Action.

As we said in our previous paper: 'Implementation is key. It needs to change the fundamentals, particularly culture and behaviours in both industry and MoD'. In this paper, we discuss three important issues bearing on implementation.

Measuring Success

People are driven by how they are measured, so measurement of success would seem to be highly important. We wondered how successful implementation of DIS was to be measured.

This is not at all clear. The main reason for this is that the perception of the overall objective of the DIS may differ from one constituency to another. Is it to provide better equipment for the

---

[78] RUSI Acquisition Focus, 'Implementation of the Defence Industrial Strategy', *RUSI Defence Systems* (Volume 9, No. 2, Autumn 2006), page 78.

[79] Names and posts of the members have in some case changed but were correct when this paper was published.

Armed Forces? Or to achieve better value-for-money for the taxpayer – or for UK plc? Or is it to ensure the preservation of industrial capabilities onshore – or just to make the defence industry feel good? Maybe it is all of these, so measurement of success is complex.

It is muddied even further by the lack of financial discussion in the DIS. As we said in our first report, the cost of retaining an onshore industry of the proportions identified, whether or not there is sufficient work for them, is likely to be significant. How much is MoD or the Government as a whole prepared to pay – and for which of the outcomes above?

However, underlying all of this is the need to change attitudes and behaviours as nothing will happen if these fundamentals are not changed. Thus, the work on 'Enabling Acquisition Change' led by Tom McKane is perhaps the most important piece of work that has been put in hand.

Main Recommendations of the Study 'Enabling Acquisition Change'

- 10-year plan to be constructed for all defence costs, including support costs.
- Imbalance between Capital and Resource DELs to be addressed.
- Introduce an uncommitted element into the Equipment Plan to improve agility.
- Every major new capability to be assigned a 2-star Senior Responsible Owner (SRO)
- Defence Procurement Agency (DPA) and Defence Logistics Organisation (DLO) to be merged without Agency status.
- A strong commercial team to be built round the new Defence Commercial Director.
- The Defence Management Board (DMB) to be involved in Initial and Main Gate decisions.
- The Investment Approvals Board (IAB) to be restructured.

We warmly welcome the report because it contains many excellent recommendations on organisational and procedural change (shown in the panel), not least of which are the restructuring of the IAB and the engagement of the DMB. However, these will not in themselves change acquisition delivery as they are enablers, not drivers. The real driver is a change of culture and the report does have an excellent section on Behaviour, Culture, Skills and Training in which many important issues are discussed. Disappointingly, though, the recommendations which flow from this section are weak, and this weakness is carried through to the Executive Summary and Recommendations, which is the only part of the report that many decision-makers will read.

Inevitably, action will centre on merging the DPA and DLO, building a strong commercial team around the new Defence Commercial Director, restructuring the IAB, changing terminology and transforming organisational responsibilities. Almost all of this will be for the good, but we should not underestimate the challenge of the DPA/DLO merger. While grappling with this challenge, there is a very real danger that cultural change will take a lower priority. Exactly this happened with the Smart Procurement Initiative in 1998 and the partial implementation of that initiative led to failure. We should not make the same mistake again. Moreover, the timescale for establishing the organisational changes is long and this will almost certainly lead to paralysis in the interim, as decisions are deferred and individuals seek to settle in their new roles and workplaces. Any delay in appointing the new head of the merged procurement and support agency will limit his opportunity to engender the right culture there.

So, the challenge is there and PUS as the owner of the implementation of DIS will need to focus clearly on culture change and not allow procedural and organisational matters to push it into the background. It is unlikely that major behavioural change can be delivered solely by Ministerial diktat in an institution with the strong 'immune system' that MoD possesses. Strong, clear drivers that can be recognised by all are almost certainly required. Although there are pockets of excellence in the DPA, clear drivers for major change there would still seem to be lacking; in contrast drivers are much more clearly perceived in the DLO.

Perhaps not surprisingly, therefore, change is already apparent in the DLO (although there is still much more to be achieved), but there is a strong view that change is less evident in the DPA, where competition is still the soft option and partnering is seen as neither easy nor necessary. Culture change is needed across the board, but changes for the better in the DLO will not necessarily transfer successfully to the DPA, nor to the rest of the DLO; each project is different and may need to tailor change to its own circumstances. It will be interesting to see whether the merger of the two organisations will stimulate or dilute the changes taking place in the DLO. It is not easy to be optimistic.

But industry, too, will have to change and this is another challenge. In the defence industry, perceptions of the drivers will vary: some will see the necessity for change, but others may not if they have alternatives to working with MoD – for example, investing increasingly either in the US or in the civil sector.

Success will only be achieved by changing culture in MoD and in the defence industry. How this is to be driven and measured is not clear, although it is absolutely certain that only strong, even ruthless, leadership will achieve anything. Lord Drayson's undoubted commitment and continuing drive is essential to the level of success which can be achieved.

Partnering

The DIS has signalled a move away from competition towards partnering. Partnering, however, is not a soft option, but a mutual dependency within which both parties may have to make significant sacrifices and to share the risk. In our last paper, we pointed out that there was no common understanding of the responsibilities of partnering either within the MoD or across the MoD–industry divide, and partnering will not be successful unless responsibilities on both sides are clearly defined, recognised and consistently put into practice. And that includes accepting the pain of significant sacrifices.

Whilst the DLO has made major moves towards effective partnering, the DPA seems ideologically opposed to it. It has taken enormous personal conviction to drive through the Westland agreement, which at least shows the way. Effective partnering is likely to be the one indicator (and eventually the measure) of DIS success, but attitudes to competition and value-for-money will need to be substantially changed if partnering is to be successfully established.

Too often the short-term view overrides all, and the long-term view is ignored, even when it is clear that the short-term solution will have significant adverse effects in the long term – particularly where budgets are concerned. Agility is required as boundary conditions change, for no project is an island; this is not possible if contract rigidity is allowed to overrule capability coherence and common sense.

The conspiracy of optimism referred to in previous NAO reports appears now, for many programmes, to be replaced by a conspiracy of opportunism. This can drive sponsor, project team and industrial partner towards the short-term fix, on the basis of a shared understanding that the urgency of current problems makes it impossible to consider the longer-term solution adequately. What appears to be needed is a method of ensuring that the long-term issues are not lost in the scrum of immediate problem-solving.

One way in which this has been addressed at Board level in both DLO and DPA is to draft in non-executives who, in addition to bringing fresh perspectives, can act as the conscience of the enterprise.

It could be worth examining this approach at programme and even at project level. This already happens in at least one programme: the Defence Fixed Telecommunications Service (DFTS) partnership, in which the Defence Fixed Networks (DFN) IPT and its BT partner are governed by a Joint Management Board with a non-executive Chair.

This arrangement is relatively heavy on overheads in comparison with a conventional customer/supplier arrangement. Nevertheless, there are considerable advantages. These advantages are particularly important in a service-oriented arrangement (like DFTS) because of the relentless emphasis on cost control and service delivery on the one hand, and on the other because a partnership without adequate governance can become too cosy. The Chair has the responsibility for ensuring that shared decisions are properly examined rather than slipped into, for ensuring that the long-term view is balanced against the short-term imperatives and for bringing to the Board a constantly questioning outside perspective.

It may be worth considering the extension of this type of arrangement to other partnering programmes. However, to make it work, the Chair must have access to the top of both partners. And what would be the 'top'? Minister? Chief Executive?

The test comes when things go wrong. The Astute submarine programme was one such example: both sides combined to dig themselves out of the hole and they did so because both were 'locked in a lethal embrace'. Some good examples of what is commonly understood as partnering are Fast Jets in the DLO and Watchkeeper in the DPA.

Small and Medium-Sized Enterprises (SMEs)

Those working in SMEs are concerned that:
- They do not have the right relationship with the prime.
- They never see the customer.
- Their components/sub-systems are often poorly integrated.
- They are neither understood nor valued.

Amongst SMEs, there is a perception that MoD treats SME IPR with arrogance; that there is a reluctance by MoD to allow stage payments which forces SMEs to shoulder all the cashflow; that the bidding process is too long; and that SMEs need to be wary of airing innovation to primes. Many SMEs find that dealing with MoD is such a time-consuming business over a long period that they find it difficult, if not impossible, to sustain. Indeed, the average life of a SME is considerably less than the duration of a project's procurement cycle. This timescale may mean that the SME's originally cutting-edge technology is obsolescent by the time that it is in the field – hardly an inducement for a small organisation. The MoD process beats innovation out of the system because it is seen as risk, which it finds difficult to handle.

There are warm words about SMEs in the DIS, as there have been in earlier initiatives, but MoD is still seen as innovation-averse and unhelpful to SMEs. In addition, primes are not eager to use SMEs and their track record of doing so is poor. There is often little incentive for primes as, for example, they have to maintain continuity of supply and SMEs are always vulnerable – not least to takeovers by other primes. The average SME views the prime with the same suspicion that primes reserve for MoD.

So, SMEs have much to be unhappy about. Unless things change, many will be swallowed by large companies, others will die and more will leave the defence sector altogether. This might not matter if this reduction in SMEs was a controlled process, but it is not, and in some defence sectors key capabilities may well disappear. It would seem that, if MoD wants SMEs, it will have to pay for them.

How does MoD assess SME value? If it doesn't, does that mean that MoD doesn't really value SMEs? Would it rather place everything at higher cost with a large company that will still be in business a decade later if MoD wants to sue?

However, if MoD does really value SMEs, what should it do? The major difficulty is how to help or protect SMEs without coming between the prime and its supply chain. A code of conduct is unlikely to have much effect unless certain parts of it are mandated in the contract, as happens in the US. Is such mandating the answer and, if it is, does MoD have the necessary supply-chain knowledge to implement it sensibly? And should the use of SMEs be mandated irrespective of the quality of those SMEs? Such mandating implies the use of targets, and we know that target-setting is fraught with difficulties.

If MoD cannot offer practical help, what can the SMEs do themselves? Articles elsewhere in this issue explore moves to cluster

SMEs, possibly under one larger company (not a traditional defence prime), to provide an expert group to bid for a contract. There is considerable activity here, but MoD's attitude towards such initiatives would need to be more positive than it has been in the past. Indeed, the DIS suggests that it is not seen as the way ahead; instead it appears to favour the attachment of SMEs to large primes, which will maintain them over a long period of time.

In reality, any artificial maintenance of SMEs will cost money as this attempts to create a dynamic that does not naturally exist in the defence market. Funding universities has not achieved what was expected as innovative SMEs are not spun out of academia, but out of industry.

Conclusion

We came to the conclusion that:

- The DIS will only be successful if culture is changed. Success of implementation will, therefore, be measured by the change of culture, and this will only be achieved by strong, consistent Ministerial leadership over a lengthy period.

- The McKane report should be warmly welcomed as it contains a great deal of important recommendations on procedures and organisation. However, while it includes much of value on culture and behaviour, this is not satisfactorily carried through to the main recommendations. This needs to be rectified.

- Partnering is not an easy option. There is a danger that it will be driven by a 'spirit of opportunism': the adoption of short-term fixes rather than working towards the best long-term outcome. One way of counter-balancing this tendency would be the appointment of a non-executive at project Board level, perhaps as Chair (as per the DFTS programme), although he would need to have access to the top of both partners.

- There is no common understanding of the responsibilities that partnering brings either within the MoD or across the MoD divide, and this needs rectifying.

- Despite the warm words in the DIS about looking after SMEs, it is difficult to see how MoD would make these work, except by mandating a quota of SMEs (and quality?) in each contract as happens in the US. This may, of course, cost money in the longer term. More practical would appear to be the banding together of a shifting alliance of SMEs under a larger firm (not a defence prime) to bid for contracts. This is already happening and MoD should consider helping these initiatives where they are likely to give good value-for-money.

- The overall objective is not clear, and it is likely that each MoD Department and each Ministry will perceive a different aim. But whatever the aim, the retention of an onshore defence industry is likely to cost significant sums of money. How this is to be funded needs to be identified. Is the prime benefit to MoD or to the defence industry or to UK plc? The answer to this question should determine who will provide the funds.

Chapter Five

DIS: The New Relationship with Industry

It is time now to look at the nuts and bolts of the DIS and how effectively they are being carried forward.

Appropriate Sovereignty

The DIS is based on the need to retain 'appropriate sovereignty' and 'operational independence'. How realistic is this?

> *We are faced with the fact that the bulk of our defence spend is being placed with big companies. And as most of them are multinational, the decision regarding where the development is carried out is made outside the United Kingdom.*[80]

The intention is not to debar non-British companies from bidding for programme work, but that a reasonable amount of high-technology work would be carried out in Britain. However, intentions are one thing, implementing them is quite another.

> *The requirements of appropriate sovereignty drive us [SAIC, a US company] to place more emphasis on onshore [UK] production in those sectors that the DIS has specified. At the same time – as the RUSI study correctly pointed out – there has to be a balance because in some cases the quality product will be offshore (we have a lot of quality products in the US), and there will have to be, even when the DIS has been implemented, an element of reach-back or reach-out to subsidiaries of US firms.*[81]

Reach-out is bound to be a feature of future acquisition whether the prime is a US company or BAE Systems with its ownership of many US companies. The amount of reach-back or reach-out will almost certainly increase in the future for two reasons. Firstly, because of the huge disparity in research and technology spending between the US and UK, more and more quality products and technology will be found in the US and less and less onshore in the UK. Secondly, because BAE Systems is progressively moving its centre of gravity towards the US and the DOD, which is where the money is and where the sizeable profits are to be

---

[80] Paul Withers, 'The Defence Industrial Strategy: The Holy Grail for SMEs?', *RUSI Defence Systems* (Volume 9, No. 2, October 2006), page 94.

[81] Robert Bell, Interview, *RUSI Defence Systems* (Volume 9, No. 3, February 2007), page 10.

made. As a result, it will be more and more difficult to ensure that enough high-technology work and technology transfer is achieved onshore.

> *Ultimately, the clever design is done offshore as well. The result, in the short term, is that the product gets designed and everyone is happy. In the long term, however, the results will be more and more primes deciding to place design offshore – the knock-on effect of that being that the majority of the build is conducted offshore and the supporting infrastructure slowly disappears, eliminating the rich and diverse skill base that SMEs bring to our nation.*[82]

Paul Withers goes on to ask how long it will be before the primes are islands of technical ability in our defence industry, employed to bolt together bits that are built offshore. But I would suspect that before we get to that point, the primes will have moved their corporate bases to other countries – probably the US – and we will be left with the single option of buying off-the-shelf from other nations.

This does not necessarily mean from the US or Europe. In the East we are seeing China and India growing at an immense pace and turning out many, many times more science and engineering graduates than we are. Their economies are growing hugely and they can now afford to buy, and in some cases make, sophisticated defence equipment in staggering numbers. This can only increase their pull in the defence market, and before long they will be making all their equipment and selling it worldwide. Will we be able to compete? Not unless we drastically increase our R&T funding and target it much more effectively than we do now.

> Is appropriate sovereignty a possibility? Yes – in the short term

Is appropriate sovereignty a possibility? Yes – in the short term. But if we are to achieve it in the longer term, our acquisition performance will have to improve greatly through MoD and industry working together.

Strategic Partnering

To do this, the old adversarial approach with its 'competition, competition, competition' mentality has to be replaced by strategic partnering. DIS makes this abundantly clear with its sustainment

---

[82] Paul Withers, 'The Defence Industrial Strategy: the Holy Grail for SMEs?', *RUSI Defence Systems* (Volume 9, No. 2, October 2006), page 95.

strategies that seek such partnering agreements with BAE Systems – for armoured vehicles, fast-jet aircraft and general munitions – and with AgustaWestland for rotary wing. In addition, MoD is seeking something similar in the maritime sector once industrial restructuring has been completed. Other partnering arrangements are sought with Team Complex Weapons, with non-BAE general munitions suppliers, and with BAE for unmanned air vehicles (UAVs) and unmanned combat air vehicles (UCAVs).

The Shift of Risk

Levene made competition the bedrock of acquisition for a couple of decades, and the MoD repeatedly claimed that competition saved £1Bn per year. This has never been substantiated and many doubt that competitions run on price could produce savings. But whether or not competition has saved money, is there not risk in moving from competition to partnering? Is this not a return to the cosy cost-plus days of the 1960s and 1970s? Possibly, if MoD fails to adopt a true partnering mentality. So, who bears the risks and has it shifted?

> MoD has not been clear on risk and whose responsibility it is

MoD has not been clear on risk and whose responsibility it is. Ultimately, the risk is borne, not by industry nor by the MoD acquisition organisation, but by the front-line sailor, soldier or airman whose ability to defeat the enemy and defend himself depends on timely delivery of enough advanced equipment which works. Without it, he is less effective and his life is thereby at greater risk.

So, when the Government trumpeted in 2004 that Bowman had entered service on time, this was not only a gross untruth, but it publicly washed its hands of responsibility for eight years of delay and the fact that it entered service with 27 major provisos, many of which would not be cleared until several years later. Who bore the penalty? Not the Permanent Under Secretary (PUS), not CDP, not industry – the serviceman bore the penalty just as he was conducting two major operations with considerable loss of life.

Bowman is not an isolated example: there are many others such as FRES, which continues to be delayed after 30 years of false starts; combat identification, which was the number one priority after the First Gulf War in 1991 but its continuing lack still imperils lives through 'blue-on-blue' engagements; Chinook helicopters for special forces, which sat in a hangar for years because someone forgot to include the software codes in the contract; the failure to allocate money for adequate numbers of helicopters and transport aircraft because jobs in politicians' constituencies ringfence funds for other equipments which may (or may not) be of lesser importance or urgency. These and other examples are all essential for the operations in Iraq and Afghanistan where lives are being lost, some of them as a direct result.

So, the serviceman ultimately bears all the risk.

But, of course, apportioning the interim risk during acquisition is important, but only if that risk is dealt with by people who understand it. MoD used to understand risk, but over the last 20 years or so has largely lost that ability. The result is that it has attempted to pass the risk to industry – not always with common sense.

> MoD used to understand risk, but has largely lost that ability

> For example, on one PPP programme, providing simulation facilities, the contractor was asked to bear the risk of the utilisation of the facility being lower than stated in the RFP, a situation where the contractor had absolutely no control over the level of demand which was totally controlled by the MoD user.[83]

The move to contracting for availability of a capability has shifted much risk to industry:

> In the past, the MoD might have bought a long-range radar system from a supplier (along with spare parts to last for an estimated lifetime) and then maintained and repaired the radar itself. Under the DIS, the MoD might instead buy the capability 'to detect air contacts at ranges over 100 nautical miles with an availability (system operating time) of x per cent. The winning supplier will provide the radar, as well as maintain and repair it throughout the lifetime to meet stated availability and performance targets – or risk not being paid. Thus, the DIS heralds the largest shift of risk from government to industry in the history of the armed forces.[84]

---

[83] John Weston, email to the author, September 2008.
[84] Len Pannett and Dean Gilmore, 'Strategic Partnering: The Emerging Relationship Between Industry and the MoD', *RUSI Defence Systems* (Volume 10, No. 2, October 2007), page 79.

This should work well as industry does understand the development and production risks better than MoD, as is repeatedly demonstrated in the UOR process. However, shifting risk to industry only makes sense if MoD is a very intelligent customer. But if not, what happens if MoD and industry get stuck in a contractual stand-off because the contract missed out essential targets or was too vague? Has this never happened? Could it happen under partnering?

> *The single biggest concern for the MoD is to ensure that industry can, in fact, deliver on the contract and maintain warfighting capability. To allay this concern and allow through-life capability to be implemented, defence companies must develop the internal capabilities needed for servicing and supporting complex warfighting products. This is a major effort that in many cases will require fundamentally new operating models and a new set of skills, tools and processes.*[85]

The biggest issue in effectively contracting for, and managing, availability is the paucity of useful data. Historical data is only an indicator and major new developments are full of unknowns. This paucity of data brings huge

> **This paucity of data brings huge potential risk**

potential risk and therefore contracting for availability is more realistic, but the risks have to be mutually understood – not just handed over or, worse still, glossed over.

This sounds like a major challenge for MoD and industry. If things go wrong, industry may bear the risk of not being paid in full, politicians may face embarrassment which they will promptly forget, and the acquisition community will pile on more process and procedural change. The front-line serviceman may lose his life. Think FRES, its forerunners, Iraq and Afghanistan.

What is Strategic Partnering?

If we are to lower the risk to the serviceman, we must improve the way we acquire equipment. The DIS rightly demands a move from the old competitive, adversarial relationship with industry to strategic partnering, but what is that?

> *That Shangri-La which has been much spoken of – a new partnership and dialogue between the defence customer and his supplier. But this is, to misquote*

---

[85] Ibid.

Da Ponte, somewhat like the phoenix – everyone has heard of it, but almost no one has seen it.[86]

There may be two reasons why no one has seen it – firstly, it is difficult to achieve and secondly, no two people understand it in the same way. When asked whether people across industry and MoD understand the same thing when they use the word partnering, Ian King of BAE Systems replied:

No. It is only when you have been working in a partnering environment that you really understand what it means. Competition has been until now the default position for everything ... Partnering will differ every time because every programme will have a different life-cycle, will have different operational requirements.[87]

This was underscored by the RUSI Acquisition Focus:

In our last paper, we pointed out that there was no common understanding of the responsibilities of partnering either within the MoD or across the MoD–industry divide, and partnering will not be successful unless responsibilities on both sides are clearly defined, recognised and consistently put into practice. And that includes accepting the pain of significant sacrifices.[88]

The key point is that partnering is not an easy option if value-for-money is to be attained. Competition is far easier – decide what you want, issue an invitation to tender (ITT), judge the results, write a contract with robust milestones around a fixed price, test the equipment and accept it (or not) into service. No need to consider the concerns of the industrial contractor.

> The key point is that partnering is not an easy option

Lord Drayson, with his commercial experience, saw strategic partnering thus:

The key point for me about the partnership is that it is a hard and demanding arrangement where both parties are driven not just to deliver jointly, but also to seek continuous improvement, efficiency and innovative approaches. It is about ensuring value-for-money for the taxpayer in environments where competition is not possible. Negotiating the agreement [with AgustaWestland] was at times

---

[86] Sir Jeremy Blackham, *RUSI Journal* (Volume 152, No. 4, August 2007), page 38.
[87] Ian King, Interview, *RUSI Defence Systems* (Volume 9, No. 1, June 2006), page 11.
[88] RUSI Acquisition Focus, 'Implementation of the Defence Industrial Strategy', *RUSI Defence Systems* (Volume 9, No. 2, October 2006), page 79.

tough, needing clear leadership and an honest, open and at times frank relationship on both sides.[89]

The NAO examined time and cost performances for oil, gas and defence projects and this is summarised in Figure 5–1. It is notable that nearly all the defence projects are out-performed by the oil and gas ones, all but one of which came in on, or below, cost and time schedules. Savings were large – 40% in one, 33% in another and 18% in a third.

> *Of course a simple graphic doesn't prove there is a causal link, but what it does is further support the conclusion from the 2005 study[90] and subsequent work that, whilst most projects use similar project management techniques, the key differentiator is the strength of the underpinning relationship. And the project teams interviewed for this study were in no doubt that their investment in collaborative relationships was worthwhile and were very clear about the hard benefits that investing in the right behaviours can bring in terms of profit and quality of delivery.*[91]

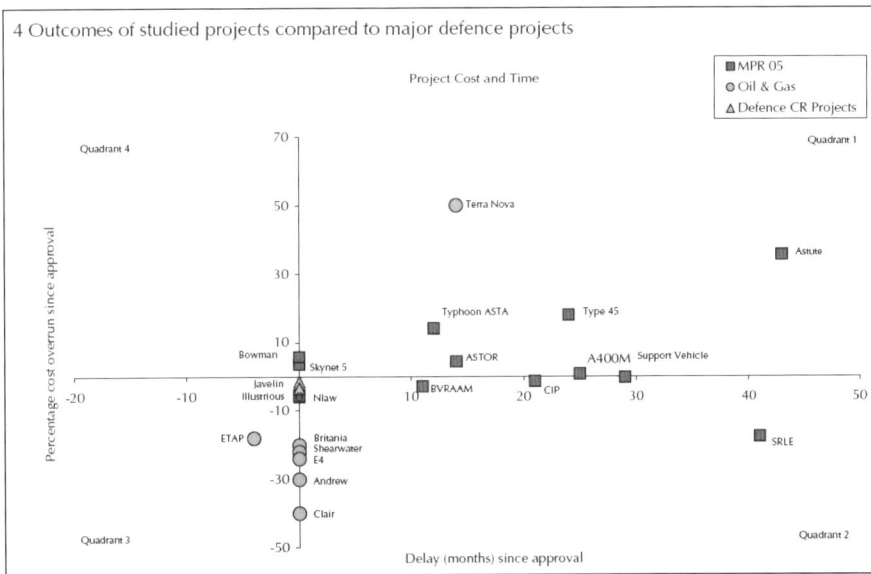

Figure 5–1: Cost and Overruns and Delays: Comparison between Defence Projects with Oil and Gas

Source: NAO, Good Governance: Measuring Success Through Collaborative Working, November 2006

---

[89] Lord Drayson, 'The Defence Industrial Strategy: Our Relationship with Industry', *RUSI Defence Systems* (Volume 9, No. 2, October 2006), page 20.

[90] National Audit Office, *Driving the Successful Delivery of Major Defence Projects*, 2005.

[91] Tim Banfield and Julie Exton, 'Investing in Relationships', *RUSI Defence Systems* (Volume 9, No. 2, October 2006), pages 86/87.

In the same article, the authors cited the refit of HMS Illustrious as an example of partnering and living the DIS's Defence Values for Acquisition. The relationship with Babcock was based on shared values and behaviours which were measured regularly. The 30-month, £120M refit came in within a very ambitious timescale and under budget – the savings were shared between partners and MoD saved £1M.[92]

However, once this programme was complete, contracting moved to competition:

> Due to the very competitive nature of the competitions, the successful working practices were replaced by commercial practices where suppliers still had cost to recover and adversarial relationships replaced working together and the partnering framework. Not surprisingly, the objectives and goals of both customer and supplier became misaligned as they set off on differing strategies.[93]

So, back to the adversarial behaviours of the past couple of decades. However, there have been examples of movement in the right direction:

> Too often MoD contracts are designed to produce an adversarial relationship where MoD is keen to interpret the specification to produce a very high level of performance, whereas the contractor is keen to provide the minimum level. This was very much in evidence on the Nimrod Mk4, until a new deal was struck whereby MoD and the contractor would share cost overruns beyond a defined figure. One of the BAE staff closely associated with the programme said that the introduction of this new approach had transformed the MoD stance and introduced considerable flexibility aimed at finding a sensible level of performance at minimum cost.[94]

So, changes for the better do occur – at least occasionally.

The Adversarial Legacy

Clearly, both industry and MoD should be investing a lot of effort in changing behaviours. Is such change difficult?

Well, it's a major change. For nearly a quarter of a century, managers in both MoD and industry have made careers in this adversarial, competitive environment. How difficult will it be for these leopards to

---

[92] For further detail on this programme, see Stuart Leonard, *RUSI Defence Systems* (Volume 9, No. 2, October 2006), page 90.
[93] Stuart Leonard, 'Development of a Collaborative Gold Standard', *RUSI Defence Systems* (Volume 9, No 2, October 2006), pages 90/91.
[94] John Weston, email to the author.

change their spots? Easy enough I suspect when programmes are running smoothly, but what is their default approach when the going gets tough?

> *It's a huge challenge. One needs to recognise that a lot of people in this business, in both MoD and industry, have grown up and built their careers on managing and succeeding in the aggressive, confrontational, competitive environment of the last 20 years. Throughout my own career, I've learned to play that game. So it's counter-cultural now to be standing up in front of our workforce, saying the rules have changed ... Frankly, this is not going to change overnight ... This poses big demands on us and raises big questions in terms of our ability and willingness to trust each other.[95]*

Does industry believe in DIS? Unless it does, the top industrialists are not likely to lead change enthusiastically. It's a good question and the answer seems somewhat indeterminate. On the one hand, many saw it as a lifeline for industry, and therefore must be made to work. Others were more cynical: would MoD make it work, or would another initiative come along to distract top officials? Would funding be found and, if not, how can it ensure retention of industrial skills onshore? Would Drayson remain long enough to embed the changes? Or was it just a short-term fix to keep industry quiet?

But let us assume that industry's fears were misguided and that DIS and strategic partnering will be successfully implemented. What is the mentality that needs to be developed?

Solving 'His' Problem Together

If partnering is going to work, the required mentality has to leave behind the 'Is that as much as I can screw out of him?' attitude of the old adversarial approach and adopt an attitude of 'His problems are mine'. It's us-us rather than me-me. That means sharing gain, but it also means sharing pain. It means considering the long term at least as much as the short term, something that neither MoD nor industry is very good at – the next election, next year's funding line, the next

> It is to solve 'his' problem. But solving 'his' problem together may well pay dividends in the longer term

---

[95] Guy Griffiths, COO MBDA, *RUSI Defence Systems* (Volume 10, No. 1, June 2007), pages 12-13.

shareholders' report. It is not in either MoD's or industry's nature to accept pain willingly in the short term, particularly if it is to solve 'his' problem. But solving 'his' problem together may well pay dividends in the longer term, with reduced costs or less cost overrun or less delay.

Many people would say that MoD and the defence industry cannot be made to work together in such a way. They ignore, however, three clear pieces of evidence:

- UOR delivery.
- The DIS Pathfinder programmes.
- Many, if a small overall minority of, programmes throughout the history of acquisition.

I will look at the Pathfinder programmes later in this chapter. As for historical examples of projects with a good partnering approach, everyone will have their own list. Mine would include the self-propelled howitzer AS 90 and Rapier. Although some might point out that AS 90 was largely developed by industry before MoD became involved, and that Rapier was very expensive, I would suggest that all showed a strong partnering approach by both MoD and industry. Both were developed pre-Smart Procurement and there was no partnering agreement in either project, but two characteristics stood out – strong leadership, particularly by the MoD project managers, was very much in evidence and, perhaps as important, both industry and MoD players understood each other very clearly. Decisions were argued over, sometimes most heatedly, before they were made, with both sides understanding the driving factors on each side.

UOR Culture

But it is the UOR culture which shows conclusively that a partnering culture is quite possible. For the Falklands, Northern Ireland, the Gulf, the Balkans, Iraq and Afghanistan, vast numbers of UORs have been delivered in staggeringly short timescales (some in days, most in weeks or a few months) and the vast majority have worked effectively, with many being retained in service for much longer than envisaged. How has this been done? Not

> It is the UOR culture which shows that a partnering culture is quite possible

through process, shorter though that might be, but by the culture of both sides working to a common end – to get a life-saving piece of equipment into the field as quickly as possible. Long hours, quick decisions and a lack of bureaucratic risk-aversion have been the dominant factors.

Of course the UOR procedures have their weaknesses – lack of support for more than a short period, reduction in commonality with other in-service or development equipment and no full consideration of all DLoDs. Some would say that value-for-money is not demonstrated, but that could be refuted by two arguments – that time is money and that lives saved are invaluable.

No one would suggest that we go to the extreme of developing an aircraft carrier under UOR procedures as they are now, but we should be able to find ways of harnessing the UOR culture to streamline procedures in 'normal' procurement.

In 1998, the SDR called for:

> *A new relationship between the Ministry of Defence and its suppliers in which both sides can operate to their strengths … and which provides industry with the greatest incentive to perform.*[96]

Sadly, nothing much happened.

The Industrial Incentive

What is the greatest incentive that can be offered to industry to perform? Profit. Whitehall needs to stop thinking of profit as a dirty word. Industry exists to make money for their shareholders. Percentage profit in the defence sector is way below that in the civil sector, and that in UK defence contracts way below that in US defence contracts. Defence companies have to make a reasonable return on investment, but they don't – except where they manage to export in quantity.

> Whitehall needs to stop thinking of profit as a dirty word

What is the result of low profit margins? Industry can no longer afford to invest in innovation and technology as they should if they are to remain healthy. As MoD doesn't either, innovation in this country is badly constrained. Our wealth was once founded on inventions – radar, the jet

---

[96] MoD, *Strategic Defence Review*, Cmnd 3999, Supporting Essay Ten, page 10-3, July 1998

engine, the computer and arguably the internet amongst a host of others. Our inventors have shown (and still show in some areas) that they are second to none. But no longer in the defence industry. There is not enough investment in R&T – and crucially no encouragement for SMEs where innovation so often occurs.

If the Whitehall mandarins do not like to think of taxpayers' money going to make money for shareholders, they should instead allow higher profits and insist that the extra is invested in R&T.

Is the attitude in the Civil Service to profit being made by industry from public money changing?

> *I think there is more enlightenment. Competition has taken industry to the edge, with decisions that reduced the industrial capability needed to sustain the UK's Armed Forces. And if there is no sustainable UK defence strategy, why would we want to invest in the UK? I think, too, that MoD has worked out that profits equals a strong company equals a capability that they want.*[97]

A 'survival guide' has been suggested by Paul Nixon and David Moore of the Defence Academy:[98]

- Profit is good.
- Strong suppliers make successful clients.
- Unpredictable workloads are the enemy of value.
- Investment in training helps everyone in the supply chain.
- Collaboration is never the wrong thing to do.

According to MoD/CBI guidelines in 1998, partnering between MoD and its suppliers is:[99]

> Collaboration is never the wrong thing to do

- A commitment to achieve excellence in the timely supply of high-quality products and services, and excellence in relationships for all those involved.
- An attitude of mind.
- A culture of trust and openness.

---

[97] Ian King, Interview, *RUSI Defence Systems* (Volume 9, No. 1, June 2006), page 10.
[98] Paul Nixon and Dr David Moore, 'BAE Systems: National Asset or Global Chameleon?', *RUSI Defence Systems* (Volume 10, No. 2, October 2007), page 85.
[99] MoD/CBI Partnering, MoD website, 26 November 1998.

Trust and Transparency

The MoD/CBI guidelines were underlined by the DIS with such statements as:

- We will start with immediate effect to deliver on our revised policy of providing industry with a better and longer-term understanding of our future plans.
- We will be looking to industry to promote the use of partnering behaviours in industry's interface with the Department at all levels, so as to encourage trust, openness, transparency and communication.
- We all must value openness and transparency and share future plans and priorities wherever possible to encourage focused investment and avoid wasted effort.

MoD Transparency

In addition, there is a whole section entitled Transparency, which sets out the sort of information that industry can expect from MoD. At sector level this would include indicative planning assumptions for each sector, an illustrative EP, research and logistics expenditure out to ten years, the types of technology required and priorities for improved military capabilities over the next two decades. At programme level, the wording is more woolly, such as an "indication of indicative funding allocation", but it does give a list of information that MoD would 'consider' sharing with industry:

- Capability requirements and planning assumptions on production quantities.
- Overall project timescales, including in- and out-of-service dates.
- Specific planned dates for inviting and receiving proposals and tenders from industry.
- Overall budgetary assumptions for the through-life capability requirement.
- Planned expenditure profiles.
- Associated procurement strategy.
- Logistic data required to support the formulation of cost-effective support solutions.
- The wider factors that will be included in the assessment of value-for-money.

Early exposure and involvement in MoD's planning ... has two great benefits: first, it means that MoD has tested its plans with industry ... that plans are soundly based and therefore robust to changes on the grounds of lack of realism. Secondly, industry has greater confidence in MoD's direction ... Together, these factors will lead to more investment for the defence enterprise overall.[100]

DIS also stated that MoD would expect industry to supply information on their future plans and business.

Industrial Transparency

The above is an excellent start, but it has two flaws. First, what MoD expects from industry in terms of transparency is sketchy indeed and suggests that knowledge of industry in Whitehall is very limited. It is better put by Guy Griffiths:

It requires industry to be equally transparent with MoD about the key elements of our business planning – what resourcing levels we have, what mix of skills, capabilities and facilities we have, and the extent to which all that is sustainable against our forward business projections in both the home and our export markets.[101]

'Wriggle Room'

But, more importantly than the paucity of the DIS wording on industrial transparency, the wording of what MoD will provide allows plenty of 'wriggle room'. Experience suggests that 'wriggle room' will be extensively used, as for example it has been during PR 08 – MoD has excused itself from providing information on future plans because of the great difficulties in this particular planning round. After PR 08 is put to bed, it is said, industry will get the information it needs. But of course tomorrow never comes. Or will it this time? Oh dear, we now have problems with PR 09. Perhaps the year after.

> Without trust the partnering mentality won't take root

The more that MoD holds back on providing the transparency it has promised, the less trust it will engender in industry. Without trust the partnering mentality won't take root.

---

[100] Ron Finlayson, industry co-chair of the NDIC's subgroup on TLCM planning, 'The Role of Industry in Capability Planning', *RUSI Defence Systems* (Volume 10, No. 1, June 2008), page 35.
[101] Guy Griffiths, COO MBDA, *RUSI Defence Systems* (Volume 10, No. 1, June 2007), page 12.

The Pathfinder Projects

The DIS set up two Pathfinder programmes:

- **The Sustained Maritime Surface Combatant Capability.** The long-term sustainment of the capabilities currently delivered by Maritime Surface Combatants alongside a solution for the Key User Requirements previously identified by the Future Surface Combatant programme.
- **The Sustained Armoured Vehicle Capability.** The long-term sustainment of the capability delivered by the current and programmed armoured vehicles.

The key features of the Pathfinder programmes are set out as follows:[102]

- Culture change through setting the right values and behaviours.
- A programme approach to TLCM.
- Effective integration across all the Defence Lines of Development to deliver sustainable military capability.
- Effective techniques for capability trade-off with early industry engagement in capability analysis.
- Defence industry joint working to understand and address the dynamics of the supply chain and sources of innovation.

The joint MoD and industry working appears to have been very successful and the involvement of industry was reported to have provided a defining characteristic of the Pathfinders, while a key lesson was that industry's perspective forms an essential component of capability planning. Certainly, the Pathfinders showed that if the involvement of industry was kept away from the 'buying end', it was possible to put six or more major players together and achieve consensus on the problems and solutions.

> Competition and partnering do not fit together comfortably

---

[102] DIS, page 136.

The Place of Competition

Competition and partnering do not fit together comfortably. Before 1985, there was little competition in the 'cosy cost-plus' world, but in 1994:

> *MoD has finally woken up to the fact that for 30 years the defence industry has been ripping off their customers.*[103]

From 1985, to eliminate any 'rip-off', competition and the adversarial approach became the primary procurement tool and "up to £1Bn per year was saved", according to MoD estimates. The Smart Procurement Initiative promoted the partnering approach but nothing much happened. Three years later the then CDP showed his view of procurement strategies other than competition:

> *The answer to the first question – is competition necessary? – is that it remains my preferred method. It is not the only method. If I cannot have competition, I would rather have the ships and get them by some other way.*[104]

Now strategic partnering is to be the norm for doing business in many sectors. If competition saves money, shouldn't we retain it? Yes, and the DIS examines ways in which competition will be used and suggests four models, though whether anyone will use these as a basis for deciding on a strategy is doubtful.

The US has a clear approach to partnering and competition:

> *Over the last ten years, we have been working long-term relationships with our contractors, particularly in sustainment, giving them contracts for a term, which might be three or five years, with evaluation points. If the evaluation shows they've done well, they'll be awarded another term; if they haven't done well, then we will go out and compete it. We like to have long-term relationships and to find ways of measuring that in terms of dollars and quality of service that is transparent to everyone.*[105]

But the DIS states that:

> *Whilst competition allows the advantage of tangible price comparison determined by market forces and the ability to compare competing proposals for compliance, it can also sometimes drive unintended behaviours and consequences*

---

[103] An anonymous industrialist quoted in the MoD *SIP Consultation Study*, March 1994.
[104] Sir Robert Walmsley giving evidence to the House of Commons Defence Committee's Report on Procurement, 2001, page 5.
[105] The Honourable Claude Bolton, Interview, *RUSI Defence Systems* (Volume 10, No. 2, October 2007), page 9.

for us [MoD] and industry. These may include unrealistic timescales, an over optimistic assessment of risk and hence cost, and the potential loss of flexibility for timely insertions of technology in the future.[106]

We will not pursue competition beyond the point where it can offer long-term advantage or where the cost of competition is demonstrably disproportionate to the benefits that might be achieved.[107]

This is no more robust in its wording than that in the Smart Procurement Initiative, after which competition remained the primary tool of procurement even when it was grossly inappropriate, at least in the DPA – in the DLO there was more willingness to embrace partnering at the expense of competition, partly because partnering over a long in-service period was easier to set up and manage than in the shorter timescales of procurement, and partly because both industry and the DLO had similar goals and a common need to sustain equipment over a long period.

So, what was to stop competition remaining the primary procurement tool? One thing only: the much more positive wording about, and instructions for implementation of, strategic partnering. But strategic partnering was driven by the paucity of new builds in the future in many sectors and the need to support and upgrade in-service equipments. So, new build procurement of all types of equipment, large or small, was likely to remain competitive unless driven hard from the top to non-competitive strategies. Would this happen?

> Strategic partnering was driven by the paucity of new builds in the future

Well, even if it was driven hard, competition might well play more of a role than is sensible.

Its [the Treasury's] senior people still cling to the 1980s' dogma of competition for everything rather than a pragmatic balance between competition and common sense ... HM Treasury seems, from recent evidence, to want both best value-for-money and competition; the two, experience shows, are not always comfortable bedfellows.[108]

---

[106] DIS, page 48.

[107] DIS, page 49.

[108] Paul Beaver, 'Is the System Ready for the Defence Industrial Strategy?', *RUSI Defence Systems*, Volume 9, No. 1, June 2006), page 17.

Over the last couple of decades, competition has borne hardest on small companies down the supply chain. For some time, MoD did not seem concerned, believing that there were too many and that the weakest would go to the wall. But as more and more went out of business or transferred to the civil sector, competition in some sectors disappeared. Small companies needed a strategy.

Small- and Medium-sized Enterprises (SMEs)

One of the major achievements of DIS is the attempt for the first time to set down which skills are required to be retained in which sector. This is driven by the need to retain 'appropriate sovereignty'. So far, so good. But while it may be clear in the case of a new-build development programme, such as the Future Rapid Effect System (FRES) or the future aircraft carrier (CVF), it is far less clear in small systems or subsystems. Should these be sourced onshore or can they be bought through open competition or off-the-shelf from offshore? What is the extent of sovereignty?

This is particularly important for the supply chain and vital for SMEs.

To many in industry and elsewhere, DIS was seen as an exercise for the preservation of large platform primes, with little in it for others. This may not be entirely true, but there is enough truth in it to undermine its effect in industry.

SMEs are of course covered:

> We fully recognise the important role played by SMEs ... In 2004/05, just over half of MoD contracts let were directly with SMEs, accounting for over half a billion pounds. Many SMEs play a crucial role in meeting UORs ... We are widening our supply chain focus below the prime level to identify critical sources of key capability and technology and further to encourage SME entry into a broader range of defence opportunities.[109]

Lord Drayson clearly understood the importance of SMEs:

> One of the criticisms that has been levelled at the DIS is that it focuses too much on the major primes. I understand this concern. From my background in industry I am very aware of the importance of a healthy supply chain, and I am clear that MoD should take an active role in ensuring it exists ... I strongly believe there is

---

[109] DIS, page 48.

great benefit in the long term from a well-structured supply chain which allows supplier substitution and clearly defines the relationship between elements of the supply chain.[110]

In addition, DIS makes reference to available support mechanisms such as the Manufacturing Advisory Service, fiscal incentives and DTI support, the Small Firms Loan Guarantee Scheme, grants for R&D, Support to Implement Best Business Practice and Grants for Investigating an Innovative Idea.

Warm words.

Of course, Smart Acquisition used warm words on SMEs, but nothing much happened. Will they be implemented this time around? I doubt it – I could not find one word on SMEs in Section C which is about implementation of the DIS. The sentiments above express a desire, not a prescription.

The RUSI Acquisition Focus, in its paper on the implementation of DIS[111] picked out the issue of MoD support for SMEs as one of the six major challenges (in addition to cost) that face MoD in implementing DIS.

The Importance of SMEs

Some will say that primes do innovate:

I don't think it fair to imply that primes do not innovate. They certainly can and often do, but in a process which strangles innovation, considering it too risky, no one innovates – if you innovate before the bid, the innovation gets stolen. Who is going to innovate in this climate? The scourge of innovation is the process itself.[112]

Nevertheless, SMEs have a major role to play in innovation and Lord Drayson has referred to smaller companies as a 'key source of innovation'. The DIS White Paper recognises the flexibility, agility and innovation that SMEs offer as well as the important role they have to play in maintaining UK's strong market position. Others have mentioned agility:

> SMEs have a major role to play in innovation

---

[110] Lord Drayson, *RUSI Defence Systems* (Volume 9, No. 2, October 2006), page 21.

[111] RUSI Acquisition Focus, *RUSI Defence Systems* (Volume 9, No. 2, October 2006), page 80.

[112] Bob Barton, email to the author, 1 September 2008.

MoD can benefit significantly from the technological innovation coupled with the pace and agility that SMEs can offer.[113]

SMEs play a vital role in defence. They can be a source of deep expertise particularly in areas of high technology and/or where there is a need to adapt commercial technologies for military applications. Many SMEs gain their strength by retaining a capability to deliver the traditional products that are vital to the building of any platform or system (castings, forgings, machined parts, fabrications, big or small, simple or complex). Niche suppliers may have a unique product or a unique process that performs such an important function that the whole platform or system would be almost pointless without it – examples might include sensors, armour, crypto and would certainly include many software algorithms. The intellectual- or research-based SME will help overcome a range of obstacles and potentially deliver that all-important technological edge. The design house will so often be the source of innovation when the design department of the major prime will stay with the tried and tested low risk approach.[114]

SMEs are, therefore, an important and very diverse group within the defence industry.

Difficulties

So why do we need to worry about SMEs?

Many of those working in SMEs are concerned that:

- They do not have the right relationship with the prime.
- They never see the customer.
- Their components/subsystems are often poorly integrated.
- They are neither understood nor valued.
- MoD treats SME Intellectual Property Rights (IPR) with arrogance.
- There is a reluctance by MoD to allow stage payments, which forces them to shoulder all the cashflow.
- The bidding process is too long.
- They need to be wary of airing innovation to primes.

> MoD must take resolute action if SMEs are to remain in the defence sector

If this is correct, or at least partially correct, then MoD must take resolute action if SMEs are to remain in the defence sector. As Lord Drayson has said:

---

[113] Dr Ben Dobson, *RUSI Defence Systems* (Volume 9, No. 2, October 2006), page 96.
[114] Chris Trout, BMT Defence Services, 'Operational Sovereignty and the Role of SMEs', *RUSI Defence Systems* (Volume 11, No. 2, October 2008).

> *It continues to surprise me how few SMEs operate in the UK market. I fear over time we may have become complacent and closed off avenues of innovation and rapidity of response at a time when security threats are evolving at an ever-greater pace.*[115]

Solving the Problem

But what action can MoD take?

Some of the above concerns should be relatively easy to resolve – stage payments to help cashflow, for example. A reduction in the length of the bidding process would help, too, and although this might be a little more difficult, we do need to speed up all elements of the acquisition cycle, and not just to help SMEs.

Other concerns are less easily rectified without MoD coming between the prime and its supply chain, but the issues of Innovation and IPR must be put to rest. We need SMEs to innovate and they need their IPR to be treated with respect – it is their lifeblood.

One suggestion that has been made is to follow the US approach and mandate a level of SME involvement in a project, but would that mean that getting a tick in the box of SME involvement became rather more important than selecting the right companies to take part?

Another suggestion is that it might be worth following the US Mentor–Protégé Program:

> *It is up to the MoD to demonstrate some leadership in this area, to set the appropriate framework, to provide a level of funding and generally set the conditions for industrial sustainability. In this respect, the US Mentor–Protégé Program could well represent a model worth emulating in the UK. In simple terms, the Mentor is a prime contractor and the Protégé is an SME and the DOD provides incentives through various means, including direct contracts. The purpose of the Program is to provide incentives for DOD Tier 1 contractors to assist small businesses in enhancing their capabilities and to increase participation of such firms in government contracts.*[116]

Not all SMEs need MoD support. But in the following circumstances, they might:[117]

> **Not all SMEs need MoD support**

---

[115] Lord Drayson, *RUSI Defence Systems* (Volume 9, No. 2, October 2006), page 22/23.
[116] Chris Trout, BMT Defence Services, 'Operational Sovereignty and the Role of SMEs', *RUSI Defence Systems* (Volume 11, No. 2, October 2008).
[117] Ibid.

- Where the natural flow of business is sporadic with the potential for long periods between orders.
- Where technology moves quickly and there is potential for more than one generation change between new projects.
- Where the preservation/maintenance of jigs and tools is vital to retain a source of supply.
- Where niche products or processes are essential.
- In any situation where security aspects limit potential sources.
- For maturing vital technologies to TRL 4/5.

While over half of MoD contracts were let to SMEs, they were worth only half a billion pounds. Can SMEs be more proactive in winning contracts?

Several SME initiatives have taken place and continue to do so, usually under the auspices of a Trade Association or prime:

- The Farnborough Aerospace Consortium hosted a MARVIN workshop in which its members came together to form new collaborations. One of these, the Silicon Valley Team, subsequently won funding from MoD to develop a solution to MoD's UGV Grand Challenge.
- The same Trade association also created Defence Ventures – a 'virtual prime' to group defence-related SMEs within southern England and promote their skills, capabilities, capacity, and intellectual and technical know-how.
- DML has created a business model in which it acts as an independent systems integrator with no vested interests and 'brigades' the collective skills and agility of a number of SMEs to compete for defence contracts as an integrated, cost-effective team.

The RUSI Acquisition Focus sees a practical approach in the banding together of a shifting alliance of SMEs under a larger company (not a defence prime) to bid for contracts. This sort of approach needs to be encouraged by MoD. If nothing else, it should alleviate the problems of cashflow and time-to-contract, which cause huge difficulties that SMEs find difficult to overcome. Indeed, the average life of an SME is considerably less than the duration of a project's procurement cycle.

Will the New Relationship Work?

The DIS will not work if the new relationship envisaged between MoD and industry does not materialise. It is the heart of DIS and the strategic partnering that is to replace high-level competition must be driven into staff at all levels within both MoD and industry. It will not be easy when things go wrong and pain has to be shared, but it is then that implementation will be clear – or not. It must be partnering between equals, not domination of one party by the other.

> It will not be easy when things go wrong and pain has to be shared

Will it work? We will see.

SUMMARY: THE RELATIONSHIP WITH INDUSTRY

Appropriate Sovereignty
- Aim to retain industrial expertise onshore.
- Should work in the short term, but will it work in the longer term?

Strategic Partnering
- Major shift of risk to industry, but ultimate risk lies with the serviceman.
- Strategic partnering is a hard and demanding arrangement.
- A major change from the previous competitive, adversarial approach.
- UOR culture and the Pathfinder Projects show that change can be made.
- MoD and industry must share both pain and gain. There must be incentives for industry.
- Trust and transparency are essential prerequisites for success.
- Competition needs to be retained, but only where there are clear benefits.

SMEs
- SMEs are vital to the health of the onshore defence industry.
- MoD must do more to help SMEs with issues of cashflow, long bidding processes, IPR and innovation – but without coming between primes and their supply chains.
- Trade Associations and others can help by setting up SME 'brigades' to collectively bid for contracts.

"I've got mixed feelings about you Jones… I'm going to empower you but make sure that you can never use it!"

Chapter Six

DIS: Reorganisation

Within MoD, the major change in organisation recommended by the Enabling Acquisition Change (EAC) study was the merging of the DPA and the DLO into Defence Equipment and Support (DE&S). Ever since the formation of the two constituent parts under the Smart Procurement Initiative in 1998, it had seemed inevitable that the two would eventually be brought together to simplify the through-life approach. For several years it had been officially taboo; now it was suddenly policy.

Defence Equipment and Support

The EAC report listed the benefits that would arise from the merger:

- The establishment of a unified approach to procurement of equipment and through-life support.
- Provision of a single point of contact with industry and MoD customers.
- Reduction in the number of internal boundaries across the acquisition system.
- Encouragement of the defence industry to bring together project and in-service support, thereby facilitating through-life capability management (TLCM) and reducing cost.
- Reduction of overheads.

Further to these benefits was the support of operations:

> *The establishment of DE&S should be seen as a major opportunity to enhance support to operations today, tomorrow and in the future.*[118]

The DPA and the DLO were very different beasts. The former had procured equipment against the capability requirements of the ECC and then 'threw them over the wall' to the DLO to support. While the DPA had had, or had wanted, little direct interface with the end-user, the DLO had been much closer to the Commanders-in-Chief because support of

---

[118] DE&S, *Establishing an Integrated Defence Procurement and Support Organisation*, page 6, MoD, January 2007.

operations was vital for success – poor performance here was high profile. This closeness to operations had engendered a different culture from the rather introverted one that had existed in DPA where, except in a few cases, it was less important to consider the end-user than the reaction of the NAO and the Public Accounts Committee. The DPA, despite Smart Acquisition initiatives, had remained dogmatically in favour of 'competition, competition, competition' but the DLO, with the advantage of much longer support timescales, had successfully pursued partnering arrangements in many areas.

The Scale of DE&S

Bringing them together was going to be difficult – not so much the nuts and bolts of organisation as the culture and the size of the merged organisation.

> The scale of the structural change involved should not be underestimated: at launch, DE&S will have around 29,000 staff. It will be responsible for spending some 40% of the UK annual defence budget … it is important that we all recognise the opportunity we now have to make a real improvement in our business … it will also provide the opportunity to take the best approaches from both the DLO and the DPA and blend those effectively to produce something that is much greater than the sum of the component parts … Ministers expect DE&S to demonstrate the highest levels of commercial astuteness in dealing with industry and of operational effectiveness in supporting the front line. To achieve that requires us **all** to provide the leadership to identify better ways of doing business.[119]

Better Support to the Front Line

The idea of better support to the front line is perhaps the key to the benefits offered by the merger. The establishment of the 3-star military Chiefs of Materiel (CofMs) is an important step forward, initially opposed by the 'system', but successfully fought for by the new Chief of Defence Materiel (CDM) – General Sir Kevin O'Donaghue, the previous Chief of Defence Logistics. His CofM (Land) reinforced this view:

> As Chief of Materiel (Land), I formally exercise [my] responsibilities through membership of the DE&S Main, Executive and Investment Boards, the Land Forces Command Board, the Army Board (on which I sit as Quartermaster

---

[119] MoD DE&S, *Establishing an Integrated Defence Procurement and Support Organisation*, Foreword by CDL and CDP, page 3, January 2007.

> *General) and the Enhanced Joint Capabilities Board. However, as important are my regular interactions with the front-line user both on operations and at home. I'm here to ensure the DE&S provides operationally effective solutions in the Land environment, making a positive difference to those deployed on operations. The effectiveness of the Joint Supply Chain is a key element in this ... we Chiefs of Materiel have a unique view across the Unified Customer [User, Sponsor and DE&S] and the Department more generally.*[120]

But better support to the front line requires changes by the end-user. The front line has ever been pretty ignorant of logistics and, particularly, procurement. In fact, many see a job in procurement as the kiss of death and most find logistics a boring fact of life, although this has changed to some extent with extended operations. Even so:

> *We now have to be much more of an intelligent customer than in the past and clearly state our requirements so that the DLO can provide them.*[121]

The CofMs cannot of course do their job by themselves, so Customer Support Teams have been formed to maintain an understanding of the user's needs and to help IPTs to understand and react to these priorities.

DE&S Organisation

CDM						
Chief Operating Officer	DG Finance	Chief of Staff	Chief Corporate Servicss	CofM(Fleet)	CofM(Land)	CofM(Air)
DG Ship		DG Change	DG Human Resources			
DG Submarines				Naval Bases		
DG Land Eqpt			DG Safety & Engineering			
DG Helicopters						
DG Combat Air			DG Commercial			
DG Air Support						
				ACDS (Log Ops)	DG Joint Supply Chain	DGISS
DG ISTAR						
DG Weapons					DSDA	

Figure 6–1: Top Level Organisation of DE&S
Source: MoD

---

[120] Lt Gen Dick Applegate, *RUSI Defence Systems* (Volume 10, No. 3, February 2008), page 93.
[121] CinC Land, *DLO News*, July 2006, page 24.

IPTs

The organisation of DE&S is shown at Figure 6–1. This will only work as well as it is hoped if the CofMs are able to improve the support to the front line. But of equal importance is the performance of the IPTs. Since Smart Procurement empowered IPT leaders (at least in part) in 1998, that empowerment has been progressively reduced, thus undermining motivation and drive – one recent IPT leader felt that he had been totally unempowered. Moreover, IPTs have been 'drowned in process' and have seen little in the way of reward compared with those with whom they work in industry. There has been little improvement in either cost increases or delay, except with UOR projects. For the DE&S to work as it should, IPTs and their leaders must be motivated, sensibly empowered and not over-encumbered with process.

> IPTs and their leaders must be motivated, sensibly empowered and not over-encumbered with process

Team Leaders will remain clearly accountable not just for the delivery of their outputs but also for the management of the often sizeable businesses they run ... the main function of IPTs – the delivery of equipment to the front line – will remain fundamentally unchanged.[122]

This last sentence is disturbing. Performance in equipment IPTs has been pretty bad, judging by the remarks made by the last CDP in May 2004 and by the performances recorded in the NAO Major Project Reports. We shall look at that in Chapter Ten.

But there is another aspect of the organisation which may adversely impinge on the empowerment of IPT Leaders. The organisation has changed the alignment of IPT groupings. With the implementation of Smart Procurement, the DPA organised its IPTs in clusters under three Directors – Land & Maritime, Information Superiority and Air, and Weapons & Support. These were to some extent capability driven, but the groupings were very different from the Equipment Capability groupings, which were truly purple, giving rise to the need for DECs to deal with far more IPT Leaders than should have been necessary – and vice versa. Industry, which had to deal with both DECs and IPT Leaders,

---

[122] MoD, DE&S, *Establishing an Integrated Defence Procurement and Support Organisation*, January 2008, page 16.

had an even bigger problem.

The new DE&S organisation appears to make few concessions to the Joint or capability approach of Smart Procurement, as it has reverted largely to the pre-Smart days of environments, and so continues to remain unaligned with ECC. We now have eight equipment Directors General (DGs): DG Ships, DG Submarines, DG Land Equipment, DG Combat Air, DG Air Support, DG Helicopters, DG ISTAR, DG Weapons. The last three are Joint, but the others are not – for example, the future carrier (CVF) sits under DG Ships, while its aircraft come under DG Combat Air.

This change in organisation is not necessarily a bad thing – but there are two weaknesses. First, the groupings still do not match those in the ECC and, more importantly, the DG structure is bound to make it more difficult for IPT Leaders to be properly empowered. Nevertheless, the reorganisation of IPTs does seem to have improved coherence. If the Smart Procurement vision represented two steps forward, its implementation could only be described as half a pace forward. Does this change to clusters and DGs not represent a pace or two backwards? What price empowerment? What price coherence?

> Does this change to clusters and DGs not represent a pace or two backwards?

Working with Industry

The new structure should make it easier for industry, which will now only have to deal with one rather than two organisations. Moreover, the DG structure should give more coherent answers to industry's questions, being the single point of contact.

Making a Difference

The DE&S document gives a list (Figure 6–2) of what will be different from April 2007:[123]

---

[123] Ibid, page 23.

DE&S: What Will Be Different from April 2007

- There will be a through-life approach to everything – plans, options, support, finance, approvals, contracts, technologies.
- No dual accountability: there will be one reporting system, one financial system, one planning process, and greater coherence between initial procurement and support.
- The Programming and Options process will be led by Sponsors and Users and not by the Centre or by DE&S.
- IPT groupings will have a clearer alignment with DIS sector strategies, and implementing these will be a driving force for project business.
- Key internal processes – finance, commercial, project management, personnel, approvals, logistics support, performance management, etc. will be owned by a designated member of the DE&S Executive and will be captured clearly and implemented consistently as part of the Acquisition Operating Framework.
- DE&S as a whole will adopt a culture of continuous improvement and performance management.
- There will be a major focus on helping staff to develop the right skills and on closing skills gaps, including allowing the necessary margin to facilitate training.
- Those performing well will be more effectively recognised and rewarded and poor performance will no longer be tolerated.
- There will be simpler, more flexible ways of managing people.

Figure 6–2: The Differences that the New DE&S Will Make

That all sounds pretty good, but the proof will be in the implementation.

Clearly, the possibility of achieving viable TLCM is increased significantly with the removal of the major interface between the old DPA and the DLO, and this must be a major improvement. As are the strong words about personal performance. But the real questions stem not from the organisation, but from merging the different cultures of the two constituent parts and the processes that staff will use, rather than be drowned in. These will be examined in Chapters Seven and Eight.

The MoD Customer

While the EAC study recommended the major organisational change of the formation of the DE&S, it made no recommendations to reorganise the MoD customer. This is perhaps not surprising as the Equipment Capability Customer was the one area that had been successfully and fully implemented, as the last CDP told the House of Commons Defence Committee in May 2004.

EAC did, however, recommend some nomenclature changes – 'customer' for the MoD as a whole, 'sponsor' for DCDS(EC)'s organisation, and 'user' for the single-Service Chiefs of Staff and the Front Line Commands ('Joint user' for the Vice Chief of the Defence Staff (VCDS) and the Permanent Joint Headquarters (PJHQ)).

EAC also recommended that *"each major new capability should be assigned a 2-star Senior Responsible Owner (SRO) residing in the Equipment Capability Customer"*. SROs would still have no authority commensurate with their responsibilities – particularly over the non-equipment DLoDs – but being in the ECC at least would give them some authority over equipment funding.

Committees

A major change in the composition and responsibilities of committees, which should right two weaknesses of Smart Acquisition, was recommended.

The first concerns the disconnect between the Investment Appraisal Board (IAB) and the Defence Management Board (DMB).[124] The latter is the governing body of defence and its responsibility should include the resolution of major equipment issues that cannot be resolved in the IAB, but this has not been happening. The EAC recommended that:

> *DMB should be involved in Initial Gate and Main Gate decisions for the highest-value and strategic investment decisions.*

This was picked up by PUS Bill Jeffrey:

> *We are now implementing changes which will give the Defence Management Board – the Department's main executive body, of which the Service Chiefs are*

---

[124] Now the Defence Board.

> *prominent members – greater involvement in acquisition and a greater degree of*
> *ownership, particularly of the largest projects.*[125]

The second weakness was the composition of IAB, which included the MoD suppliers (CDL and CDP) as full members of IAB, while DCDS(EC) was not – the MoD customer being VCDS. EAC recommended that CDM should no longer be a full member of IAB but should be 'in attendance' to provide *"assurance to the Board on the procurement and support arrangements"*. It did not, however, recommend the inclusion of DCDS(EC).

Instead, it recommended that the Defence Commercial Director be a full member and become the 'owner' of the procurement process and that consideration be given to appointing the Finance Director as a full member instead of 2nd PUS. It was also recommended that one non-executive director be appointed to the Board.

This still left the MoD user's position weak, given that VCDS with his myriad of other responsibilities had to take the lead for the MoD customer, while the expert MoD supplier (CDM) would be in attendance to provide expert advice. But it was an improvement.

Will the Reorganisation be an Improvement?

The bringing together of the former DPA and DLO should make the whole-life approach to acquisition much easier to implement and help in the relationship with industry as the latter will have to deal with only one organisation, not two, but the size of the resultant DE&S will make it very difficult for its chief to command and control. The reversion to the 2-star DGs will help here, but there is a potential clash between 2-star control and IPT Leader empowerment that will need to be satisfactorily resolved.

The 3-star Chiefs of Materiel appear to be creating a much closer link between the acquisition system and the front-line commands, particularly as regards operational matters, and this is a clear step forward.

The extended use of SROs is an advantage, but in reality they will not be able to carry out their full responsibility without further authority over all DLoDs.

The changes to the committee structure is of minor impact as the user's position is still weak, and decision by committee consensus is one

---

[125] Bill Jeffrey, *RUSI Defence Systems* (Volume 9, No. 2, October 2006), page 23.

of the barriers to clear accountability.

Overall these changes should be for the better, particularly the formation of DE&S, but are unlikely to achieve a great deal without a change of culture throughout the acquisition chain.

SUMMARY: REORGANISATION

Creation of DE&S

Strengths

- Merger of the Defence Procurement Agency (DPA) and the Defence Logistics Organisation (DLO) will remove many barriers to Through-Life Capability Management (TLCM).
- Removal of dual accountability.
- Better alignment with industry sectors creating single points of contact.
- Alignment of Director General (DG) areas with DIS sector strategies.
- Stronger links with the front line.

Weaknesses

- DG areas not generally Joint and not aligned with Directors of Equipment Capability (DECs).
- Creation of DGs pose problems for empowerment of IPT Leaders.

Equipment Capability

Strengths

- Each major new capability should be assigned a 2-star Senior Responsible Owner (SRO).

Weakness

- SROs have no clear authority over non-equipment Defence Lines of Development (DLoDs).

Committee Changes

Strengths

- Greater involvement of the Defence Management Board (DMB) in major decisions.
- Weakening of MoD supplier's position on Investment Appraisals Board (IAB).

Weakness

- User's voice on IAB not strengthened.

Chapter Seven

DIS: Process and Procedures

Process had featured very heavily in the Smart Procurement Initiative and had been fiddled with a great deal since. However, much of it had not been properly implemented with the result that the advantages of the changes were far fewer than envisaged and many of the disadvantages remained. The DIS reinforced many of the recommendations of the Smart Procurement Initiative.

DIS Recommendations on Process

DIS proposed to make the acquisition approach more innovative, agile and flexible at the project level by:[126]

- Streamlining decision-making, recognising that delays have a cost.
- Greater assurance that risk is progressively reduced through the project's life.
- Being prepared to cancel projects, if necessary before Main Gate.
- Increasing the tempo of procurement to match the speed of technology and operational change.
- An improved approach to technology insertion.
- Improving the pull-through of technology from research into capabilities.
- Exploiting synthetic environments and experimentation to reduce risk.
- Working with industry and universities to identify sources of innovation.

But the headline change was the through-life approach with industry and TLCM. This was, of course, one of the Smart Procurement initiatives that had never been properly implemented, but the formation of DE&S should now make TLCM easier to implement.

EAC Recommendations

Following on from DIS, EAC recommendations on process stated, inter alia:

- **Planning.** The Department's planning system needs to be improved to enable Ministers and the DMB to take a more

---

[126] DIS, page 138.

strategic view of the defence budget across 10 years and beyond. This involves the reintroduction of a 10-year view of defence spending, across the board, without returning to the nugatory detail of the Long Term Costing.

- **Realism.** An increased emphasis on realism in the planning of defence capability ... The solution lies in part in introducing greater realism into project planning, but also an acceptance that we need to maintain, at the Departmental level, a contingency of unallocated funds.

- **Support.** The Department needs to programme equipment support costs over 10 years ... We recommend that the Front Line Commands should programme the costs of supporting in-service equipment over the first four years of the defence planning period ... The ECC should be responsible for the support costs of new equipment over ten years and of in-service equipment beyond the first four years.

- **Other Costs.** The ECC should also assume responsibility for programming other significant net additional costs associated with new capability (such as infrastructure and training).

- **Clarification of Roles.** New clarity should be given to the roles of DCDS(EC), the Chiefs of Staff, the Front Line Commands and PJHQ in exercising their customer responsibilities.

- **Senior Responsible Owner.** More use should be made of the SRO approach to programme management inside the ECC, which should become more focused on through-life capability planning.

> These changes, together with others of organisational nature, needed to be considered as a package

- **Governance.** Changes should be made to the governance of the procurement process, including changes in the relationship between the DMB and the IAB, and an improved, more focused approach to scrutiny of major investment decisions.

The EAC report went on to say that these changes, together with others of organisational nature, needed to be considered as a package.

Faster Procurement

Perhaps the most important thing to get right is the procurement time cycle.[127] Major development programmes often take about two decades from the start of the Concept stage to fielding, while smaller, less complex programmes, although they may enter service more quickly, are too often held up unnecessarily by bureaucracy and slow decision-making.

> *It does seem extraordinary that a programme such as the Army's Future Rapid Effect System (FRES) takes so long to introduce. It is the Army's highest priority future procurement programme and has been talked about for years. If it had been in service, the FRES system would have saved lives in Iraq and Afghanistan. It is desperately needed … Bureaucracy and a laborious process are largely responsible … one is bound to wonder whether it is not in some people's interest to delay.*[128]

Two decades is far too long a period, far longer than either technology generations or operational change, and DIS was quite right to state clearly that MoD will *"take action to make our acquisition approach more innovative, agile and flexible at the project level"*.[129]

The Importance of the Time Cycle

Why is cycle time so important?

To start with, time is money. For decades, the official mind ignored this, and the Treasury and MoD central financiers argued that delay saved money. This was a fallacious argument. While moving things to the right might reduce the financial requirement in Year One or Year Four or over the whole ten-year period, it did not save money **overall**. In fact, because of the need to keep teams together for longer and the

> Delays cost money – long delays cost lots of money

higher inflation rate in defence, delays cost money – long delays cost lots of money.

The higher level of defence inflation compared with national inflation is not a new phenomenon, but it has not been clearly quantified until now. The result has been that government politicians, because they

---

[127] The RUSI Acquisition Focus paper 'Why Does it all Take So Long?' is at Appendix 7–2.
[128] General the Lord Guthrie of Craigiebank, *RUSI Defence Systems* (Volume 10, No. 1, June 2007), page 16.
[129] DIS, page 138.

have to find the money for the defence budget, have conveniently ignored it, while others who point to it as a reason to increase the defence budget (opposition politicians, MoD and defence analysts) have no firm figures to present as evidence and their arguments are dismissed.

However, Professor David Kirkpatrick has recently carried out some work on defence inflation[130] and, although his figures are not definitive (more authoritative figures could only be produced through access to data on MoD expenditure that is not available in the public domain), they suggest that defence inflation is likely to be consistently about 3% above the GDP deflator. Not all defence expenditure is subject to this level of inflation as is shown by Kirkpatrick's final table at Figure 7–1.

Category	Fraction of MoD Budget	Category Price Growth Relative to GDP Deflator	Overall Price Growth Relative to GDP Deflator
Personnel	0.36	1.7%	0.61%
Military Equipment	0.36	6.2%	2.23%
Other Supplies	0.28	0.3%	0.08%
Total			2.92%

Figure 7–1: Defence Inflation Broken Down by Category [David Kirkpatrick]

It can be seen from Figure 7–1 that defence inflation in equipment acquisition is far higher than in personnel costs or non-equipment supplies, although all categories are higher than the GDP deflator.

So, when the Government trumpets an **increase** in the defence budget of 1.5% per year for three years, it actually means that they will limit the annual **cut** to the budget of 1.5%.

Let us take military equipment. Price growth is shown to be about 6.2% above the GDP deflator which, in effect, means that in real terms the equipment programme has to be cut by that figure every year, unless some extra pain is borne by costs of personnel and other supplies. Think

---

[130] Professor David Kirkpatrick, 'Is Defence Inflation Really as High as Claimed?', *RUSI Defence Systems* (Volume 11, No. 2, October 2008).

how long this has been going on and work out the 'real' cut in the equipment budget that has had to be made over, say, the last couple of decades since the end of the Cold War. Is it any surprise that the equipment programme experiences so much turbulence and lack of commitment? Is it a surprise that, in dealing with these increasing costs, things are moved to the right and an unaffordable hump just beyond the end of the 10-year programme (the so-called bow wave) builds up?

Kirkpatrick's full paper is at Appendix 7–1.

But it is not just the high level of defence inflation which dictates that delays or long cycle times raise costs.

A view from a foreigner is instructive:

> *I know I am an outsider, but I've done a lot of work in UK over the years and, as an interested observer, it seems to me that often when a new system is being considered for procurement, the proponents start with a grand plan and a very optimistic estimate of the amount of funding that will be available. They then go to great lengths to establish the validity of the operational need and the effectiveness of their system in meeting it. As time goes on and more potential users and other interested parties are heard from, 'requirements creep' often sets in. This, in turn, requires bid updates from the contractor(s) and, as a result of adding the requested capabilities and the re-bidding process itself, prices go up. Meanwhile, other priorities and demands for funding drive down the available funds and the programme managers suddenly realise that the new costs exceed the budget and they have to get more money authorised at some level (1-star, 2-star, ministerial ... etc.). This effort takes time, and time means two things – costs increase again (they never go down) and/or the schedule slips to the right. This, in turn, makes Treasury functionaries, scrutineers and other observers, some of whom have agendas of their own, question the validity of the requirement or the management of the effort and the cycle starts all over again. It makes one wonder how anything gets fielded on time and on budget.*[131]

The Light Mobile Artillery Weapon System (LIMAWS) was the subject of a Feasibility Study in 1996, with an ISD of 2006. It was subsequently broken down into LIMAWS (Rocket) and LIMAWS (Gun). LIMAWS(R) was to fire proven MLRS munitions (as does the UK's MLRS system which has been in service for many years) and was therefore a fairly straightforward project. However:

> *The slip in LIMAWS' ISD was largely a function of requirements creep, the*

---

[131] Colonel Jon Schreyach, 'The One That Got Away', *RUSI Defence Systems* (Volume 11, No. 2, October 2008)

yearly budget battles and the unending meddling of the 'scrutineers' over time. As, for example, when in the budget deliberations of 2007 the LIMAWS(R) programme managers agreed to stretch the programme in order to save it by spreading the costs over a further seven years – thereby giving budget cutters the ammunition they needed to label the system 'irrelevant'. This is what we, in the US, call a self-inflicted wound! If the programme had been executed without all the hand-wringing and mucking about, it would probably be in theatre right now.[132]

Delay undermines commitment, which in turn produces slower progress and more delay – how do you keep the best industrial people on the programme if there are lengthy discontinuities caused by financial or operational uncertainties? Delay introduces increased risk of obsolescence on fielding (Phoenix is a good example here[133]), with the need to upgrade earlier or, worse, change subsystems, components or software; or, even worse, the need to buy interim systems off-the-shelf to fill a gap (UAVs, interim armoured vehicles, small arms etc.) – with, of course, more cost.

But even more important than the unnecessary cost increases is the delay of new capability being made available for operations. Lord Guthrie cites the lives that might have been saved if FRES had come in earlier. FRES has been delayed for very many years through the inability to decide what is wanted and the repeated delays to funding. The financial bottom line in Whitehall clearly takes priority over safeguarding lives.

> The financial bottom line takes priority over safeguarding lives

Learning from the Civil Sector

Much shorter timescales are fairly normal in the civil sector, even for major state-of-the-art systems. The A340 aircraft was bought by airlines off the drawing board and was in service, on time, within budget in less than four years. BP's Andrew Platform came on stream six months ahead

---

[132] Ibid.

[133] The unmanned air vehicle Phoenix had an original ISD of 14 February 1989. If it had met this with the performance specified, it would have had good export potential. However, a bad contract and poor management by both MoD and industry led to a slip in ISD of a decade with a final performance that was inadequate, particularly in hot and high environments. By the time it did come into service, the UAV world had moved on. It was removed from service in 2008.

of schedule in four years. The car industry just could not function at all on the sort of timescales that are typical of MoD. And those in the motorsport industry win races only if they modify, upgrade or redesign between one race and the next.

Can MoD learn from the civil sector? Lord Drayson, with his background in the motorsport industry believed it could.

> *The advantage is the brilliance of the [motorsport] engineering, the speed and the get up and go. The difference with motorsport is that people make decisions quickly because they have to be there on Saturday to race. How is it that a Le Mans team can recognise it has a problem with its dampers and they can design, manufacture and fit a new set of dampers the next morning? If you want a new design of dampers for an armoured vehicle you are waiting years.*[134]

Why? The bureaucracy justified by 'due diligence'? More like a waste of taxpayers' money.

Rapid Procurement

Can procurement be drastically speeded up? Of course it can. Performance and culture in the delivery of UORs show most plainly that it can. While the Falklands War, the Balkans, and the First Gulf War demanded many UORs over short periods, Northern Ireland, Iraq and Afghanistan show that the pace of UOR delivery can be kept up over extended periods of years, possibly decades.

> The bureaucracy justified by 'due diligence'? More like a waste of taxpayers' money

There are other examples: the Experimental Aircraft Programme, set against Air Staff Target 403, was first contracted to BAe in 1982 after ten days of contractual negotiations, and was to be designed, built and flown at Farnborough in 1986. How was this possible? Professor Lynn Davies who was centrally involved in the project said:[135]

> *MoD laid down the rules and BAe did it. There was no MoD heavy hand and industry shared the risks, the costs and the benefits.*

---

[134] Lord Drayson in an article by Gavin Ireland, 'Accelerating Defence Acquisition: What Defence Can Learn from the World of Motorsport', *RUSI Defence Systems* (Volume 10, No. 1, June 2008), page 82.
[135] Dr Lynn Davies, interview with the author, 2002.

In other words, it was done by Smart Procurement – 12 years before Smart Procurement was born.

The US has a similar process for rapid acquisition for operations. But they can also make their 'normal' system work faster. The example already quoted bears repeating:

> Going through the normal process, the Stryker, a brand-new vehicle, took about two years from an idea to a production model, and from an idea to a deployed fighting brigade in northern Iraq, four years … In 1100 attacks – IEDs, suicide bombers, RPGs – six soldiers have been injured and all have been returned to duty; no one in that vehicle has been killed or seriously injured.[136]

A vehicle that saves many lives and is procured in a couple of years seems to me to be a triumphant success and great value-for-money – not to say a literal life-saver.

But the UK has its own examples of rapid procurement. The Loitering Munition (LM), part of the Indirect Fire Precision Attack (IFPA) programme, went from drawing board to its first test-firing in only 15 months, and is now progressing through its Assessment Phase with the potential for the introduction of an Early Operational Capability (EOC) into operational theatres by 2011. Of course, there may be future delays, but Team Complex Weapons (Team CW) has embraced rapid procurement philosophy from the beginning. This includes:[137]

> The Loitering Munition went from drawing board to its first test-firing in only 15 months

- Low-cost rapid development techniques including considerable use of proven technology.
- An MoD/industry 'one team' ethos which focuses on the following:
  - ➤ A rapid and flexible approach to requirements development.
  - ➤ An early focus on a streamlined approach to certification and acceptance.
  - ➤ Effective stakeholder management based on a close, early

---

[136] The Honourable Claude Bolton, *RUSI Defence Systems* (Volume 10, No. 2, October 2007), page 8.

[137] Dr Akram Ghulam and Colonel Peter Tomlinson, 'A Big Step Towards Rapid Acquisition', *RUSI Defence Systems* (Volume 11, No. 2, October 2008).

and continuous engagement with all stakeholders, with the mindset of listening and understanding before responding to solutions.

- ➢ The use of concurrent engineering and re-use of MOTS and COTS.
- ➢ A quick, timely and flexible approach to joint trade-offs.
- Trust

The Team learned that Relationship Management is not a quick fix and requires perseverance, courage and hard work and that continuous communication is essential.

The UOR Example

The LM is urgently required for operations in Afghanistan, but is not a UOR. Much operational equipment has been fielded in Iraq and Afghanistan over the last five years or so, but the UOR process is not suitable in many ways for 'normal' procurement – the short support timescale, the risk of failing to get value-for-money, and lack of coherence and interoperability with other systems. But there is scrutiny and decision-making at the appropriate level. So surely process and culture can be read across. What is usually thrown up as an argument against is cost risk. But if we reduce the procurement cycle significantly, we will save money as argued above. Moreover, if we reduce the time cycles of all projects by, say, 50%, then we could reduce the staff in MoD by a considerable number – and at a considerable cost saving. Would it not also lead to a reduction of staff in industry with a cost saving as well? Set all that against the occasional cost risk and the argument is clearly in favour of incorporating UOR processes and culture.

In fact, the NAO has recommended that MoD does just that:[138]

- **NAO Recommendation:** Apply lessons from the procurement of capabilities through UORs more widely, for example flexible procurement and rapid competition techniques.
- **MoD Implementation.** The Department is considering how best to transfer lessons to wider procurement practice, and the

---

[138] National Audit Office, 'The Rapid Procurement of Capability to Support Operations', HC 1161 Session 2003–2004, The Stationery Office, London, 19 November 2004.

Acquisition for Network Enabled Capability Project has started to roll out amended procurement processes.

So, clearly MoD accepted NAO recommendations four years ago, but we still have to wait and see whether 'normal' procurement will be speeded up.

The 'normal' process must produce equipment far more quickly than it does now, or we will continue to fight wars with a peacetime mentality, allowing the tempo and culture to be tied to the general budget round. What needs to be transferred from the UOR process into 'normal' procurement is firmer commitment, faster decision-making, a sense of urgency, use of mature technology and empowerment. Crying for the moon? No – crying for common sense.

> Incorporating a UOR mindset into 'normal' procurement is crucial

Incorporating a UOR mindset into 'normal' procurement is crucial – without that change of culture nothing much will change. But there are two other major blocks to shorter timescales: programme affordability and technical risk.

Programme Affordability

We know that the current equipment programme is grossly underfunded, but even if it wasn't, the high rate of defence inflation would soon make it so. If the defence budget remains flat in real terms (i.e. inflated by the national inflation figure or GDP deflator), this amounts to a 3% cut in what perhaps we should call 'real-real' terms. However, inflation in defence **equipment acquisition** runs at over 6% above the GDP deflator, so every year the cost of the equipment programme is increased by 6% in 'real-real' terms[139] – or in other words it has to be **cut by 6% every year** to remain within provision.

Thus, an annual exercise has to be carried out for the programme to remain within budget. If we then add on cost increases for other reasons, this exercise becomes a very large one and undermines commitment to the programme by both MoD and industry. This in turn leads to delays while the programme is re-examined, the capability

---

[139] For further explanation of these figures see Appendix 7-3.

requirement revalidated and the updated arguments accepted by the user, the supplier, industry and the Treasury. No wonder programmes slip.

Technical Risk

Another major block is technical risk. All too often, programmes approach Main Gate with too much of it, with the result that either Main Gate is delayed or, worse still, hits additional problems in the final stages before production.

> Another major block is technical risk

> *Technology must be brought to maturity before MoD finalises its requirements and before industry is forced to make fixed-price bids. Bids based on uncertain technology can never be honest and will always contain the seeds of time slip and price escalation, fuelling mistrust, preventing openness and breeding confrontation.*[140]

We need to do much more much earlier if we are to approach Main Gate with the risks fully understood and minimised, enabling decisions to be made much more quickly with greater certainty. Lord Drayson, with his links with the motor racing world, believes that there are lessons that could be learned by defence, including making more use of rapid prototyping. Others agree. In motor sports,

> *They really do have to use rapid prototyping when, say, they have to produce a necessary system enhancement between two races one week apart. They seem to be able to do it very effectively. Are there techniques that might be applied in our sector? In my company [MBDA] we have a cell that is looking at rapid prototyping techniques and applying them to particular programmes, and the results on occasion are quite astounding.*[141]

I will come back to technical risk in Chapter Nine, and to affordability in Chapter Eleven.

DIS and Agility in Acquisition

As a start, DIS directed that decision-making be streamlined, and that the tempo of procurement be increased using technology insertion or incremental acquisition. Sadly, this was not taken forward in EAC, although it was later addressed in the refocusing of the DACP in 2008 (of which more later).

---

[140] RUSI Acquisition Focus, *RUSI Defence Systems* (Volume 10, No. 1, June 2007), page 32.
[141] Guy Griffiths, Interview, *RUSI Defence Systems* (Volume 10, No. 1, June 2007), page 15.

The Acquisition Cycle

Unlike the Smart Procurement Initiative, DIS quite correctly did not fiddle with the acquisition cycle but retained the CADMID cycle.

Incremental Approvals

However, one of the strengths of the CADMID cycle vision was the reduction from four to just two committee submissions – at Initial Gate and Main Gate. The idea of this was to speed the process up, but of course it never happened. Many projects now adopt 'incremental approvals' to reduce the risks involved in complex projects. This may be a pragmatic approach but, unless sensibly handled, could cause additional delay, particularly if the right issues at each point are not properly identified. In effect, the main advantage of the CADMID cycle seems to have been squandered.

> The main advantage of the CADMID cycle seems to have been squandered.

One Size for All

'One size fits all' has tended to be the view of the process mongers. The process is designed to fit the big projects and then, if at all, footnotes are added to account for small projects – lower levels of authorisation, for example. This is not sensible as one size clearly does not fit all.

The majority of contracts are 'small' with a worth under £100M, but this is generally ignored because the fewer, very large programmes gain all the attention of the media, Parliament and Ministers. Maybe this is all to the good as many of the small projects have relatively little 'hassle' as a result and produce good time, cost and performance outcomes.[142]

But too often the process police try and stuff the two into the same box. Yet the two require utterly different approaches:

> The 'wicked' programmes (including IT programmes) need different management skills from smaller, less complex projects, and a different approach, led by a different style with a wider breadth of understanding, greater initiative and less process constraint.[143]

---

[142] There is, however, much less data in the public domain (and I suspect within the MoD) on small programmes than there is on the large ones.
[143] RUSI Acquisition Focus, *RUSI Defence Systems* (Volume 10, No. 2, October 2007), page 64.

The cry: 'We are all drowning in process' is common. Process needs to be rolled back. This is particularly important for the complex, 'wicked' programmes. If MoD cannot find a dozen or so talented, experienced IPT Leaders, excelling at leadership, then we really do have a problem. But I believe that they are there. Such people do not need to be ruled by process – indeed it holds them back and demotivates them.

For the less competent or inexperienced IPT Leaders, more process regulation is perhaps needed. But surely not as much as now.

Incremental Acquisition

Although it was officially blessed by the Smart Procurement Initiative, incremental acquisition (IA) had been a fairly common procurement route for a long time. The Rapier surface-to-air missile is a good example with its Field Standards (FS) A, B1, B2 and C, the development stage of each overlapping with the production and fielding of its predecessor, and then in due course informing the design of its successor. FS A was deployed in the Falklands and some weaknesses became apparent. It was too late to incorporate the solutions to its operational weaknesses in FS B1, which was due in service shortly afterwards, but those that couldn't be solved by 'quick fixes' were resolved in the next acquisition increment, FS B2.

The Incremental Approach

The Rapier incremental approach was not driven by spreading financial commitment over a longer period, but by the availability of mature technology to meet the requirement. This approach meant that the Army and RAF did not have to wait until the full requirement could be met, but could deploy the 50% or 60% or 70% solutions much earlier.

Although it might well be difficult to persuade the military to accept a 60% solution with the current defence budget problems, the greater difficulty with incremental acquisition lies in persuading committees to endorse large amounts of money for, say, a 60% solution as the first step on the way to the final full solution without knowing the risks, costs and timescales of following increments. Incremental acquisition must have an endorsed plan and funding for full implementation – all the increments must be seen as a whole and not as useful savings measures.

That's what happened too much in the past – the Army's Air Defence Command and Information System (ADCIS) and Phoenix UAV are examples. ADCIS Stage 1 was a 40% solution to bring Army air defence into the 1980s, while Stages 2 and 3 were to provide a 1990s' solution and a turn-of-the-century performance in due course. ADCIS Stage 1 went into service, but not before Stages 2 and 3 had been cancelled as savings measures. That made little sense, for without the later stages ADCIS was obsolescent.

Phoenix was originally designed to carry many different sensor pods in addition to the artillery target acquisition pod – for surveillance, intelligence, EW and others. The Phoenix project was dogged by bad management and a bad contract, but before these became evident, all the other pods had been cancelled as savings measures. It is worth a thought that, had those follow-on pods not been cancelled, MoD would have had much more leverage on the prime contractor when it came to a stand-off between the Ministry and prime.

There are plenty more examples of incremental acquisition pre-Smart Procurement, some successful like Rapier, some less so like ADCIS and Phoenix. Nevertheless, the view overall was that incremental acquisition was a 'good thing' and come Smart Procurement it was officially embraced as a good way of reducing risk and of speeding up the fielding of equipment.

> Committees became increasingly reluctant to sign up to incremental acquisition

Despite this official endorsement, committees became increasingly reluctant to sign up to incremental acquisition. Challenged to name some post-Smart incremental projects, a senior DPA official could name only one – and that one a pretty dubious one. There have been one or two (JOCS, for example) but fewer than previously. Committees have taken the short-term, rather than the long-term, view.

DIS confirmed that incremental acquisition was officially favoured:

> *All projects* should use more flexible approaches (such as incremental or evolutionary acquisition).[144]

This seems to be the only reference to incremental acquisition in DIS,

---

[144] DIS, page 138.

while it was not covered by any recommendations in EAC. Perhaps the theory was still in favour but the practicalities of getting incremental acquisition through committees forced it out of court.

Technology Insertion

Instead there was much greater emphasis on Technology Insertion (TI), which is similar and shares some of the advantages of incremental acquisition.

> *The time between major platform procurements is increasing, as is proliferation and rate of change in R&T. The UK must increase the pace of technology insertion … this will allow us to respond to both evolution (the norm) and revolution (the exception) in capability. We should look to open architectures that facilitate incremental technology insertion (i.e. 'plug and play'). Platforms and systems should be designed with upgrade and flexibility in mind, noting that new roles for existing equipment will be identified to respond to changing threats.*[145]

The chief aims of incremental acquisition were to reduce technical risk and to speed up procurement. The aims of TI, on the other hand, are much more to do with upgrading in-service equipment and prolonging platform life. Both are important; both share many of the same characteristics; both have decided advantages. Neither should replace the other. Has incremental acquisition been quietly dropped? And if so, why? Pragmatism? Defeatism? Or just terminology? Probably the last as I am told that it features heavily in the forthcoming MoD publication – *The Defence Acquisition High Level Blueprint*.

Even so, the lack of true incremental acquisition projects suggests that they have been replaced by TI. If this is so, this implies that those responsible believe the latter to be more straightforward than the former. Maybe it is in terms of MoD processes and decision-making, but it is not a simple matter, as is demonstrated by the 'contention' section in the October 2008 edition of *RUSI Defence Systems*: those contributing were clear why.

> *The theory of Technical Insertion is straightforward enough; the complexity comes from putting it into practice. In this regard it would be easy to think the main issues associated with implementation are about the 'technicalities' – i.e. the engineering aspects of technology readiness, systems architectures, interface*

---

[145] DIS, page 43.

compatibility, programme scheduling, and so on. Whilst all this is undoubtedly important, the Team CW case is a good illustration of the importance of getting the strategic environment right first ... sufficient scale, a long-term planning horizon, an appropriate commercial framework and joint management ethos between customer and industry are the essential strategic ingredients to allow the engineers to get on with the job.[146]

> At what point you go firm on exactly the right piece of technology you want to insert

Andrew Brookes, in the same issue, asks at what point you go firm on exactly the right piece of technology you want to insert – an important point when even MoD TI programmes are outpaced by rapid technology change. He adds that there are security and technology transfer issues, particularly within an international framework.

Cost, too, needs to be carefully considered across all DLoDs before any decision is made.

Any Technology Insertion requires an assessment of the resulting improvement in the effectiveness of the equipment considered, and some test and evaluation to demonstrate that the improvement has been delivered and that the system's safety has not been compromised. This assessment must estimate the cost of the implementation of the TI by a defence contractor, withdrawing some systems from service and temporarily reducing the military capabilities of the operating Services (which reduction may need to be offset by procuring additional weapon systems, depending on the frequency and duration of the TI processes) ... the significant effects of the Technology Insertion on all of the Defence Lines of Development must be considered before it is approved.[147]

And, as Andrew Sleigh of QinetiQ says in the same issue,

Trends suggest that technology insertion will become the dominant approach in future acquisition strategies. It is probably the only way the nation can square the circle between affordability, operational sovereignty and the agility essential to 21st Century security needs.

If it is to become the dominant approach, then we had better not underestimate the very real complexities.

---

[146] Tony Bourne, MBDA, *RUSI Defence Systems* (Volume 11, No. 2, October 2008).
[147] Professor David Kirkpatrick, *RUSI Defence Systems* (Volume 11, No. 2, October 2008).

Spiral Development and Spin-Outs

Spiral development was devised in the mid-1980s by the then Chief Scientist at TRW Inc. to reduce risk on large software projects. He recommended a cyclical approach in which customers evaluated early results and in-house engineers identified potential trouble spots at an early stage. There were two major differences from IA – the spiral was aimed at development, not fielding by stages; and it was applied to large IT projects.

More recently, it has been read across to non-IT programmes, most notably the US Future Combat System (FCS). This major system of systems is a family of manned and unmanned systems, connected by a common network, which will provide the US Army with leading-edge technologies and capabilities. The key here is the Spin-Out of key capabilities for early deployment in the field – exactly what is needed in Iraq and

> The key here is the Spin-Out of key capabilities for early deployment in the field

Afghanistan now. So far, Spin-Out 1 has produced micro-UAVs, unattended ground sensors and a non-line-of-sight precision munition launcher ('rocket-in-a-box').

So, spiral development, depending on the context, can be an approach to reducing risk in development, or speeding up the fielding of capabilities. But there are problems.

> *Spiral development of Bowman and other systems means that there will be constant upgrades of AFV electronic systems through life. The UK's TCIS (Bowman) is in service, but new versions are being planned on a 3–4 year cycle. So, by the time FRES appears, a second new version should be extant.[148]*

This drives us towards open architectures to enable insertion of new technologies as they become available across a range of platforms. So, no 'big bang', but we do need a planned approach.

New equipment rushed into the field under UOR procedures has the ability to destroy coherence of capability. However, this can be alleviated, although not entirely eliminated, by Spin-Out from planned development. If the planned approach uses open architectures, new

---

[148] Dr Sandy Wilson, *RUSI Defence Systems* (Volume 10, No. 2, October 2007), page 20.

technology spun out from projects in development could be incorporated relatively smoothly.

> *It's important that these urgent pressures don't completely override a planned approach to sustainment – and enhancement – of military capability across all Defence Lines of Development (DLoDs). For instance, 'traditional' insertion of extra capability usually brings with it an extra control box or display, which has to be housed in an already cramped crewspace. This inevitably causes ergonomic, workload, information management, training and crew-tasking problems.*[149]

In addition to open architectures, we need to make greater use of commercial off-the-shelf (COTS) products. This may be self-evident, but there are risks.

> *Whilst industry and the wider supply chain can provide the innovation required to make extensive use of COTS in the submarine environment, leadership from MoD will be required to encourage the use of this technology. Much of the resistance to modifying the standards applied to submarine build and operation are based on valid concerns of safety and capability. Nevertheless, there are likely to be areas in which innovation can be introduced without compromising safety or performance. In some of these cases, the existing defence standards may need to be re-examined and modified.*[150]

The rapid spinning out of technology in a useable form is important. In the US, the Defense Advanced Research Projects Agency (DARPA) has a licence to push the boundaries of military technology and the expertise to feed its promising new technologies directly into the acquisition pipeline. It pursues research and technology where risk and pay-off are both very high and where success may provide dramatic advances for traditional military roles and missions. In contrast, in the UK our approach to high-risk technology, whether high pay-off or not, tends to be rather less determined and draw rather less funding.

Through-Life Capability Management

DIS was rather vague about the through-life approach and TLCM as if it wasn't quite sure what it was all about. We had seen this previously with Smart Procurement – the first edition of the Smart Procurement

---

[149] David Leslie, *RUSI Defence Systems* (Volume 10, No 2, October 2007), page 21.
[150] Gavin Ireland, 'Beyond *Artful*: Government and Industry Roles in Britain's Future Submarine Design, Build and Support', *RUSI Whitehall Report* 3-07, 2007.

Handbook stated that one of the key features was:

> *A whole-life approach, embodied in a single Integrated Project Team (IPT) bringing together the main stakeholders and involving industry except during the assessment of competitive bids.*[151]

The Handbook also described the Through-Life Management Plan. However, by January 2004, perhaps conscious that not much progress was being achieved, the Fifth edition devoted 13 pages out of a total of 44 to Through-Life Management. It defined it as: managing the Cost of Ownership (whole-life costs) of defence capability; ensuring that investment decisions take full account of the longer-term implications across all DLoDs; and developing and using a realistic, costed whole-life plan.

DIS does discuss through-life relationships with industry and it does state that the implementation plan has specific initiatives to address the objective of achieving "the primacy of through-life considerations". EAC had this to say:

> *Our recommendations need to be considered as a package. Taken together, they should produce an acquisition system which is better fitted to meet the needs of the Armed Forces and to engage with industry in a manner consistent with the principles of Through-Life Capability Management.*[152]

But little else.

There appears to be considerable differences in what different people mean and understand by TLCM. Indeed, DIS referred not only to TLCM, but also to through-life **equipment** management, which is much less complicated, as if the two were synonymous. They aren't. Just as equipment is not synonymous with capability, many talk of a ship (Type 45 or CVF) as a capability, although ships are equipments that are key in providing, along with other equipments, capability. Until this is resolved, TLCM is likely to face uncertain implementation.

The formation of the DE&S is indeed a giant step in enabling TLCM.

> *If we get the merger right, there is every prospect that we can bring the Through-Life Capability Management concept to life.*[153]

---

[151] MoD, *The Acquisition Handbook*, Edition 1, April 1999, page 6.
[152] MoD, *Enabling Acquisition Change*, page 5.
[153] Bill Jeffrey, *RUSI Defence Systems* (Volume 9, No. 2, October 2006), page 23.

So, what is TLCM?

TLCM represents a completely different way of working – with an emphasis on long-term capability management. If the DE&S change is a 'simple' organisational move, it is the profound cultural shift of TLCM, which the formation of DE&S underpins, that will shape future acquisition practice.

While TLCM was hardly central to the DIS, it has assumed a greater and greater importance as DIS and its follow-on studies are implemented. But is it being implemented effectively?

> While TLCM was hardly central to the DIS, it has assumed a greater and greater importance

Is TLCM a new idea? No. It's what we have been trying to do for decades, but have not done well. The Downey Cycle covered cradle to grave from 1968; DLoDs were considered in the past, although the accountability and authority were too fractured to do it well; and MoD did try to pull together procurement and in-service aspects, although this was much more difficult without a unified acquisition and support organisation. So, TLCM is not a new idea as such.

Not a new idea, perhaps, but it is certainly a new approach:

If the financial pressures and competing demands on the MoD's finances tell us anything, they tell us that we need a rigorous, broad approach to how capability is delivered. Not only how it is delivered, but what opportunity exists to deliver the same capability in a more effective manner, balancing current and future capability in the optimum way. In the equipment capability area we need to have a view that is not solely focused on replacing one piece of equipment with another, but a view that challenges how we get the most out of the resources that we have and how we can deliver capability in a more intelligent, informed and timely manner. TLCM is an approach to the acquisition of military capability in which every aspect of new and existing military capability is planned and managed coherently across all lines of development from cradle to grave.[154]

This is a major undertaking and one that will need considerable leadership, effort and focus. It will take a long time to embed. It is not just about organisation and process, but about culture change too.

Jon Brittain, MoD's Director of Capability Improvement, goes on to

---

[154] Brigadier Jon Brittain, Director Capability Improvement, UK MoD, 'Through-Life Capability Management – One Year On', *RUSI Defence Systems* (Volume 11, No. 1, June 2008), page 30.

say that behavioural change is not yet consistent, that there are weaknesses in thinking and working and that the following challenges[155] must be addressed:

- Lack of leadership and correct governance structures.
- Poor visibility of through-life costs across all DLoDs.
- Inconsistency in the way information is managed.
- Inconsistent capability delivery.

Additionally, while these challenges are being confronted within the ECC, a consistent approach across the Unified Customer is not apparent. This is a major weakness that has to be addressed quickly. But it is not an easy task.

> *The Sponsor – me – is responsible for TLCM and for ensuring that it is coordinated with the DE&S, with the Front Line Commands, with the Centre and the SIT [science, innovation and technology] community. The biggest challenge is the size of the enterprise. We've made great progress on this, but there are a lot of people to educate and train. It's pretty difficult to get the 400 people in the ECC spun up on this, let alone the rest.*[156]

Changes at the 'Top-of-the-Shop'

MoD may have made some – I would query the word 'great' – progress, but there is still a very long way to go before any progress is translated into improved capability management output. In truth, it is a huge job. Such change (and much of it is about cultural or behavioural change) is only ever successful if it is led from the very top, rather than imposed with an attitude of 'do as I say, not do as I do'. Change at the very top is not at all apparent – for a good example, note the political edicts during the 2008 Planning Round (PR 08) that no programmes were to be cancelled.

> Change is only ever successful if it is led from the very top

So, while implementation of much of the process is perfectly possible, there must be change at the 'top-of-the-shop' as well as all the way down the acquisition community, and this is where it may well fail.

---

[155] Ibid.

[156] Lieutenant General Andrew Figgures, Deputy Chief of the Defence Staff (Equipment Capability), Interview, *RUSI Defence Systems* (Volume 11, No. 1, June 2008), pages 76–77.

The RUSI Acquisition Focus has identified three 'top-of-the-shop' issues that will have to be resolved if TLCM and acquisition change are to be effectively implemented: the top-level organisation and accountability, culture change and the overheated defence programme:

> First and foremost [MoD] needs a new top structure that aligns real power and real accountability with the responsibilities of top officials. This must be under a minister with the relevant expertise and experience as well as the visible and consistent backing of the Secretary of State and the Prime Minister. This full accountability means ending the ability of other officials to stop decisions being made – they would provide advice only. We believe that we were getting tantalisingly close to that condition under Lord Drayson.[157]

And, on culture:

> Once clear accountability is in place, we could see a change in culture at the top. Decision-making should be faster, the 'Whitehall delay mentality' could be bypassed and much of the culture (but clearly not all) of UOR delivery could be adopted. Mission command should become the order of the day: tell leaders and managers what they have to do, let them get on with it, measure their results and hold them accountable.[158]

And, on the overheated defence budget:

> The overheating of the defence budget needs to be resolved as soon as possible, because it is distorting all other initiatives and work. The root cause(s) must be determined and eliminated, and TLCM has the pre-eminent role to play here in deciding affordability, relevance and value of what should remain in the programme.[159]

> Clearly these changes will be very uncomfortable and will require vision and leadership

Clearly these changes will be very uncomfortable and will require vision and leadership. Equally clearly, they must be effectively introduced.

The full paper on TLCM by the RUSI Acquisition Focus is at Appendix 7–3.

---

[157] RUSI Acquisition Focus, 'Implementing Through-Life Capability Management', *RUSI Defence Systems* (Volume 11, No. 1, June 2008), page 29.
[158] Ibid.
[159] Ibid.

Through-Life Costs

If changes in culture and accountability at the top are difficult, other more detailed issues are also difficult to resolve, one of which is identifying through-life costs with any accuracy – at least with the accuracy necessary to make cost-conscious decisions during the design and development stages.

> Today, funding must take into account maintenance costs. With sophisticated CIS merging into high-tech weaponry, complex capabilities have an ever higher maintenance cost. In fact, maintenance includes a wide spectrum of overlapping operations whose boundaries are not clearly determined: upgrading of the early production batches, implementation of new standards, improvement of technical interfaces, mitigation of obsolescence which may appear even before the end of the production phase, and, obviously, in-service maintenance.[160]

Whole Life Costing (WLC) is indeed difficult, particularly early on before the design is clear. MoD has defined WLC as:

> A continuous process of forecasting, recording and managing costs throughout the life of an equipment with the specific aim of optimising its whole life costs and its military output.[161]

Although there are similar instances in non-defence fields, MoD has often been spectacularly bad at producing development and production costs at the start of a project. While there are difficulties here, particularly with a new capability rather than a replacement ship, armoured vehicle or fast jet aircraft, estimation has been woefully inaccurate. Part of this is caused by the 'Conspiracy of Optimism' by which estimates are deliberately reduced to get them into the overheated Equipment Plan (EP), and by industry to land the

> MoD has often been spectacularly bad at producing development and production costs

contract – we will return to this later in this Chapter. Not surprisingly, costs escalate during the procurement stages. But it's not all due to this 'conspiracy'.

According to the National Audit Office's MoD Major Project

---

[160] Major General Jean-Tristan Verna, *RUSI Defence Systems* (Volume 9, No. 3, February 2007), page 69.
[161] MoD, *The Smart Acquisition Handbook*, Edition 5, January 2004, page 14.

Reports (MPR) 2007, the cost increase since Main Gate for the top 19 projects is some £2.8Bn. However, this includes some very dubious figurework – £609M has been 'saved' in-year by transferring certain costs to other budgets (with no saving at all to the overall defence budget), and a further £81M has been 'saved' by 're-evaluating' quantities and delivery dates required. The previous report (MPR 2006) showed similar, but much larger 'savings' and 're-evaluations'. Some of these changes or re-evaluations are large – for example, the reduction of Nimrod MRA4 aircraft from 18 to 12 'saved' £155M. The overall figure for 'savings' brought about by reductions in capability is about £1Bn, but this could hardly be called a reduction in the acquisition costs. Nor could the re-evaluation of the risk differential figures in the 2006 MPR (approximately £1.8Bn), or the transfers to other budgets with no overall savings to the defence budget (£448M in MPR 2006).

Cost Increases since Main Gate of Top 19 Projects (excluding Typhoon)	
MoD figures from MPR 2006	**£2,670M (11%)**
Reduction in capability (approx.)	£1,000M
Transfers to other budgets with no overall savings to defence	£448M
Re-evaluation of risk differential	£1,836M
True cost increase	**£5,954M (24%)**

Figure 7–2: True Cost Increase Compared with Declared Cost Increase

The net effect is that the true cost increases since Main Gate are far higher than those reported by MoD as shown in Figure 7–2. Moreover, this does not include either the cost increases before Main Gate for any of the projects. Neither are the cost increases for Typhoon, either before or after Main Gate, included as these are not given in the MoD figures because they are 'commercially sensitive'. Are they? Or are they so large as to make the cost increases unattractive for publication? Given the monkeying about with the other figures, we cannot be blamed for being sceptical. I will return to this in Chapter Ten.

If MoD cannot come close to estimating procurement costs early on, how much less credible will their cost estimates be for whole-life costs? Are they likely to be too inaccurate to act as a basis for any rational decision? Estimating whole-life costs in, say, the Concept stage when there is no firm design and therefore no firm manning figure or training approach or ease of maintenance, must be the very devil. Of course it will get more accurate as the project progresses through demonstration and maturation, but by then several crucial decisions will have been taken that bear on the in-service costs. Are we really pretending that those decisions will have a strong WLC base? Some will argue that WLCs will be accurate enough, but they will be outnumbered by those who disagree – including those who are not motivated by the desire to stay in their traditional comfort zones.

So, WLC is a real problem, but there are other difficulties too:

> *While the entire SIB [Submarine Industrial Base] accepts the imperative of reduced through-life cost, the trade-offs between unit cost and through-life support, due to a number of industrial and platform-specific factors, are uniquely challenging in the submarine context, as illustrated in the Astute programme. Particular new build techniques, such as modular build and vertical outfit, which have accelerated the Astute build and helped bring the programme on track, may yet complicate the upkeep of the submarine once they are in service.*[162]

Trading-Off Cost, Time and Performance

Cost and performance are issues throughout the procurement stages. As time is money, and because ISDs very often are about saving lives in operations (think FRES, Iraq and Afghanistan), we have a threesome – cost, time and performance.

We need to be alive to the opportunities for trading-off these three factors. Indeed, MoD is aware. But trading-off should be an objective exercise in producing the best overall result when any of the three change.

> *MoD contracting arrangements have also not been helpful in aligning the objectives of the procurement authority and the contractor. Inevitably in high technology development programmes there needs to be some flexibility in the outcomes, rather than slavish adherence to every detail of performance targets.*

---

[162] Gavin Ireland, 'Beyond Artful: Government and Industry Roles in Britain's Future Submarine Design, Build and Support', *RUSI Whitehall Report 3-07*, 2007, page 22.

ASRAAM was a good example of this, where a highly capable weapon was produced which exceeded the specification in some measurements, but fell marginally short in others. Any balanced assessment would have concluded that overall the development programme had been a success, and a weapon produced with orders of magnitude more capability than the weapon that it was designed to replace. However, there was a 12- or 18-month stand-off between MoD and the contractor, whilst the former tried to force some very expensive changes to meet every detail of the original specification, despite the fact that the RAF was keen to take delivery of the weapon to meet current operational requirements.[163]

> Trades should not be exercises in masking cost increases or slips in ISD

In some cases, no trades would be the correct answer – with cost increasing, or ISD slipping, or performance reducing. But in other cases, it might make sense to limit a threatened cost increase by reducing performance requirement that now seems less important to attain.

Trades, however, should not be exercises in masking cost increases or slips in ISD. Too often, cost escalation is reduced by lowering performance specifications, rather than examining the reason for the cost increase itself. Changes in cost and time are easy for the media and opposition politicians to spot, but reductions in performance are less easy to understand – even the effect of reducing production numbers can be difficult to quantify.

The Conspiracy of Optimism

The term 'Conspiracy of Optimism' has been in use since at least the mid-1990s and probably dates back to much earlier. It is said to exist between MoD and the defence industry, each side striking unrealistic agreements, later recognising, but not necessarily admitting, that the basis of the agreement was highly optimistic. Although there are many reasons for this, two – one on each side – are likely to be the main drivers.

The EP has become increasingly overheated over the last decade or two, due particularly to the 'peace dividend' after the fall of communism, the 1997 SDR which was badly underfunded, and operational commitments that year-on-year exceed Defence Planning Assumptions

---

[163] John Weston, email to the author.

on which funding is based. In an overheated programme, it is difficult to get new capabilities funded. The bigger the programme cost, the more difficult it is to get the new capability funded. There is, therefore, very strong pressure on staff to reduce the cost to a minimum and, perhaps not surprisingly, a match between capability and cost is not always achieved – sometimes knowingly, sometimes not. In addition, costs of development and testing of interfaces, technology demonstration and industrialisation, training and/or manpower are too often overlooked. In particular, costs of demonstrating and de-risking technology are frequently under-estimated.

A good example of this so-called 'entryism' is the future aircraft carrier CVF. The original MoD estimate was £2.9Bn, whereas non-MoD estimators set it at £3.9Bn or more. Immediately, there was a potential cost increase (since realised) of more than 30%.

> A good example of this so-called 'entryism' is the future aircraft carrier CVF

The other main driver occurs on the industrial side. Always in competitive bids, and often during negotiations for non-competitive contracts, there is intense pressure on industry to reduce price. In an effort to win the contract, the negotiating company will come down to the lowest possible price, but this often proves too low once the contract is in place. The result is a hiatus while the company tries to find contractual loopholes or persuade MoD to give it more money. As this happens during development when significant sums of public money have already been spent, MoD is not in a strong position to resist – MoD seldom cancels projects.

There are other, lesser but still important drivers – poor cost estimation techniques, bad programme management and a lack of transparency between MoD and industry.

The subject was examined by the RUSI Acquisition Focus,[164] whose paper is at Appendix 7–4.

---

[164] RUSI Acquisition Focus, *RUSI Defence Systems* (Volume 10, No. 2, October 2007), page 60.

Time and Cost Estimating

It seems unlikely that WLC will become accurate enough to clearly inform decisions during development which will reduce the overall cost of ownership. But should we not do better than we do with estimating procurement costs at Initial Gate? Arguably, actual cost growth during procurement is less than it seems because a sizeable chunk of it is caused by the Conspiracy of Optimism.

Is the bulk of the remainder down to poor management? Not so, some will claim:

> Cost growth is the product not of slack project management, but of the conspiracy of optimism ... Measuring management performance in terms of year-on-year changes in forecast costs and timescales makes matters worse. At best it encourages project management to postpone declaration of the truth as to likely costs and dates. At worst, it encourages 'descoping' in which more and more money is spent on less and less capability.[165]

> Are the faults in the Bowman programme not down to poor management?

Others might claim that the Conspiracy of Optimism, suppression of the real state of the project and fear of a blame culture – in both MoD and industry – is in fact weak project management.

For example, are the faults in the Bowman programme not down to poor management? A House of Commons Defence Committee report made the following points:[166]

- The secure radio capability provided by Bowman had only just begun to enter service, some 10 years late,[167] resulting in the armed forces having to operate with insecure, outdated analogue radios for far longer than they should have done.
- Bowman CIP was accepted into service in March 2004 with 27 major provisos that reduce the capability of the system. Substantial technical challenges remain to be overcome before all the required capabilities are in place.

---

[165] Philip Pugh, 'Delusions of Management', *RUSI Defence Systems* (Volume 9, No. 3, February 2007), pages 64/65.

[166] House of Commons Committee of Public Accounts, *Delivering digital Tactical Communications through the Bowman CIP Programme*, 14th Report 2006/07, HC 358, 27 February 2007.

[167] The original ISD was 1995.

- MoD seriously under-estimated the challenges involved in delivering it and sustaining it in service.
- Support costs such as the provision of spares and training requirements were severely under-estimated.
- MoD failed to appoint an SRO with responsibility, funding and authority to deliver the programme.

Several more failings were noted. It should also be pointed out that the Bowman programme was launched in about 1982, so the inadequacies above have arisen after 25 years in the procurement mill, starting with a procurement strategy that was known to be unworkable. It's a pretty grisly story. But it's not uncommon.

The International Dimension

Lewis Page, amongst others, has suggested[168] that we buy American, rather than UK equipment which is more expensive, less good and far too late. We have bought a lot of US kit – for example, much artillery: the 155mm M109, the 8-inch M110, the M107, the Honest John and Lance nuclear rocket systems, and the MLRS. We have also bought artillery systems off-the-shelf from elsewhere: the Swedish 5.5 inch and the Italian 105mm pack howitzer; even the UK AS 90 was originally developed as a private venture for a foreign country. We've been pretty satisfied with what we've bought; and, as buying American will almost always be cheaper for large programmes, we seem to have got really good value-for-money.

Many believe that DIS will cost a great deal and that this will make UK-developed kit even more expensive. So, there is much to support Page's view – except for one thing: operational sovereignty and the need to be able to deliver UORs to operational theatres. Buying more off-the-shelf would make this much more difficult.

> Many believe that DIS will make UK-developed kit even more expensive

In the field of very large programmes, there is another trend that pushes us towards collaboration or buying kit off-the-shelf – the rising

---

[168] Lewis Page, *Lions, Donkeys and Dinosaurs*, Chapter 10, (William Heinemann, London, 2006).

inter-generational costs (increasing from one generation to another by a factor of between three and ten)[169] which means that, increasingly, single nations can no longer afford, nor have the capability, to produce national solutions. This has been so in UK with fast-jet aircraft for some time, but we still choose to make the next generation of all our major naval assets (aircraft carriers, destroyers, submarines), although whether this will break the MoD bank we will have to see. This is a much greater difficulty for smaller nations, who find that collaboration is the only alternative to buying foreign that they can afford if they wish to both retain high-performance military equipment and maintain a defence industrial base.

But large commercial companies also find large programmes difficult.

EADS has indicated there will be delays and cost increases to the A400M military transport programme. Carlos Suárez, chairman of EADS Casa and head of the group's military transport aircraft division, said the company would never again attempt a programme 'of this scale and magnitude'.[170]

> There are concerns, other than that of operational sovereignty, about buying American

If a very large company like EADS, with the backing of the major European nations, will not in the future make transport aircraft, and if we are to collaborate with, or buy off-the-shelf from, other nations, the first port of call will inevitably be the US. But there are concerns, other than that of operational sovereignty, about buying American:

Firstly, the Americans are going to be much keener to provide more advanced technology if the customer has a realistic alternative to buying from the US. Without this the difficulties experienced in accessing the necessary software codes and integration data, already widely experienced on a number of programmes, can only become worse. Without a domestic capability we will be obliged to buy what the Americans are prepared to supply, at a price which they set. Secondly, it is a fact of life in the defence market that, when spending very large sums of the taxpayers' money, politicians like to see some benefit of this expenditure accruing to those that vote for them. There is, in my view, a clear link between the government's willingness to spend, and the local employment considerations. The carriers are a recent unfortunate example.[171]

---

[169] Professor David Kirkpatrick, 'Is Defence Inflation Really as High as Claimed?', *RUSI Defence Systems* (Volume 11, No. 2, October 2008).
[170] *The Financial Times*, www.ft.com, 22 April 2008.
[171] John Weston, email to the author, 11 September 2008.

How likely are these concerns to restrain us? Will technology transfer happen? Will the US make it difficult for US-sourced equipment to be used in operations that the US does not approve of? Will we be 'over a barrel' financially when it comes to supporting and upgrading the equipment? Do we really have cause for concern?

Collaboration with the US

The alternative to buying American or UK-developed equipment is to collaborate with allies. Collaborating with the US is the obvious answer as that would give us

> Will we be 'over a barrel' financially when it comes to supporting and upgrading the equipment?

the best equipment very early (often too early for our funding profiles) at a good price, and if we play our cards right, a share of the high-technology design and development. We have tried that and there have been some successes, but there have also been failures. The terminally guided warhead for MLRS which, just at the point of successful demonstration (one launch, one hit), was sunk when the US pulled out in favour of one of their 'black' programmes.

On our own, we cannot be a very strong partner to the US as our likely offtake will be grossly inferior to that of the US, except in a few areas. Nuclear submarines is one.

> With the UK SIB [submarine industrial base] under pressure to deliver highly capable, yet affordable submarines, and with the US programme tasked with cost-reduction and de-risking of new technology, there is real potential in further collaboration on both the state-to-state and the business-to-business levels.[172]

We are also collaborating with the US on the Joint Strike Fighter (JSF). However, other nations are involved too, so the amount of non-US investment is a much greater percentage. There has been concern over whether we shall get the necessary technology transfer to support it in the future, without being tied to the US. Lord Drayson, after robust discussions in Washington, gave us the assurance that we will. But will the JSF be a cost-effective buy? The Australians have recently looked closely at costs for their involvement in JSF and have concluded that:[173]

---

[172] Gavin Ireland, 'Beyond *Artful*: Government and Industry Roles in Britain's Future Submarine Design, Build and Support', *RUSI Whitehall Report 3-07*, page 19, 2007.
[173] Dr Andrew Davies, *RUSI Defence Systems* (Volume 11, No. 1, June 2008), page 36.

The natural response for prospective JSF customers is to wait and see how the costs shape up as the programme nears delivery of a fully operational aircraft. But that may set the scene for a self-fulfilling prophecy. If the curve continues to rise [see Figure 7–3], the possibility of cuts to planned acquisitions will increase. That will, in turn, drive unit prices further upwards and risk still further cuts to numbers – a phenomenon known to US acquisition commentators as a 'death spiral' ... Given the importance of the JSF programme to the USAF and Marine Corps, there is good reason to think that the JSF programme will be resourced well enough to succeed in delivering a capable product. But, like many aircraft before it, the JSF will likely cost more than was budgeted for. The initial aim of producing a fifth-generation capability at a less than fourth-generation cost seems to have been overly ambitious. Cost is not an independent variable after all.[174]

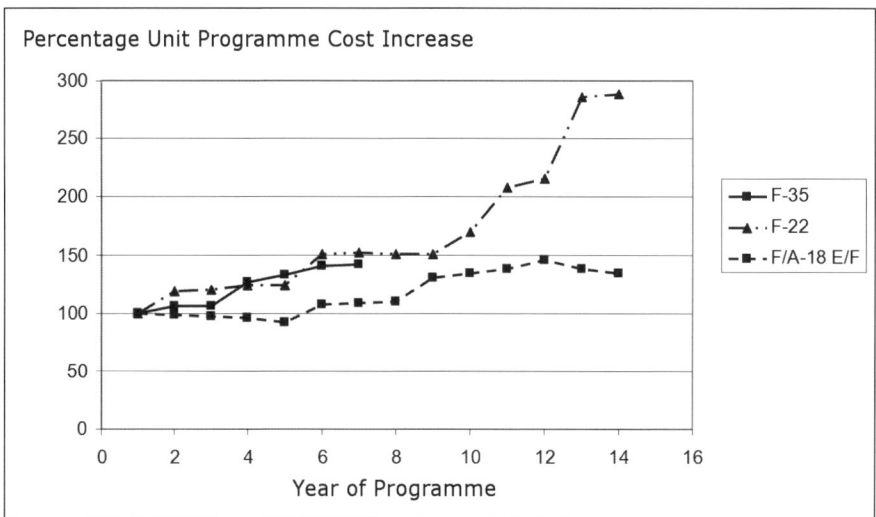

Figure 7–3: Cost Growth of US Aircraft Projects
Source: Australian Strategic Policy Institute

Figure 7–3 shows a cost growth of nearly 50% over the first six years of the project. At what point will the UK or other nations want to reduce numbers or pull out altogether?

European Collaboration

But what about collaborating within Europe? This has also been tried extensively, but has proved expensive and long-winded. Several nations, if

---

[174] Dr Andrew Davies, Australian Strategic Policy Institute, 'JSF Costs: Taking Off or Levelling Out?', *RUSI Defence Systems* (Volume 10, No. 1, June 2008), page 38.

there is no clear dominant partner, make decision-making very time-consuming. Moreover, too many compromises have to be made over design, schedule, cost and procurement strategy (particularly competition) to make for an easy ride. A good example is the SP70, the self-propelled 155mm artillery howitzer. The design, insisted upon by Germany, used the Leopard tank chassis. This, however, meant lifting ammunition up and over the vehicle engine and necessitated a large number of micro-switches, the reliability of the whole being fatally compromised. After years of effort and much expenditure, the project was cancelled.

European development programmes are not necessarily more expensive than US equivalents, but most are for three reasons. Firstly, because the US DOD is more likely to cancel a poorly performing programme than is a group of European nations, who see continuation as important for the future of European collaboration; secondly, because of the slow decision-making processes in Europe and hence delay that brings cost escalation; and thirdly because the US government spends much more on research and development than do European nations.

The UK has a history of pulling out of European collaborative programmes after investing considerable sums of money – the Horizon frigate, the long-range version of TRIGAT, the MRAV armoured vehicle, TriMilSat are a few examples – and this hardly endears us to other European nations as a partner.

It sometimes works better on a bilateral basis – the French are usually quick to mention the Anglo-French helicopter projects and the Jaguar aircraft, but they were a long time ago. It can work with a greater number of participants, but usually with cost overruns and delays – the EFA or Typhoon aircraft has shown a major cost increase and some delay, and the A400M continues to show significant slippage.

Smart Procurement claimed that collaboration was of increasing importance, but did not introduce any measures that added weight to the claim. *The Acquisition Handbook* had only this to say:

> *An increasing proportion of equipment expenditure is likely to be spent on collaborative projects. Smart procurement will bring some advantages over previous practices for UK teams engaged in collaborative projects. The UK wil have more flexibility than before in trading-off time, whole-life cost and performance. In addition, the relationship between UK project staff and industry*

is likely to be closer to that found in our main European partners than our previous arms-length approach. However, there will also be challenges. The tough performance targets placed on MoD may make the UK less ready to accept a risk of a cost or time overrun. To meet these targets all the implications and risks associated with collaborative projects will need to be properly considered and planned for.[175]

This is not a very helpful guide to collaborative projects under Smart Procurement. Was this because MoD did not know how to square the circle of savings by doing things 'faster, cheaper, better' with a Prime Minister who wanted to operate at the heart of Europe, or was it because it did not wish to? DIS hardly mentions collaboration. If Smart Procurement was caught in a collaborative bind, then DIS with its emphasis on appropriate sovereignty will only find it more difficult. Add to that the increasing disinclination both to pay much for defence and to take part in dangerous operations, collaboration within Europe seems an increasingly unattractive prospect.

> Government-to-government collaboration is neither a recipe for success nor an attractive prospect

The DIS makes remarkably few ritual genuflections towards the nascent European Defence Agency (EDA) and the proposed European Defence Equipment Market, or other gestures towards consolidating defence procurement at European level. I hope this reflects a hard-headed realisation that most of our EU partners are under too much fiscal pressure to increase defence spending meaningfully.[176]

So, government-to-government collaboration is neither a recipe for success nor an attractive prospect. Yet many believe that the only alternative to becoming an offshoot of the US is collaboration within Europe.

Most significantly perhaps, we have to re-examine our industrial needs and capabilities on a Europe-wide basis – not a national and somewhat protectionist one, as the recent British Defence Industrial Strategy appears to do – to ensure the preservation of the right capabilities across Europe and to give Europe the

---

[175] MoD, *The Acquisition Handbook: A Guide to Smart Procurement*, Edition 1, April 1999, page 21.

[176] Antonia Feuchtwanger, 'Inching Towards the Best Kit', *RUSI Defence Systems* (Volume 9, No. 1, June 2006), page 19.

opportunity to produce the capability that its wealth and size should allow, instead of being the very poor relations of the USA.[177]

Industry-Led Collaboration

The real problem with European collaboration is the collaborating governments, which have different requirements, different approval procedures and different attitudes to industry. So it's not surprising that it takes much longer and costs much more. If we really want the fruits of collaboration within Europe – equipment commonality and/or interoperability, reduced prices from longer production runs, more orders for European industry – then perhaps we should do it without government interference.

How?

Well, to start with, we should look at the Storm Shadow/Scalp EG missile programme. UK MoD had a requirement for a Conventionally Armed Stand-Off Missile (CASOM), whose history says it all.

> *Approval was given in 1982 for a Feasibility Study into Naval Ground Air Staff Target 1236 (NGAST 1236), the Long Range Stand Off Missile (LRSOM) programme undertaken jointly with the US and Germany. In 1986 LRSOM was subsumed in favour of the Modular Stand Off Weapon (MSOW) 7-nation collaborative programme. The MSOW programme collapsed in 1989 when the US and UK withdrew. Following this withdrawal the requirement was reviewed as part of Options for Change. In 1993 the requirement was revived in the form of Staff Requirement (Air) 1236 (SR(A) 1236) and an invitation to tender was issued in 1994, with bids received from 7 companies. In February 1997 a development and production contract was placed with Matra BAe (UK) Ltd.*[178]

The competition for the Storm Shadow contract was won by MBDA (formerly Matra BAe). It then transpired that France had an almost identical requirement (Scalp EG) and MBDA harmonised the requirements and produced a merged specification, combining the best features of each. Each country retained its own project office and managed its own project independently. Later, Italy bought Storm Shadow. Storm Shadow was used operationally by the UK in Iraq in 2003.

---

[177] Sir Jeremy Blackham, 'Rebalancing at the Expense of High-Level Capability', *RUSI Defence Systems* (Volume 9, No. 2, October 2006), page 16.
[178] National Audit Office, *Ministry of Defence: Major Projects Report 1998*, HC 519, Session 1998/9, 30 June 1999, page 129

What does all this show? It took various government-to-government collaborations seven years to get precisely nowhere. It then took the UK government a further eight years before it was ready to let a national contract to industry, stipulating an ISD of 2001 – only four years after contract signing. Not surprisingly, that ISD could not be met, but was achieved in 2003. Governments had messed about for 15 years without result, and then industry had achieved it in six.

Why can't industry-led collaboration become the norm?

It must be said that it probably would not have happened if MBDA had not been an Anglo-French company and if consolidation of the European missile industry had not been a priority of European nations at that time. Nevertheless, it seems to make sense to let industry do the harmonising of similar requirements and specifications direct to each government, as they will see the business opportunities. Once two nations have a combined production line, then other nations may well buy into the programme – and longer production runs can only benefit both governments and industry.

> Why can't industry-led collaboration become the norm?

As the UK IPT Leader said:

> The programme had set a new template for international cooperation which did not involve the bureaucracy and complex decision-making processes inherent in traditional collaborative projects.[179]

So, why hasn't this become the norm for collaborative programmes? Given that there have been many government collaborations, it can't be because there are no similar requirements to be harmonised by industry.

No, it's because of the greater European dream and the determination of the EU and national governments to play to it. So, for the greater glory of their dream, they set up another bureaucratic institution dedicated to government-to-government collaboration with its built-in cost overruns, delay and requirement compromises. It's called the European Defence Agency (EDA).

---

[179] *Preview*, Journal of the Defence Procurement Agency (No. 59, 1 April 1999), page 17.

The European Defence Agency

Initially the UK was in favour:

> *The creation of the European Defence Agency is a ground-breaking venture …*
> *The [British] Government are confident that the agency will play a key role in*
> *improving the delivery of future European military capabilities.*[180]

This initial enthusiasm did not last long and there has been British reluctance to play a full part. It has opposed small increases in the EDA budget and has exempted itself from some leading EDA initiatives.

Will it become more attractive? Only if it becomes more successful in attracting more investment from all European nations.

> *The challenge facing EDA is significant. European defence budgets are generally*
> *shrinking, different countries have different priorities … and a few key defence*
> *ministries have proven less willing (and able) than others to work with the*
> *Agency. The lesson of experience to date is that if EDA wishes to build big, it*
> *must start small.*[181]

So, perhaps we shouldn't hold our breath.

The Future for Collaboration

It seems that DIS has reduced the push for collaboration since 1998 when it was predicted that in the future 40% of all projects would be collaborative.[182] Now the push for appropriate sovereignty and operational independence has made collaboration less attractive and it would need something pretty major – such as EDA projects repeatedly coming in cheaply and quickly, or the US bending over backwards to collaborate on more favourable terms for its partners than for itself – to reverse this trend. How unlikely is that?

> It was predicted that in the future 40% of all projects would be collaborative

In some cases, collaboration with the US makes sense – I have

---

[180] Rt Hon Geoffrey Hoon MP, Secretary of State for Defence, 'Establishing a European Defence Agency', European Standing Committee B, 22 June 2004.

[181] Ibid, page 70.

[182] John Spellar, Under Secretary of State for Defence, Speech to a RUSI Seminar on Smart Procurement, 29 January 1998.

already mentioned nuclear submarines – but the likely areas are limited. Nevertheless, where it does happen, we would get the best equipment cheaper and more quickly than we can make it ourselves (with or without collaboration in Europe), and would help to maintain interoperability with our main ally.

In contrast, government-to-government collaboration in Europe seems to make no military or commercial sense, although many would maintain that it has political incentives. But if we do want to maintain an alternative to US collaboration of buying American, we can only do that at the moment by collaborating in Europe, at least until India or, less likely, China become alternative collaborators.

> Government-to-government collaboration in Europe seems to make no military or commercial sense

If government-to-government collaboration is ruled out on military and commercial grounds, we must look to industry-led collaboration along the lines of the successful Storm Shadow / Scalp EG model.

Why have we not done so?

Interoperability and Commonality

There can be no doubt that, in this age of multinational operations, the ability to communicate with, understand and operate with each other is essential – interoperability is key. So why are we so poor at it?

Part of the problem is that, unlike in the Cold War days, many operations involve national forces that are not used to working together and have no common procedures. It is understandable in these circumstances if interoperability is poor. But why is interoperability between, say, NATO nations also less effective than it should be?

> *The key to success is determining from the mission what level of interoperability is required with whom. This is far from simple: is it interoperability at the network level, or in applications, or simply the ability to interpret a flag hoist in the same way as the ship approaching? What bearers and bandwidth are available, and does the information need to be protected, and if so at what level? And even if all those issues are resolved, the softer aspects of information management and ways of working cultures may also cause difficulties.*[183]

---

[183] Captain Al Adams RN and LCDR Krist Zimmerman USN, 'Interoperability: A Maritime Perspective', *RUSI Defence Systems* (Volume 11, No 1, June 2008), page 50.

Is commonality of equipment necessary? It would certainly help, but does this mean buying American? And if it does, who can afford to do so across the board? And how would the non-US defence industry survive in the long term?

Commonality certainly helps and can be achieved in some areas with some allies – Typhoon and JSF are examples. Another area is artillery ammunition. It certainly helps in multinational operations if one nation can fire another's ammunition out of its own national artillery pieces **and know where it is going to land**. This was largely achieved within NATO in the 1980s, but would be impossible to achieve now with all coalition nations. Moreover, other ammunition types (e.g. small arms) have never been interoperable.

Across the board, commonality is unaffordable and, if non-US defence industries are to survive, inefficient. So, although collaboration has some operational benefit, the main driver is financial – and if cost reduction is not achieved, then the only outcomes are delay and job creation schemes.

> although collaboration has some operational benefit, the main driver is financial

What, then, is the answer?

As it is so difficult to make national systems, with a variety of security accreditation, classification and gateway constraints, interoperate at any useful and timely level, the proven way to meet the multinational requirement is to purchase bespoke equipment (i.e. additional servers, computers, routers, cryptos) common to all nations connected to a bespoke, common network.[184]

A pragmatic view. NATO Standardisation Agreements (STANAGs) and common equipment might have made sense during Cold War days – even then we achieved very little – but with shifting coalitions of the willing, common or even interoperable equipment is unlikely to be achievable. We should do what we can to remain interoperable with US forces and produce bespoke solutions elsewhere.

---

[184] Ibid.

Process and Delivery

As already mentioned, 'drowning in process' has been a plaintive cry for some time and it does seem that the MoD has a mania for playing around with process. Why is this? Why should the way people do their jobs take precedence over what they achieve? Is it because managers and mandarins are frightened to allow empowered people to get on with it, in case they make a mistake? Or in case they do something that the manager or mandarin doesn't understand and can't explain to a politician? Is the 'long screwdriver' a favourite tool in Whitehall and Abbey Wood?

There are other issues to resolve. For example, the programme Military Training through Distributed Simulation (MTDS), generally regarded as a success story, has left a series of question marks in its wake:[185]

- How do you avoid overpaying for upgrades to a training system as new platforms are added to the inventory?
- How do you account for costs necessary to ensure connectivity remains possible?
- How do you contract for availability when in multinational exercises a system failure occurs and it is impossible to prove whose equipment was responsible for the fault?
- If the system is to be used for concept assessment or tactics development, how do you include 'research-type' activities in a training service?

Similar issues arise in the course of most programmes and are generally resolved in due course. But think of the totality of these issues – is it possible to write a process that covers them all, particularly when many of these issues will only emerge as the procurement cycle progresses? An incomplete process mandated for all programmes, big or small, is obviously the wrong answer.

A process of some sort is clearly necessary, but it must not bind the hands and minds of the real workers – the DECs, the IPT Leaders – whose work should be judged by achievements rather than ticks in a myriad of boxes. Interestingly, neither Smart Procurement nor DIS (and its associated study EAC) added much unnecessary process. The real

---

[185] Jon Saltmarsh and Sheena MacKenzie, 'Mission Training through Distributed Simulation', *RUSI Defence Systems* (Volume 11, No. 2, October 2008).

problem is that they didn't remove the encrustations that had built up before. Is there anything in Smart Procurement, DIS or EAC which makes it imperative that a military sponsor has to obtain 17 signatures while negotiating 17 gates for a release of £250k on a £1.1M contract, a task which took him six months?[186]

How much did that cost and what was the activity worth? Given that an SME nearly went to the wall with the delay, I suspect that the potential risk far outweighed the maximum benefit. Yet the sponsor was only following the process, no doubt laid down by someone with little or no experience in the real, commercial world.

If we really want to improve acquisition, we need to do many things – but one of the most important is to simplify and downgrade the grip of 'Process' so that 'Delivery' is king, and to pour the time and energy saved into managing culture change.

---

[186] Bill Robins, 'The Value of SMEs', *RUSI Defence Systems* (Volume 10, No. 3, February 2008), page 15.

SUMMARY: PROCESS AND PROCEDURES
DIS RECOMMENDATIONS

DIS Recommendations

- Streamline decision-making, recognising that delays have a cost.
- Assure that risk is progressively reduced through the project's life.
- Be prepared to cancel projects, if necessary before Main Gate.
- Increase the tempo of procurement to match the speed of technology and operational change.
- Improve approach to technology insertion.
- Improve pull-through of technology from research into capabilities.
- Exploit synthetic environments and experimentation to reduce risk.
- Work with industry and universities to identify sources of innovation.
- Embrace the vision of Through-Life Capability Management (TLCM).

EAC Recommendations

- Improve the Department's planning system.
- Increase emphasis on realism.
- Programme equipment support costs over 10 years.
- More use to be made of Senior Responsible Owners (SROs).
- Improve governance of the procurement process.

SOME MAJOR ISSUES

Time

- Importance of greater agility in procurement.
- Need to cut cycle time by at least 50%.
- Import some of the Urgent Operational Requirements (UOR) culture and process into 'normal' procurement.

Acquisition Cycle

- One size does not fit all.

Through-Life Capability Management

- TLCM is a major change programme.
- Changes are needed at the 'Top-of-the-Shop'.

Conspiracy of Optimism

- Needs to be rooted out.

International Dimension

- Difficulties in collaborating with US and in Europe.
- Industry-led programmes have attractions (e.g. Storm Shadow).
- Interoperability may need a pragmatic, bespoke approach.

Process and Delivery

- Shift emphasis from process to delivery.

Appendix 7–1

Is Defence Inflation Really as High as Claimed?
by **Professor David Kirkpatrick**

David Kirkpatrick is an Associate Fellow of RUSI. In this article he examines the facts behind the claims that defence inflation is higher than the national GDP deflator and provides illumination on the heat generated by others.

When the UK government publishes its plans for public expenditure, the future annual budgets for defence are eagerly reviewed by various interested stakeholders (particularly by the Armed Forces and by defence contractors) and are compared with the present defence budget. If the planned annual increases in the level of the public expenditure allocated to the Ministry of Defence (MoD) exceed the expected annual increases in the Gross Domestic Product (GDP) deflator (an index which represents the average change in the prices of UK goods and services), the government announces its plan as a 'real' increase in defence spending.

This announcement is regularly followed by a debate about whether the actual price inflation in the goods and services procured by the MoD is greater than that of the GDP deflator, and hence whether the government's planned expenditure will really enhance the military capability of its armed forces. More often in recent years, the debate has centred on whether the government's planned expenditure is sufficient to avoid a significant decrease in the UK's military capability, and corresponding danger to its national security. Some assert that defence inflation is larger than the GDP deflator, while others assert that it isn't or that if it is it ought not to be. In this debate special pleading by interested parties often generates more heat than illumination.

To provide a better basis for this recurrent debate, this paper discusses the construction of a simple price index, the price indices now used by the UK Government to assist economic management, and how the price inflation in the MoD's budget might relate to the GDP deflator and other national price indices. The conclusions rely on published data, and should be refined by more detailed analysis.

I am grateful to Professor Ron Smith of Birkbeck College, University of London, for much helpful advice, but any remaining errors and misconceptions are my own responsibility.

Construction of price indices
Retail price index
To illustrate the construction of price indices, consider the example of a medieval town which derives its income from the production and sale of salt, and in which the population now spends its disposable income on bread, beer and firewood in proportions 5:3:2. If between this year and the next the prices of these goods rose by 10%, 40% and 20% respectively, the town's retail price index for next year can be calculated by first multiplying the price increase for each item by a weighting factor proportional to the town's relative expenditure on that item, and then adding the results.

Retail price index = (0.5 x 1.1) + (0.3 x 1.4) + (0.2 x 1.2) = 1.21

This calculation takes no account of any fish or fruit which the inhabitants might catch or gather for themselves since these items are not marketed; it also excludes the expenditure of the local baron on armour and French wine, since his expenditure is atypical, and would distort the index if it were included.

The figure of 21% retail price inflation implies that next year the town's inhabitants would be able to afford less bread and firewood, and much less beer, or that they would have to increase the quantity and/or the price of the salt produced next year in order to sustain their living standards. However, these price increases would not have the same effect on all of the town's inhabitants, since the figure of 21% is an average and not universally applicable. The abstemious priest, for example, drinks no beer and spends equal shares of his meagre income on bread and firewood so he would face an inflation rate of only 15%; on the other hand the town drunk would be more severely affected.

Consumer Price Index
The town's retail price index for next year was calculated above as the arithmetic mean (weighted according to the town's expenditure) of the increases in the prices of bread, beer and firewood, and assumes that the quantities of those items consumed by the population would remain constant from one year to the next (in statistical terminology, it is a Laspeyres' index). Alternatively, the town's 'consumer price index' can be calculated as the geometric mean of the changes in the prices of the three items, weighted in proportion to the town's expenditure.

Consumer price index = antilog [0.5log1.1 + 0.3log1.4 + 0.2log1.2] = 1.203

The difference between the arithmetic mean and the geometric mean depends on the difference between the price increases for different commodities; if all prices rose at the same rate, the arithmetic and geometric means would be equal.

GDP Deflator

Although the concepts of a national Gross Domestic Product (GDP) and of a GDP deflator were not developed until modern times, it is illuminating to calculate these values for the medieval town. The town's GDP (= total expenditure = total income) includes not only the value of goods and services purchased by the population for immediate consumption but also the values of investments in capital equipment and of non-marketed public services. Investments (such as expenditure on new equipment for salt production) are assumed for simplicity to be zero. Public services are provided by the local baron, who levies a 10% tax on the sale of salt and spends equal shares of the resulting income in supporting a monastery and a contingent of mercenary men-at-arms. The monks consume only bread and firewood (in the same proportions as the priest) and use herbal remedies to treat sick citizens in the infirmary. The men-at-arms traditionally supply their own weapons and their annual wages are linked to the town's retail price index. The public services, then as now, are valued by their input costs (though in modern times employees providing health and military services would expect their wages to rise, like other workers in a modern economy, faster than the retail price index).

The quantities of bread, beer and firewood consumed, and of health and military services provided, represent a better measure of the town's welfare than the value of its GDP measured in money. The GDP deflator, which links the money value of GDP to the volume of goods and services, is equal to the value of the town's goods and services in Year 2 divided by the value of the same goods and services at Year 1 prices. The GDP deflator derived from the assumptions above for the medieval town is:

$$\text{Deflator} = 100 \,/\, [45/1.1 + 27/1.4 + 18/1.2 + 5/1.21 + 5/1.15] = 1.195$$

This calculation of the GDP deflator assumes that the town adjusts its pattern of consumption each year to maximise its welfare obtainable from the available income.

The three alternative measures of monetary inflation in the medieval town yield different values:

Retail price index (RPI)	+21%
Consumer price index (CPI)	+20.4%
GDP deflator	+19.5%

The increase in the CPI is smaller than that of the RPI because of the ways they are calculated. The increase in the GDP deflator is even smaller in this case, partly because of the way it is calculated and partly because of the frugality of the monks providing health services. In principle the GDP deflator can rise more or less than the RPI depending on the scale of the non-marketed public services, and the relative price inflation in those services.

UK Price Indices

Today in the UK there are now two principal measures[i] of the general level of market prices for goods and services bought for consumption. The Consumer Price Index (CPI) is used in association with the government's target level of 2% price inflation per year. The more familiar Retail Price Index (RPI) is used in adjusting many pensions and state benefits to maintain their buying power. Both of these indices represent the average change of the prices of a wide range of consumer goods and services, recognising that within this range some prices may rise more quickly than average, while other prices may fall.

Retail Price Index (RPI)

The range of items used to construct the RPI includes some 650 items which are representative of the much larger number of consumer goods and services in the market. These items include some goods and services which are 'essentials' and some which are 'luxuries', the distinction being largely subjective, and is updated annually to reflect the changing tastes and priorities of most of the UK population. The RPI includes council taxes and rates, but excludes national taxes and national insurance contributions.

The current price of each item in the RPI is assessed monthly by drawing data from retail shops, large commercial suppliers and government organisations. No attempt is made to differentiate between normal free market prices and those prices which may have been artificially raised by a monopolist or a cartel, or those which have been reduced by discounting or by illegal employment practices. For each item the price is what it is.

In those areas of the market (such as consumer electronics) where obsolescent products are rapidly replaced by newer products with superior performance, the price of the new product is adjusted downward to allow for the change in its quality relative to that of its predecessor, the increase in quality being measured in terms of additional benefits to the consumer. The change in retail price is thus based as far as possible on a like-for-like comparison.

The weighting factor allocated to each item in the RPI represents its relative importance in the typical household budget. This excludes the expenditures of the very rich and the very poor – i.e. households with the top 4% of incomes and pensioners on low incomes (both groups having atypical patterns of consumption which would distort the index). The change in the cost of each item is multiplied by the corresponding weighting factor, and the results are added to obtain the RPI. It thus follows the same principles, albeit on a much larger scale, as the retail price index for the medieval town described above.

Consumer Price Index (CPI)

The CPI is calculated according to harmonised European rules. It uses much of the same price information as the RPI, but its weighting factors are based on a broader proportion of the population and it covers a different range of goods and services. For example, the CPI excludes council taxes and rates, vehicle taxes, mortgage interest payments and the depreciation of dwelling houses. Because the range of included items and the weighting factors in the RPI and CPI are different, and because they are calculated as arithmetic and geometric indices respectively, the two indices have different values: over the last decade in the UK the RPI has been about 1% higher than the CPI, but a fall in the price of houses or in interest rates could reverse that situation.

Other Inflation Indices

The UK Government calculates other inflation indices to assist its management of the national economy, and to guide its budgets for social services expenditure. The RPIX index excludes mortgage interest payments, and is thus decoupled from fluctuations in the housing and financial markets. The RPIY index also excludes all indirect taxes (such as value-added tax and excise duties) and thus reflects underlying price changes in the commercial market for goods and services, undistorted by the government's fiscal policy. The Tax and Prices Index (TPI) includes all direct and indirect taxes as well as national insurance contributions, and is used along with data on national incomes to calculate the extent by which a typical taxpayer's standard of living is likely to be increasing or decreasing. Other indices are calculated, by the government and by various charities, to show how current price inflation affects particular groups within society having patterns of consumption significantly different from the average.

The GDP deflator covers the whole UK economy, including about 40% of total expenditure which is now allocated to a wide range of public services (education, health, defence, highways, etc.) provided by national and local government organisations. Over the last decade the GDP deflator has been very similar to the RPIX index.[ii]

All of these indices are designed for different purposes and all show different values of inflation. None of these values is more 'right' than any other, and different individual households are differently affected by current changes in the prices of the myriad of goods and services in the market. Similarly, each of the government's Departments of State, each of which procures a different mix of goods and services, is differently affected by current changes in prices.

The Price of Labour

In recent decades the index of personal earned income in the form of wages and salaries (i.e. the price of labour) in the UK economy has risen about 1.7% faster than the GDP deflator, because of ongoing improvements in labour productivity which have continued since the Industrial Revolution. Such improvements tend to be larger in production industries than in personal services (output per worker in manufacturing industry has increased over the past decade by about 4% per year). The price of each item in the RPI is built up by increments of value added in production, distribution, marketing etc., so the prices of different items are variously affected (according to the proportions of value added) by increases in the productivity of those activities. Items which incorporate a particularly high proportion of their value added from personal services (such as residential care for the elderly) tend to rise more rapidly than others.

The various UK price indices[iii] can be ranked according to average annual growth over the decade 1997–2007, as shown below.

	% Average Annual Price Growth 1997–2007	% Average Annual Price Growth, Relative to the GDP Deflator
Labour	4.2	+1.7
Retail Price Index	2.8	+0.3
GDP Deflator	2.5	0
Consumer Price Index	1.9	
Inputs to mfg. industry	2.0	
Output from mfg. industry	1.4	−1.1

Although the price of output from UK factories has grown by only 1.4% per year, the retail prices of the manufactured items within the RPI may have grown faster because of higher price growth in services (such as distribution).

The MoD Budget and Defence Price Inflation

The MoD budget can be divided into three principal categories – personnel, military equipment, and other goods and services. Military equipment can be further divided into combat and non-combat equipment. Combat equipment is directly involved in active operations, so that its effectiveness depends both on its own performance and on the threats presented by enemies. Non-combat equipment (such as transport vehicles) fulfils a distinctively military function, but its ability to fulfil that function satisfactorily does not depend significantly on the threat. The category of other goods and services covers items (food, fuel, office equipment, etc.) which perform essentially civilian functions and which appear also in the RPI. Even those items sometimes have to have special features to meet MoD requirements; anything likely to be deployed overseas must be robust and securely packaged, and even equipment for MoD offices in the UK may have more security features than the corresponding commercial equipment. The boundaries between the three main categories are not explicitly presented in current MoD accounts,[iv] but estimates are presented in the table below.

	£Bn	
MoD's Net Cash Requirement, 2006-07	31.4	
Annually Managed Expenditure (mostly pensions)	0.6	
Cash Expenditure on Defence Capability	30.8	
Expenditure on Personnel	11.2	36%
Expenditure on Military Equipment	11.0	36%
Expenditure on Other Goods and Services	8.6	28%

Personnel
The MoD spends about 36% of its annual budget on the services provided by its Service and civilian personnel, and their wages must (to maintain satisfactory levels of recruitment and retention) rise broadly in line with the general level of wages in the UK economy. During periods of arduous and/or unpopular operations, Service wages and associated expenditure on Service personnel may have to rise faster than the general level of wages. In commercial organisations progressive improvements in productivity allow their business to be undertaken with ever fewer staff, but MoD personnel levels are set by the demands of future operational scenarios and must remain at those levels, even if its peacetime activities could be done more efficiently. For these reasons, the level of price inflation affecting this part of the MoD budget must be larger than the GDP deflator, probably about 1.7% higher.

Military Equipment
Almost all of the items in the category of military equipment (development and production of bespoke equipment, procurement of equipment off-the-shelf, and support of equipment in service) are delivered by manufacturing industry, and accordingly their prices might, other things being equal (which of course they are not, because of the particular characteristics of the defence equipment market), rise about 1.1% more slowly than the GDP deflator because of the impact of greater productivity on the manufacturing processes, which ought to affect the defence sector of manufacturing industry as well as the civil sector.

However, because most types of defence equipment are manufactured over a long period to rigorous and pre-agreed specifications, defence contractors have less scope than their civilian counterparts for adjusting the design or manufacture of such equipment to minimise the impact of input price increases (for example, of rare materials) and it is appropriate to make an (arbitrary) additional allowance of 0.5%. The actual size of this allowance could be calculated from a detailed analysis of the volatility of the prices of inputs to the defence sector of manufacturing industry.

Military Equipment – Inter-Generational Escalation
Part of the MoD budget (probably amounting to two-thirds of the expenditure on military equipment) is spent on the acquisition of combat equipment for its armed forces. It is understood that within most classes of combat equipment (such as fighter aircraft) the unit cost of equipment increases from one generation to the next[v] by a factor of between three and ten (with a few exceptional classes outside this range), equivalent to a trend of 5–10% per year.[vi] Equipment incorporating mature technologies tends to appear at or below the lower end of this range, and equipment exploiting rapidly advancing technologies tends to appear at or above the higher end. Such increases in unit cost occur in each class of equipment only infrequently, when a new design replaces its obsolescent predecessor in military service, but in the whole of the MoD's equipment acquisition programme such increases occur in a virtually continuous stream, and provide an average underlying cost growth of around 7.5% per year in the budget for the acquisition of combat equipment.

Because the new combat equipment generally provides the same military capability against an enhanced threat (e.g. an acceptable probability of victory in aircraft v. aircraft or in tank v. tank battles during conventional warfare, or an acceptable probability of survival in a patrol vehicle exposed to the hazards of asymmetric warfare), it would be inappropriate to adjust the cost of the new equipment to allow for quality change (as is done within the RPI when successor products provide superior performance to the consumer). In some exceptional cases, where a new class of military equipment is introduced or where a breakthrough in military technology (such as stealth or Chobham armour) does provide a substantial increase in military capability against the threat, some price adjustment for quality could be calculated, but such exceptions are neglected in this analysis.

A more accurate figure (than the assumption of around 7.5%) could be derived from the proportions of the equipment budget devoted to different classes of equipment and from parametric analysis of the current trend of inter-generational price growth within each class. This calculation would require access to classified MoD data and even then the result could not be rigorously accurate, since there would be doubts about current price growth in the various classes and about any possible adjustments for quality. But even an approximate figure for the underlying price growth would be superior to the current practice of neglecting it entirely.

The price of non-combat military equipment need not increase to match ongoing developments in the threat. The quality of successive generations of such equipment may have to rise to match the expectations of recruits, but this factor will not be considered here. It may therefore be concluded that the price of military equipment increases, due to inter-generational price growth, by (7.5% x 2/3) = 5% per year.

It is relevant that the MoD is not the only Department of State to be affected by this problem. The NHS has to spend part of its budget on ever more sophisticated and expensive drugs to counteract increasingly virulent bacteria that have now evolved to resist the cheaper drugs which have been used for some years. However, the NHS spends a smaller proportion of its budget on clinical supplies than the MoD spends on military equipment, so for the NHS this problem is less severe.

Military Equipment – Escalation During Procurement
The price of military equipment also tends to vary during the development and manufacturing phases of the equipment life cycle, as technical and management problems are resolved favourably or unfavourably. In principle, such variations could be upward or downward, but in practice the initial forecasts of cost tend to be over-optimistic and most revisions are upward. The National Audit Office regularly presents, as part of its annual Major Projects Report, the in-year variation in the reported procurement cost of the MoD's largest projects (about 20 in each year). These reports show that the reported procurement costs of the largest projects have increased in recent years by an average of 1.1% of their approved budgets. However, these reported costs are often distorted by reductions in the specification and/or the number of equipment to be procured and by accounting adjustments which allocate costs from a project to another part of MoD's budget. Allowing for such distortions, it appears that in recent years the actual increase in the MoD budget required to maintain the planned procurement programme for major projects has averaged

2.7% per year (though there is considerable variation from one project to another and from one year to the next). This number is assumed to be representative of the whole equipment programme.

Ideally there would be no 'conspiracy of optimism' between Service customers and industrial suppliers in the initial forecasts of equipment project costs; such cost forecasts would be unbiased, and the average annual increase in the cost of the MoD's equipment programme would be zero (masking some inevitable upward and downward variations in the costs of individual projects). In practice, however, the 'conspiracy of optimism' does exist and has endured through several well-meaning reforms of MoD procedures,[vii] as the responsible stakeholders seem unable or unwilling to correct it. Whatever the reason, the tendency for the prices of equipment projects to rise during procurement is an observed fact (which is regrettable, but is as real as any increase in retail prices caused by a monopolist extorting excess profits) and thus should be included in a defence inflation index.

Assuming that the upward trend in projects' costs affects their procurement budgets but not their budgets for in-service support (which amount to some £3.8Bn of the £11Bn spent on military equipment), its overall effect on the budget for military equipment would be:

(2.7% x 7.2 / 11.0) = 1.8%

This section suggests that the price of military equipment acquisition might be expected to increase at an annual rate above the GDP deflator of:

(-1.1 + 0.5 + 5.0 +1.8) = 6.2%.

Other Goods and Services

The remainder of the MoD budget is spent on other, essentially civilian, goods and services which are not subject to the same military imperative to match enhanced threats, do not present the same problems of cost forecasting, and can be procured under relatively short-term contracts. While the composition of this sector of the MoD budget is very different from the range of goods and services in the RPI and, therefore, its price index will reflect differently the current variations in market prices of particular goods and services in any particular year, the price index for this category is likely to increase broadly in line with the GDP deflator.

Caveat

It must be emphasised that all of the figures in this section are illustrative and not definitive; the argument has been put in a numerical format only in order to clarify the issues and to facilitate further discussion. The annual argument over whether a planned increase in the defence budget is 'real' could be more constructive if the MoD undertook (or commissioned) a review of its expenditure to generate more authoritative data.

Conclusion

A detailed comparison between defence inflation and the GDP deflator would demand more detailed data on MoD expenditure than is available in the public domain, and is accordingly beyond the scope of this paper. However, the speculative and approximate calculation in the table below suggests that defence inflation is likely to be consistently about three percentage points above the GDP deflator.

Category	Fraction of MoD Budget	Category Price Growth Relative to GDP Deflator	Contribution to Price Growth Relative to GDP Deflator
Personnel	0.36	1.7%	0.61%
Military Equipment	0.36	6.2%	2.23%
Other Supplies	0.28	0.3%	0.08%
Total			2.92%

It follows that if the UK Government intends to maintain the nation's military capabilities at their planned levels, it must provide increases in the annual MoD budget which are about 3% (or whatever similar percentage is derived from a more rigorous analysis) higher than the predicted values of the GDP deflator. If the government decides to provide a smaller increase, it should explicitly agree with the MoD the resulting savings in personnel and/or equipment, and acknowledge the associated reductions in the UK's military capabilities. If it fails to acknowledge those reductions, and the defence budget is accordingly overstretched by a mismatch between the MoD's resources and its aspirations, it is tempting for the MoD to make false economies (e.g. via delays to projects or inadequate risk management) which solve its immediate budgetary problems, but which in the longer term degrade the cost-effectiveness of the UK's armed forces.

[i] Office of National Statistics, *Consumer Price Indices – a Brief Guide*, Unpublished

[ii] Anis Chowdhury, 'The GDP Implied Deflator', *Economic & Labour Market Review* (Volume 2, No. 6, June 2008), pages 53–56.

[iii] Office of National Statistics website, www.statistics.gov.uk.

[iv] DASA, *UK Defence Statistics 2007*, The Stationery Office, London 2007.

[v] D. L. I. Kirkpatrick, 'The Rising Cost of Defence Equipment – the Reasons and the Results', *Defence & Peace Economics* (Volume 6, 1995), pages 263–288.

[vi] P. G. Pugh, Performance-based Cost Estimating, Unpublished.

[vii] W. A. Chin, *British Weapons Acquisition Policy and the Futility of Reform*, (Ashgate, England 2004).

Appendix 7–2

RUSI ACQUISITION FOCUS PAPER[187]

WHY DOES IT ALL TAKE SO LONG?

The RUSI Acquisition Focus was formed in March 2006 to provide expert, objective views on aspects of defence equipment acquisition. The Focus meets three times a year and cannot, therefore, provide detailed solutions to the issues discussed, but it does pinpoint the essential arguments as viewed by a widely experienced group. This, its fourth paper, considers the length of time that defence equipment procurement takes and how it can be speeded up.

The members of the RUSI Acquisition Focus are: John Weston (Chairman), Tim Banfield (NAO), Bob Barton (co-chair of the MoD/Industry Equipment Capability Group), Vice Admiral (retd) Jeremy Blackham (recently EADS UK President), John Dowdy (Director, McKinsey), Professor Christopher Elliott (GD UK), Air Marshal Lord Garden (House of Lords), Graham Jordan (formerly S&T Director, MoD), Gerry Paulus (Managing Director, SVGC Ltd), Major General (retd) Bill Robins (formerly DGICS, MoD), Professor Trevor Taylor (Head of Defence Management and Security Analysis, Cranfield University), Bill Kincaid (Editor RUSI Defence Systems)

SUMMARY

Collapsing the length of the procurement cycle will bring huge benefits. Achieving this will not be easy, but the recent Pathfinders show it is possible.

Dedicating a realistic budget within a properly funded defence programme, selecting the key industrial players on a capability basis, and forming a joint MoD–industry project team charged with producing the best system for the money, in a challenging timescale, against a cardinal points specification, and with governance reduced to a minimum based on a process re-engineering approach derived beforehand, would produce some dramatic results. It does of course need real will, a much more

---

[187] RUSI Acquisition Focus, 'Why Does It All Take So Long?', *RUSI Defence Systems* (Volume 10 No. 1, June 2007), page 32.

trusting approach and above all some courage, but industrial members of the team will be quite capable of adopting the aims of the customer in such an endeavour.

But to open the road towards this modern way of doing things, two road blocks must be removed. Technology must be brought to maturity before the MoD finalises its requirements and before industry is forced to make fixed price bids. Bids based on uncertain technology can never be honest and will always contain the seeds of time slip and price escalation, fuelling mistrust, preventing openness and breeding confrontation. Building a sound technology base before price is fixed will mirror best practice outside defence. But it will require extra investment before Main Gate and in Technology Demonstrators before projects start. To pull money to the front end of projects like this can only be achieved within the kind of radical programme and policy review we advocated in our last article.

The Length of Equipment Procurement Cycles

MoD has produced a number of initiatives to improve defence equipment procurement, the most recent of which are Smart Procurement (1998, later Smart Acquisition), the Defence Industrial Strategy (2005), Enabling Acquisition Change (2006) and the Defence Technology Strategy (2006). These initiatives have been welcomed and generally perceived as significant steps towards better procurement. However, Smart Procurement was never properly implemented and the remainder are, as yet, far from being realised, with the result that little demonstrable improvement in output, in terms of reduced cost and time, is apparent.

Costs have received a great deal of scrutiny, but overall procurement timescales have not, so in this paper we look at the time it takes to bring major programmes into service and what can be done to reduce it.

Major MoD procurement programmes exhibit a number of differentiating characteristics. The solutions are often complex, non-repetitive and contain unproven technology. Not surprisingly, this leads to lengthy and drawn out acquisition processes to establish their integrity. Programmes that require full development often take a couple of decades from start to ISD: Bowman 20 years, Typhoon 20 years, A400M 17 years, CVF 15 years, FRES 19 years, JCA 16 years. The lengths of the last four procurements are currently less than two decades, but if delays are of historical size they may well take that long.

Not all complex projects take as long as two decades: for example, Rapier FSC, HVM, Trident and Tomahawk, albeit that the first two still suffered severe delays within the shorter timescale. It is particularly noteworthy that Trident, one of the biggest and most complex programmes of all, was delivered reasonably quickly. Why should these programmes have been successfully concluded more quickly than others, such as FRES and A400M, which are arguably no more complex? Are there reasons that can be applied to other, less time-successful programmes? One obvious reason is that these examples were either off-the-shelf buys or based on more mature technology that had been developed earlier. But are there other, perhaps cultural, reasons? Trident was the one programme that **had** to finish on time to avoid a gap which would have undermined the whole *raison d'etre* of the deterrent. Is there something in this – do some programmes slip because they can, whereas Trident didn't because it couldn't? Maybe, but Trident this time around suggests that lessons have not been learned – first time around it took 14 years from the White Paper decision to ISD for all three elements (boats, missiles and warheads), whereas this time the White Paper allows 17 years for just the boats.

But do lengthy procurement timescales matter? And, if they do, to whom?

The Importance of Time

Since the end of the Cold War our operations have been increasingly wide-ranging, and asymmetric where our opponents make quick use of new technology. In the same period technology gestations have been growing far shorter. This is particularly stark in the world of IT – and almost all programmes now contain a large amount of IT. Our acquisition system (process, organisation and culture), which is still geared to a symmetrical world, needs greater agility to confront these changes.

Time is money. The longer a project takes:

- The longer project staff are tied to that project and the larger the procurement organisation has to be.
- The greater the chance of obsolescence.
- The more likely that the requirement will change.
- The less the agility that can be achieved.
- The greater the difficulty of exporting.
- The greater the industrial costs, which ultimately must be borne by MoD.

- The greater the uncertainty of continuity, undermining commitment within industry and increasing costs through consequential delay.
- The greater the risk to the survival of the design, engineering and industrial capacity.

Delays after programme launch create further cost increases. Delays increase the degree of obsolescence on fielding, which induces operational risk and increases support costs as old equipment becomes more and more expensive to support. And it is not only the extra costs, but the increased risk to forces operating with equipment where its performance is no longer adequate – the lack of FRES to replace CVR(T) is an obvious example.

National Audit Office (NAO) reports on MoD major projects, as well as media reporting, have concentrated on delay rather than on overall length of the procurement schedule. Recently, these NAO reports have focused on delays only post-Main Gate (for example it has been nearly 10 years since the CVF programme was announced but since it has not yet passed Main Gate, no delay has 'officially' occurred). However, delay is a secondary issue: it is the total time that a programme takes from concept to ISD (which of course includes delay) that is more important. The NAO should consider whether their project reports in the future should look at overall timescales and costs from concept to ISD, rather than delay and cost overruns post-Main Gate.

In today's fluid, and increasingly asymmetric, defence environment, collapsing the current procurement cycle of two decades for a major system would yield huge benefits. We need not just a two- or three-year reduction, but much more – a cut of, say, 50% should be the aim so that the largest programmes take a decade and smaller ones much less. We know this is possible through the example of UORs and wartime programmes, but we should not hide behind the comfortable feeling that, in peacetime, things can take as long as is comfortable. We are engaged in several challenging conflicts, but we are providing equipment with a peacetime mentality.

Can we cut procurement times by 50%? What are the reasons that govern the time successful programmes take? And can those reasons be read across to other programmes?

Reasons for Extended Schedules and Delay
There are many reasons for the long schedule times. Some of them, such as process and technical complexity, testing and evaluation and

risk reduction cannot be significantly reduced without adding undue risk. There are others, however, that can and should be actively targeted.

The reasons for these lengthy schedules are many and varied. Some have been recognised by MoD initiatives, but others have not, while many problems in industry have remained 'below the radar'.

Affordability and Technical Risk

Perhaps the two most significant reasons for long procurement timescales and delay are overall affordability of the equipment programme and the use of immature technology in the later stages of the procurement cycle.

In our last paper, we concluded that the defence equipment programme was significantly underfunded, and that a properly costed Defence Review was urgently needed if major cuts, which would seriously undermine the coherence of the equipment programme, were to be avoided. Continued underfunding is responsible for uncertain commitment, changes in requirement and specification, delays for financial reasons and repeated discontinuities in industrial activity – all of which contribute to cost increases that in turn lead to further delay.

Discontinuities in programmes, often lengthy, are also caused by the use of immature technology. Technology must be brought to maturity before MoD finalises its requirements and before industry is forced to make fixed price bids. Too often, programmes approach Main Gate with too much technical risk, with the result that either Main Gate is delayed, or worse still, the programme passes but hits additional problems in the final stages before production. The longer high technical risk remains, the greater the potential for major delay in the later stages when much greater sums of money are being spent.

These are perhaps the two most powerful reasons for major delay and, therefore, lengthening procurement timescales. But there are also many softer issues that contribute heavily to the long, drawn out timescales, and these can be categorised as issues of culture, the relationship between MoD and industry, and process and organisation.

Issues of Culture – MoD

Many cultural issues have major adverse impacts on lengthy procurement schedules.

In MoD, these include dilatory decision-making (often to have yet another study) and the need to achieve consensus not only from the wide range of stakeholders, but also from those with no authority – but with the ability to say no. There is a lack of acquisition expertise – in May 2005, the Chief of Defence Procurement of the day, Sir Peter Spencer, said that poor performance in the Defence Procurement Agency was 'endemic'; it is generally recognised that this is caused by several things, including lack of personal qualities, inadequate experience and expertise, and minimal training. There is a lack of true accountability – although IPT leaders and Directors of Equipment Capability (DEC) were 'empowered' under Smart Acquisition, it is only a partial empowerment because they cannot make many of the essential decisions as these have to be referred up the management chain or to committees – there is an excessive commitment to 'process'. Empowerment is clearly the way to go, but the terms of delegated powers are not sophisticated enough. A note of caution is necessary, however, as empowerment of DECs and IPTs has led to a lack of consistency in areas where it is essential and this aspect only serves to confuse and confound industry. Cluster level management (e.g. across all maritime platforms and related programmes) must be paramount to ensure coherence.

Other cultural issues include a poor understanding of industry and its commercial drivers. This is endemic in the MoD and leads to a blind pursuance of the competition dogma, especially where a partnering approach would clearly develop faster solutions. Moreover, a lack of urgency and drive, caused by poor leadership, high post turnover and the lack of a performance-based reward system, generate a culture of little or no true accountability. In a world where 'time to market' is of little or no account – even though servicemen's lives are at risk if equipment is delivered to service after it is required – we can have little wonder why performance procurement timescales remain too lengthy. The MoD is, bluntly, not an output-focused organisation.

Smart Procurement called for the primacy of the customer and EAC acknowledged the need for the customer to take the lead in committees. However, the real issue is between operational need and acquisition process, and the merging of the procurement and support organisations into the even more powerful Defence Equipment and Support (DE&S) seems to be tipping the balance the wrong way. DCDS(EC) as the Sponsor is junior in rank and influence to the Chief of Defence Materiel (CDM). As a result, even now, we understand that arguments about 'who calls the shots' are developing along the M4 in direct contradiction of Smart Acquisition and EAC. In addition, the Treasury's view that competition equals value-for-money puts it on a collision course with MoD. The resultant clashes, both intra- and extra-MoD, take a great deal of time to resolve, often with compromises that are not really in anyone's interests.

There is also a clear culture of 'do what is deemed to be right' – no one has ever been fired for running an unnecessary competition or being over careful; conversely, the 'system' – including successive Chiefs of Defence Procurement (CDPs) – has consistently encouraged caution, over emphasis on detail and avoidance of risk/opportunity management.

As we have argued previously, we have a defence programme that is unaffordable within the sums of money that the Government and its successors are likely to provide. Some programmes suffer long delays in the early phases simply because there is no money to take them forward any faster. This creates not only a sense of unreality and uncertain commitment, but also a 'delay mentality' in Whitehall – the greater the perceived funding shortfall, the stronger the instinct for delay. The recent practice of not setting an ISD until Main Gate reinforces this delay mentality – if there is no stated ISD, there can be no delay. The imperative to deliver Trident by a certain, clearly understood and logical date reinforces this. Can we replicate this imperative elsewhere?

Issues of Culture – Industry

There are cultural issues in industry as well. While a huge range of very different companies can hardly be lumped into a single generalised entity, there are certain problems, which affect the time it all takes, that seem to be common to many defence companies. A contract won as a 'must win' is invariably a 'loss-leader' or, more correctly, a 'loss starter'. Subsequent behaviour is often compounded by changes of personnel generating a mentality to 'bury bad news'. The root of this is a poor competitive policy which distorts the nature of the competition. The fear/blame culture clearly leads to suppression of bad news for as long as possible, so that remedial activity starts far too late.

There is, too, a lack of management skills in many areas in industry. Many companies have insufficient understanding of the customer/end user, with the result that they get their priorities wrong and spend too much time on less important issues and too little on the key factors. Among other things, it makes it likely that projects will be launched on the basis of nominally fixed prices long before the technological foundations are in place to make accurate cost estimation feasible. Allied to this is the 'PERT chart mentality' where the urgent, time-based goal gets lost in the detailed planning and management of the many component activities of the programme. The question – 'what have I got to do to hit the end date?' – ceases to be central. Overly detailed PERT charts for long programmes give an illusory view of control.

Issues of Culture – MoD and Industry

Both MoD and industry are guilty of other cultural weaknesses. These include the concentration on minimising the downside, rather than maximising the gains, but for different reasons – MoD because it is pressurised by media, NAO and Treasury, industry by the demands of their shareholders to maximise profits. Neither MoD nor industry devotes enough effort to examining successful programmes to identify the reasons for success so that they can be applied to other projects. While much work has been done in this area in MoD, industry and, particularly, the NAO, lessons identified too seldom become lessons learned. This transition to lessons learned applies equally to lessons identified from failures. Much time is spent in 'reinventing the wheel'.

Leadership is not generally conspicuous in either MoD or industry. Without a high standard of leadership, motivation, determination, a sense of urgency and pride in achieving the necessary quality in the necessary time frame are unlikely to be much in evidence. Leadership is a complex quality: it is not just an ability to motivate others and imbue them with determination to achieve the goal, but it demands an expert understanding of the job and the seasoned expertise to go with it. Do we have such people? It is notable that, when UORs are being met, leadership within both MoD and industry, much of it of a very high standard, is much in evidence. Maybe with the UOR process it is the removal of the fear factor, the lower priority given to cost considerations and the focus on the end result that leads to their success. So it would appear that our peacetime procedures suppress leadership skills to a counter-productive extent.

Often, both MoD and Industry show a pre-occupation with cost that borders on the unhealthy, but this appears too much of a cultural black hole, particularly for the Treasury, whose own pre-occupation with competition and price, to the detriment of other ways of demonstrating value-for-money, remains a dominant factor in delay and paradoxically, cost overruns. It is a fallacy that controlling cost requires you to concentrate on cost itself: quite the reverse is true. Concentrate on the result, focus on what is needed to deliver it, and cost will look after itself. There is plenty of evidence to show that, by doing it quicker, the overall cost will be less.

The Relationship with Industry

The DIS is intended to change the direction of MoD's main procurement strategy from one of adversarial competition to one of strategic partnering. Less competition suggests that time can be saved, but that will depend on where and in what way competition is applied. More importantly, partnering should instil in both partners a greater joint stakeholder mentality with a greater sense of urgency and understanding. The questions are whether both sides are serious about developing a partnering mentality and whether they can do so successfully in a relatively short time after decades of adversarial behaviour, which has been responsible for a great deal of unnecessary delay in many programmes. Both will need to change from an attitude of 'That's his problem, not mine', to one of 'His problem is mine, so we had better resolve it together'.

Competition is important, but its application must differ from project to project. Inappropriate use of competition has in the past been responsible for considerable extension of timescales, particularly irritating when competition is unnecessary but decreed for 'safe' policy reasons. In the future, competition should be used only when there are very good reasons. The major cultural change here, however, is an emphasis on early and rapidly completed competition. By getting it out of the way early in the procurement cycle all parties can then concentrate on the result. Drawn-out competitive processes increase costs for all concerned and are a major factor in extending schedules significantly. But if early competition is to be combined with fixed price, technological risks must be dealt with earlier – we return to this later.

Process and Organisation

Changes to process and organisation tend to get more attention than changes to culture. This is hardly surprising as they can be altered relatively quickly (certainly faster than culture change) and can provide the 'quick wins' beloved of politicians and senior officials. Although less vital than culture change, they are still important. Many of the most important are detailed in the study Enabling Acquisition Change (EAC). But there are others that need addressing.

There is an unsatisfactory audit trail from the Defence Concepts and Doctrine Centre (DCDC)'s overall operational concepts to the capability requirements produced by the Equipment Capability Customer (ECC). This can give rise to poor or late operational concepts, which then cause delay at the start of a programme and also further downstream. FRES is a case in point.

The 'validating' and 'verifying' of the requirement and regular re-iterative examination of the potential solution using long-winded Operational Analysis causes early drag in the OE part of the Concept and Assessment Phases, especially should the SAG scenario set change owing to revised strategic guidance. Whilst shipbuilders can build in five years from knowing the requirement, it takes MoD nine years to provide and agree it (the standard Concept, Assessment and Demonstration (CAD) Phases rolled together). Add to this the constant (annual) re-examination of the money and possible deferral due to funding bow waves. Many of the problems we are seeing (but the public are not) are the delays of programmes long before Main Gate and often long before Initial Gate. It is more often the money profile that drives planned ISDs of programmes and not the ability of industry to build, or even of MoD to decide. Such planned delay is accepted (the only option when overheating a department budget) without full knowledge of the cost of maintaining legacy kit or, at least, with a blind eye to the increasing support elements of the whole-life costs of existing equipment from the point of delay onwards. And sometimes this phase is drawn out because the ambitions of the Armed Forces lead to systems that cost more than can be justified by the potential operational benefits. This can lead to repeated studies in the hope that a different result will emerge with different assumptions – it rarely does. The MoD has to find a swifter way to resolve such conflicts between cost and ambition.

As the procurement cycle progresses, further issues emerge. The two-gate process has become a multi-gate one; while this is not necessarily a bad thing, the right issues for examination at each mini-gate are not always identified. This adds time without progress. Annuality or bienniality remains a constraint on timely decision-making. Low spend on the early stages of a project links to low technology readiness levels at Main Gate, with consequential delay either to Main Gate or afterwards. It also leads to bid prices being fixed before technological risk areas have been mastered, building in something close to inevitability that supposedly fixed times and costs will not stay that way.

The 'conspiracy of optimism', by which projects are inserted into the equipment programme with insufficient funding and unrealistic timescales, is responsible for much delay as programmers, DECs and IPT leaders struggle to stay within unrealistic time and cost boundaries, or spend time in finding more funding and trading off performance against time. Unrealistic bid prices from industry reinforce this 'conspiracy of optimism' and, eventually, the programme may well need restructuring with the further delay that that entails.

Trade-offs between cost, time and performance are well established, but are usually done to reduce cost and time overrun. However, as we have already pointed out, costs cannot be controlled simply by concentrating on cost itself. Concentrating on time, and trading off performance against time would be more productive. As part of this, a harder look should be taken at whether the capability advantages associated with the riskiest technology areas are really needed or could be provided in another way. Industry has a major responsibility here.

Trading off performance to reduce technological risk will pay dividends later in terms of reduced time and cost overruns. If the technological risk areas are essential to delivering the required performance, then the whole project should be put on hold (or cancelled) until a separate Technology Demonstrator programme has been carried to a successful completion. Better still, this should be done before the programme starts, or at any rate before Main Gate. If none of this is acceptable on timescale grounds, then the only alternative is to buy the best available off-the-shelf.

Programmes that are in deep trouble should be considered for cancellation as early as makes sense and replaced with a buy-off-the-shelf. Phoenix should have been cancelled around 1990; perhaps FRES should be cancelled now and the existing funding used for a buy-off-the-shelf. The problem here is that cancellation leads to the confiscation of funds for that capability and further delay as a new programme is restarted (the delay caused by restarting a programme is well illustrated by the Type 45 destroyer, which will not enter service until after the Horizon frigate, from which UK withdrew partly because the ISD was too late). To that can be added not only the politicians' dislike of cancelling projects when public money has already been spent, even if continuation will waste yet more of the public's money, but also the fact that often (but not always) significant extra money is required – Nimrod being a case in point.

The industrial response to a distorted bidding process also contributes to increased timescales. Companies naturally feel the need to bid compliant and at the lowest price to win and then spend a great deal of time looking at how to claw back costs. The fact is that as most defence acquisitions seek something new, and as the solution is unproven, the cost is what it says – an estimate. Estimates for the unknown have a tendency to be optimistic, and 'scrubbed' estimates invariably increase optimism rather than reducing cost. This is compounded when major technological uncertainties mean that industrial bidders have no firm foundations on which to base their estimates – adding in sufficiently large contingencies would lose the bid, so the conspiracy of optimism is fuelled, with the inevitable consequences of future time slip and cost overrun. A difficult starting position is then often compounded by restructuring, reorganisation and personnel changes, which also have a delaying effect.

What To Do?

There is much work going on in MoD to improve procurement processes and organisation. However, we are concerned that reorganisation of structure and process is taking precedence over culture change, which we regard as the more important lever on performance. But over and above this work, there are many other things that can be done to speed up programmes. These can be divided into those for MoD to do, those for industry to do, and those for both to do together.

We have identified a long list in each category. It is too long for listing here, but is included in the electronic version of this paper at www.rusi.org/defencesystems. The most important are discussed below.

Things for MoD to Do

First, we believe that decisions must be made by those with knowledge and responsibility – not by a wide consensus of those without. The committee culture needs to be minimised and a 'single controlling mind' (the Senior Responsible Owner (SRO) but with greater authority over all aspects of the programme) be given the full authority to make all but a handful of major decisions that will still have to be taken by committees. Committees must be customer-led.

Second, technological risks must be evaluated early in the programme cycle and eliminated well before Main Gate is reached. Technology must be 'on-the-shelf' and not developed while the programme is being advanced. This will require more funding to be made available for both the research and technology budget, and for the early stages of procurement. Technological ambition for the wrong reasons (e.g. keeping up with the US in the majority of capabilities, although it is clearly necessary in some) should be avoided; if it is needed but the technology is not mature in UK, a buy-off-the-shelf may be a better course. Another option might be greater use of incremental acquisition.

Third, MoD needs to instil a sense of urgency into the procurement process with 'time-to-market' drivers. Set a challenging, but realistic, ISD early and strive to meet it. The process needs to be transformed to combine the agility of the UOR process with the greater rigour of the full procurement cycle in whole-life and integration issues. The really key issue here is for the MoD to become far more output-focused as a norm, forcing a genuine accountability for timely delivery.

Fourth, compete (but only where it makes sense to do so) early, and then partner while there is still time in the procurement stages to benefit from partnering. Create transparency of operational, procurement and financial planning for the industrial partner(s).

Things for Industry to Do

Industry has a major responsibility to match MoD's progress but, as yet, the ways in which it needs to change have not been clearly articulated.

As a partner of MoD, it needs to create transparency in the key elements of its business planning – resourcing levels, mix of skills, capabilities and facilities, and the extent to which all of that is sustainable against forward business projections. In addition, it needs to improve the 'honesty' of its bids and be prepared to tell MoD when the capability it seeks implies the need for a technology demonstration phase before prices are fixed.

Industry needs to improve management skills at many levels, and offer high quality staff for MoD training courses. It needs to better understand the customer's organisation, process, constraints and aspirations in order to design suitable commercial structures.

Primes must flow down benefits fairly and promptly through the whole supply chain to reduce SME cash flow problems that import unnecessary risk downstream and stifle innovation. SMEs in return must concentrate on various improvements (see the full list) to improve company health so that they can accept greater risk sharing and invest more up-front.

Things for MoD and Industry to Do Together

It will be of little use if MoD and industry make changes in a vacuum. They need to work closely together.

Most importantly, they need to develop a strategic partnering mentality, in which problems are addressed jointly within a joint structure with agreed assumptions, a single data set and a single governing body with the authority to solve problems rapidly. The recent Pathfinders have shown how valuable the early involvement of industry can be.

Both will need to jointly agree effective, innovative 'gainshare' methods of working, and identify what can be imported from the UOR methods to speed up the process.

Elimination of the 'conspiracy of optimism' is vital, and both MoD and industry will need to work at getting rid of the cause by jointly agreeing realistic costs and schedules from the start. Output focus must become the norm.

Reducing the Time Cycle

The actions described above and listed in the electronic version of this paper will shorten project cycles, but not halve them as we suggest is required, unless it is combined with an even greater shift in outlook in both MoD and industry.

Previous acquisition reforms have concentrated on the MoD side of the equation, whilst exhorting industry to 'help' and support the effort. No reform to date has addressed the entire process, including the industrial part, on an end-to-end basis. The partner approach of the DIS gives a perfect backdrop to a major effort to address this – as has been demonstrated by the Pathfinder programmes. Dedicating a realistic budget within an adequately funded defence programme, selecting the key industrial players on a capability basis, and forming a joint project team charged with producing the best system for the money, in a challenging timescale, against a cardinal points specification, and with governance reduced to a minimum based on a process re-engineering approach derived beforehand, would produce some dramatic results. It does of course need real will, a much more trusting approach and above all some courage, but industrial members of the team will be quite capable of adopting the aims of the customer in such an endeavour.

But to open the road towards this modern way of doing things, two road blocks must be removed. Technology must be brought to maturity before the MoD finalises its requirements and before industry is forced to make fixed price bids. Bids based on uncertain technology can never be honest and will always contain the seeds of time slip and price escalation, fuelling mistrust, preventing openness and breeding confrontation. Building a sound technology base before price is fixed will mirror best practice outside defence. But it will require extra investment before Main Gate and in Technology Demonstrators before projects start. To pull money to the front end of projects like this can only be achieved within the kind of radical programme and policy review we advocated in our last article.

All of this will need strong, consistent leadership and a greater continuity of the leaders themselves (e.g. longer postings which only end at some point of assessment or measurement). This leadership must come not only from politicians, but also from top management in MoD and industry – not just now but for several years to come – if a major reduction in timescale is to be achieved with all its benefits, not least in reduced costs.

Above all, it needs an integrated approach – all of these things need to be done together, because they have the potential to reinforce each other and generate a virtuous spiral. For example, changing the culture will be easier if bids are honest and less likely to lead to conflict later; bids will be more likely to be honest if technological risk is eliminated before fixing prices; removing technological risk will be easier if the armed services are more ready to compromise on capability; and compromising on capability will also help to reduce budget overheating and projects being pushed to the right for budgetary reasons, which will feed back into a culture of doing things faster. And to do this, industry and all the MoD stakeholders have to jointly recognise the portfolio of problems and jointly own the solutions. With many examples from the civil sector and recent experience of the Pathfinder projects, we can be confident that it is possible.

Appendix 7–3

RUSI ACQUISITION FOCUS PAPER[188]

IMPLEMENTING THROUGH-LIFE CAPABILITY MANAGEMENT

The members of the RUSI Acquisition Focus are: John Weston (Chairman),
Tim Banfield (NAO), Bob Barton (co-chair of the MoD/Industry Equipment
Capability Group), Vice Admiral (retd) Jeremy Blackham (recently EADS UK
President), John Dowdy (Director, McKinsey), Professor Christopher Elliott
(GD UK), Graham Jordan (formerly S&T Director, MoD), Gerry Paulus
(Managing Director, SVGC Ltd), Major General (retd) Bill Robins (formerly
DGICS, MoD), Professor Trevor Taylor (Head of Defence Management and
Security Analysis, Cranfield University), Bill Kincaid (Editor RUSI Defence
Systems)[189]

The word 'capability' in through-life capability management (TLCM) changes the emphasis away from just equipment acquisition to cover all Defence Lines of Development and this change is far-reaching and concerns both MoD and industry.

The TLCM initiative comes at a time of critical funding concerns that adds difficulty to its implementation. However, much effort is being devoted to implementing this important initiative and progress has been made in a number of areas – within the Equipment Capability Customer (ECC), with coherence across the Unified Customer, in decision-making and in the willingness to confront unpleasant realities and find innovative solutions – but elsewhere progress is patchy or slower than envisaged.

However, even if the current progress is maintained and embedded across the board, we believe that the improvement in acquisition output will fall well short of what is needed unless three high-level issues are effectively tackled – high-level organisation and accountability, culture, and the overheated defence programme.

---

[188] *RUSI Defence Systems* (Volume 11, No. 1, June 2008), page 26.
[189] Names and posts of the members have in some case changed but were correct when this paper was published.

TLCM requires major change but cannot simply be layered on top of existing organisations, as these ensure that several people share accountability for acquisition. Recent changes have not resolved this. What is required is a structure that aligns real power and real accountability throughout the organisation.

Changes in culture at the top are essential: the import of some of the urgent operational requirements (UOR) culture into 'normal' procurement is desperately needed and Mission Command should become the order of the day.

The overheating of the defence programme has been recognised for some years, but little has been done to overcome the problem. PR08 has not helped. The root cause of overheating must be identified and eliminated, as it distorts all other initiatives and work.

We believe that fully implementing TLCM will be an uncomfortable process and will require vision and leadership. It is vital for the future of our Armed Forces.

The UK defence acquisition process has been in a constant state of change for decades. The latest innovation to be introduced has the potential to be the most far-reaching of all – the introduction of a coherent scheme for the management of a capability throughout its life, or through-life capability management (TLCM). The MoD defines it as:

> An approach to the acquisition and in-service management of military capability in which every aspect of new and existing military capability is planned and managed coherently across all lines of development from cradle to grave.

The word 'capability' changes the emphasis away from just equipment acquisition to cover all Defence Lines of Development (DLoDs). This explicitly broadens the role of the Equipment Capability Customer (ECC) to responsibility for coordinating all DLoDs. But the word 'capability' is mired in confusion. Are the two new aircraft carriers a **capability**? Or are they equipments that contribute to a capability over a period of years? We believe that the latter should be the answer and TLCM should be about the enduring provision of such **capability** –

not individual equipments. It should result in the smooth fielding of systems, without detriment to the end user, introduced at the most appropriate time, in order to ensure the lowest cost across legacy and new build taken together.

Implementation of TLCM will require industry to be treated more inclusively – inside the tent rather than contractually held at arm's length – since trade-offs across the DLoD spectrum will require a full understanding of the implications for all stakeholders. Both MoD and industry desperately need TLCM fully implemented, and this must be achieved jointly through a controlled and iterative process over a period of time. The Pathfinder programmes should have ignited the second iteration but, sadly, have clearly not yet done so.

The definition above is, of course, a statement of the direction to go – many would see it as more of a philosophy rather than how to get there. Few would disagree with it, but most would agree that MoD has been more successful at producing the right initiatives than carrying them through to a successful conclusion – a process which in the nature of things may often take several years.

Moreover, the definition does not mention change but TLCM, if it is to be effective, is nothing if not a massive change programme and this is where the going gets tough for a large and complex department.

The initiative has also come at a time of critical funding concerns. TLCM itself does not offer any respite in the short term – indeed, by including sustainment costs for the new period 4–10 years, it makes matters worse – but it does offer the prospect of more informed decisions if judgements have to be made about relative affordability and value.

Implementing TLCM

For TLCM to succeed there will need to be a change of mindset and this was recognised by the Defence Industrial Strategy (DIS). It falls to MoD, as the very powerful monopsony customer, to lead and set the example here, but changes in MoD must be mirrored by changes in industry.

Work at McKinsey's shows that 70% of major change programmes in industry fail, but those that *do* succeed have invariably been led over a period of years by one top man or woman. It is arguable that Lord Drayson could have provided that single-minded focus and authority, but this will clearly be much more difficult following his departure late last year.

Where Are We Now?

MoD has a list of where it claims TLCM has made a difference so far:

- Consistency and continuous improvement in the core business of ECC.
- Coherence across the Unified Customer.
- More effective decision-making.
- Improved behaviours – knowledge sharing, performance metrics, training, learning from experience.

To this we would add that we see a greater willingness to accept unpleasant realities, ask tougher questions and offer up more innovative solutions. There is also much good work going on in the MoD in implementing DIS including that on strategic partnering, organisation at all levels below the top, process improvements and some culture change.

Against this, however, needs to be set those areas where progress is patchy or slower than envisaged, including culture change, creation of transparency and trust, and genuine understanding that enduring capability management may, as a result of technological innovation, involve the capability being fielded at times by different Services than those that do it today. This last is a real challenge and will seriously test the Defence Board and the Chiefs of Staff (COS).

What is Needed to Make TLCM Succeed?

It is quite clear that, even if these weaknesses are eliminated, the overall improvement in acquisition output will fall well short of what is needed unless three high-level issues are effectively tackled.

Top Level Organisation and Accountability

TLCM requires major change and cannot simply be layered on top of existing organisations – indeed, such an approach would only add to the difficulty in effectively implementing TLCM. There are currently several people who share accountability for acquisition at MoD, in contrast to the US where, for example, the US Assistant Secretary of the Army for Acquisition, Logistics and Technology has singular responsibility for Army acquisition. In MoD, acquisition is directed by an informal acquisition group, but whether this can provide the clear accountability needed is questionable.

Who is finally accountable for MoD acquisition decisions with the power and authority to follow them through? The Minister for Defence Equipment and Support (DE&S) potentially has the power, but few politicians have the unique combination of industrial understanding, political awareness and the experience to use that power to take on and face down opposition from senior officers and officials. The recent reorganisation of the MoD into a Defence Board has not led to the creation of a single focus for TLCM, nor has it achieved clear accountability – in this regard there will, of course, always be a difficulty arising from the position of the PUS as Accounting Officer. Once the top-level responsibilities and accountabilities are clarified, subsidiary responsibilities and accountabilities must then be identified.

Sorting out top-level responsibility for TLCM will also require that the relationships between the ECC, DES, single Services and the RP staff are made clear and unambiguous. A cross-unified customer body or 'Sponsor Group' is needed to drive cross-departmental progress and, more importantly, consistency.

Culture

Once clear accountability is in place, we could see a change in culture at the top. Decision-making should be faster, the 'Whitehall delay mentality' could be bypassed and much of the culture (but clearly not all) of UOR delivery could be adopted. Mission Command should become the order of the day: tell leaders and managers what they have to do, let them get on with it, measure their results and hold them accountable.

Mission Command works well in warfighting and other military operations. There is no reason why it should not work well in MoD, although financial constraints and accountabilities, particularly of the PUS, would need rather more consideration – selective incorporation of the UOR culture and process might serve the purpose. But it demands a single leader, accountable and responsible when all the arguments are over. It is odd that the military profession should have such a clear understanding of this issue, but the ministry controlling the profession should have such difficulty applying it.

The Overheated Defence Programme

The defence programme has long been overheated, but has become progressively more so over the last decade. This year has generally been seen as the critical one to match budgets and plans. This hasn't happened.

But is the overstuffed programme the cause or is it just a symptom? Whichever it is, it has got to be fixed – and quickly, as it is well known that saving a pound by delaying a project now will cost two pounds in the future. At a time when the MoD budget is so stretched, and the probability of any real increase so small, the consequences of generating extra cost through slow implementation should be a real focus of attention for the management of MoD. Instead it appears that this is seen as the short-term solution to the problem, which can only result in further serious consequences in the future. We appear to have missed the chance to fix things this year, so it seems essential to do so next. However, this year's decisions to delay programmes, rather than cut them, are actually contrary to the basic tenets of TLCM, and will have a serious financial knock-on effect for PR09 and PR10.

Once the programme has been properly matched to budget forecasts, we must ensure that it doesn't overheat again. That means finding the root cause and dealing with that, rather than continuing to delay programmes with the consequence of increased costs and yet more programme turbulence.

Many possible causes of overheating spring to mind – the 'conspiracy of optimism', high defence inflation, poor cost estimation, use of immature technology, loss of funding through underspending, poorly executed competitions, lasting commitment to very large and expensive 'totem' programmes and many others. But if we fix these (which will not be easy), will we have eliminated the root cause(s)? Or is there something else? We need to find out.

Conclusion

To concentrate on the 20% that will make 80% difference, what are the issues surrounding TLCM that MoD has to resolve?

First and foremost, it needs a new top structure that aligns real power and real accountability with the responsibilities of top officials. This must be under a minister with the relevant expertise and experience as well as with the visible and consistent backing of the Secretary of State and the Prime Minister. This full accountability means ending the ability of other officials to stop decisions being made – they would provide advice only. We believe that we were getting tantalisingly close to that condition under Lord Drayson.

Mission Command and full accountability would then be the way of conducting business, with managers being told what is required and then left to get on with it. They would need authority to match their responsibility and they would be held fully accountable.

The overheating of the equipment programme needs to be resolved as soon as possible, because it is distorting all other initiatives and work. The root cause(s) must be determined and eliminated and

TLCM has the pre-eminent role to play here in deciding affordability, relevance and value of what should remain in the programme.

A specified sense of how TLCM will actually work, including the place of mission command and delegation techniques, is urgently needed. However, we believe that if TLCM is to work, we must remove the paralysis that appears to grip the decision process around the defence equipment programme. We suggest that this can be done only if the first of our recommendations is addressed. This will be very uncomfortable. It will require vision and leadership but it is vital for the future of our Armed Forces.

Appendix 7–4

RUSI ACQUISITION FOCUS PAPER[190]

THE CONSPIRACY OF OPTIMISM

The members of the RUSI Acquisition Focus are: John Weston (Chairman), Tim Banfield (NAO), Bob Barton (co-chair of the MoD/Industry Equipment Capability Group), Vice Admiral (retd) Jeremy Blackham (recently EADS UK President), John Dowdy (Director, McKinsey), Professor Christopher Elliott (GD UK), Graham Jordan (formerly S&T Director, MoD), Gerry Paulus (Managing Director, SVGC Ltd), Major General (retd) Bill Robins (formerly DGICS, MoD), Professor Trevor Taylor (Head of Defence Management and Security Analysis, Cranfield University), Bill Kincaid (Editor RUSI Defence Systems) [191]

SUMMARY

A 'conspiracy of optimism' exists between MoD and industry, each having a propensity, in many cases knowingly, to strike agreements that are so optimistic as to be unsustainable in terms of cost, timescale or performance.

The causes are several. Optimistic defence assumptions based on policy dogma, Service aspirations, and Government reluctance to fully fund commitments lead to an overheated defence programme. To get new projects funded is therefore difficult, leading to 'entryism' when the initial cost and schedule are deliberately under-estimated. This is compounded by poor cost-estimation techniques, which frequently omit costs for development and testing of interfaces, technology demonstration and industrialisation, training and/or manpower. Technology risks are too often under-estimated.

Because of the decline in the number and frequency of contracts for large, intellectually rich development programmes, industry

---

[190] *RUSI Defence Systems* (Volume 10, No. 2, October 2007), page 60.
[191] Names and posts of the members have in some cases changed but were correct when this paper was published.

sees many of these as 'must win' and, in step with optimistic MoD budgeting, bids an optimistic price on an optimistic schedule, expecting to claw back some of the shortfall during subsequent phases. Often both sides know that the basis of the contract is unrealistic.

Projects are seldom cancelled once they are fully launched, and the lack of transparency shelters those who make poor decisions.

If the 'conspiracy of optimism' is to be eliminated, MoD and industry must ensure that: defence planning assumptions and equipment aspirations are realistic; independent cost estimates are produced; transparency is improved; programmes with large cost overruns and delay are considered for cancellation; interfaces and technology risks are properly identified and managed; large complex programmes are managed with greater initiative and less process constraint; and all this is carried through into acquisitio

Delays and cost overruns to defence programmes have many causes. One cause, however, does not seem to have been much debated although it is universally recognised – the 'conspiracy of optimism'. The term has been in use since at least the mid-1990s and its existence may date back further.

General Rob Fulton, when he was DCDS(EC) saw it as a bipartite behavioural problem, with MoD and industry as co-conspirators. Essentially, both sides had a propensity to strike unrealistic agreements, later recognising, but not necessarily admitting, that the basis on which contracts had been let was highly optimistic. In many cases both parties knew very well at the time that the offer made was unrealistic in terms of either cost, timescale or delivered performance. Neither side would acknowledge that it was actively part of a conspiracy, but the behaviours clearly exhibited all the same characteristics. The result is that the contracted cost and schedule are almost always far too low, thereby causing apparent cost growth and schedule overruns as the programme proceeds, when in reality these were inevitable outcomes of the bidding process.

Agreeing to unrealistic programme parameters is a fact (much reported by successive NAO Major Project Reports), but what has sustained the practice and why does the 'system' encourage such behaviour?

The Causes

Aspirations

During the Cold War, quality of defence equipment was paramount: we needed equipment that was as good as, or better than, Soviet equipment. Timeliness was less important. This was the mindset in which most of today's top military and industrial leaders learned their job.

Since the end of Communism, we aspire to equip our forces with the best, which in effect means US quality, in a world of much faster technological change; time therefore does matter. The aspiration to keep up with the US at the tactical and operational level, if not the strategic level, places a huge strain on our much reduced defence budget, yet the war on terror has dissimilar demands, not least a rather different balance between quality and numbers.

The UK policy to 'punch above its weight' without the resources to do so places a premium both on the *quantity* of key equipments (to replace battle casualties, e.g. Chinook and Warrior) and on the *quality* and level of sophistication (in the case of CIS to handle coalition interoperability, particularly with the US). With our limited spend and, particularly, our drastic reduction in R&T funding, we are now in danger of falling between the two stools of quantity and quality.

The defence planning assumptions (DPAs) begin as a rigorous analysis of what threats face the country and what defence capability is required to meet them. Unfortunately, that rigour breaks down when confronted by real-world issues of affordability and selective trade-offs are made between different DPAs. This happens because the DPAs are assumptions, not facts and are, as such, open to interpretation and debate. Finally, real-world events unfold more quickly than MoD seems able to change DPAs – they are, after all, a snapshot frozen in time – and they very soon become dated. All this means that the DPAs give a veneer of scientific support to decisions that are rather more determined by cost and political judgement; the DPAs are used in these arguments with false precision in order to substantiate important procurement decisions made elsewhere. The result is that we plan for defence capability that proves inadequate for the task when it arrives and which is then expensively expanded at short notice, playing havoc with the financial cohesion of the long-term equipment programme. As evidence, our present commitment to two continuing operations overseas has breached the DPAs that created the military capability to fight them. Since 2002, the scenarios on which DPAs are based may not have changed, but equipment numbers have been repeatedly reduced and commitment levels have continuously exceeded planning assumptions, undermining the logic of scenarios and assumptions.

Another contribution to the overheated equipment programme is the desire to develop equipment from scratch in the UK. This is at the heart of the Defence Industrial Strategy (DIS) and UK jobs, IPR ownership and European solidarity often override the economic and schedule advantages of buying off-the-shelf. The balance of arguments for buying C-17 off-the-shelf against the European development of A400M illustrates this issue.

Entryism

This optimism in the DPAs, the desire to punch above our weight with the reluctance to pay for it, and the bias against buying off-the-shelf all create an overheated equipment programme. Overheating is also fuelled by deliberate over-programming to avoid underspend, inaccurate costing of non-equipment defence lines of development, and Service aspirations to maintain size and shape. Overheating is not a transient problem, but is with us to stay unless substantially different practices are adopted. An overheated programme is 'unaffordable', but for the MoD this may seem preferable to accepting cuts early. It may also act as a weapon in the continuing battle with the Treasury for increased funds – in many cases to match the increasing (and underfunded) commitments of the Government. It also means that existing programmes can be kept alive, albeit artificially, but reduced in scale or capability or further delayed, despite the high risk of technological obsolescence this brings.

Getting new projects into an overheated equipment programme, or seeking increased funding for existing projects, is difficult as it requires the deletion, delay or reduction of another project or projects – the larger the sum of money, the more difficult it is to get it into the equipment plan, particularly if the programme is to meet an emerging requirement with funding required in the immediate future. Consequently, there is positive pressure to reduce the estimate of the cost to, or beyond, the minimum.

Examples are legion. For example, the original British Aerospace (BAe) estimate for the cost of the Nimrod MRA4 programme was around £2.9Bn. Squeezed through several 'best and final' offer rounds it was eventually contracted at around £1.8Bn. The final outcome is expected to be over £3.5Bn. Again, the Tornado mid-life update was originally estimated at around £800M. The scope was reduced to get the costs down to around £400M to get it into the equipment programme, with both MoD and BAE Systems recognising that additional work, not included in the reduced scope, would have to be funded separately to produce an effective system. Once this was added back, the programme came in close to the original estimate. The post-project analysis conveniently forgets that the outturn was pretty close to the original 'unacceptable' estimate.

Poor Cost Estimation

Estimating costs, including support over perhaps a 40-year period, at the start of a complex development programme is difficult. In the past, estimated costs have often left out essentials such as development of interfaces with other programmes, interface testing, technology demonstration and industrialisation, training and manpower costs. An obvious example is the exclusion of dockyard construction costs at Devonport when considering certain nuclear submarine issues. This exclusion of certain costs is nothing new, but the withdrawal of MoD from active participation in design and the reliance on competition over the last quarter of a century has degraded MoD's ability to understand costs and to estimate them with any accuracy.

The problem here is that more accurate cost estimation will normally arrive at a much higher figure than is budgeted, and 'creative accounting' may be used just to get the project into the equipment programme. A good example (see Figure 1) is the future aircraft carrier programme (CVF) where MoD 'estimated' the cost as about £2.9Bn, whereas non-MoD estimators set it at £3.9Bn or more (and this figure was a multi-source view).

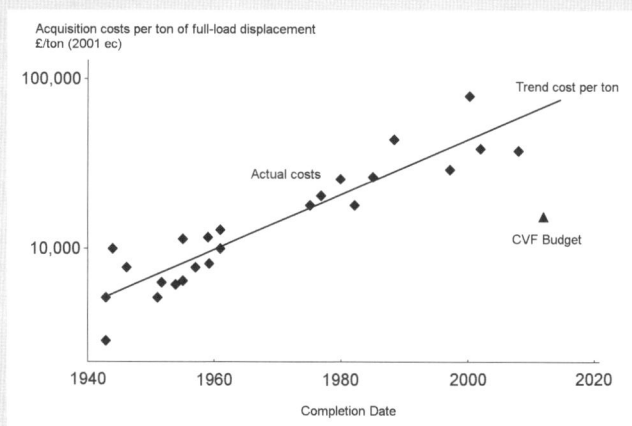

Figure 1: CVF and historical costs [HVR]

The latter figure is now in the programme. But would another programme with less political sensitivity and weaker Service proponency have stayed in the programme without major surgery or delay to the In-Service Date (ISD)?

Programme Management

The MoD acquisition cycle tends to treat all projects (except UORs and Special Projects) in the same way. However, small projects or buys off-the-shelf are totally different from large programmes with a major development element, and the failure to treat non-repetitive, intellectually-rich procurement differently from that of smaller, less complex projects (which generally come in on estimate and largely on time) is at the heart of the problem.

The NAO Major Project Reports have repeatedly shown failings in the management of large, complex programmes; these, almost without exception, are the 'problem children' (some have called them 'wicked programmes'). Managing such programmes requires totally different skills to ensure that effective problem exploration, option generation and analysis are undertaken before decisions are made on solutions. PERT Management here will fail: what is needed is joint, goal-directed management with trades being a fundamental part of the progression.

Industry's 'Must Win' Approach

Large programmes, delivering major improvements to capability, are let infrequently and have inherently long cycle times. Consequently, each new major programme suffers from a 'collective loss of memory' – either because the industrial capability has decayed or has been lost through natural wastage of the original deliverers. Industry, faced with such infrequent specialist acquisitions, sees a stark reality of 'existence or bust' relating to win/lose and with it the secondary effect of loss of capability that is needed to sustain the existing equipment and services. A 'must win' mentality is created and this is a primary breeder of optimism, which is often reinforced by dubious competitive practices.

In step with the MoD's minimum costings, defence companies will bid a minimum price in order to win a competition that they feel is a 'must win'. Once the competition is won, there is pressure to recover costs through whatever mechanisms exist in the contract so as to increase (or in many cases restore) the tiny profit margin in the bid price.

Prior to DIS, there was little recognition that this drive to recover costs after unrealistic bids and fixed-price contracting existed, and even now it appears that the Treasury either cannot recognise it or will not accept it.

Technology Risk

One of the major causes of delay and cost increase is the failure to drive out technology risk early enough in the procurement cycle. Too often the necessary funds are not included in the original cost estimates, as mentioned above, and early commitment is inevitably made against optimistic cost forecasts. Technology demonstration is essential, but can only be done if enough time and funding are available in the early project stages. There appears to be a lack of understanding in MoD, and a reluctant acceptance on the part of industry, of the paucity of funding for this.

Many years ago, it was MoD policy to pay for development, the de-risking of technology and the development of prototypes, even pre-production models. Some highly successful programmes, with a joint and well-developed estimating process, came through this system and, in our view, delivered better Value-for-Money (VfM) than more recent programmes. The process was based on gradually increasing certainty, not expecting it at the outset. An excellent example is Rapier Field Standard C. Wherever there are unknown technology, manufacturing, integration and performance risks the now familiar 'first-of-class direct build' approach (effectively a prototype taken directly into service) will inevitably meet optimistic schedules head on, and there seems to be little recognition of this in the timescale available – the huge delays in the early stages of the acquisition process of Bowman and FRES contribute hugely to compressed timescales in the Demonstration and Manufacture stages. Moreover, first-of-class build compounds the problems because, in the absence, in many areas, of any controlled environment in which to de-bug prior to further build, any problems get compounded into the second and subsequent builds, so multiplying delays and cost escalation.

The desire for premature certainty is exemplified by the practice of fixed-price contracting; the expectation of accuracy is quite unrealistic in the early stages of a programme when the risks cannot be clearly defined. This fixed-price obsession is a significant reason for apparent cost escalation and delay. The US dropped such contracting after a number of disasters, but HM Treasury appears to demand its retention despite all the evidence to the contrary.

Project Are Seldom Cancelled

The Smart Procurement Initiative in 1998 stated that projects would be cancelled more readily at Main Gate than hitherto at a similar approval point. This has not happened. Of course, Ministers are not keen on cancelling things on which significant sums of public money have already been spent, even when much greater sums of public money may be needed to put it all right.

Reluctance to cancel, even when other options are available off-the-shelf, can only encourage over-optimistic cost and schedule estimates at the start, with those responsible knowing that more money will eventually be made available and that ISD slippage will be accepted.

Of course major projects are cancelled from time to time – for example MLRS Phase III, Tracer and Horizon – but invariably for reasons that do not appear to discredit MoD: the examples mentioned were all blamed on other countries. Have any UK projects been cancelled because of slippage and cost overruns stemming from unrealistic MoD estimates at the start? We cannot think of any in the last decade or two. Is bad management thereby rewarded or at least uncensured?

Elsewhere in this edition, the US Assistant Secretary for the Army, the Honourable Claude Bolton, says that he has terminated 76 Army programmes in the last five years and expects to get to three figures before he leaves. He does make the point, though, that where the project manager has done all the right things, he should not be blamed for a failed project. But in deciding whether a UK IPT leader has done all the right things, more transparency in decision-making is required than currently exists.

Lack of Transparency

A lack of transparency shelters those who make poor decisions, whether individuals or committees. If decision-makers, whether IPT leaders, Directors of Equipment Capability, programmers, industrial managers or committees, are sheltered from blame, it can only encourage optimistic decisions on cost and time in the early stages if that helps to get funding into the programme, or helps to win a competition.

Lack of transparency also makes it difficult to see what is deleted from the equipment plan when realism increases the inadequate initial budget as a programme continues, and raises the question of whether that programme is still Value-for-Money.

We believe that the UK is the only country with major development programmes to withhold future equipment programme details. Experience shows that few organisations are more adept than MoD at hiding embarrassing developments from scrutiny for long periods. The National Audit Office (NAO) has managed to prise out important facts and force lessons to be learned, but this has taken time and concentrated effort. Few organisations other than NAO have the resources to do this, and even their resources are strictly limited.

The defence acquisition values propounded in the DIS include the statement that 'we all must value openness and transparency; share future plans and priorities wherever possible to encourage focused investment and avoid wasted effort'. There is a long way to go.

Are there lessons to be learned from the oversight that Congress exercises over the DOD in the US? The dilemma here will be to avoid the paralysis and bureaucratic overhead that DOD experiences from such oversight. But maybe some of the US practice could translate to UK in a productive way.

Solutions

Whilst optimism describes the mood that allows wrong decisions to be accepted, the key word in the phrase is conspiracy, which describes a behavioural process between several parties, with looping reinforcement. Conspiracy here might be defined as: 'collaborative behaviour, hidden from view'. The collaboration is more often by accident than common purpose (and can even occur under different aims), and perversely it is recognised that later in the development cycle it can be entirely beneficial.

This damaging 'conspiracy' can be halted by two means: by driving the processes into the open, so that it is no longer hidden from view; and by cutting or recrafting the process loops that allow the collaboration to be self-reinforcing.

If Whitehall and Abbey Wood really want to remove this 'conspiracy of optimism' – and we wonder if they do – then there are several things that must be done.

Planning Assumptions and Aspirations

While forecasting the future is not an exact science, DPAs are of little use if they are exceeded year on year. They need to be more honest and recognise reality. Serious underfunding positively encourages 'entryism'.

The aspiration, whether conscious or subconscious, to keep up with US standards of equipment needs to be tempered with reality. We cannot afford the most capable equipment in sufficient numbers across the board and, indeed, we have already abdicated from some capability areas where we now expect the US to supply.

We need to identify and declare in DPAs those areas where:

- We do not need the most capable equipment.
- Greater numbers are essential.
- Improvements are desperately needed in the short term.
- The ISD could slip without too much penalty.
- Greater priority and funding needs to be concentrated.

Cost Estimation

More accurate cost estimating from the start will mean less cost escalation downstream and less delay while extra funding is approved. Conversely, it will reduce the number of projects that can be taken into the equipment programme. This will reduce the turbulence in procurement, allow greater commitment to programmes once they are in, and gain greater commitment and investment from industry.

Although difficult, reasonably accurate cost estimation is not impossible. Independent cost estimators, used by leading defence primes, have proved approximately right over many programmes, and there is no reason why MoD should not use them too. Parameterised estimates are often pretty accurate – but are rejected for 'lack of detail'. It seems that MoD has now understood the need for independent cost estimation as Paragraph 9.22 of the McKane report states that Main Gate Business Cases for Category A projects should contain an independent estimate, and this is now written into the guidance on the Acquisition Operating Framework website.

We are poor at learning lessons, so MoD should set up a process for the continuous 10-year examination of past projects and other procurement issues and use the results to forecast the future, including early cost and schedule estimates.

Transparency and Accountability

Visibility of decisions needs to be improved. The equipment programme should be published with identification of those responsible for each project and how their responsibility is circumscribed. Committee decisions, too, need to be more open.

As fixing more than one, or possibly two, of the variables of cost, time and performance is not possible, the key criterion for each programme should be identified so that trades can be made when necessary between the three.

Cancellation of Programmes

In the US when a programme breaches its cost ceilings, DOD has to testify before Congress that there are no alternatives to continuation. MoD should adopt a similar process and be more willing to cancel programmes where cost or schedule have escalated unacceptably and where there are viable alternatives – the prospect of cancellation should concentrate minds, particularly when early cost and schedule estimates are made and agreed. However, decisions to cancel must not be based only on cost and schedule overruns, but must take into account realistic alternatives and military imperatives, otherwise there is a danger that cancellations could lead to an unbalanced equipment programme where the main criterion is good financial and schedule management of projects.

Integration and Technology Risk

The low level of funding for research and technology (R&T) starves projects of a flow of mature technology as well as the ability to demonstrate technology early in the cycle. There is a need to separate, in time, technology development from programme development while bringing management of technology and programmes closer together and making more frequent and more informed use of spiral development.

Greater funding of the early stages of a project's procurement cycle has been called for over many years. The importance of this is now generally recognised and a higher level of funding is now provided for many projects, but it is still too low. Technology options must not initially be costed as mature unless they clearly are.

Technical interfaces will not come right without a full understanding of the technical and operational factors. As few systems are not networked, effective and imaginative test environments for the interfaces that networked systems have to handle must be used. The cost and schedule implications of interface design and testing must be built in from the start. Integration remains a poorly considered aspect until it becomes an imperative, which gives rise to increased cost over what might have been achieved had it been tackled proactively.

Programme Management

The 'wicked programmes' (including IT programmes) need different management skills from smaller, less complex projects, and a different approach, led by a different style with a wider breadth of understanding, greater initiative and less process constraint. As a senior, and highly respected, civilian manager of a very complex project said: 'The trick is to understand what rules you cannot break, then bend all the others if necessary to destruction.'

And since many more programmes now are information rich, they deserve the same degree of holistic risk management as much larger programmes. Networking the battlespace inevitably increases the number and importance of interfaces between projects. The Equipment Capability Customer (ECC) should exercise an imaginative determination to envisage the battlespace and insist on interfaces being managed properly. This may lead to a requirement for more staff for the chronically undermanned ECC.

Strategic partnering with industry could well improve the quality and pace of joint decision-making, as was demonstrated in the DIS Pathfinder programmes, but whether this will improve management of interfaces with other programmes in DE&S and on contract to other defence companies is doubtful. But clearly, changes to both organisation and process are needed.

Education

It is widely held in the USA that the US Defense Acquisition University at Fort Belvoir has blown a fresh wind through the US DOD and has created a body of shared expertise and open-minded approach that reduces the tendency to run defence acquisition as if it were a conspiracy against the public.

If the conclusions of this paper and similar work were to be factored into the teaching at DMTC Shrivenham, we may build a body of professionals who conduct acquisition in a more open-minded and less conspiratorial manner.

Conclusion

It could be asked whether we would want anything other than optimism within the equipment programme. Would a 'conspiracy of pessimism' be preferable? The answer is yes and no. The 'conspiracy of optimism' drives a bow wave that is now threatening to become a tsunami and will at the very least mean that many projects will be further delayed for funding reasons downstream (risking obsolescence or irrelevance) or severely reduced in numbers or capability. The latest NAO Major Projects Report shows that, since approval at Main Gate, the top 20 programmes have been reduced in capability/numbers by £1Bn as part of the effort to stay within cost constraints, caused partly by optimistic estimates. What effect these reductions have on each programme or the overall defence capability is not clear, and it is doubtful whether value judgements have been rigorously made in all cases.

On the other hand, a 'conspiracy of optimism' does get more programmes into the equipment programme, and to some extent, therefore, is beneficial to the Armed Forces. However, the optimistic climate not only drives behaviours but leads to dishonest decision-making. Everyone knew, or should have known, that the initial costings for CVF were wrong, but they accepted them as a price for getting the carriers into the equipment programme. This could be called 'institutional dishonesty'.

This term is a far more accurate reflection of the behaviours at play because of the perception that being honest won't get the job started, and this is compounded by the view: 'Don't worry, once we've started they won't be able to stop it, and when the real cost comes out later, they'll have to find the extra funds'. This attitude prevails on both sides of the MoD/industry divide, despite individual protestations to the contrary.

Although the 'conspiracy of optimism', or 'institutionalised dishonesty', does help to get programmes into the equipment programme, the unrealistically low initial cost and schedule estimates cause large cost variances to budget and delay to in-service dates, fuelling turbulence in the equipment programme and undermining commitment to particular projects.

Several improvements, which are shown in Table 1, can be made to reduce, or eliminate, this 'conspiracy'. We do not believe it is possible to 'cherry pick' these: it is all or nothing. The key is whether Whitehall and Abbey Wood really wish to tackle it or whether they prefer to live with it.

Table 1: Solutions

Breaking the 'Conspiracy of Optimism'

Solutions

Improve Transparency and Accountability
- Publish the equipment programme.
- Increase transparency of decisions to expose accountability.

Improve Reality in Assumptions and Aspirations
- Make Defence Planning Assumptions realistic rather than 'affordable'.
- Trim aspirations to reality.

Improve Cost Estimating
- Provide independent cost estimations. Make more use of parameterised techniques.
- Carry out a 10-year examination of projects to help in forecasting the future.

Cancel Programmes More Readily if Viable Alternatives Exist

De-risk Technology and Technical Interfaces Earlier
- Understand and test technical interfaces better.
- De-risk technology earlier and only cost technology as mature if it clearly is.

Improve Management of Complex Development Programmes
- Manage risk holistically – financial, integration, obsolescence, operational and political.
- Manage the large, complex development programmes with a different skill set and a greater emphasis on problem exploration, option generation and analysis before decisions on solutions are made.
- Ensure that interfaces between projects are better managed.

Abandon Fixed-Price Development Contracting
- Adopt a more incremental approach to funding.
- Use more joint teams to develop and assess options.

Education
- Factor in the above solutions to teaching at DMTC Shrivenham.

"How on earth can we address this consensus culture of weak decision making?"

"...let's form a committee!"

Chapter Eight

DIS: Culture and People

There are three main facets of any major change – reorganisation, process modification and culture change. The first two are relatively straightforward and can be imposed quite quickly, but the third – culture change – is much more difficult to implement, takes much longer, but is a *sine qua non* for enduring change.

DIS appears to be following the path of Smart Procurement: wide-ranging changes to organisation and process have made considerable progress but culture change, after nearly three years, is only beginning. And, as with Smart Procurement, it has been the organisational and process changes that have received the lion's share of effort. Whether this is because these can produce the 'quick wins' desired by top officials and their political masters, or because they are more straightforward to implement than culture change is not clear, although it is a reasonable bet that both are likely to have been a significant factor.

But you neglect forcing necessary culture change at your peril.

> *Restructuring on its own is never a substitute for necessary management change, and can sometimes be a distraction.*[192]

> *Past experience in government and industry shows that you can play around with the organograms as much as you like, but if the people keep doing the same things, nothing will improve.*[193]

In general terms, reorganisation and process modification are enablers for, in themselves, they will not lead to much, if any, improvement. It is culture change that will, on its own, make considerable improvement, but to make all its potential improvement, the two enablers are essential. So, culture change needs the greatest attention and it needs it early and continuously.

But culture change is a nebulous subject and difficult to implement.

---

[192] Bill Jeffrey, 'Implementing the Defence Industrial Strategy', *RUSI Defence Systems* (Volume 9, No. 2, October 2006), page 23.
[193] Derek Marshall, 'The Defence Industrial Strategy: Will it Make a Difference?', *RUSI Defence Systems* (Volume 9, No. 1, June 2006), pages 33/34.

People want the benefits of change without the inconvenience and risks of having to change themselves. Change is threatening to the existing senior structures and inevitably involves shifts in power and influence. [194]

Admiral Blackham goes on to say that the most important aspects of change management are:

- It must be led from the top and the top man must show by his behaviour that he is committed to change.
- The top man must be prepared to change senior managers who do not 'join the party'.
- The top man must encourage initiative, innovation and new thinking at all levels, but especially amongst the lower levels where it most often can be found.

It is well worth bearing these three points in mind as this chapter progresses.

The Existing Culture

We have already discussed the problem of changing from the adversarial world, in which MoD officials and industrialists have built their careers, to one of cooperation and strategic partnering. In some cases, changing from one to the other has been quick and painless – but in general it has been reversible. In other areas, no change has been obvious.

In other words, culture change is not being given the impetus it needs. While Smart Procurement and DIS trumpeted the need for culture change, implementation was not clearly defined, so not surprisingly it is not being carried forward. DIS did lay down Defence Values for Acquisition (DVA), but these did not really amount to anything definitive about a change of culture – much of it was about process, and the rest was airy-fairy as far as the implementation of the values. It talks about 'emphasis on joint team behaviours', 'emphasis on partnering behaviours' and 'understanding of industry'. But not much that is definitive.

Of course, the DIS spawned the EAC which was to advise on what

> Culture change is not being given the impetus it needs

---

[194] Sir Jeremy Blackham, 'MoD and Industry: Changing the Mind-Set', *RUSI Defence Systems* (Volume 8, No. 3, February 2006), page 54.

changes should be made to MoD's structures, organisation, process and culture. EAC did indeed recommend a series of changes to organisation and process, but it steered a wide berth around culture. According to the report, it *"focuses on structure, organisation and processes. This is not to understate the paramount importance of skills, training, culture and behaviours"*. In other words, culture is of top priority, but we don't know how to change it. Or should that be: "It's all too difficult, so let's forget about it".

The Cultural Problems

So, what are the cultural problems?

> *The official mind is outstandingly good at dealing with 'tame' problems ... it is trained and honed for this purpose. It is less well adapted, indeed almost wholly unsuitable, for thinking 'out of the box'.*[195]

This suggests that the official mind does indeed find it very difficult, if not impossible, to deal with culture change and identify the most important problems which need to be resolved. What are these?

The RUSI Acquisition Focus has identified them as follows:[196]

> The official mind does indeed find it very difficult to deal with culture change

- Poor leadership.
- Official encouragement of caution, emphasis on detail and avoidance of risk.
- Whitehall's delay mentality.
- A fear/blame culture.
- Concentration on the minimisation of the downside rather than the maximisation of the upside.
- Preoccupation with unit cost and a refusal to see the overall cost picture.
- A refusal to learn from experience.

It is these cultural issues that need to be met head on and changed, for

---

[195] Sir Jeremy Blackham, 'Dealing with Wicked Problems', *RUSI Journal* (Volume 152, No. 4, August 2007), page 37.
[196] RUSI Acquisition Focus, 'Why Does It All Take So Long?', *RUSI Defence Systems* (Volume 10, No. 1, June 2007), pages 32–37.

unless they are, no amount of 'emphasis on partnering' or on 'joint team behaviours' will be achieved.

With these weaknesses, it is hardly surprising that major projects generally take a couple of decades – A400M 17 years, CVF 16 years, Astute 17 years, Bowman 20 years, Joint Combat Aircraft 16 years, Typhoon 19 years. The Type 45 Destroyer has taken less, but much of the early work had already been done in the NATO Frigate (subsequently aborted) and the Horizon programmes (from which UK withdrew). And FRES has arguably taken (with its several aborted predecessors) three decades. In most of these examples, there is still time for historic levels of delay to stretch them to two decades. This leads to the inherent expectation that schedules of two decades for major programmes are the norm – not only in MoD, but in industry, too.

> Within the build sector, there is already an awareness that 17 years to design, build and commission a new class of SSBN – particularly one that is required to be substantially cheaper to support – is a stern challenge.[197]

This ingrained feeling that things must necessarily take a long time – *"You cannot take even one day out of a programme schedule without importing unacceptable risk"*, as one senior official put it to me a while ago – will need a great deal of leadership to overcome. And this ingrained feeling must now be getting worse with the recent practice of not setting an ISD until Main Gate and withholding escalating cost detail (e.g. Typhoon) so as to apparently minimise the bad news. If there is no ISD, there can be no delay. If costs are withheld, no one can prove cost overruns.

With the faults bulleted above, it is hardly surprising that many people see MoD as incapable of effectively supporting the Armed Forces, particularly when they are involved in major operations.

> 'Admiral's logic' should trump 'accountants' logic'. That is not to deny the value of accountants' logic; merely to demand that it be kept in its proper, subordinate place. This goes to the heart of the dysfunctionality of the contemporary MoD. As its behaviour over the current Afghan operations in its generally inept support

---

[197] Gavin Ireland, 'Beyond Artful: Government and Industry Roles in Britain's Future Submarine Design, Build and Support', *RUSI Whitehall Report* 3–07, page 15, 2007

of General Richards' campaign plan of 2006 has publicly shown, it is at war employing a peacetime (accountants') mentality.[198]

But how are we to account for the difference in culture between UOR procurement and 'normal' procurement? The NAO lists the following as characteristic of UOR culture and processes:

- UORs are driven by the dynamic interaction of individuals helping multiple activities to be progressed concurrently.

> How are we to account for the difference in culture between UOR procurement and 'normal' procurement?

- The people involved in the UOR process are highly committed to making it deliver.
- MoD is flexible in the techniques it uses to source UORs (innovative solutions, commercial off-the-shelf, military off-the-shelf, accelerated programmes, leasing).[199]

Why can't 'normal' procurement be driven by dynamic interaction, concurrent activities, high commitment and flexibility? Is it because that's 'not the way MoD does it'?

In industry, and to a much smaller extent in MoD, there is another problem.

> *The biggest cultural issue is addressing the human frailty that believes that information is power. The more you do things jointly – joint teams, collocation and so on – you create an atmosphere where everyone wants to share data.*[200]

The problem of course is not just an industrial one, but one that exists between MoD and industry and has to be solved if we are going to have satisfactory partnering arrangements.

So what needs to be done? First of all we need strong and consistent leadership, and this has been acknowledged by the PUS, Bill Jeffrey.[201]

---

[198] Sir Jeremy Blackham and Professor Gwyn Prins, 'The Royal Navy at the Brink', *RUSI Journal* (Volume 152, No. 2, April 2007), page 12.
[199] National Audit Office, '*The Rapid Procurement of Capability to Support Operations*', HC 1161 Session 2003–2004, The Stationery Office, London, 19 November 2004.
[200] Ian King, Interview, *RUSI Defence Systems* (Volume 9, No. 1, June 2006), page 12.
[201] Bill Jeffrey, 'Implementing the Defence Industrial Strategy', *RUSI Defence Systems* (Volume 9, No. 2, October 2006), page 23.

Addressing the Cultural Problems

Smart Procurement made much about changing culture, but the section on People and 'Smart Procurement' in the first edition of *The Acquisition Handbook* was almost totally about the structures and processes for managing staff – it was not about changing culture. The same was true of later editions, although Edition 4 (January 2002) laid down five 'building blocks' for performance management:

- A bold aspiration, to stretch and motivate the organisation.
- A coherent set of performance measures, and a demanding set of targets based on these, to translate this aspiration into a set of specific metrics against which performance and progress can be measured.
- Clear accountability for these targets at an appropriate level within the organisation so that individuals who are best placed to ensure their delivery have real ownership for doing so.
- A rigorous performance review process to ensure that continuously improving performance is being delivered in line with expectations.
- Meaningful reinforcements and incentives to motivate individuals to deliver the targeted performance.

> Clear accountability and metrics against which progress can be measured are most obviously missing

Smart Procurement delivered only bits of the above. In particular, clear accountability and metrics against which progress can be measured are most obviously missing.

DIS Recommendations

As already discussed, DIS and the subsequent DACP are very light on culture change. Not only that, but what direction they give does not seem to have been accorded a great deal of priority.

However, a few months before DIS was published, the NAO produced a report on delivering major projects successfully. It defined a 'gold standard' against which projects should be judged. This 'gold standard' for establishing and sustaining the right cultural environment is as follows:[202]

---

[202] National Audit Office, *Driving the Successful Delivery of Major Defence Projects: Effective Project Control is a Key Factor in Successful Projects*, HC 30 2005/06, The Stationery Office, London, 20 May 2005.

- Open, trusting and honest relationships between client, prime contractor and supply chain:
  - ➢ Explicit 'no surprises/no blame' culture (defined as not penalising staff for bringing potential problems to light early) between all parties.
  - ➢ Regular and timely discussion of all matters that affect the project with no no-go areas.
  - ➢ Mutual benefits through shared ownership of end product or outcome between all parties.
  - ➢ Clarity of purpose and common understanding at all levels throughout all organisations.
  - ➢ Agreements between the parties to undertake a project as a partnership or alliance.
- Measurement of client–contractor relationships:
  - ➢ Regular independent assessments of client-contractor relationships as these develop during a project.
- Supportive and open corporate environment:
  - ➢ Explicit no surprises/no blame culture (defined as not penalising staff for bringing potential problems to light early) on the project and within the wider project organisation.
  - ➢ Clear information requirements with clear purpose.
  - ➢ Clear boundaries of authority and action.
  - ➢ Clear link between corporate and project governance.

It is surprising that so few of these have found their way into DIS culture. Without clarity of purpose, common understanding, clear information requirements and clear boundaries of authority, project control will be ineffective and, more importantly, decision-making both within the project and by those outside, will be less than coherent.

Decision-Making

As we have seen, the time taken in making decisions lies at the heart of the unacceptably long procurement cycles in major programmes.

> *It then took a further nine months to get approval for this new way forward. This time was consumed by discussions within the Department prior to approval by its Investment Approvals Board, followed by discussions with the Treasury because*

the adjustment required their approval. The Department recognises that its decision-making processes are more complicated than they need to be and is looking at its internal approvals process to slim down the layers of consideration, whilst retaining the due diligence that is needed to spend taxpayers' money sensibly.[203]

However, neither DIS nor EAC specifically recommended slimming down the layers of consideration, nor did they look at the time taken in discussions with the Treasury. This could be inferred perhaps from some of the wording on agility, but that is hardly a strong basis for action, which is surely needed to break through the inertia in the system.

This is a far cry from what Smart Procurement envisaged – where an individual becomes accountable for delivering a project and is given authority to do so; makes decisions and implements them, manages his team and motivates them; thinks radically about trade-offs within given parameters; and finally delivers. Although implementation of such a vision was begun, it never made enough progress. It was apparently 'all too difficult'. But is it? The BP's Andrew Platform integrated management team:

Sought to create an environment which encouraged people to come forward with ideas and question proposals in the knowledge that there would be no adverse reaction, no threat to their security on the team. As people realised they were able to behave openly and that Andrew was not constrained by traditional client-contractor hierarchies, their desire to communicate came to the fore – contribution was their ticket, their entitlement to be on the team. This led to a sense of shared ownership of the project which fired their enthusiasm to participate even more. A culture soon developed where people set their own targets and then sought ways to improve on them still further; once success followed, it became a habit.[204]

> But maybe – just maybe – it was professional pride at achieving the very difficult

There is massive motivation at work here. Maybe it is the thought of large bonuses from delivering on or below time and budget. But maybe – just maybe – it was professional pride at achieving, if not the impossible, the very difficult. Not a far cry from the esprit de corps that exists in a

---

[203] House of Commons Committee of Public Accounts, *Delivering Digital Tactical Communications through the Bowman CIP Programme*, Fourteenth Report of Session 2006–07, HC 358, 8 March 2007, page 8.

[204] Terry Knott, *No Business As Usual, an Extraordinary North Sea Result*, 1996.

good military unit.

> *Decision-making should be faster, the 'Whitehall delay mentality' could be bypassed and much of the culture (but clearly not all) of UOR delivery could be adopted. Mission Command should become the order of the day: tell leaders and managers what they have to do, let them get on with it, measure their results and hold them accountable.*[205]

Mission Command is, of course, alien to Whitehall's culture, but there is no clear reason why it should not work, although financial constraints and accountabilities, particularly of the PUS, would need particular consideration.

> *It is odd that the military profession should have such a clear understanding of this issue, but the ministry controlling the profession should have such difficulty applying it.*[206]

However, Mission Command requires a single accountable leader, but vague accountability in MoD is at the heart of the problem.

The RUSI Acquisition Focus considered[207] the difference between decision-making in MoD and in industry. It found the major differences to be:

> **Vague account-ability in MoD is at the heart of the problem**

- **Focus.** In industry this is clear – shareholder value. In MoD, the focus is less clear – is it benefit for the Armed Forces or value-for-money from the defence budget? Or benefit for UK plc or political issues? Nor is the focus clear on whether the priority is for current operations or longer-term, high-intensity warfighting.
- **Planning Chain.** In MoD the links between strategy and capability are weak, with no clear action plan or financial plan to achieve the strategy; whereas industrial companies maintain a clear strategy and from that develop an action plan, a long-

---

[205] RUSI Acquisition Focus, 'Implementing Through-Life Capability Management', *RUSI Defence Systems* (Volume 10, No. 1, June 2008), page 29.
[206] Ibid.
[207] RUSI Acquisition Focus, 'Decision-Making in MoD and Industry', *RUSI Defence Systems* (Volume 11, No. 2, October 2008).

term financial plan and a budget, with the executive team given considerable flexibility within them.

- **Refreshing the Plan.** Things change. In industry, plans are revisited regularly and changed when necessary. In MoD, plans and projects once agreed are stuck to rigidly and MoD regularly commits to what it cannot afford.
- **Politics.** Although industry is affected by political decisions, it has a free hand in how it reacts to them. MoD has less room for manoeuvre as decisions are subject to agreement by other Departments.
- **Continuity in Post.** Because the procurement cycle is so long, repeated changes in personnel in MoD dilutes accountability, whereas in industry accountable individuals are in post for much longer.
- **Data and Information.** Industry makes decisions on the basis of good data, which it turns into relevant information. MoD collects a mountain of data but little of it is turned into useful information. Moreover, this data is 'spun' too often.
- **Readiness to Take Decisions.** In Whitehall, the culture is not conducive to making timely decisions. In industry, decision-makers are much readier to make decisions because of the perception that time is money.

It concluded that, although there are many differences, MoD could usefully study the way that industry turns strategy into clear plans, updates them on an annual basis, makes timely decisions, achieves continuity in post, maintains a clear focus, changes things that are not working, collects relevant data and creates the necessary information with which to work.

The full paper is at Appendix 8–1.

Empowerment

Empowerment was another Smart Procurement theme, and it was successfully introduced, but only patchily. It was then progressively undermined so that by the time of DIS it had largely reverted to that in pre-Smart days, except perhaps in the ECC.

However, DIS is not clearly supportive of empowerment, nor is EAC, yet it is essential if decisions are to be made more quickly by those best placed to make them.

> *Although IPT leaders and DECs were 'empowered' under Smart Acquisition, it is only a partial empowerment because they cannot make any of the essential decisions as these have to be referred up the management chain or to committees – there is excessive commitment to 'process'. Empowerment is clearly the way to go, but the terms of delegated powers are not sophisticated enough.*[208]

There are two main difficulties – one imagined, one real. The imagined one is the old chestnut of due diligence. Imagined because all the time lost by the scrutiny, the discussions with all and sundry and the briefing up and questions back down actually cost more than the possible savings. Time really is money – even in Whitehall.

The real problem is a little more difficult: empowerment creates stovepipes. An IPT Leader, with empowerment and difficult targets to meet, is not likely to look beyond his own programme(s) when he makes decisions. And these decisions could well have adverse effects on other programmes – everything is networked now. Programmes have become more and more complex because they have to interface with a large number of other development programmes and in-service platforms – Bowman is a good example. This has been happening over the last few years to the detriment of acquisition coherence and subsystem and component commonality. Competition, too, has had the same effect. However, if someone above the IPT Leaders, such as a 2-star DG, interferes in such decisions, does this not limit empowerment? So, can empowerment of individual IPT Leaders and DECs be made to work in this networked environment?

> Time really is money – even in Whitehall

The SRO has a role to play here, but he will not necessarily be sighted on all other programmes that could be affected by one of the IPT Leaders in his capability area, although he may well be able to anticipate such effects. In addition, he sits in the ECC area and would need to be careful as to how he plays his part. And, crucially, he lacks the financial authority that he would need to overrule an IPT Leader.

So, stovepipes are a bad thing, and empowerment is a good thing, but they are difficult bedfellows. It should not, however, be beyond the ability of MoD to solve. Perhaps 'Mission Command' is the word.

---

[208] RUSI Acquisition Focus, 'Why Does It All Take So Long?', *RUSI Defence Systems* (Volume 10, No. 1, June 2007), page 34.

Mission Command would seem to have been at least partially adopted as the way to do business in ECC, but even here DECs do not have real control over what they are doing as they do not have control over cuts and delays imposed each year in the planning rounds, although they do have much greater influence than a decade ago. But ECC is a largely military organisation, and its staff are used to operating Mission Command. But even if Mission Command was successfully implemented throughout the acquisition community, the workers at the coalface would still be bound by the culture above.

Two aspects of culture that do need to be changed at the top are attitudes to risk and innovation.

Risk Aversion

MoD is generally perceived as risk-averse. DIS has little to say about risk, but in the section on Defence Values for Acquisition, it states:

> *In delivering this Vision in Acquisition, we all must quantify risk and reduce it by placing it where it can be managed most effectively.*[209]

> Risk can always be reduced further with further work, but this also carries a cost

The emphasis here is on quantifying and reducing risk – two good things to do as risk carries both cost and time penalties. However, there is a line below which it may not be cost-effective to go. Risk can always be reduced further with further work, but this also carries a cost. Where is that line? Who draws it?

Ministers and senior officials do not generally feel comfortable with risk. The lower it is, the better, would be their feeling. But this is not necessarily the right answer. Reducing risk further takes time, and time is money. And time also places lives at risk.

> *It is interesting to note that the difficulties with risk and decision-making within the procurement process are in dramatic contrast to the ethos of the military customer, which is to take risks and make decisions, and that of the industrial supplier base, which also has to take risks and [make] decisions in order to remain competitive ... It is apparent that far too often [MoD] decisions are based upon risk avoidance, rather than risk management. Considering why this is so*

---

[209] DIS, page 132.

> *highlights that there are few incentives to do otherwise, as for many staff there is a perceived personal and professional risk to making decisions ... MoD sometimes attempts to 'buy-off' the risk by passing it to industry. However, that has proved to be of limited effectiveness, very expensive, and has undoubtedly resulted in longer timescales.*[210]

And, as I have discussed earlier, the ultimate risk is borne by the front-line serviceman.

Rick Hussey also makes the point that reducing risk piecemeal may be inefficient and that *"the overall global risk may be less by introducing a less than perfect capability early"*. This, of course, links back to the importance of incremental acquisition and technology insertion.

It also links into the UOR process. UORs are developed and delivered extremely quickly, and the need to take greater, but reasonable, risk in doing so is accepted. Yet how much greater is that risk? The vast majority of delivered UORs work well enough, are safe to use and easy to train on and operate. So, where is the evidence of increased risk? Cost? Maybe, but it is difficult to equate the cost of a quick buy off-the-shelf with a much slower development, even if each was as operationally effective as the other.

No, the real risks lie in the constraints in the UOR process – short-term support and the need for the MoD to buy back UORs from the Treasury to take into the core programme after the first year or two – this might have made sense for the Falklands or the First Gulf War, but for persistent operations in Iraq and Afghanistan it does not. There is also the risk in the reduction of interoperability and equipment coherence. But have we a good record here with 'normal' procurement? I think not.

> We have only to look at many projects to see that risk has not been managed properly

For 'normal' procurement, we have only to look at many projects to see that risk has not been managed properly, that delays have been frequent and often needless, while costs have soared. I have already mentioned Bowman, but what about the following?

- The eight Chinook helicopters which sat in a hangar for eight

---

[210] Rick Hussey, 'Are Programme Delays and Overruns Caused by MoD's Approach to Risk Management?', *RUSI Defence Systems* (Volume 10, No. 1, June 2007), pages 20/21.

years after software changes costing millions had made them virtually unflyable.

- The long delays and huge cost overruns in the Astute and the Nimrod programmes as technical risks were not reduced early enough.
- The lack of progress in Combat Identification after it had been declared a top priority in the wake of the First Gulf War in 1991. More than a decade later the Committee of Public Accounts stated that, *"It is unsatisfactory that the Department has made such slow progress ..."*, and in 2006, the NAO recommended that MoD should develop a strategy.[211] [No strategy after 15 years?]
- The 30-year prevarication over replacements for the FV430 and CVR series of armoured vehicles and the continuing delay to the latest incarnation, FRES.
- Apache, where the remaining risks shortly before ISD, not least in the non-equipment DLoDs, were extensive and detailed in the NAO report of 2002.[212]
- Delays so far of more than 3 years to the ISD of A400M, more than 8 years to BVRAAM (Meteor), over 3 years on NLAW and over 4 years to the Type 45 Destroyer – all measured from Initial Gate.
- The large growth in assessment phase costs since Initial Gate: CVF +153%; FRES +447%; FSTA +185%; IFPA +179%; SAR Helicopter 1100%. The MARS figures are not given. Of the 10 Assessment Phase projects in the NAO MPR 2007, only two are within the approved cost. Much of the cost increase is due to incomplete assessment phase scoping.

It could be said that many of these had their roots way back, but certainly not all. The fact remains that 'normal' procurement throws up plenty of examples where risk has not been properly quantified or managed. So much for the much-trumpeted Whitehall excuse of ensuring taxpayers' money is spent prudently.

I see no obviously greater risk in delivering UORs, but I do see

[211] National Audit Office, *Progress in Combat Identification*, HC 936, 2005/06, 3 March 2006, The Stationery Office, London.
[212] National Audit Office, *Building an Air Manoeuvre Capability*, HC 1246, 2001/02, 31 October 2002, The Stationery Office, London.

reduced timescales, leading to cost savings, and a saving of lives. So, if this is correct, why is there such a cultural difference in attitude to risk between UOR and 'normal' procurement?

It is not only in MoD, but in industry too, that the aversion to risk exists.

> *We have got a risk-averse culture within our sector. Not for one minute am I suggesting cutting corners on such fundamental issues as safety, but the testing and validation regimes that we subject our systems to may need to be challenged.*[213]

So, MoD and primes are risk-averse. SMEs would claim that they are not, but are forced by the big boys to eschew risk. And it is SMEs who are the key innovators:[214]

> *SMEs are perfectly placed to deliver the innovation and evolve ideas into products or system designs. With the appropriate intellectual stock and the right environmental conditions, it is relatively cheap, via SMEs, to achieve a maturity of TRL 4 or 5 and establish a 'technology bank'.*[215]

Innovation Reluctance

Another high-level cultural barrier to cost-effective procurement is a reluctance to embrace innovation, and to equate innovation with risk. Innovation and its importance is discussed in Chapter Nine.

However, equating innovation with risk by a risk-averse MoD is a cultural issue and if we are to embrace innovation as we must, then this is a cultural change that must be made.

Target Setting

Decision-making should be objective and balance the long-term effects of that decision with the effects in the shorter term. The target-setting culture pursued so enthusiastically by the Labour governments over the last ten years makes that very difficult. Targets are usually expressed in the short term and managers are well aware that their performance will be judged very largely on whether those targets are met or not. It is

---

[213] Guy Griffiths, Interview, *RUSI Defence Systems* (Volume 10, No. 1, June 2007), page 15.
[214] See Chapter Five.
[215] Chris Trout, BMT Defence Services, 'Operational Sovereignty and the Role of SMEs', *RUSI Defence Systems* (Volume 11, No. 2, October 2008).

significant that several police forces have decided to ignore targets, scrap the paperwork and concentrate on effective police work.

MoD is different, however. While hospital trusts that fail to meet targets find themselves falling down the league tables and/or get fined, IPT Leaders who fail to meet targets do not get fined, nor do they find themselves at the bottom of a league table. Even if this was tried, it would be easy to argue that new problems have their root in decisions made by others over the years. FRES? Bowman? The Chinook debacle?

So, target-setting in MoD dos not seem to achieve much. So why do it?

> Target-setting in MoD dos not seem to achieve much. So why do it?

The answer is because it gives the impression of control. Maybe it would act as a control mechanism if, firstly, the targets set were demanding but not so demanding that all efforts go into trying to achieve targets, which may be out of reach, at the expense of other vital activities.

This raises the question of who should set targets. We know that the 'Conspiracy of Optimism' makes cost overruns and delays almost certain, so cost and time targets are likely to be impossible to meet without reducing performance and/or numbers to a significant degree. Who knows how much optimism remains?

It is also clear that the target-setter needs to have a detailed knowledge of the project if he is to set reasonable targets of cost, time and performance. That means the IPT Leader or his boss. Both will have a vested interest in meeting them, so they will be set low – the fact that they are so often missed shows how difficult targets are to set. Once set, officials and politicians all the way up the chain want to see them met. Does a politician really want to see improvement, or would he rather stand up and claim targets are being met?

> *If 'failure' is synonymous with missed targets, it will generate a culture in which targets are set too low (to ensure 'success') and in which results are massaged for presentation to superiors and the public. In such a world, it is deemed better to achieve a 6% improvement against a 5% target than to make a 12% improvement against a 15% target. Badly set targets and fear of failure to meet them are counter-productive.[216]*

---

[216] Bill Kincaid, *Dinosaur in Permafrost* (TheSauras Ltd, 2002), page 58.

> *So many, particularly politicians, do not know their job and spend an inordinate amount of effort and resources – cash, to you and me – on consultants, surveys and advice from interest and pressure groups. The puritanical obsession with league tables, audits, performance indicators, targets and other statistics, as part of centralised and financial control, is delaying decision-making and stifling progress ... any company or organisation that continually demands data, hoards information, keeps records and statistics and sets targets is showing weakness and distrust in its employees ...[217]*

Setting targets is very difficult in defence acquisition. No one is sacked or fined when they are not met. So what is the point? Motivation by pressure or leadership by numbers? Whatever it is, it is not working.

Burying Bad News

We are all well aware of the tactic favoured by politicians and others of burying bad news by letting it out when some very big story breaks or when Parliament is in recess. Dubious ethics, perhaps, but not exactly a lie.

What is a lie is the manipulation of figures in reports or answers to questions so as to give a false impression of the Government's progress. No doubt it has always been done, but surely never as much as over the last decade. Year after year the headlines in Part 1 of the MoD Major Project Reports (which is all most people read) give a far more optimistic account (a new meaning for creative accounting?) than the detailed figures in Part 2.[218] But even here it does not give the whole story.

	ISD at Initial Gate	Forecast ISD Now	Total Delay	Delay Recorded in NAO Report
Type 45	Dec 2002	Nov 2010	95 months	25 months
NLAW	Jun 2005	July 2008	37 months	0 months
BVRAAM	Mar 2005	Aug 2013	101 months	12 months
A400M	Dec 2007	Mar 2011	39 months	15 months

Figure 8–1: Difference between MoD Figures and Reality
Source: National Audit Office, MoD: Major Project Report 2006

---

[217] Kenneth Armitage, letter to *The Times*, 27 February 2008.

[218] It must be emphasised that the Major Project Reports are MoD reports to Parliament which the NAO can only analyse and draw attention to, but cannot alter the base data. So criticism of some of the more 'creative' aspects of the figures must be directed at MoD and not NAO.

All these programmes are 'Smart' – that is, they hit Initial Gate after the Smart Procurement Initiative had been introduced and do not therefore carry a lot of baggage from the 'bad old days'.

The figures in the report are actually correct, but a lot has been left out – for example, the MoD report only measures delay from the last major submission (e.g. Main Gate) rather than for the whole project. If a lie is the intention to mislead, then the figures are a lie.

This is not an isolated example. Right across government, figures are massaged to present achievement as better than it is, and shortfalls as less important than they are. This culture of deception – or lying[219] – is so pervasive that it is now done without much thought. How else can we explain the crude reduction in cost overruns in the same report already discussed? Someone had the idea of moving certain expenditure from procurement to other budgets in the MoD and calling them procurement 'savings', thus reducing both the overall 'expenditure' and the cost increases. Of course, there was no saving in the overall defence budget.

> If a lie is the intention to mislead, then the figures are a lie

What a wheeze! It'll make things look better, won't it? No one will notice.

Well, they do notice because the deception is so transparent. It seems some people cannot do deception sensibly.

> The headline figure from the MoD [in the MPR 2007] suggests that the total in-year cost increase for its nineteen largest projects was £43M, which is a minute fraction of the total fraction of the total budgeted cost of these projects and appears to be a creditable performance. However, the figure of £43M was only achieved after subtracting £609M, representing funds transferred to a different budget line … These transfers do not represent any savings to MoD and should have been excluded … Other spurious savings have been achieved by reducing the quantities of equipment being procured (e.g. fewer anti-aircraft missiles for the Royal Navy's new Type 45 destroyers) by reducing the specification of equipment (e.g. deleting a communications system originally required for the A400M transport aircraft) and by delaying the delivery of some other equipment.[220]

---

[219] Collins English Dictionary defines 'lie' as 'an untrue or deceptive statement deliberately used to mislead'.
[220] David Kirkpatrick, 'More Spurious Savings by the MoD', *Newsbrief* (Volume 28, No. 1, January 2008), RUSI, page 3.

Add this to the previous year's manipulations when the MoD report showed an in-year **saving** on the top 19 projects of £781M, when there was an **increase** of £667M – a difference of over £1.5Bn between figures produced by MoD and reality.

The DIS's move to strategic partnering is dependent on, amongst other things, trust and transparency. What hope is there for success, then, if everyone knows that MoD doctors its figures?

Learning from Experience

We are very bad at learning lessons. Oh yes, we **identify lessons** well and often, but there is no culture of **learning lessons** so that their fruit can be applied next time around, which might be next year, next decade or later. We keep reinventing the wheel, occasionally coming up with a square one.

Lessons remain in the brains of individuals and as soon as the turnover of staff is complete, those identified lessons cease to be known. After the Iraq war in 2003, I was told by the Tank Support IPT that they found it impossible to access any information, relevant to them, about the the First Gulf War. I asked how they solved the problem. He told me that he was fortunate to have a major who had been a tank commander in the the First Gulf War – the relevant information was still in that officer's head. Whether that information existed anywhere except in the brains of those involved 12 years before is not clear. What is clear is that it was not easily accessible.

We have never learned lessons properly, so we have no culture of using past experience as a help in making decisions. Staffs tend to use their own experience which may or may not be relevant. Too many people 'know best' when clearly they don't.

> We have never learned lessons properly

There is a problem in industry as well. As gaps between procurement orders grow ever wider, and production runs continue to reduce, fewer and fewer people will have the experience of last time around. Can a 20- or 30-year gap between major builds, filled only with technology insertion, be efficiently managed without a better system of identifying lessons and making them accessible many years hence?

We are in danger of forgetting increasingly more lessons that we should have learned but haven't. This may be a procedural issue – how, where and when to learn and store lessons, but if the culture is not there, it won't happen.

Smart People

Smart Acquisition laid much emphasis on producing Smart People, although it largely failed to achieve much improvement. MoD has a lot of smart people, but it also has many more who are less than smart (for various reasons) and some that are not smart at all. Are the smart ones adequately rewarded? Are the less-than-smart given the push? Are high-quality people recruited? Probably not.

> MoD needs leaders at all levels, but it must let them lead

MoD needs leaders at all levels, but it must let them lead. Leaders and followers must have the right skills. All need to be motivated. We know from the UOR process that there are leaders and staff with the right skills and motivation.

Leadership

Leadership is an area where the Armed Forces excel. It is surprising, then, that officers, in particular many senior officers, seem to shed their leadership credentials once they pass through the portals of the Main Building or Abbey Wood. Is it because so many are not experienced in MoD ways and find themselves outgunned by civil servants who have lived in the Whitehall environment for many, many years? Is it because they are mindful of their next job and fear to make waves? Or is it because leadership is clearly discouraged in the MoD? Probably a bit of all three, but the last may be the most powerful of those reasons.

> *Leadership is not generally conspicuous in either MoD or industry. Without a high standard of leadership, motivation, determination, a sense of urgency and pride in achieving the necessary quality in the necessary time frame are unlikely to be much in evidence. Leadership is a complex quality: it is not just an ability to motivate others and imbue them with determination, but it demands an expert understanding of the job and the seasoned expertise that goes with it. Do we have such people?[221]*

---

[221] RUSI Acquisition Focus, 'Why Does It All Take So Long?', *RUSI Defence Systems* (Volume 10, No. 1, June 2007), pages 34–35.

The answer to this is a qualified yes. And the evidence is the way in which UORs are articulated, met and delivered, for leadership is widely visible in this process both in MoD and industry. So, if leadership qualities abound during the UOR process, why is it markedly lacking in 'normal procurement'? There can only be one answer – it is discouraged by the culture and processes in MoD, and in industry, too.

I said that the answer was a qualified yes. There are good leaders in the acquisition community, but also plenty who are not – whether through the lack of personal qualities or because they are marking time and want a quiet life. What is the proportion? I don't know, but I would suspect more than half. This would not be surprising as acquisition posts are not often filled with the best officers or officials – acquisition is seen as near the bottom of the barrel. Until an IPT Leader's job is seen as more attractive

> There are good leaders in the acquisition community, but also plenty who are not

than that of a Military Assistant (MA) to a 4-star general, it is unlikely to change. The MA is selected with an eye on his early promotion towards a 4-star general in due course, while the IPT leader is thrown into a much more difficult job with less likelihood of promotion however well he does. Is this the same with civil servants?

Acquisition Skills

Lord Drayson was clear that people counted, and not just in MoD:

> ... it's people who make the difference. For example, from industry Guy Griffiths at MBDA and Alan Johnston at AgustaWestland have shown an ability to lead their sectors and to act as personal examples of the behaviours and willingness to transform that we need to see across the whole industrial base. In other parts of industry we have a way to go.[222]

In MoD there is also a variable mix:

> Our best project managers stand comparison with any in the public or private sector – but we need more of them, and we need to develop a self-confident cadre of acquisition specialists in the Department. That will require both a

---

[222] Lord Drayson, 'The Defence Industrial Strategy: Our Relationship with Industry', *RUSI Defence Systems* (Volume 9, No. 2, October 2006), page 21.

concentrated effort to grow our own and a readiness to bring in capable people from outside.[223]

Yes, the best are good. Bill Jeffrey's analysis above is a little more optimistic than that of the then Chief of Defence Procurement's in 2004, which was that poor performance in the then Defence Procurement Agency was endemic. Did this judgement show a decline in performance from earlier decades?

> *There is no substitute in acquisition for having skilled individuals with real experience. It is noticeable that over the years the level of expertise of the MoD practitioners has declined. In the 1970s and 1980s, many of the senior officials in the procurement executive had had experience on a number of key programmes, and were familiar with the challenges of development, production investment and production launches. This did give them a modicum of understanding of the challenges being faced by the contractors. In addition they did have sufficient empowerment to exercise the flexibility needed to manage difficult high-technology development programmes. Despite more recent claims to have 'empowered' individual project managers, my observation would be that MoD is now less flexible, and project managers less empowered, than they had been traditionally.*[224]

Poor performance can be caused by several things – in combination or even singly. Even those with high personal qualities will struggle (at least for longer than they might) if they lack the necessary expertise and experience. Experience is vital and the practice over the last decade or so of moving people from sector to sector does not help. It may give the individual greater width of experience, but it is unlikely to give him the depth that he will need to evaluate properly advice from his subordinates or from industry, or to press a course of action with his superiors.

Anyone in a new job takes time to find his feet – the better his personal qualities, the quicker he will be up and running. Even someone with lesser qualities, however, will be coping with his new job if it is an area where he has already had experience. But in such favourable circumstances how long will it take an average person to give of his best? Three months? Six months? Longer? It will of course depend on the individual, his new job, his relevant experience and his current expertise.

---

[223] Bill Jeffrey, 'Implementing the Defence Industrial Strategy', *RUSI Defence Systems* (Volume 9, No. 2, October 2006), page 23.

[224] John Weston, email to the author, 11 September 2008.

Let us say four months, although I would say this was on the low side except for the very best. Many tenures are two or three years in post, although recently they have tended to be longer. Let us say three years. For the last few months, he may well be looking towards his next job, particularly if he has a chance of going to it on promotion.

So, if we take away the first four months and the last four months from a tenure of three years, he will only be fully effective for about 78% of his time. If he is moved after only two years (as many of those up for promotion are), this proportion drops to 67%. On the other hand, if his tenure is for four years, the proportion will increase to over 83%.

> *Upon one thing, all can agree. This is that, when the acquisition phases of major projects last for 20 years or more, it must be detrimental to their management that leaders of project teams remain in post for a mere three years upon average. That can only exacerbate the tendency for their conduct of the project to be judged not upon the achievement of value-for-money in the items eventually procured, but upon much shorter-term criteria. When a project has six, seven or more leaders before its success or failure is properly known, credit or blame for that outcome attaches to none of them. For each, 'success' comes to mean getting the project past whatever review point falls within their brief tenure.*[225]

Specialising within sectors and staying in post for longer will give individuals the right experience, and the right experience will furnish the right expertise. But this is more process than culture. DIS, as I have pointed out already, said very little about culture and people – and EAC even less – but it did cover the question of acquisition skills:

> The right experience, and the right experience will furnish the right expertise

> *Learning the requisite behaviours and skills, as well as other professional procurement competencies, takes time and experience ... We are committed to retraining and developing our people to develop the competencies required ... We recognise that in the short term we may not be able to find internally all the individuals we require who have or can quickly develop the requisite skills and experience, and would therefore need to recruit externally.*[226]

---

[225] Philip Pugh, 'Delusions of Management', *RUSI Defence Systems* (Vol. 9, No. 3, February 2007), page 65.
[226] DIS, page 133.

So, what are these skills and competencies that are needed?

Neither DIS nor EAC pinpointed them. It can be inferred that MoD didn't know, as one aim of the Project Delivery Skills Strategy was to identify the gaps. But if we look back 20 years or more at the skills MoD had then, but doesn't have now, we might produce a list something like this:

- Technical costing.
- Expertise in technologies and systems.
- Industrial knowledge and understanding.
- Intelligent customer status in all technical and programme areas.
- Experience of project and programme management.
- Leadership.

To this list should be added commercial (rather than just contractual) skills.

This list is no doubt incomplete. However, it shows two things quite clearly. First, it points to the paucity of skills in the MoD acquisition community today; second, it reveals the huge task that MoD faces in upskilling its people. It is neither a trivial nor a straightforward problem.

> How much can industry, in the form of the 'customer's friend' or 'system of systems integrator' provide?

Another question raises its head. Given that upskilling to the level of, say, a couple of decades ago is a major challenge, how far do we need to go? How much can industry, in the form of the 'customer's friend' or 'system of systems integrator' provide? How far should MoD allow itself to lean on industry? Is it cheaper to employ industry to provide those skills for each and every project than to upskill the MoD acquisition workforce?

These are difficult questions to answer, but answered they must be. My initial thought is that all the above capabilities are needed by MoD, but perhaps not to the extent that has been the case in the past. Some dependence on industry may be sensible and may be the cost-effective option, but the customer must understand what its advisers are doing.

Training

Unlike culture, there is a relatively long passage on professional delivery skills in the 'Taking Forward the DIS' section.

> *The Acquisition Leadership Development Scheme is key to achieving [competence] and provides a clear career anchor and development structure for acquisition professionals. There are currently some 664 members. Senior leaders in their respective professional fields have been identified as development partners to: determine the future skills need; develop and advise on career paths; and inspire individuals to acquire the skills the acquisition community requires.*[227]

The passage then goes on to other current training initiatives, including the MSc in Defence Acquisition Management at the Defence Academy, the Business Graduate Development Scheme and graduate recruitment schemes. It also describes the Civilian Workforce Plan under which the MoD will:

- Address shortages in project delivery skills.
- Improve recruitment, reward and recognition practices.
- Make increased professional accreditation schemes.
- Improve the science and technology skills base.
- Increase the investment in systems engineering.
- Place greater emphasis on staff continuity.

DIS then goes on to say that MoD will also work closely with industry in developing acquisition skills and professionalism, and will explore alternative models for independent project management of major projects, with two pilot schemes.

Some of this was set in place in the Smart Procurement Initiative (e.g. the Acquisition Leadership Development Scheme (ALDS)), but most has been set up during the implementation of DIS.

The EAC, although it acknowledged that it did not focus on culture, behaviours, skills and training, nevertheless recommended that MoD should:

- Reinforce the message at every level of the acquisition system that improved skills are key to improving MoD's TLCM performance.
- Ensure that the skills agenda is given prominence in the programme of implementing the changes recommended elsewhere in this [EAC] report.

---

[227] DIS, page 139.

The Defence Academy was given the responsibility for delivering the training and education required. This is being implemented by the Defence Acquisition Management Education Programme (DAMEP), which is shown at Figure 8–1, and is described in some detail by Commander Stuart Young in a RUSI Defence Systems article.[228] He says that within the DE&S,

> Allocation of time to continuing professional development is mandated. Ultimately, though, it will depend on the recognition by staff of the value of personal development, training and education, both for themselves and for all members of their organisation.

This last sentence is of great importance because many staff, particularly at the lower levels, will need to be motivated if training and education is to achieve the necessary effect.

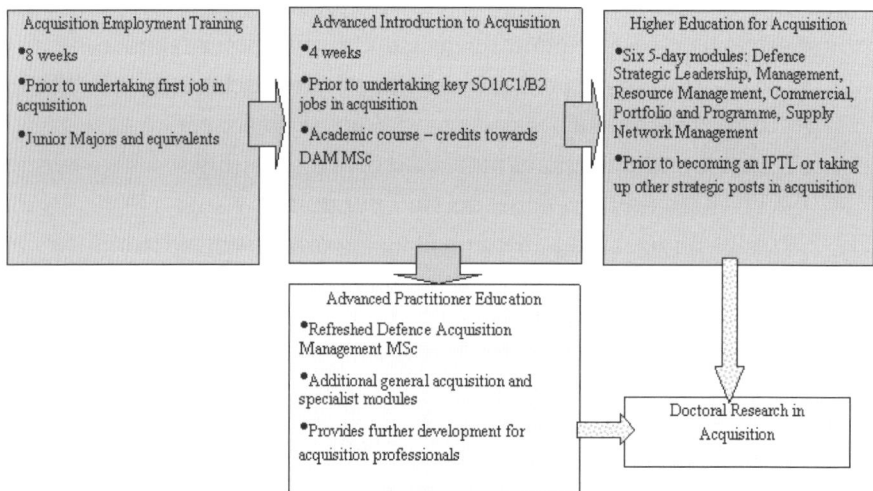

Figure 8–1: The Defence Acquisition Management Education Programme
Source: Cdr Stuart Young, The Defence Academy, RUSI Defence Systems, Vol. 10, No. 2, October 2007

---

[228] Commander Stuart Young, 'Defence Acquisition Change: Developing the Skills and Behaviours', *RUSI Defence Systems* (Volume 10, No. 2, October 2007), pages 75–77.

Pay and Rewards

Motivation of staff is primarily achieved by the personal qualities of the leader. The leader needs to lead by personality and example – he should only have to drive occasionally. 'Kick-ass' and the 'fear/blame culture' can be motivating to some extent, but they invariably have adverse effects, such as fear of making mistakes, risk aversion and the burying of bad news for as long as possible.

Motivation also depends on tangible rewards and recognition by senior managers. Those that work with industry, particularly those in DE&S, constantly see their opposite numbers gaining greater financial reward than they do – both in terms of salary and bonuses. This may have little effect on some, but most people when they start a family find it hard to make ends meet, and the short-term attraction of greater financial reward, rather than longer-term job security, may be too powerful to resist. It may also stop the inflow of recruits with both qualifications and experience. So, what happens? Many of the best will leave for industry, but most of the weak will stay and hope for a quiet life. Hardly the way to improve staff capabilities.

Smart Procurement proposed a special performance-related bonus scheme, with team and individual rewards, but this never really got off the ground to any meaningful extent as it achieved only a scale of reward between 0.2% and 0.4% of salary. Hardly an impressive amount.

More recently, MoD has announced that it will take a fresh look at the benefits and rewards structure to introduce a more performance-focused arrangement. But it is a difficult area. Pay, both military and civilian, is governed across a wider field than just DE&S and, perhaps more immediately important, any pay increase or rewards have to come out of the defence budget, which as we all know is highly overheated.

However, with the upskilling of the acquisition staff, will there not be a possibility to reduce the very large number of specialist advisors, consultants and systems houses that are employed at huge fees? And if we have to employ these large numbers, should we not be able to reduce the MoD's acquisition staff, whose job the consultants are doing? And if so, could not the savings made from such reductions be ring-fenced for increasing pay or rewards? And would higher pay not attract a higher grade of staff, who could work more effectively so that things are only done once? And would that not mean that more staff could be cut? There is a magic circle here which we should aim to break into.

Will we? Probably not, because of the two issues above, and a third that is threatening to become a major headache. With the increasing shortage of scientists and engineers coming out of our national education system, MoD is trying to recruit in the same inadequate pool as academia and industry – not just the defence industry, but the civil sector as well.

So, don't hold your breath about breaking into magic circles.

Changing Culture

It is widely agreed that changing culture is:

- Essential if delivery is to improve; changing organisations and processes without changing culture will achieve little.
- Difficult – far more so than reorganising or fiddling with process.
- A lengthy business – it is likely to take five to ten years rather than one or two.

MoD does not dispute any of the above. Indeed, the necessity of culture change has been clearly stated in both Smart Procurement and the DIS initiatives. I have already quoted what John Spellar, then Under Secretary of State for Defence Procurement, said in 1999, but it is worth repeating:

> The [Smart Procurement Initiative] will not succeed unless we change the culture and our people respond to the circumstances we create for them … we need to become more flexible, responsive and receptive to new ideas. We need to depend less on rulebooks or precedent and more on judgement and experience.[229]

Although he was writing nearly a decade ago, he could have been speaking today. Yes, acquisition change will not happen without culture change (bullet 1 above). He also said at a RUSI lecture that culture change might take more than five years (bullet 3 above).

But what about the difficulty (bullet 2 above)? It is not quite as clear what MoD thinks on this.

> Although there have been plenty of warm words, there has been little about implementing culture change

Although there have been plenty of warm words, there has been little about **implementing** culture change. The DIS White Paper lays

---

[229] John Spellar, *RUSI Journal* (Volume 144, No. 3, June 1999).

down Defence Values for Acquisition and some of these hover around the required new culture, but many of them can gain a 'tick in the box' through changes in process. It does, however, go on to say:

> We will **embed these values** for acquisition <u>in our partnering arrangements</u> through clear leadership at all levels ....[230]

Only in our partnering arrangements?

There is more on strategic partnering culture, and a significant section on skills and training. It also states that MoD will place real effort and priority on driving forward a programme of cultural and behavioural change to embed Defence Values for Acquisition and address shortages in project delivery skills.

We should not criticise DIS too much as it was written to a very tight timetable. What perhaps is disappointing is that the follow-on EAC study did not, and admitted that it did not, cover culture change.

The one really bright culture spot in DIS was the setting up of the two Pathfinder Programmes, one aim of which was culture change through setting the right values and behaviours.[231] These were outstandingly successful, but how was this culture change to be carried forward?

> The one really bright culture spot in DIS was the setting up of the two Pathfinder Programmes

Many of the problems discussed in this chapter have not been mentioned at all in DIS and its associated studies, much less identified how they might be overcome. How are we to deal with:

- Whitehall's 'delay mentality'?
- MoD's suppression of leadership?
- A culture of minimising the downside rather than maximising the upside?
- A mindset that is risk-averse and equates innovation with risk?
- The bad target culture?
- Spin-doctoring of figures which undermines trust and transparency?

---

[230] DIS, page 132.
[231] See Chapter Five.

- The clash between true empowerment and stovepipes?
- The repeated failure to learn, rather than just identify, lessons?
- The difficulty of recruiting, and retaining, high-quality staff?

No doubt there are many more.

It is, of course, perfectly possible for MoD to change its culture. We know this from examples in the civil sector, from the Pathfinder Programmes and, above all, from the UOR culture which has exhibited the answers to most of the above for several decades. Surely all we have to do is to find the way to import the best of the UOR culture into 'normal procurement'.

> **All we have to do is to find the way to import the best of the UOR culture into 'normal procurement'**

But, however we intend to change culture, it needs far more thought and dedication than MoD has given it in the wake of either Smart Procurement or DIS. Here is a US view:

> *How do you manage culture change? This is one of the most, if not the most, important questions to be answered and answered well. I don't think we do a good enough job here … You really do need a person on your staff whose full-time job is to manage change … When I say this, folks may nod their heads, but we aren't communicating. As I said it's a full-time job – not additional – a full-time job for someone who is experienced, educated and trained in this area called 'change management'.*[232]

How will we know when, or if, implementation of DIS has been successful in five or ten years' time?

> *This is not at all clear. The main reason for this is that the perception of the overall objective of the DIS may differ from one constituency to another. Is it to provide better for the Armed Forces? Or to achieve better value-for-money for the taxpayer – or for UK plc? Or is it to ensure the preservation of industrial capabilities onshore – or just to make the defence industry feel good? Maybe it is all of these, so measurement of success is complex.*[233]

And if measuring success overall is complex, how much more difficult is it to measure culture change as that is the most nebulous part of all?

---

[232] The Honourable Claude Bolton, Interview, *RUSI Defence Systems* (Volume 10, No. 2, October 2007), page 8.
[233] RUSI Acquisition Focus, 'Implementation of the Defence Industrial Strategy', *RUSI Defence Systems* (Volume 9, No. 2, October 2006), page 78.

It is perhaps worth repeating, from near the beginning of the chapter, Jeremy Blackham's three main points about culture change:

- It must be led from the top and the top man must show by his behaviour that he is committed to change.
- The top man must be prepared to change senior managers who do not 'join the party'.
- The top man must encourage initiative, innovation and new thinking at all levels, but especially amongst the lower levels where it most often can be found.

We will have to wait and see whether culture will be changed significantly and for good. If it is not, who do we blame? The top man, obviously. But which top man? Politician or official? And which of those, as they will all have changed in the five or more years it will take?

> No one to blame? Now there's a surprise

No one to blame? Now there's a surprise.

SUMMARY: CULTURE AND PEOPLE

DIS and EAC
- Both the Defence Industrial Strategy (DIS) and the Enabling Acquisition Change (EAC) study stated the importance of culture change.
- Neither DIS nor EAC tackled culture change adequately.

MoD Culture – Problems
- Poor leadership.
- Official encouragement of caution, emphasis on detail and avoidance of risk.
- Whitehall's delay mentality.
- A fear/blame culture.
- Concentration on the minimisation of the downside rather than the maximisation of the upside.
- Preoccupation with cost and a refusal to see the overall financial picture.
- A refusal to learn from experience.
- The difficulty in recruiting, and retaining, high-quality staff.

Change Management

- It must be led from the top and the top man must show by his behaviour that he is committed to change.
- He must be prepared to change senior managers who do not 'join the party'.
- He must encourage initiative, innovation and new thinking at all levels, but especially amongst the lower levels where it most often can be found.

Upskilling MoD Workforce – What Needs To Be Improved

- Technical costing.
- Expertise in technologies and systems.
- Industrial knowledge and understanding.
- Intelligent customer status in all technical and programme areas.
- Experience of project and programme management.
- Leadership.
- Commercial, rather than just contractual, skills.
- Reduction of external consultants etc., reduction of internal manpower, increase in pay.

Changing the Mindset at the Top

- Understand and be convinced that:
  - Delay is costly.
  - Innovation has attractions.
  - Strong leadership is essential.
  - Empowerment and Mission Command must be given priority.
  - Clear accountability is desperately needed.
  - Uncomfortable decisions should not be postponed.
  - Speed in decision-making will save money and reduce obsolescence.
  - Trust and transparency must be fostered.
  - A high quality workforce will be cheaper than retaining dead-beats.
  - Strategic partnerships with industry mean sharing both gain and pain.

Appendix 8–1

RUSI ACQUISITION FOCUS

DECISION-MAKING IN MoD AND INDUSTRY

*The members of the RUSI Acquisition Focus are: John Weston (Chairman),
Tim Banfield (NAO), Bob Barton (co-chair of the MoD/Industry Equipment
Capability Group), Vice Admiral (retd) Jeremy Blackham (recently EADS UK
President), John Dowdy (Director, McKinsey), Professor Christopher Elliott
(GD UK), Graham Jordan (formerly S&T Director, MoD), Gerry Paulus
(Managing Director, SVGC Ltd), Major General (retd) Bill Robins (formerly
DGICS, MoD), Professor Trevor Taylor (Head of Defence Management and
Security Analysis, Cranfield University), Bill Kincaid (Editor RUSI
Defence Systems)*[234]

SUMMARY

One of the biggest differences between MoD and industry lies in the
way decisions are made. It is often said that decision-making in the
former is slow and cumbersome compared with that in industry
but, if this is so, is it because of factors that cannot be altered or is
it because of a culture that can be changed? In this paper, the RUSI
Acquisition Focus examines seven key facets of decision-making.

Decision-Making Focus. In industry this is clear – shareholder
value. In MoD the focus is not sharp – is it the benefit for the Armed
Forces or value-for-money from the defence budget? Is it benefit for
UK plc or is it political issues? Moreover, MoD does not seem clear
as to whether the focus should be on current operations or on a very
unclear future.

The Planning Chain. We believe that MoD is generally good at
producing strategy but weak at turning this into the effective
delivery of equipment capability: the links between strategy and
capability are weak, broken or simply too long. As a result there is
no clear action plan or financial plan to achieve the strategy, nor to
adapt it. In contrast, industrial companies produce and maintain a
clear strategy and from that develop an action plan, a long-term
financial plan, and a budget. Once the budget is set and targets
given, the executive team is then given considerable flexibility.

---

[234] Names and posts of the members have in some case changed but were correct when
this paper was published.

Refreshing the Plan. Things change. In industry, plans will be revisited regularly and changed when necessary – commercial organisations that don't adapt, don't survive. In MoD, plans and projects once agreed are stuck to rigidly, often because the commercial and political implications of cancellation are too tough to confront. Making decisions to cancel programmes is politically unattractive and, as a result, MoD regularly commits to what it cannot afford.

Politics. Industry is affected by political decisions but has a free hand in how it reacts to them. MoD, on the other hand, has less room for manoeuvre – decisions are subject to agreement or veto by other Departments. In addition, some MoD 'tribes' have political profiles, whereas individual capability areas do not. While tribal politics exist in industry, the CEO has the power to manage them.

Continuity in Post. The procurement cycle is so long that repeated changes can only dilute any accountability initiatives that are established. This applies at every level within the MoD. In industry, accountable individuals are in post for much longer.

Data and Information. Industry in general terms makes decisions on the basis of good data, which it turns into relevant information. MoD collects a mountain of data but little of it is turned into useable information and, even more worrying, much of it is 'unknown'. Moreover, data is extensively manipulated for public consumption and there is still evidence to support the view that the 'conspiracy of optimism' is alive and well.

Readiness to Take Decisions. In Whitehall, the culture is not wholly conducive to making timely decisions – no one is ever sacked for postponing a decision or for following the rules. Nor are officials well rewarded for taking well-judged risks, and whose decisions may bring censure for getting it 'wrong'. The result is a leadership chain that lacks confidence. In industry, decision-makers are much readier to change course.

Conclusion. We believe that MoD could usefully study the way industry turns strategy into clear plans, updates them on an annual basis, makes timely decisions, achieves continuity in post, maintains a clear focus, changes things that are not working, collects relevant data and creates the necessary information with which to work.

MoD and industry are different: they have different goals, a different set of external influences and different cultures, particularly in the knowledge economy and similar fast-paced sectors. But there are also similarities: the major firms are similar to MoD in that both are large organisations with comparable global reach, are concerned with delivery and sustainment of complex equipment in the long and short terms, and in some cases are constrained by safeguards that are designed to ensure that public funds are spent wisely.

One of the biggest contrasts is in decision-making. It is often said that decision-making in MoD is too slow and cumbersome, and does not always come up with the right answers. People bemoan the fact that MoD does not behave more like industry in the way that decisions are taken and in the timeliness of those decisions. But is this a realistic criticism? In this paper, we compare seven facets of acquisition decision-making in MoD with those in industry, identify the differences in the business environment of each and suggest areas where MoD could benefit from incorporating industrial practices.

Decision-Making Focus

In industry, the decision-making focus is the benefit for shareholders both in the short term and, to a lesser extent, the longer term. The share price of a publicly quoted company gives a short-term reaction to the company's performance, effectively the product of the company's expected earnings for the current year, the P/E ratio, driven by the perceived sustainability of the earnings, the growth prospects based on the market's assessment of the companies strategy, and the perceived strength of the management team.

In MoD, whilst the processes to make decisions are set out, the reality of what drives decisions is less clear – is it the benefit for the Armed Forces or value-for-money from the defence budget, whatever that means? Is it benefit for UK plc or is it political issues such as jobs in marginal constituencies? Is it avoidance of political embarrassment from such things as cost overruns and delays or is it the future viability of the defence industry?

Perhaps it is a mix of all these – a mix which changes with time depending on political imperatives, the desire to limit 'bad' acquisition news or the laudable desire to support operations. Even if it is the last of these, MoD does not seem clear as to whether the focus should be on current operations (largely ground forces and their supporting air assets), or on a very unclear future (aircraft carriers, Terrier, Typhoon, JSF). Both must be achieved and the defence budget managed accordingly. Although much equipment has value in both types of operations, affordability of alternative capabilities must be a key consideration.

This uncertainty is encapsulated, for example, in the argument over the capability requirements for, and numbers of, the Future Surface Combatant (FSC), which will also have long-term/permanent implications for the future of industrial capacity, support infrastructure, manpower and training, and may determine any future ability to expand or adapt capability if allowed to atrophy. Yet the acquisition case will be built using the tools at the disposal of MoD acquisition and support planners: the biennial Defence Strategic Guidance (DSG) and supporting doctrinal publications. These are incomplete instruments and, while Capability Management Groups (CMGs) are being tasked to think completely in capability terms, as indeed the ECC was under Smart Acquisition, there seems to be no clearly defined capability goal that the FSC and all the Defence Lines of Development (DLoD) associated with it are being jointly shaped to meet.

Money and authority flow through enabler organisations, not effectors and, as a result, there is no clear output focus in MoD. Organisations and processes are diverted from concentrating on the needs of the front line.

The Planning Chain

Whilst all commercial companies have their own ways, most produce and maintain a clear strategy and from that develop an action plan with specific objectives. This gives rise to long-term financial plans, into which a detailed set of numbers are injected to produce the budget. There is a clear chain from strategy to annual budget. Annually – more often if required – strategic and objective changes would be reflected in the amended financial plan. Once the budget is set and targets given, the executive team is then given considerable flexibility as to how to navigate the commercial reefs and currents as the year unfolds.

In contrast, whilst we believe that MoD is generally good at producing strategy in the form of the Defence Strategic Guidance (DSG) but, despite re-drafting DSG every two years, it is weak at turning this strategy into the effective delivery of equipment capability, especially when this requires the coordination of multiple DLoDs: the links between strategy and capability are either weak, broken or simply too long. Despite the strategic guidance, there is no clear action plan or financial plan to achieve the strategy by delivering a coherent and costed package of capabilities, nor to adapt and recycle the strategy to a more affordable shape, if delivering the matching capability package proves too expensive. The Equipment Capability Customer (ECC) has to provide the linkage from strategy to capability as best it can, without having the necessary authority over the non-equipment DLoDs or the single Services. Neither does it have the expertise and the resources to do so. It does not, in most cases, even have explicit costings of all the DLoDs associated with the items of equipment for which it is directly responsible. Seen from the direction of MoD financial planning, there is no mechanism that takes the Defence Plan and demonstrates that, year by year, it delivers a costed (and affordable) capability profile that meets the MoD's strategy goals in the short and long term. The current aspiration of Director Commercial to produce a single electronic data resource in the equipment area, visible to both MoD and industry, is especially welcome in this respect.

Whose is the responsibility in MoD for producing such a strategy action plan? The answer appears to be 'no one' at the moment, although the responsibility must be vested in the Secretary of State who, after all, is the Government's appointee to implement defence strategy. Should it be done by the Defence Board? Would the Board agree? Is it capable, given its make-up, of making the necessary tough decisions? Or should it merely endorse the Plan produced by someone else? If so, who? (We note that the Defence Management Board (DMB) now seems to have lost its 'M'; whatever the intentions behind this, we hope that the present article makes it clear that Management from the top level downwards is needed to fill the current gap between strategy and capability delivery.)

Refreshing the Plan

There is only one certainty in the environment within which MoD and the major primes work: that things will change, often very quickly and in unexpected ways. Both MoD and industry therefore have to make many major assumptions when they plan. Some of these assumptions will change and in so doing undermine the agreed strategy. In industry, the plans will be revisited regularly and changed when necessary – commercial organisations that don't adapt, don't survive. In MoD, flexibility is frowned upon, in part because of the political reluctance to make a 'U-Turn' – once agreed, plans and projects are stuck to rigidly, often because the commercial and political implications of cancellation are too tough to confront. J.M. Keynes once wisely said, when accused of changing his views, "When the facts change, I change my mind".

The Strategic Defence Review (SDR) was produced in 1998 and is still the top level guidance on defence policy and plans. Yet, in the meantime we have had 9/11 (which led to the addition of a New Chapter to the SDR but not a fundamental revision), Iraq and Afghanistan, and without any expectation that we would now be struggling to fight two enduring, medium operations with insufficient funds, manpower and equipment whilst still maintaining the ability to meet other standing Military Tasks. The SDR (politically, a strategy designed to maximise the post-Cold War peace dividend, while keeping both the services and industry 'on board') was never adequately funded and the gap between funds and defence commitments has since grown considerably. The result is strategy with unrealistic elements within it that weaken it fatally.

The SDR should have been regularly updated when required to provide new departure points for the DSG, but politically this has been a non-starter. There is a strong case for a proper (government?) review at regular intervals – and/or when external developments dictate – with the will to make necessary changes. Given the rate of change of external parameters, is there not a case for annual review of strategy? This is normal practice in industry and allows for revisions where the facts (economic environment, demand etc.) have changed. Strategy by definition should not and generally does not shift dramatically – but the drivers and the implementation do change during a year.

An out-of-date strategy is a disaster waiting to happen.

Because the core assumptions – assumptions only, not even facts – have not been tested or revisited frequently enough, the Strategic Guidance, once reasonable, has becomes dangerously dated. The absurdity of the still extant Strategic Guidance that we will only fight a single, enduring brigade-sized operation at one time in the face of the demands of Afghanistan and Iraq proves this so.

The Future Rapid Effect System (FRES) is a classic example of pursuing an out-of-date strategy. FRES emerged from the ashes of several projects that had been aborted over the last 30 years. As uncertainties or technological advances presented themselves, it was easier to delay than decide. Further, the FRES community was, from the beginning, heavily influenced by the technological ambitions of the much more far-reaching US Future Combat System (FCS) programme, when what was needed was a relatively cheap, fairly simple armoured vehicle capable of being deployed quickly and effectively in various scenarios and able to be procured quickly; instead, the solution was for too long aimed at having something as technologically advanced – if not better than – the US FCS. Its ISD was originally set, unrealistically given the expectation, as 2007 but is unlikely now to be achieved, even with a lesser capability, until 2013 at the earliest.

Meanwhile, the Army has been fighting two wars with inferior legacy equipment and emergency purchases of military off-the-shelf (MOTS) substitutes. This has caused enormous frustration to the front line, yet once FRES was in the programme, it became an obsession for the Army to protect the concept that had been produced – particularly the push for air-deployed medium-weight armour – lest the funds for that capability be removed.

The Defence Industrial Strategy initiated two 'Pathfinder' programmes to reflect its Values for Acquisition. One of these – the Sustained Armoured Vehicle Capability (SAVC) Pathfinder, which included six industrial players in the core team – recognised that, given the primacy of financial constraints, the most expedient and balanced solution would come from a mixture of upgrade and new vehicles, delivering a balanced budget and an acceptable through-life programme. This was deemed 'unacceptable' – arguably not for reasons of front line focus and need. The lesson here is that the process by which decisions are reached does not always place military imperatives at the top of the list – even when it is clearly pressing and unavoidable.

Will aircraft carriers become another example of obsessive protectionism, irrespective of the benefits and strategic priorities?

What might industry have done if they had charge of FRES? Well, they would probably have made time-to-market a very high priority and considered both upgrade and export possibilities. They would then have produced a basic and incremental design with room for growth, and continually assessed what was really needed.

It is this lack of continual assessment and willingness to redesign or even cancel programmes, together with constant changes that undermine their coherence, that cause problems in MoD. Making decisions to cancel programmes is politically unattractive and, as a result, we regularly commit to what we cannot afford. In contrast, no commercial organisation has a strategy that it cannot afford – if it does, it does not survive for long.

Politics

Political pressures play a large role in MoD – whether practised by politicians or by the tribes in the defence organisation or the rest of

Whitehall. Internal politics is also at work in industry. Companies are subject to changes in tax, government fiscal policy and laws governing the workplace. However, companies, and in particular the Chief Executive Officer (CEO) who is the focus of authority, have relatively unfettered ability to make decisions to cope with these changes. In comparison, MoD has less room for manoeuvre – decisions are subject to agreement or veto by other Departments, notably the Treasury and Number Ten.

Defence Acquisition is a complex and difficult process, but it is not clear who is in charge of acquisition in MoD. While the organisation of the MoD is based on dual leadership (the military Chief of the Defence Staff and the civil service Permanent Secretary), the tribal base is much wider and includes the three Services that are inevitably far from 'purple', especially in times of severe financial pressure. Moreover, some MoD tribes have political and public profiles, whereas individual capabilities do not.

The effects are particularly malign in acquisition where decisions are affected by the scratching of uniformed backs. This may be inevitable, given the current structure, but the programmes that get into the Equipment Plan, and stay there with adequate funding, tend to be those that have the very strongest single-Service proponency or political backing – for example, aircraft carriers, fast jets and armoured vehicles, but not helicopters, transport, much C4ISTAR, and combat ID, all of which are desperately required now in Iraq and Afghanistan – and none of which are a single-Service 'must have'.

Organisational change is necessary if MoD is to make good decisions in a timely manner, but what is the answer? More non-executive directors on the Defence Board? Removal of the single-Service Chiefs of Staff from the Defence Board? The current Defence Board structure would appear to make clear, timely decisions unlikely.

Data and Information

Industry in general terms makes decisions on the basis of good data, which it turns into relevant information. MoD collects a mountain of data but little of it is turned into useable information and, even more worryingly, much of it is 'unknown'– i.e. those who need it often do not know what data is available and, when they do, cannot find it. The lack of relevant information is a major weakness and hampers good decision-making – the lack of data on DLoD costs associated with particular equipments has already been mentioned. In contrast, a huge amount of less useful data is routinely collected at great cost and is either never used or, potentially, leads to poor decisions or undue reliance on personal perspectives or gut feeling. The answer is not to demand yet more data, but to decide what data is needed, whether it exists, collect it if not and then use it to produce helpful analysis to support informed debate.

The required information has to be reasonably accurate. Defence companies calculate costs better than MoD before committing – cost overruns in MoD projects are large and ubiquitous, with repeated observations from the National Audit Office that information is not mature enough at Main Gate – a reflection in part of the technological immaturity of many projects at this point.[1] We believe that in MoD there is little P&L discipline or firm basis of costing. Costs are extensively manipulated for public consumption and to support the arguments of particular tribes in MoD, as we have seen in the Major Projects Reports of the last two years. There is still evidence to support the view that the 'conspiracy of optimism' is alive and well.[2] Indeed, it is likely that MoD falls into the fatal trap of believing its own propaganda!

The lack of quality information only helps those whose minds are made up before a decision is debated – as the SAVC Pathfinder experience shows.

Continuity in Post

We have discussed in previous papers the importance of establishing proper accountability. There are many facets to this, but one central one is the continuity in post of those accountable. The procurement cycle is so long that repeated changes can only dilute any accountability initiatives that are established. This applies at every level within the MoD.

In industry, individuals usually remain in post for much longer but, in the limit, the pressure for shareholder value, of which delivery is a key driver, ensures that output focus is retained.

Readiness to Take Decisions

In Whitehall, the culture is not wholly conducive to making timely decisions – no one is ever sacked for postponing a decision or for following the rules. Nor are officials well rewarded for taking well-judged risks, and whose decisions may bring censure for getting it 'wrong' – a subjective term usually applied with the benefit of hindsight. The result is a leadership chain that lacks confidence: indeed, at the present time, many decisions are side-stepped by both the Investment Approvals Board and the Defence Board, with options offered instead. Moreover, non-decisions tend to move programmes to the right and thus 'save' money in the ten-year Equipment Programme – at the expense of course of increased cost overall and, importantly, delaying the availability of the capability. The lack of data to quantify this point illustrates the negative impact of the paucity of information.

Making decisions may expose Ministers to difficult justification and strong opposition – even severe embarrassment. Those civil servants who see their job as to spare Ministers embarrassment will obviously see non-decisions as preferable to decisions. The result is that promotion will often go to the 'safe pair of hands' – often a euphemism for not making decisions that could cause debate or controversy.

Such decisions include any that cancel or make major changes to programmes where significant sums of public money have already been spent. Once a programme has been fully launched, it is supported obsessively even when it is in severe trouble and when it would make more sense to cancel it and buy 'off-the-shelf' – ignoring spiralling costs, greater delays and increasing obsolescence. There is always a tribe to support it wholeheartedly.

In industry, decision-makers are much readier to change course, abandon a programme that is costing more money than it is worth, and adopt a new course. In the defence sector, this may not happen as often as in the civil sector because, once a programme is on contract, there is reluctance on the part of MoD to change course, and industry can usually make the case for greater funding with the support of Service or political champions to argue their corner.

Conclusion

In the 1980s Peter (now Lord) Levene championed a seismic shift in the way MoD approached procurement by introducing a more commercial approach. There are many differences between decision-making in MoD and industry and our analysis shines a light on some of the specific characteristics of the MoD decision-making process and highlights aspects where MoD could become more effective by adopting a more commercial approach. In particular, MoD could usefully study the way industry turns strategy into clear plans, updates them on an annual basis, makes timely decisions, achieves continuity in post, maintains a clear focus, changes things that are not working, collects relevant data and creates the necessary information with which to work. The political issues do not affect industry as much as MoD, but the tribal nature is handled more effectively in industry.

But this is not to say that MoD acquisition is uniformly poor –

examples such as the procurement of many Urgent Operational Requirements (UOR) show how agile the system can be. The problem is how to reflect the relevant lessons from the best of these examples.

MoD has a reputation for not understanding industry. It needs to show that it is putting that behind it.

---

[1] Graham Jordan and John Dowdy, *RUSI Defence Systems*, (Volume 10, No. 2, October 2007), page 16.

[2] RUSI Acquisition Focus, *RUSI Defence Systems*, (Volume 10, No. 2, October 2007), page 60.

Chapter Nine

Research and Technology

With the low level of pull-through from defence research to projects, many people ask the question "What's it for?" because defence research doesn't seem to be very cost-effective. But, although the pay-off is often far in the future, it is vital for the following reasons:

- To provide the basis for equipping our Armed Forces with battle-winning equipment.
- To maintain a strong, healthy industrial base with appropriate sovereignty and good prospects for exports, which keeps MoD prices down.
- To grow and maintain the expertise for the UK to be an intelligent customer when evaluating bids from UK or foreign companies, and when partnering industry.
- To counter new and emerging threats by developing effective – particularly UOR – equipment quickly.
- To carry out research in vital areas where industry won't because of high risk and little certainty of profit overall.
- To identify and evaluate defence uses for civil research and technology.

To those who would claim that such spending is unnecessary because we could buy better equipment more cheaply and more quickly from abroad – in particular the US – the answer is that this would, if it became the norm, destroy the defence industry in this country. "So what?" might be the reply. Economically, there may not be much of a case for spending money to prop up the industry – after all, the increasing shortages of scientists and engineers threatens to lead to a shortage right across the civil and defence sectors, so the demise of the defence industry might just be a good thing in that respect.

But how would we maintain the intelligent customer expertise to buy cost-effective equipment from abroad? How would we produce vital UOR equipment in the extremely short time frames they demand? Expertise does not come from reading reports of research carried out by others – it comes from doing leading-edge research.

> *There is an acceptance that some research funding must be allocated to maintaining intelligent customer skills, and the argument further runs that this can only be achieved by undertaking actual research. But research to do what? Because if it is only to build a body of knowledge, then this is a high premium indeed … Surely, though, the main value of research is to provide innovative, cutting-edge equipment for our front-line forces.*[235]

Maintaining intelligent customer expertise and the ability to deliver cutting-edge equipment in short timescales under UOR procedures make an onshore research base essential. And the DIS is aimed at retaining, in many sectors, a strong onshore defence industry, for which a strong research base is vital. That means at least an element of government funding because industry will not carry out research – particularly far-term research – which will not clearly produce payback in a reasonable time frame.

The Defence Industrial Strategy and Research

Given that a strong onshore research base is essential if DIS is to be successful, it is surprising that R&T is so poorly covered in the White Paper. I have noted already that DIS was produced in a very short timescale, but if the industrial strategies could be produced in that amount of time, why couldn't R&T have been considered equally well?

> It is surprising that R&T is so poorly covered in the White Paper

But this is all of a piece with the way MoD has played with R&T ever since the fall of Communism nearly two decades ago – no money for research that's not immediately needed and little understanding of the subject except by those very close to it. Research is not a player in 'accountants' logic'.

It is true that DIS has a whole chapter on R&T and innovation, and that chapter repeatedly underlines the importance of R&T in achieving an advantage in military capability from R&D investment. Unfortunately, this is rather undermined by the muddling of R&T with R&D but, no matter, the point is made.

---

[235] David Lynam, 'Research: Where Now?', *RUSI Defence Systems* (Volume 8, No. 3, February 2006), page 17.

The DIS report then goes on to look at key R&T challenges for UK defence, which it lists as:

- Maintaining technological advantage to counter emerging threats.
- Sustaining investment levels to maintain the UK's relative global position.
- Developing knowledge management and systems integration skills in the defence sector so that technologies can be matured and integrated into war-winning systems for the future.
- Recruiting and retaining skilled people to act as the MoD intelligent customer for R&T acquisition to meet defence needs.
- Developing design and acquisition processes to enable technology insertion throughout equipment life.

While this chapter is fairly full, the implementation section is weak on R&T. It says that MoD will:

- Review the alignment of the research programme with MoD needs.
- Conduct further work to understand better the underpinning technologies that the UK must have for security and sovereignty reasons.
- Update its Defence Technology Strategy (DTS) to reflect the conclusions of the DIS.
- Develop a better understanding of the innovation process.

This is disappointing. It seems as if MoD did not want to lay down a future path for R&T, but to leave the whole thing to the update of the DTS. This is a mistake as the new DTS surely needed strong direction from DIS, not least in terms of the scale of investment – DIS states the challenge of "sustaining investment levels to maintain the UK's relative global position". With the rise of China and India, to say nothing of the huge US investment, does this not mean increasing defence R&T spend in the UK?

> Does this not mean increasing defence R&T spend in the UK?

The Defence Technology Strategy

The DIS promised that MoD would update its DTS, and this was completed quickly and was published in 2006. It listed as challenges:

- The MoD emphasis on maturing current technologies to the detriment of the new.
- The need for MoD to own and control key technologies.
- The low level of industrial investment in R&D compared with MoD.
- The need for greater combined MoD and industry investment in R&D with more emphasis on research.

The key here was the acknowledgement of the need for greater investment in R&D – including more emphasis on research. However, the weasel words allow MoD a way out as it points to industry primarily to increase investment. I will return to this later in the chapter.

The DTS then listed its priorities as shown in Figure 9–1.

DEFENCE TECHNOLOGY STRATEGY
PRIORITIES FOR SCIENCE & TECHNOLOGY (S&T)

Advancing S&T in:
- Man-portable biological detection systems.
- Radar.
- Modular open systems.
- Modelling and simulation.
- Propulsion.
- Generic medical countermeasures.
- Satellites for information collection and analysis.
- Gallium Nitride circuit technology.
- Materials and structures for protection and through-life support.

Setting up communities of practice in core technologies that will continue to shape future capability in:
- Signal and data processing.
- Geolocation and synchronisation.

Creating university centres of excellence in critical areas such as:
- Sensors.
- Technologies to support C4ISTAR.

Speed up R&D exploitation
- "MoD will ensure that a planning process is in place involving key MoD and industry stakeholders based on technology roadmaps by September 2007".

Create joint MoD/industry framework for investment
- "DTS is affordable provided both MoD and industry invest together ... industry needs to invest more ..."

Figure 9–1: DTS Priorities for S&T

Implementation of DTS

The DTS states that it will:

- Sustain vital defence S&T in the long term by harnessing all parts of the research and development chain through government, industry, academia and, where there is mutual advantage, with our key allies.

- Develop a coherent structure and process to ensure S&T requirements are defined and pursued effectively.
- Create structures within the R&D programme that are capable of flexible and rapid responses to the changing defence environment, and develop processes and architectures that allow rapid technology insertion.
- Build on existing, and develop new, joint working practices to fulfil and deliver the R&D programme and to exploit R&D to deliver world-class military capability.

Note the emphasis on structures, processes, practices and architectures. Is this really what the DTS needs to do? Will it improve the R&T output? Will it close the transatlantic technology gap, or even stop it widening as quickly as it is at the moment?

> Fiddling at the edges cannot be the answer

No, I fear it will make little difference. Oh, I expect that it might make slightly better use of the tiny pot of R&T funds, but that is not the real issue. MoD must understand that DTS implementation will make little difference to the health of defence R&T without a major increase in funding. Fiddling at the edges cannot be the answer.

The Funding Issue

If we look back at the Priorities for R&T laid down in the DTS, it is the last one which is the key. However, the full wording (as reproduced in Figure 9–2) is not reassuring.

Defence Technology Strategy

Statement on Increasing R&D Investment

The position of industrial funding of defence R&D needs to be contrasted with industrial R&D funding in the civil sector. By way of example, the level of UK aerospace industry self-financed R&D in the civil sector in 2005 was approximately 6% of its £10.5Bn turnover. However, its self-financed R&D in the defence sector was only approximately 2% of its £12.2Bn turnover. This should be compared with UK MoD's total R&D investment of over 8% of the defence budget.

Furthermore, the UK aerospace sector only spends 8% of its total R&D budget on research.

By way of comparison between UK R&D funding for defence and for the civil and defence sectors combined, the UK government national target is to increase R&D investment from the 2005 figure of 1.9% (£22Bn) to 2.5% of GDP by 2014 … As HMG increases its R&D investment to meet the 2014 target, it is looking to business enterprise (industry) to play its part. It is important to note, however, whilst overall industry does invest in R&D, defence industry investment is low.

Figure 9–2: Defence Technology Strategy and Investment

This may not strike you as a model of clarity. Nor is it – for two reasons: it is comparing apples with both oranges and bananas and coming up with a lemon; and it leaves a lot unsaid:

- MoD constrains the defence industry in the amount of profit it makes from each contract and this is a lot less than civil industry can and does make. This directly depresses the amount defence companies can invest in, inter alia, research, technology and development.
- The long cycle times of defence programmes postpone the industrial pay-off (primarily exports, as not much money is made on sales to UK MoD), compared to the much faster pay-off that civil industry receives with its time-to-market priority.
- MoD commitment to programmes, and particularly schedules, is neither strong nor consistent (FRES, IFPA and FIST are

examples) so it is difficult for defence companies to make strong cases to their Boards. This contrasts strongly with the civil sector where a programme, once launched, is driven hard by the time-to-market priority.

- Defence projects are driven by the needs of UK MoD (and to some extent by foreign MoDs) whether or not they are likely to be profitable for industry; the civil sector, in contrast, is driven by profit in the marketplace.

- R&D is perhaps the wrong category to choose for comparing the defence and civil sectors, or indeed for comparing MoD and defence industry funding. R&T might make for more useful comparisons.

- It is not at all clear whether the target of extra government funding on R&D will be met (eight years is a lifetime of failing to meet targets) or, even if it is, whether any of it will be directed at defence.

The statement above does not make a clear case for showing that the defence industry is any more culpable than MoD for what is unarguably the unacceptably low overall spend on either defence R&T or defence R&D. More money must be invested in both. There is also nothing that categorically makes the case for increased industrial spending rather than MoD funding. It's difficult to see how it can make a strong case, unless procurement cycles are speeded up and/or defence companies are able to make more profit on contracts. The latter could flow from more enlightened commercial arrangements for gainsharing.

> More profit on contracts could flow from more enlightened commercial arrangements for gainsharing

A particularly chastening experience for industry was the Merlin millimetric wave guided mortar bomb:

> *British Aerospace (BAe) was told that the Army had a definite requirement for Merlin, but could not afford to fund the development programme. If BAe developed it the company was assured that the Army would buy it. After a particularly difficult development programme, costing some £110M, BAe finally had a solution which performed. At this point the Army decided that it could not fit Merlin into the procurement programme leaving BAe to write off the £110M – a pretty painful experience, even for a company of BAe's size.*[236]

---

[236] John Weston, email to the author, 11 September 2008.

Perhaps not surprisingly, spending on R&D by the largest defence and aerospace companies fell in 2005–06 by 5.7% of sales.[237] This hardly suggests that the defence industry is in the mood for raising R&D spending significantly.

> *The Government has failed to stem a long-term decline in the proportion of cash that companies plough into research and development, despite public subsidies worth £1.8Bn since 2000 … The report draws into question both the effectiveness of the Government's R&D strategy, on which £600M has been spent in the last year alone.*[238]

Clearly, much research can only be done with MoD funding.

> *Since capability advantage from military equipment in 2020 will predominantly be determined by what the MoD is spending on R&D now, I suggest that the amount of cash allocated to long-term R&D, **which is the prerogative of government**, requires urgent review. Only by this investment will we achieve the smaller, smarter forces we require with their enhanced agility to respond to uncertainty.*[239]

The first step must be for MoD to up its R&T funding now, if we are not to rely on buying in US technology and equipment in the future in many sectors. Spending on R&T leads capability output by some 20 years so that, if we

> If we don't act now, we will be undermining appropriate sovereignty required under DIS

don't act now, we will be undermining appropriate sovereignty required under DIS over the next two decades.

The bottom line is that, unless MoD increases its funding now, the joint MoD/industry framework may not achieve much, if anything.

Later in the chapter I will come back to this vital issue to see how it would be possible to increase very markedly R&T spend without upsetting the overall defence budget.

---

[237] R&D Scoreboard 2007.

[238] Gabriel Rozenberg, *The Times*, Monday 12 November 2007.

[239] Richard Maudslay, Chairman Dstl, 'UK Defence Research and Technology', UK Defence Forum, CP 64, March 2007, page 4/5.

Technology Pull-Through and the Acquisition Cycle

One of the weaknesses in R&T has been for a long time the difficulty in pulling through government-funded technology into winning projects. Not surprisingly, therefore, those responsible for funding R&T have seen research as a waste of money.

Competition

A major barrier to pull-through has been MoD's emphasis on competition, which has placed the importance of a level-playing field for competition later in the acquisition cycle as more important than either making cost-effective use of government-funded research or producing world-class technology. The result has been minimal pull-through, wasted money and a decline in scientific expertise in MoD.

This has been exacerbated by the privatisation of the majority of the former DERA into QinetiQ[240]. This removed three-quarters of MoD's scientific staff leaving behind a rump as the Defence Science and Technology Laboratory (Dstl), consisting mainly of those working in sensitive technologies. That left very little expertise to carry out the necessary work in MoD.

No problem – buy in the expertise. But can this really provide impartial advice? Maybe, maybe not. It must be admitted that DERA advice was often partial as the Not Invented Here (NIH) culture was widespread.

The Valley of Death

An even greater barrier has been the so-called 'Valley of Death'. This refers to the almost total gap in funding between the research phase and the start of a programme (as shown in Figure 9–3). Too often, this gap lasts several years, by which time it is, if not obsolescent, at least overtaken by other research. Not only that, but the research has not been taken beyond the laboratory, and no proper demonstration has been done for lack of money.

---

[240] For a fuller discussion of the privatisation, see Bill Kincaid, *Dancing with the Dinosaur*, UK Defence Forum, 1999; and Bill Kincaid, *Dinosaur in Permafrost* (TheSauras Ltd, 2002).

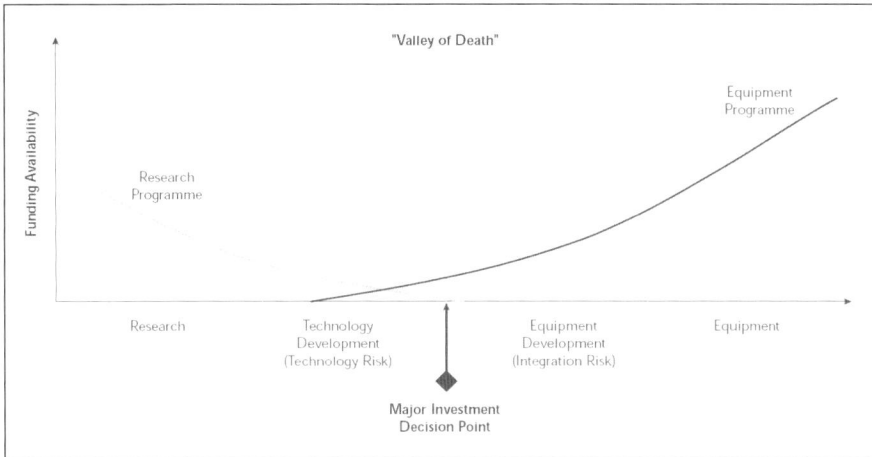

Figure 9–3: The Valley of Death
Source: National Audit Office, The Management of Defence Research and Technology, HC 360, 10 March 2004, page 32, The Stationery Office

Let us imagine a procurement competition between three company proposals. One might be proposing a design based on some good government-funded research which was completed some years ago but never properly demonstrated; a second might be fronting US technology that was newer and fully demonstrated; while the third might be offering a cheap and cheerful solution. Guess which one will **not** win.

In an earlier book I gave an example.[241] In the aftermath of the announcement that Raytheon had won the ASTOR contract:

> [Raytheon Systems Ltd] had been anticipating a request by MoD for it to accommodate Racal into its ASTOR team at the last moment. 'We were surprised it never came', a Raytheon official told Jane's Defence Weekly. Racal had bid an advanced synthetic aperture radar/moving target indicator (SAR/MTI) package based on more than a decade's worth of UK-funded technology demonstration work, within the rival Lockheed Martin team bid.[242]

No doubt there were good reasons for this decision in a narrow context, but was this the right answer overall? I don't know, but it illustrates an area where we should perhaps look more sympathetically on the potential fruits of UK-funded research – always provided that it

---

[241] Bill Kincaid, *Dancing with the Dinosaur*, UK Defence Forum, 1999, page 138.
[242] *Jane's Defence Weekly*, 23 June 1999, page 3.

meets the requirement.

In this case, money had been spent on demonstration but was now wasted. As this has been all too common, it is hardly surprising that financiers look none too kindly on requests for more research funding.

Technology Transfer to Industry

The issue of technology transfer is generally taken to refer to transatlantic transfer of technology, and I will come to that shortly.

But there is another transfer problem – that of transferring technology from MoD to industry, or transferring technology, funded by MoD, from one company or team to another. There are two major difficulties here.

The first is that technology is not easy to transfer. Moving documents from one to another does not transfer technology – in the early stages technology exists primarily in the brains of scientists and engineers who have been working on it, whether or not large amounts of information have been passed from one body to another.

This leads to the second difficulty – IPR, contracts and competition. Now that DERA has largely become QinetiQ in the private sector, with its various teaming arrangements with manufacturing companies, it would seem that QinetiQ's UK-funded research can only be readily transferred to the companies with which QinetiQ is teamed. Although more and more MoD research work is being competed, and although QinetiQ may win a decreasing amount in the future, this problem will not go away. Any commercial company that wins future research work will be unwilling to transfer the results to other companies unless they are teamed with them. This is one of the bitter fruits of privatising so much of defence research.

Widening the Research Base

The DIS states that:

> The MoD is moving away from doing most of its research in-house and is encouraging competition from industry and the university sector ... In 2002/03 around 90% of our applied research was done in Dstl or QinetiQ. By 2009/10 we plan to compete around 60% of the research budget that equated to our applied

and corporate research programme, retaining only 35% in Dstl … QinetiQ is free to compete with companies in bidding for competed research.[243]

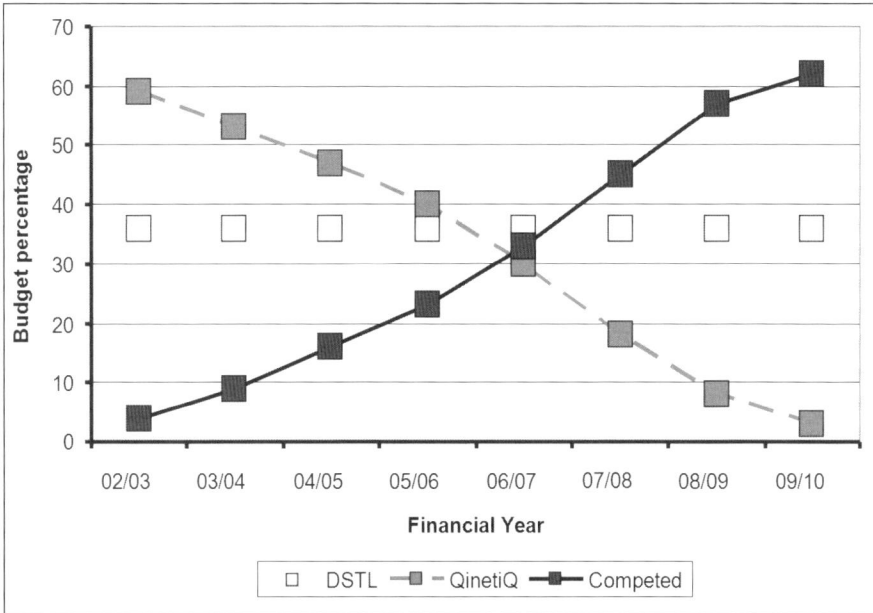

Figure 9–4: Increase in competition in the MoD research programme
Source: Defence Industrial Strategy, page 42

At first sight it seems a good idea to compete much of the MoD research work (Figure 9–4) and in many ways it is. However, there is one danger. If a large number of different companies win infrequent work, will the research base lose coherence and expertise? Research scientists and engineers need continuous work in related fields if they are to build up and retain their expertise – small amounts of work in dribs and drabs will not do that, although the mobility of staff in industry may offset that to some extent. As will repeated wins in particular areas by one company.

We need to be building centres of excellence, which will not be done by blanket competition. This policy seems to be at odds with the whole thrust of DIS. Let's have strategic partnering with centres of excellence, whether that be with QinetiQ, manufacturing companies or academia – or a combination of some or all of them.

---

[243] DIS, pages 41/42.

Deepening, rather than widening, the research base should be the aim.

Technology Maturity

One of the major problems that continues to beset acquisition approvals is the inadequate reduction of risk, and chief amongst the reasons for this is the use of immature technology.

> Aggregated across all MoD major projects, problems to do with immature technology have caused more project slippage than anything else in every year from 2000 to 2007. Typically, this cause has accounted for half of all slippage that occurred in a given year.[244]

Unlike the MoD, the civil aircraft and automobile industries recognise that development of new technology is an uncertain process and keep it separate from development of new models – only technology that is fully mature is used when a new model is launched. In contrast, MoD defines the capability it requires, launches the project to deliver it and develops new technology along the way.

> What user would want to be given a system that incorporated technology that had been brought to maturity 20 years previously?

The risks in developing new technology are not easy to identify, so should MoD change its approach to that of the aircraft and automobile industries? In theory at least, yes. But if it is to do so successfully, it must achieve three things.

Firstly, it must reduce the over-lengthy procurement cycle drastically. What user would want to be given a system that incorporated technology that had been brought to maturity 20 years previously? To avoid that happening we would have to bring down the time from concept to fielding to something similar to those that obtain in the civil sector – that is to say by 50% or more – but that is still way short of civil 'times to market'. But let us suppose that we reduced major programme procurement cycle times to ten years (a big ask), technology generations

---

[244] Graham Jordon and John Dowdy, 'Acquisition and Technology: The Problem that Won't Go Away', *RUSI Defence Systems* (Volume 10, No. 2, October 2007), page 16.

are still much shorter, as are operational change time frames in a world far removed from the static world of the Cold War. If we insist on using only fully matured technology **before** we launch a project, how will we achieve the greater acquisition agility we so desperately need?

Secondly, MoD would need to eliminate the 'valley of death' and commit much larger funds for technology demonstration and 'industrialisation'. These funds must be targeted at R&T, not at project(s) that the technology will support.

Thirdly, MoD must move competition from the project stage to the research stage – or eliminate it altogether. If we spend much more on maturing technology before the launch of a project, we do not want to see that money wasted as a competitor bids a different design using different technology. Again this emphasises the need for partnering.

Having done all this with immense effort and great leadership from the top, it is still doubtful if we will achieve what we want – agile acquisition that delivers to time and cost.

So, do we continue to use immature technology and cross our fingers that things will get better? No. The key lies in heeding the consistently repeated advice from a series of acquisition studies over 40 years – to invest more in the early stages of a programme. The figure repeatedly recommended is up to 15% of development costs, which we have never come close to achieving except in one or two isolated cases.

But is 15% adequate today? If we cannot develop mature technology before we launch a project, then we will have to spend much more in maturing it during development. We know this is risky, and we need to reduce risks well before Main Gate. This means that we will have to mature the technology in the early stages of the CADMID cycle. And that probably means greater funding before Main Gate. But, if the technology risks are really reduced by then, there will be much less cost overrun and there may not be a requirement for any more funding overall.

> That probably means greater funding before Main Gate

Of course, industry will not want to sign up to a programme with large risks in using immature technology, without either slapping on a large premium or being given a contract that has a cost-plus element for technology maturation. MoD may baulk at this because the full cost is not tied down. But is it now? No.

> At present, however, only a minority of DOD major projects are fully conformable with best practice [in civil industry]. But this allows some very illuminating comparisons to be made – between projects that enter development with all key technologies fully mature, and those that do not. Whether measured by acquisition cost increase, or in the cost of development itself, projects starting with mature technology do at least ten times better than other projects.[245]

It seems, therefore, that there are two options, excluding 'do nothing', which is not really an option at all:

- Mature all technology before the programme starts by cost-plus contract(s), then use a process with UOR attributes to bring the programme into service in a handful of years.
- Start the programme, but make much larger funds available (>15% of development costs) for maturation of technology in the early stages (well before Main Gate) using a cost-plus element in the contract. This option will also need elements of the UOR approach to defeat obsolescence on fielding.

Whichever of the two options is pursued, it will be essential to achieve a short procurement timescale, with little or no delay. Not only will it be necessary to incorporate much of the UOR culture and process, but annuality and continuous disruption of the equipment programme will have to be overcome.

Integration

Getting to Main Gate with mature technology and to ISD without obsolescence would be a major improvement, but how do we integrate the programme into the networked force and be certain that it will function as we want it to once it is in the field?

The Army is engaged, and will be engaged for quite some time, in fielding Bowman.

> But Bowman pales into insignificance when set against the procedural changes demanded by JC2SP and DII(FD) and a cascade of new capabilities hitting operational theatres in the same time frame ... most relying on information from

---

[245] Graham Jordan and John Dowdy, 'Acquisition and Technology: The Problem That Won't Go Away', *RUSI Defence Systems* (Volume 10, No. 2, October 2007), page 17.

each other and from several new intelligence systems. We don't yet know how these systems will interact technically with each other. We are still unable to model the effects of latency across battlefield networks, neither can we be confident that a map reference will remain the same as it crosses a number of systems before being used for targeting. And when we find that systems don't work as they should in Maysan or Helmand, how long will it take to put them right?[246]

Bill Robins goes on to say that, despite the Centre for Experimentation, De-risking and Integration of C4I Capability (CEDRIC) and the Land Systems Reference Centre (LSRC), there is a vital element missing. It should be filled by the Joint Command and Control Integration Facility (JC2CIF). Without it, DII(FD) and JC2CIF will not be put through a sufficiently aggressive assurance regime to work out how the total system will function on operations and how to get the best performance prior to handing it over to troops in the field.

To describe this as high risk is putting it mildly: there is no way of even measuring the risk. And handing out a system without exploring its full dependencies, inter-linkages and vulnerabilities, and without at least relatively mature working practices, will mean that risk is lobbed into the most unstable environment, the 'sharp end', for UK troops to manage as best they can. However, this is still fixable – just. Despite the severely limited time available to complete this work, proposals to set up a JC2CIF to interrogate how the DII–JC2SP will work in real operational environments are sufficiently well developed and endorsed to allow the years of procurement work already completed to make it over the last 'tactical mile' and deliver a system that is 'fit for purpose'.[247]

> To describe this as high risk is putting it mildly: there is no way of even measuring the risk

Integration is becoming top priority as our network-enabled capability (NEC) vision is slowly being implemented. NEC without the proper integration is, if not a dead duck, at least a flawed operational concept, with which operators in the field will soon lose patience and belief. We cannot allow that to happen.

---

[246] Bill Robins, 'Integration Matters – So Does Agility', *RUSI Defence Systems* (Volume 10, No. 2, October 2007), page 17.
[247] Christiaan Hesse, 'Procuring ICS to Meet Warfighting Realities', *RUSI Defence Systems* (Volume 10, No. 2, October 2007), page 72.

While integration of C4ISTAR systems within NEC may be the extreme challenge, all systems need to be integrated into the battlespace. Today all ships, aircraft and armoured vehicles incorporate huge amounts of software in the command systems, weapon systems and management systems, so electronic integration is important, but it is not the only integration necessary.

> Wiring black boxes together – vehicle installation – is only one small part of the role. A vehicle integrator must understand that, to paraphrase the UK Defence Industrial Strategy, integration is not just for Christmas – it's for life. It must span front line to factory, cradle to grave and pan-fleet dimensions.[248]

The DIS has a whole chapter on Systems Engineering. It defines it as the general term for the methods used to provide optimally engineered, operationally effective, complex systems, balancing capability, risk, complexity, cost and technological choices to provide a solution which best meets the customer's needs.

It goes on to discuss the importance of systems engineering and the expertise in each of the industrial sectors, but the sustainment of systems engineering expertise is broken down into the chapters on the different sectors, where it rather gets lost.

> There is a general perception that NEC is moving too slowly and is repeatedly being over-taken by events

Despite all this, there is a general perception that NEC is moving too slowly and is repeatedly being overtaken by events. Part of the problem is the inability, over many years, for the MoD customer to decide exactly what he wants in operational terms. Unlike aircraft or ships or armoured vehicles, he tends to approach the problem as a pseudo-geek, looking at what is technically possible and solutionising without deciding on the requirement.

Another part of the problem is the inability to produce a coherent procurement strategy. Is it a form of the 'big bang' approach to ensure that all elements fit together once they are produced, or is it a bottom-up approach to get the pieces and then wire them together? Both approaches

---

[248] David Leslie, 'Vehicle Integration – Playing 3D Chess in the Real World', *RUSI Defence Systems* (Volume 10, No. 2, October 2007), page 20.

have major risks, not helped by the speed at which technology moves.

But remembering the advice of Al Adams and Krist Zimmerman,[249] producing bespoke systems for every requirement and then tying them together might be the only way forward.

Northrop Grumman might agree. "I've heard a lot about NEC, but I've never seen it until now", was the observation of a senior RAF officer attending Northrop Grumman's Agile Thunder exercise in October 2007. This says a lot about the lack of progress over the last 20 years.

> *Agile Thunder was not a technology demonstration, it was an operational demonstration of what can be accomplished by tying together UK weapons in a way that is not done today ... The AIA [Advanced Information Architecture] makes everyone's information discoverable within the network ... soldiers on the ground can obtain airborne imagery in real time. In turn, data gathered on the ground can be presented in the cockpit as timely, critical intelligence and targeting information.[250]*

Gold-plating has long been a criticism of the requirements staff, and it seems that NEC is a prime example of the gold-plated, 'big bang' approach which is repeatedly overtaken by operational and technological changes. As noted above

> It seems that NEC is a prime example of the gold-plated, 'big bang' approach

and again in Chapter Seven, a simpler approach might just defeat the rapid pace of technology.

Innovation

The MoD culture is antipathetic to innovation, equating it to increased risk. So, although the DIS apparently champions innovation, agility and flexibility, it is disappointing that the words on innovation in R&T are not translated into robust actions in the implementation section. It is true that the DTS does take this forward to some extent – recommending communities of practice and university centres of excellence in some sectors, and a joint MoD/industry framework for investment. But none of this will amount to much without a major improvement in process

---

[249] Captain Al Adams and LCDR Krist Zimmerman USN, 'Interoperability: A Maritime Perspective', *RUSI Defence Systems* (Volume 11, No. 1, June 2008), page 50.
[250] Rich Mercadente, 'Providing Near-Term NEC with Existing Systems', *RUSI Defence Systems* (Volume 10, No. 1, June 2008), page 56.

(eliminating the 'valley of death' and investing much more in the early procurement stages), in culture (identifying and managing risk in the round rather than in the short term), and above all in R&T funding – of which more anon.

The importance of innovation and pull-through into capability is clear from a very telling passage in the DIS. It says that a recent MoD-sponsored study analysing 11 major defence-capable nations has uncovered,

> A highly significant correlation between equipment capability and R&T investment in the last 5 to 30 years ... shows that there is a simple 'you get what you pay for' relationship between R&T spend and equipment quality, with a sharp law of diminishing returns, and that R&T investment buys a time advantage over open market equipment.[251]

UK has been reducing its R&T spend and pulling through less and less of that R&T for the last decade-and-a-half

This passage is accompanied by a figure which shows equipment capability against **R&D** spend, not R&T, but in a healthy onshore industry, spend on R, T and D are all important so the quoted passage may well be acceptable. However, UK has been reducing its R&T spend and pulling through less and less of that R&T for the last decade-and-a-half. The above study demonstrates that this has been completely the wrong thing to do. The study also confirms what anyone with an ounce of intelligence knows.[252] So, why are we so intent on destroying our future capability? The reason, of course, is the overheated defence budget.

MoD produced its Innovation Strategy at the end of 2007 – rather belatedly perhaps, but better late than never. It lays down six Pillars of Innovation:

---

[251] DIS, page 39. The DIS text states R&T, but the accompanying figure is marked R&D.
[252] Over the last decade, I have discussed this with many senior MoD officers and officials and all have acknowledged the need for more funding, but none have expressed a determination to do anything about it. Short-termism, *par excellence*. In addition, since I have been Editor of *RUSI Defence Systems*, I have many times highlighted the inadequate R&T spend with articles from many distinguished people (including Sir John Chisholm, Graham Jordan and Professor David Kirkpatrick) in the editions of February 2006, October 2006, February 2007, June 2007 and October 2007.

- **Sharing the Vision for Defence Capability.** Identify needs early, articulate future capability aspirations to academia and industry, and foster an environment where promising innovative ideas are taken forward rapidly.
- **Capability and Technology Road Mapping.** Engage a wider number of suppliers and share capability and technology plans with them better.
- **Smarter Systems Engineering.** Design systems with upgrade and flexibility in mind to allow insertion of innovative technology and transition to 'open' innovation models.
- **Improved Business Models.** Encourage greater financial contribution to R&D from other sources of funding and from within the technological supplier network.
- **Need for Speed.** Increase the pace that technology is taken forward, and improve flexibility of MoD's processes and commercial models.
- **Innovation Culture.** Develop an innovation culture [see below].

All good stuff, but will it happen? The first three are relatively straightforward and should be easily achieved, but the next two will be severe challenges and will not be met without greater determination than MoD has shown over the last decade or more. Greater financial contribution is one prerequisite for success, but as important is the last. As with all other aspects of DIS, culture change is the key. The Innovation Strategy states that:

> Greater financial contribution is one prerequisite for success

- An innovation culture is one that focuses on problem-solving and allows individuals to challenge and apply independent thinking.
- There is a perception that MoD is not receptive to innovation as it leads to risk.
- There is a need to develop a culture in which we engage suppliers and the end-user in forming requirements with a greater emphasis on experimentation.
- We will only succeed if we develop a **culture** where conventions can be challenged, information is shared and valued as much as tangible assets, and **where a value is put on the speed of**

decision-making over any delays stemming from a fear of making the wrong decision.

This last phrase in bold perhaps encapsulates the culture change that is necessary in MoD – not just in innovation but across the board. It must be achieved.

The Innovation Strategy, with its call for greater emphasis on experimentation, was perhaps key to the saving of Niteworks, the partnership between MoD and industry that was established to "provide an integration and experimental environment to assess the benefits of NEC and the options for its effective and timely delivery". In December 2007, there was a very real danger that Niteworks' funding would be sacrificed on the altar of savings but, about this time, the Innovation Strategy was produced. Niteworks was saved, refocused to remove the emphasis on NEC and funding rethought. It is now to concentrate on providing evidence-based decision support to front-line operations, Joint Capability Board decision-making and capability-based acquisition programmes.

Niteworks has, over the last five years:[253]

- Brought together industry, MoD and the Armed Forces to examine the challenges of NEC.
- Developed innovative commercial arrangements allowing all partners to access intellectual property generated.
- Provided value to MoD while industry partners' understanding of MoD has grown.
- Created a culture and set of behaviours unique in the defence sector.
- Embraced best practice from across its membership.
- Demonstrated that it has the scope to be a flexible and responsive decision-making tool.

Inadequate Funding for R&T

And now to the really important issue – R&T funding.

It has variously been estimated that the shortfall of funds in the defence budget against commitments is between £10Bn and £30Bn over the next ten years. This not only causes annual turbulence in planning and

---

[253] Simon Jewell, 'Niteworks: Finding its Voice', *RUSI Defence Systems* (Volume 11, No. 2, October 2008)

contract letting, but it also leads to many difficult decisions. As politicians and MoD top management find tough decisions hard (PR 08 was no exception), this usually ends up with continued slips, and performance and quantity reductions.

The early years are always the most difficult as so much is on contract, so the weight of savings tends to fall on training, but R&T spend is also a soft target. Not that R&T can offer up much because it has so little in the first place. So, much harm is done for little return.

It is less the annual savings measures that are the problem, but more the planned reduction over the last decade-and-a-half, even though it is generally acknowledged that the world has become a riskier and less predictable place. Much of the R&T investment now will only pay off in 10 to 20 years' time, so inadequate investment now will have an adverse effect in the decade 2020 to 2030. Unless we increase our investment, we are unlikely to achieve the more agile and more capable forces that we need to respond to uncertainty.

> Unless we increase our investment, we are unlikely to achieve the more agile and more capable forces that we need

This was recognised by the Labour Party in 1995 before coming to power, as they criticised Conservative R&D spending:

> Decline in government-sponsored R&D has not been compensated for by an increase in civil research, which has indeed decreased at an even faster rate ... Fears that the erosion of Britain's defence capability will become irreversible, and that the UK industry will become no more than an 'offset graveyard' with only a minor manufacturing role in 'off-the-shelf' orders placed abroad, have been voiced repeatedly.[254]

On forming a government, they did nothing about it; indeed, things continued to get worse. Research spending reduced from £700M in 1994/95 to £450M in 2001/02 (price base 2001/02).

> What is now needed is the courage to turn the improved understanding of what needs to be done into a bold and decisive change of direction, and reverse more than a decade of counter-productive defence research reduction.[255]

---

[254] Labour's Approach to the Defence Industry, *Strategy for a Secure Future*, The Labour Party, October 1995.
[255] Sir John Chisholm, 'The Rebirth of UK Research and Technology', *RUSI Defence Systems* (Volume 9, No. 2, October 2006), page 29.

The DIS makes clear that the Government aims to achieve appropriate sovereignty. But to do that, a strong onshore industrial base is essential, and that base will only be strong enough if innovation is more widely promoted. That can only happen if R&T spend is increased significantly.

> *Extra-territorial dependence is clearly a risk, particularly if it is the sole source of supply. The example of Tornado in recent years illustrated the point. Tornado was developed against a requirement for low-level penetration of Soviet air defence and to attack airfields with cluster bombs. When first deployed in anger in the First Gulf War it proved ineffective in the modern scenario. By the Second Gulf War it had been converted into a high-level precision strike platform, a role it performed with great success. The transformation was only possible because the designs and codes were held in the UK together with the expertise and know-how relating to an airframe 30 years past its original development.[256]*

If we don't increase R&T spend, what is the outcome?

> *The increasing disparity between the annual US expenditure on R&T and the corresponding expenditure by other nations, implies that the products of defence contractors based outside the US will become progressively outclassed and uncompetitive.[257]*

And the gap will continue to widen. It has been said that the UK spends its R&T budget much more efficiently than does the US. Whether this is true is debateable.

> *The UK spend of £2.3Bn per year [R&D figure, 2006] needs to be compared with the £29Bn the US spends. As the DIS makes clear, much of this US spend goes into de-risking technology and driving innovation in a way that the UK simply does not do.[258]*

> More than 75% of UK research spending goes on advice to key decision-makers

In fact, according to the NAO, more than 75% of UK research spending goes on advice to key decision-makers, while only 14% is spent on technology in the supplier base and a mere 6% goes on innovation.[259]

---

[256] Ibid, page 29.

[257] Professor David Kirkpatrick, 'The Multiple Crises Afflicting UK Defence Equipment Acquisition', *RUSI Defence Systems* (Volume 9, No. 1, June 2006), page 17.

[258] Graham Jordan, 'The UK's Research and Development Spend', *RUSI Defence Systems* (Volume 9, No. 2, October 2006), page 30.

[259] National Audit Office, *The Management of Defence Research and Development*, The Stationery Office, London, March 2004, page 7.

The report says that:

> *The Department's strategy is increasingly changing from one of creating the Technology Base to one of accessing and exploiting it.*[260]

If you are not prepared to put enough money in, it's probably the only way of doing it. But it cannot be a more efficient way of obtaining useful output than the US approach of de-risking technology and driving innovation.

So, MoD spends about 0.3% of its total defence budget on what might be called 'fundamental research' – i.e. excluding the amount that goes on providing advice to decision-makers. In comparison, the US spends about six to eight times this proportion of its far bigger defence budget, so it stands to reason that the technology gap must continue to widen very quickly.

> MoD spends about 0.3% of its total defence budget on what might be called 'fundamental research'

That figure of 0.3% of the defence budget spent on 'fundamental research' is derisory. Clearly, MoD neither understands nor wants to understand the importance to the future of the defence industry in this country of research and innovation – a fundamental tenet of the DIS. Neither does it want to understand that calling on industry to invest more is hardly likely to achieve much – industry will need larger orders or higher profit margins to do so. While strategic partnering just might provide the latter, larger orders can only come from maintaining the high level of exports. And that will only be possible if enough money is put into technology generation and innovation.

The alternative is a decline in the UK's defence industry as it faces being increasingly left behind by the US and, in the not too distant future, by China and India.

How Much is Enough?

How much should we spend? This is difficult to answer. But it is clear that we need to spend a great deal more than we are doing at the moment. As a rough rule of thumb, we might say that we should spend at least as much as we did in the Cold War – while we still aspire to remain at the

---

[260] Ibid, page 1.

top table of warfighting, the asymmetrical threat is greater and more diverse. A smaller set of armed forces does not save much, if anything, on R&T because fewer platforms only bring savings in terms of procurement and in-service support.

It is estimated that our R&T funding has been halved since 1991. It may not appear so from official government figures because what has been included has been changed significantly twice over the last decade – for example, the budget for Porton Down was added in during the 1990s, and there were plenty of other changes, all of which pushed the figures up. The official figures apparently show that the spend on R&T has remained steady since the end of the Cold War, despite the reduction in the defence budget

Yet the House of Commons Defence Committee (HCDC), in a comprehensive report, found a picture of continuing decline:

> The pattern [of reducing defence research expenditure as a matter of policy] was set in 1987, however, and six years later, in 1993, the White Paper Realising Our Potential anticipated that the decline then under way in government-funded defence research would continue, with a reduction of a third by the turn of the century.[261]

The report continued:

> From a high point in 1993–94, MoD research expenditure is projected to be 31% less in real terms by 2001–02. The MoD records expenditure on 'research' in a slightly different way, and compared with the OST figures the MoD's data shows a more dramatic decline in its research expenditure of 40% in real terms since 1992–93.[262]

In about 1993–94, defence research expenditure appears from the statistics to have received a significant boost. But a redefinition of statistics that took place then (both technical, and with the inclusion of places like Porton Down for the first time) is almost certainly the cause, rather than a real increase. If statistics could be produced on a truly consistent basis, then they would probably show a continuous decline from 1987 onwards.

The NAO assesses[263] that research funding fell from around £700M

---

[261] *Defence Research*, Ninth Report of the HCDC, November 1999, HC 616, Paragraph 6.
[262] Ibid, Paragraph 7.
[263] National Audit Office, *The Management of Defence Research and Development*, The Stationery Office, London, March 2004, page 9.

in 1994/95 to around £470M in 2001/02 – a reduction of 33%. Assuming that it also fell between 1990/91 and 1994/95, this probably confirms – at least in general terms – a halving of research expenditure through the 1990s, despite the official figures that apparently show little or no reduction. This is yet another example of the government spin doctors cloaking the uncomfortable truth.

If we accept this argument above that we need to spend more on R&T, then we should at least double it to bring it back up to the level of the Cold War, given that we are now fighting two major operations.

How do we compare with other countries? This is a difficult comparison because most figures are of R&D, while what we really want is a comparison of R&T. Not only that, but what falls into R, T and D in each nation tends to vary.

Figures for R&D spending on defence are generally not available now, although if we go back to the figures for 1996, UK is below the US and France, but above Germany and Japan, as shown in Figure 9–5; however, it should be borne in mind that, since 1996, UK government spending on defence R&D has fallen further.

Country	Defence R&D	Civil R&D	Total R&D
US	24.092	19.938	44.028
France	2.491	6.097	8.587
UK	2.144	3.616	5.761
Germany	0.943	8.632	9.575
Japan	0.601	9.625	10.226

Figure 9–5: International Comparison of Government Expenditure on Defence and Civil R&D (£Bn, 1996 prices)
Source: SET Statistics 1998, Cm 4006, Table 7.6, July 1998

But the last column in Figure 9–5 shows UK as bottom of the table when both civil and defence R&D is added together. Updating this and including non-government funded R&D, the position is even worse as shown in Figure 9–6:

Country	Government- Funded R&D	Non-Government- Funded R&D	Total R&D
Japan	0.59	2.62	3.21
US	0.83	1.84	2.67
Germany	0.76	1.75	2.51
France	0.85	1.33	2.18
Canada	0.65	1.37	2.02
UK	0.58	1.20	1.78

Figure 9–6: International Comparisons of All R&D as % GDP in 2003
Source: www.berr-ec.com/cgibin/perlcon.pl URN 07/P6

While we will never catch up with the US – indeed we will fall further behind – we should at least aim to slow the rate at which the transatlantic gap is widening. That means an R&D budget perhaps some three to four times its present level.

But Can We Spend Much More?

Despite the repeated statements that we cannot spend any more on research because the defence budget is badly overheated and because we have to find huge savings every year, we can of course find more to invest in research. Indeed, the DTS states the need for greater investment in R&D and the figures above suggest we should be spending much more – at least twice if not four times as much. And if we want to stop the gap with the US widening so fast, we need to do even more.

Can we? Yes.

How?

The first thing we can do is rebalance the way the research budget is divided by reducing the proportion spent on advice-related work (75%). If we were to reverse the proportions so that 'fundamental research' had 75% and 'advice' 25%, we would have trebled useful research spend without affecting the overall sum in the defence budget devoted to it.

If we now doubled this sum, we would have to find a further £330M from elsewhere in the defence budget. Can't be done? But that's less than 1% of the total budget. Three Typhoons? But of course that's three

Typhoons every year, or 30 over the period of the ten-year equipment plan. Not possible?

There are, of course, two objections to moving money from Typhoons to R&T, even if the convoluted processes allow it. First, any savings on Typhoons are needed to chip away at the overheating problem, or offset the cost of new requirements. Secondly, money is so tight in the short term, that spending money on R&T which doesn't have a pay-off for 10 to 20 years is not sensible under 'accountants' logic'. Short-termism strikes again!

The real argument should be about the relative importance of that R&T pay-off in, say, 20 years and the 30 Typhoons that were never bought; or of that R&T pay-off compared with any £330M equipment saving made in the next ten years. That is probably too difficult to do objectively but, subjectively, it can be answered if we project ourselves into the future.

The answer, however, may be that an extra £330M a year would not be enough to save our defence industry and defence research base, so why bother? Two reasons. One, both are essential for appropriate sovereignty on which DIS is based. Two, we can find yet more money without calling further on the defence budget.

I have already mentioned the need to pull through more of our research output (real research, not technical advice) into the equipment programme. What proportion is pulled through now? I don't know and I can't find any reliable figures. 10%? 20%? 30%? I doubt if it's more. Let us rather generously take 30% as the figure, and then seek to increase it. Clearly we cannot get anywhere near 100% pull-through as some research will be bound to fail. Could we get it to, say, 60% – doubling it? This would not in itself provide more funds, but it would avoid much waste and would achieve a better conduit to industry, allowing them greater encouragement to invest in MoD-focused research.

We could only do this if we go all out for strategic partnering and change the culture in the procurement parts of DE&S and in Whitehall, particularly the Treasury, from 'competition, competition, competition' as the prime approach – especially for R&T. For the next step in increasing R&T funding requires the cooperation of industry.

The DTS states that industry should spend more on research as its investment is low compared with MoD's. From this it can be inferred that MoD wants industry to increase its investment – without increasing its own funding. But industry will only do so if it can see value for its shareholders in the not too distant future. It is no good preaching the value of it without exploring what is in it for them.

In general terms this means that industry must be paid at least part of the cost of doing research, and this research must be linked to that which is likely to be pulled through into products – i.e. near-term research. For other research, MoD must pay at least most of the cost.

> *Industry is weak at research, but good at pulling through to products or systems. Understanding differences and linking players can engage the national intellect in creating solutions today to the problems of tomorrow. The maturing DTC [Defence Technology Centres] concept is linking the best characteristics of university research environments with the best of industrial development environments, forming a synergistic relationship, developing genuinely new ideas and concepts and taking them forward to industrial exploitation.[264]*

There is an obvious partnering prospect here, but MoD needs to be clear where the best opportunities lie. Academia and companies towards the bottom of the supply chain need MoD money to provide the innovative research, but the pulling through of that research is best done by larger industrial companies which have a clearer view of where the end profits may lie. If SMEs really are important in producing innovation, it is a sorry comment on MoD's views on innovation and its distrust of small companies that only 8% of its research budget is placed with SMEs.[265]

> There is an obvious partnering prospect here, but MoD needs to be clear where the best opportunities lie

> *We need to enable a culture which is not merely tolerant of innovation but actively embraces it. Two factors make this difficult for MoD: firstly, government accounting rules. These classify research as current expenditure whereas equipment procurement is classed as capital expenditure. This can lead to a mindset of research being an expense while equipment procurement is an investment. Secondly, the increasing focus on risk management in the procurement process can create a climate where innovation, especially in SMEs, is regarded as just too risky.[266]*

---

[264] Jim Ironside, 'Amplifying Industrial Research and Development', *RUSI Defence Systems* (Volume 8, No. 3, February 2006), page 19.
[265] Richard Maudslay, Chairman Dstl, 'UK Defence Research and Technology', UK Defence Forum, CP 64, March 2007, page 4.
[266] Ibid.

In general terms, industry may do some research without MoD funding; in other cases it would expect to share the financial burden; but there will also be some which would not attract industrial funds. Industry is only likely to make substantial investment if one or more of the following applies:

- Competition is not to be held, either at the end of the research industrialisation work, or later in the procurement phases.
- There is a good chance that eventual profits will be substantial.
- The work would lead to further substantial work in related areas.

Focused and partnered investment by industry would increase the overall defence research funds – probably not by half as much again, but by a significant amount. Let us say 30%.

Increased Funding

By following the trail above, we will have increased funding for 'fundamental research' by some 750% for less than an extra 1% of the defence budget (Figure 9–7). Can't be done?

INCREASING THE 'FUNDAMENTAL RESEARCH' BUDGET					
		Fundamental Research Funding	New MoD R&T Funding	Total MoD R&T Funding	Increase in proportion of defence budget
Budget for 'Fundamental Research'	25% of total	£115M		£450M	
Reverse Proportions Research/Advice	25% to 75%	£335M			
Increase Budget	Double	£670M	£330M	£780M	<1%
Partner Industry	+30%	£870M			
Increases		+750%		+75%	<1%

Figure 9–7: Increasing the 'Fundamental Research' Budget

Many may be surprised that I have not included in the above any proposal to increase the research funding by collaborating internationally. This does happen in research and some collaborations are successful – with both the US and Europe. But at the moment these collaborations are very few and relatively small.

The International Dimension

UK/US Collaboration

If we are to collaborate, the obvious international partner would seem to be the US, which is where a very large proportion of the world's cutting-edge R&T is carried out. We have, of course, collaborated extensively in the past, but most of it has been under NATO auspices in areas where allied collaboration is essential – C3, NEC/NCW and modelling and simulation (alliance-wide e-training). But in recent years bilateral UK/US research or technology collaboration has been far less fruitful.

> A year or two ago the JSF project seemed to represent a new level of technology collaboration with the US. But reports in the media and the language of DIS itself indicate fundamental difficulties over UK access to sensitive US technology.[267]

This does not seem to me to be very surprising. Why would any country spend a much bigger proportion of its public money on R&T than any other country and then give away the fruits to other countries which will not help themselves? Of course the US will collaborate in some areas where we have focused investment, but these areas are getting progressively fewer as the technology gap grows. Fewer areas of US-class expertise in UK means fewer collaborative R&T opportunities. We could still join US programmes if we invest heavily in them, but will the sensitive technologies be exported?

A genuine research partnership between the US and the UK would appear to be of benefit to both and much work has gone into achieving it, but it has been a hard road with no end in sight.

> At the level of government scientist talking to government scientist, relationships have always been cordial and open: UK scientists have always enjoyed access to a wide range of US research, including classified programmes. But all of this is strictly on a government scientist to government scientist basis – only rarely is it permissible to pass anything to industry.[268]

---

[267] Graham Jordan, 'The UK's Research and Development Spend', *RUSI Defence Systems* (Volume 9, No. 2, October 2006), page 30.
[268] Graham Jordan, former MoD S&T Director, email to the author, 31 August 2008.

Much effort had gone in to UK/US research collaboration, but little hardware had come out of it apart from test equipment, research supporting techniques of no direct military or industrial significance, work on international military standards and C3 interfaces, and highly specialised niche items. Attempts to widen this to jointly developed technology that could be turned into equipment by both UK and US industries, appeared to be making progress in the early part of the decade, but quickly stalled:

> Sources in the US Army told me in 2007 that the US had entered into joint technology development agreements on the basis of existing UK/US research and R&D MOUs and treaties. But soon afterwards the State Department ruled that no treaty can override US domestic law so ITAR applied to all this collaboration. Everything had stopped dead.[269]

An International Traffic in Arms Regulations (ITAR) waiver for the UK foundered, but there is now a UK/US Defense Trade Cooperation Treaty waiting Senate approval, but it is not likely to be signed until well after the 2008 presidential election – hopefully in 2009. In addition, finding a way for the Treaty to work well in respect of research, as opposed to equipment projects, seems likely to be challenging.

Notwithstanding the general lack of progress so far, the UK and US in September 2006 formally launched a landmark collaborative venture in network and information sciences. This International Technology Alliance (ITA) brings together government, academia and industry from both countries in a five-year research programme.

> It has never been more important or necessary that we should work together to jointly develop and utilise technology, concepts and understanding that can not only improve the effectiveness and survivability of our military forces, but also their ability to operate seamlessly together as a coalition ... the successes and impact of this programme will ultimately be judged on the tangible improvements that will be a benefit to UK and US soldiers conducting military operations.[270]

The ITA is continuing with its programme. It has defined twelve cross-area research projects with teams that consist of at least one industrial

---

[269] Ibid.
[270] Dr Thomas Killion, Professor Phil Sutton, Dr Michael Frame and Pearl Gendason, 'A New Paradigm in International Collaboration', *RUSI Defence Systems* (Volume 10, No. 1, June 2007), page 46.

and one academic consortium member from each of the two countries. The active participation of US Army Research Laboratory (ARL) and UK MoD scientists as team members on each of these projects is welcome. However:

> The ITA seems to be an example of the US using an ITAR exemption for basic (i.e. quasi-academic) research to get out of the bind that both nations are in – but this only works until the research starts to get within hailing distance of something militarily useful.[271]

This exemption is the one other area of potential UK/US research collaboration:

> Some research generally avoids the constraints of ITAR. By a Presidential Directive of 1985 that still operates, basic research is generally exempt from ITAR. This constitutes more than a quarter of US defence research, and might be expected to provide a particularly attractive field for trans-Atlantic collaborative projects. It is therefore remarkable that neither the UK nor France show any expenditure in this category in the official figures for defence R&D.[272]

Collaboration in Europe

If collaboration with the US is not fruitful, can we collaborate in Europe? The problem here is similar, but in reverse: although Europe has the economic clout to rival the US in defence spending, including research and development, it spends only about half as much as the US on defence, about a third as much on equipment and about a third as much on R&D – and expenditure is split between numerous nations. Moreover, France and UK account for about two-thirds of all EU government defence expenditure. Four other nations (Germany, Spain, Italy and Sweden) account for another quarter. The remaining few per cent are contributed by the rest. Why would we want to collaborate with most of these? Even with Germany, Italy, Spain and Sweden, would we want to collaborate except in a few niche areas?

> Would we want to collaborate except in a few niche areas?

The only viable R&T partner is France. France and the UK spend

---

[271] Graham Jordan, former MoD S&T Director, email to the author, 5 July 2008.
[272] Graham Jordan and Tim Williams, 'Defence Research and Development in the Atlantic Nations', *RUSI Occasional Paper*, RUSI, London.

much the same, both have a similar defence strategy, both have collaborated in many areas in the past and still do. Bilateral arrangements work best. However, just as in collaborative procurement, collaboration is slower than going it alone – and increasingly so as the numbers of collaborating countries increase. While the base is larger and firmer, it takes more time to set up, particularly if each nation is at a different stage in some areas and has different priorities. The time saved by pooling work to date is often less than the time needed to set up the arrangements in the first place. And time is not on our side with the short technology generations and the fast-changing battlefield.

The European Defence Agency

The purpose of the European Defence Agency (EDA) is to improve the military capabilities of member states, and technology is a fundamental building block of capability.

> At birth the Agency was an unhappy compromise and slow progress to date has reflected a rather muddy raison d'être. EDA has neither pleased those who saw it as a 'dating agency' charged with identifying innovative solutions to capability gaps, nor those that expected major European equipment programmes to flow from it.[273]

One of the most important, but most difficult, subjects has been, and still is, R&T.

> The 24 European Defence Ministries that participate in the EDA are this year [2006] planning to spend a total of €2.3Bn on defence R&T – or about 1.25% of their defence spending. Industry has long been arguing that we have been living off the fat of investments made in the Cold War era; these figures prove the point. As Solana reported back to the June summit in Brussels: 'This level of investment is clearly inadequate to sustain an internationally competitive defence technological and industrial base in Europe'. Meeting as the EDA Steering Board, EU Defence Ministers readily agreed that when it comes to defence R&T in Europe, the need is to 'spend more, spend better and spend more together'.[274]

Two nations (UK and France) account for two-thirds of all European

---

[273] Graham Jordan and Tim Williams, 'Hope Deferred? The European Defence Agency after Three Years', *RUSI Journal* (Volume 152, No. 3, June 2007), page 68.
[274] Nick Whitney, Chief Executive of the EDA, 'The Challenge for European Defence R&T', *RUSI Defence Systems* (Volume 9, No. 2, October 2006), page 26.

defence R&T. Adding Germany, Italy, Spain and Sweden, the total rises to 90%. The rest spend virtually nothing. How can they contribute even if they do spend more, which is unlikely given shrinking defence budgets? Why should UK and France increase their R&T spend within Europe?

> *Given that the EDA has no R&T budget of its own, cooperation in R&T mostly means cooperation between France and the UK, and is almost entirely a matter for cooperation between the LoI six.*[275]

> **Why should UK and France increase their R&T spend within Europe?**

So, European collaboration in R&T boils down in the main to bilateral cooperation between France and the UK, with some cooperation with the other LoI nations.

In 2005, EU defence ministers called for increased spending on R&T and greater European collaboration on R&T projects. But can the EDA deliver successful R&T output as well as, or better than, bilateral arrangements, or will it just add a complicating bureaucratic layer? Will wrangling over the priorities lead to messy compromises? Or more importantly, will R&T programmes suffer a 'valley of death' when the prospect of moving outputs into projects fails to attract national support and funds?

Not surprisingly, perhaps, the EDA seems to be largely irrelevant in R&T collaboration. Add to that its poor progress on armaments, and it is not surprising that UK is not very enthusiastic.

A Defence Technology Plan

The DIS failed to cover R&T adequately, but it did direct that the DTS was to be updated and this update, published only a short while afterwards, did fill in many of the gaps. However,

> *It is a disappointing document in that, while it states the need for more investment from both industry and MoD, it does not say how this extra investment is to be produced. Without it, little improvement will be possible.*[276]

---

[275] Graham Jordan and Tim Williams, 'Hope Deferred? The European Defence Agency after Three Years', *RUSI Journal* (Volume 152, No. 3), page 68.
[276] RUSI Acquisition Focus, 'Defence Acquisition after Drayson', *RUSI Defence Systems* (Volume 10, No. 3, February 2008), page 26.

Clearly, the DTS needs to be taken further. It needs to be translated into a Defence Technology Plan, with a clear implementation plan and an endorsed strategy for significantly increased R&T investment by **both** MoD and industry. It has been announced that a Defence Technology Plan will be published at the end of 2008. Will it?

The R&T Challenge

International collaboration on R&T is neither straightforward nor does it necessarily lead to better cost-effectiveness. Moreover, collaboration with Europe is bound to be slower and more constrained financially in comparison with US national R&T. Hence European R&T, except in a few areas, is bound to fall increasingly behind that of the US. As a result, it seems that there are three possible avenues that, if pursued, would offer a ray of hope for UK R&T:

> European R&T is bound to fall increasingly behind that of the US

- First and foremost, spend much more on national R&T programmes – it is possible to get a major uplift in spending without a major increase in MoD funding, as described earlier.
- Second, collaborate with the US where this is possible and where it will deliver true technology transfer.
- Finally, collaborate bilaterally in specific areas with France and, in a very few niche areas, with Germany, Spain, Italy and Sweden.

But unless funding for R&T is given a major uplift and those increased funds spent on technology generation and demonstration, UK R&T will fall further and further behind that of the US – and in due course of China and India – and totter largely into irrelevance. Such a course would sound the death knell for the majority of defence exports, UK appropriate sovereignty and our current UOR policy. And, of course, the DIS.

SUMMARY: RESEARCH AND TECHNOLOGY

DIS Recommendations

- Review the alignment of the research programme with MoD needs.
- Conduct further work to understand better the underpinning technologies that the UK must have for security and sovereignty reasons.
- Update the Defence Technology Strategy (DTS) to reflect the conclusions of the Defence Industrial Strategy (DIS).
- Develop a better understanding of the innovation process.

DTS Recommendations

- Advance Science and Technology (S&T) in specific areas.
- Set up communities of practice in core technologies.
- Create university centres of excellence.
- Speed up Research and Development (R&D) exploitation.
- Create joint MoD/industry framework for investment.

Issues To Be Resolved

- Poor pull-through into procurement programmes of MoD-funded research.
- The 'Valley of Death'.
- Difficulties in transferring technology to, and between, commercial companies.
- Maturity of technology available before Main Gate.
- Integration of hi-tech equipment.
- Support for innovation and the Small- and Medium-sized Enterprises (SMEs) that produce it.

But none of this will matter if the one major issue is not resolved

Major Issue

- The lack of adequate funding for Research, Technology and Development (R, T & D), which will inevitably lead to a widening transatlantic technology gap, declining competitiveness in the export market, a further weakening of the onshore defence industry and undermining of the DIS itself.

PART THREE

WHERE ARE WE NOW?

"We've distilled the acquisition 'conspiracy of optimism' into a pill… we're going to make a killing in the anti-depressant market!"

Chapter Ten

Progress and Stagnation

It is now getting on for three years since Lord Drayson launched the DIS and we should have seen enough to hazard a good guess as to whether the reforms he outlined within it are on course for a successful conclusion, or whether it, together with the EAC, DACP and DTS, will remain good ideas that are never properly implemented – like so many previous MoD initiatives.[277]

Not surprisingly, there has been a great deal of activity and some real progress. MoD must be congratulated – change is never easy and requires a great deal of thought, planning and following through. But equally unsurprising is the lack of progress in other areas. Of course, not everything can be fully addressed in such a short time – it has been said that significant change will take much longer to implement fully – and we would be foolish in the extreme if we condemned MoD for not having fully implemented everything by now.

However, some things are easier to achieve than others, and it is the besetting sin of politicians and their officials, to drive for 'quick wins', rather than make ordered progress towards those measures, which will provide the greatest improvement overall. That is, the implementation of the 20% which will achieve 80% improvement, rather than the quicker and easier management of the 80% which will make only a 20% improvement. The former, of course, almost always involves the most difficult measures, and that is why they are not grasped. Consequently, that is why so many initiatives fail.

It is perhaps worth repeating the observation that has been made by Sir Jeremy Blackham:

> *The official mind is outstandingly good at dealing with 'tame' problems … it is trained and honed for this purpose. It is less well adapted, indeed almost wholly unsuitable, for thinking 'out of the box'.*[278]

---

[277] Unlike the first two parts of this book, Part Three does not comment on history, but on events as they are unfolding with a resulting paucity of clear evidence and greater speculative comment.

[278] Sir Jeremy Blackham, 'Dealing with Wicked problems', *RUSI Journal* (Volume 152, No. 4, August 2007), page 37.

So, if politicians and senior officials are wedded to 'quick wins', and if officials are less good at dealing with the really difficult problems, is it surprising if an individual first embraces the 'easier' 80% and leaves the difficult 20% for later? No doubt he will have a thought, conscious or unconscious, that delay will make it his successor's problem, or that another initiative will be along before he gets to the really difficult issues.

Has officialdom followed the easier route in its implementation of DIS? Let us look at the state of play in 2008.

The Defence Board

The Defence Management Board has now become the Defence Board. It is the MoD's senior executive committee. Chaired by the PUS, it provides senior level leadership and top-level management of defence. Military operations are the responsibility of the Chief of the Defence Staff (CDS) who draws on the advice of the three single-Service Chiefs of Staff. Defence activity is managed through eight Top Level Budget (TLB) holders and four Trading Funds.

One recent change is the creation of the three Service TLBs. For these, the objectives are set by the Defence Board, decided in the final analysis by the PUS and the CDS, and laid on the Service Chiefs, who are funded to carry out those objectives and who will be held accountable by the Board. But are they really accountable? What happens if they fail to meet their objectives? And who is accountable for acquisition?

> *As for acquisition, I think it is pulled together pretty well. What we have now is an informal acquisition group, chaired by the PUS with VCDS, the Chief of Defence Materiel (CDM), 2nd PUS, the Finance Director, the Defence Commercial Director and myself [DCDS(EC)] and this engages all the main players. Needless to say, it doesn't do the detail.*[279]

It is not clear who is held to account or how, given that decisions are by committee.

> *You may think that may be rather cosy, but I wouldn't describe it as cosy.*

---

[279] Lieutenant General Andrew Figgures, Deputy Chief of the Defence Staff (Equipment Capability), Interview, *RUSI Defence Systems* (Volume 11, No. 1, June 2008), page 15.

> *Individuals are under pressure to deliver but it is not so much the disciplinary pressure that is effective, it is the peer pressure around the Board table.*[280]

However, it is still difficult to see who is really accountable, and for what, in acquisition at the top level.

> *The recent reorganisation into the Defence Board has not led to a single focus for TLCM, nor has it achieved clear accountability.*[281]

Clear accountability remains a real weakness.

Amalgamating Procurement and Support

Much of the early DIS implementation effort was expended on the amalgamation of the existing DPA and the DLO – two separate organisations each under its own 4-star official, with different sources of funding and with significantly different cultures. Clearly, amalgamation of the two would be a very big task.

However, the bringing together of the two has been achieved in pretty quick time under the direction of the new CDM, General Sir Kevin O'Donaghue.

The joining together of both procurement and support IPTs is a major enabler of through-life management.

> *We found that the merger of the two organisations ... has provided impetus to the implementation of the Maritime Industrial Strategy. It has created a more coherent and streamlined structure which facilitates a more joined up approach in that key individuals already putting the Strategy into practice are now in a better position to deploy key players' existing skills and experience better ....*[282]

> A new relationship with the front line has been a welcome strand of the DE&S amalgamation

As well as improving through-life management and other procedures, a new relationship with the front line has been a welcome strand of the DE&S amalgamation. The three Chiefs of Materiel act on behalf of the front-line user within the DE&S and are

---

[280] Ibid.

[281] RUSI Acquisition Focus, 'Implementing Through-Life Capability Management', *RUSI Defence Systems* (Volume 11, No 1, June 2008), page 28.

[282] National Audit Office, *Ministry of Defence: Major Projects Report 2007*, HC 98-1 2007–2008, Volume 1, The Stationery Office, London , 26 November 2007, page 23.

responsible to the Front-Line Commands for the DE&S output. This has given DE&S a much clearer relationship with the end-user, one that was lacking in the old DPA and that was less than clear in the old DLO.

> *The DE&S is demonstrating an ability to combine a sharp operational focus with commercial astuteness – the best of DPA and DLO.*[283]

Another change has been the introduction of the 'industry-facing' clusters of IPTs led by 'fully empowered' 2-stars who report direct to the Chief Operating Officer. It will be interesting to see how this pans out – will the 2-stars manage to reduce the negative effect of 'stovepiping' without undermining the empowerment of the IPT leaders? Time will tell.

And time is the key.

> *I would argue that we are already making a difference; behaviours are changing, but we have only just begun; operational effectiveness must be our key measure of success; and that we will not succeed without a changed relationship with industry and the front line.*[284]

But how long do we wait for clear signs that the improvement is not confined to parts of the organisation, rather than the whole, and that the progress is not reversible?

> *It has taken six months to get the higher levels of the DE&S organisation in place and now we're taking the next year to get processes and systems sorted out for a much smoother operation. You don't do that kind of thing without some turbulence along the way, but I'm confident that it will settle down within a year or so. Melding the cultures of the DPA and DLO into a single, through-life capability management and equipment system management organisation will take longer; if we do that in two or three years, we will have done well.*[285]

We should not expect too much too soon. But equally, MoD must not allow things to drift. It is this culture change that will take the longest to instil throughout the organisation. Two or three years is perhaps an optimistic view.

---

[283] Lieutenant General Dick Applegate, 'Equipping and Supporting our Armed Forces for Operations', *RUSI Defence Systems* (Volume 10, No. 3, February 2008), page 94.
[284] Ibid, page 95.
[285] Rear Admiral Rees Ward, Interview, *Defence Director*, September 2007, GovNet Communications.

Commercial Practices

One of the acknowledged weaknesses in MoD is the lack of commercial expertise. DIS decreed the appointment of a Defence Commercial Director (and the creation of the Defence Commercial Directorate) to be responsible for *"driving forward the commercial aspects of the Defence Industrial Strategy and, in particular, for developing partnering arrangements with industry that embed the right behaviours and incentives for all parties".*[286]

MoD believes this appointment has been the trigger for major reform of its commercial practices, bringing together the development of acquisition and commercial policy, management of supplier relations and intellectual property. All this is badly needed. Substantial improvement cannot be made without such reform of commercial practices but, equally, this reform is unlikely to take root unless the traditional Whitehall antipathy to commerce is changed. Once again it is culture change that is more important than the procedural or organisational change.

Culture Shift

The need to change culture and relationships is the most important of all the elements of the changes that are being made in the wake of the DIS, EAC and DACP. And, as has already been discussed, culture change has been the chief failure of previous initiatives, because it is the most difficult, takes the longest and needs consistent and determined leadership from the top over a long period of time.

Culture and Inertia

In Chapter Eight, I discussed the DIS and EAC views on what culture changes were needed and found them wanting, because they failed to cover many major issues of culture. These bear repeating for without changing these, nothing much will change:

- Whitehall's 'delay mentality'.
- MoD's suppression of leadership.
- A culture of minimising the downside rather than maximising the upside.
- A mindset that is risk-averse and equates innovation with risk.

---

[286] DIS, page 134.

- The bad target culture.
- Spin-doctoring of figures which undermines trust and transparency.
- The clash between true empowerment and stovepipes.
- The repeated failure to learn, rather than just identify, lessons.
- The difficulty of recruiting, and retaining, high-quality staff.

In addition to the culture issues in MoD listed above, many of which have a knock-on effect on industry's attitudes to change, there are many which are common to both MoD and industry including:

- The aversion to change and innovation in MoD and Primes.
- The lack of leadership in both MoD and industry.
- Lack of clear motivation – no MoD 'time-to-market' ethos, contractual straitjackets and industry's seeking of loopholes.
- Blindness to the need for change – "I already do it".
- Industry's 'wait and see' attitude.

Overcoming this inertia needs plenty of hard work. It is worrying that the top men do not seem to have understood that at the beginning, and may not now. Writing in October 2006, the PUS said:

> *The Defence Values for Acquisition were launched by Lord Drayson in October last year at the RUSI Defence Project Management Conference, but we need to do more to explain them to staff and get them into the bloodstream of the organisation.*[287]

There are aspects of culture that are deeply ingrained and will take some shifting

This was specifically aimed at MoD where there are aspects of culture that are deeply ingrained and will take some shifting. Can they be shifted?

While much work has gone on within MoD on procedures and organisations, there has been less emphasis on culture change. Has the extra effort that the PUS called for two years ago been made? Or has it been shelved as too difficult?

It is not too difficult. The Pathfinder Programmes showed that culture can be changed. However, these were two special programmes that were set up to see what could be done. The lessons from them

---

[287] Bill Jeffrey, 'Implementing the Defence Industrial Strategy', *RUSI Defence Systems* (Volume 9, No. 2, October 2006), page 23.

should have been learned and instigated across the board. But have they? Will they?

The Refocused DACP

The DACP has a vision: *To bring about a step change improvement in acquisition performance – i.e. in the delivery of capability to the front line and value-for-money for the taxpayer – through creating a more agile acquisition system and managing capability through life.*

According to the MoD website, DACP has been refocused for 2009 and has five objectives, which are given as:[288]

- An equipment and support plan that is more stable, affordable and realistic whilst allowing greater agility. This will require better costing and forecasting, and more focus on in-service support costs. Delivering this objective will result in less disruption and delay to the programme.

- Significantly (30% to 50%) shorter acquisition cycle time – reducing the time from 'decision to effect'. To deliver this we will move to alternative, more incremental approaches to acquisition. In parallel, existing acquisition processes will be streamlined. There will be greater emphasis on open systems architectures and technology insertion.

- Reduced cost of doing business for both MoD and industry. This will require us all to have a stronger focus on the value of time, and will be enabled by the work to reduce acquisition cycle time. Both MoD and industry overheads will be reduced.

- More effective delivery. This will be delivered, in part, by further reform under way in DE&S. Much of this is dependent on greater empowerment and accountability, better use of staff with higher skills levels and changing cultures and behaviours – 'Team Defence'.

- These objectives will be delivered hand-in-hand with the industrial transformation set out in the DIS.

The new approach of DACP work has four major thrusts:

- Planning and TLCM.
- Alternative acquisition approaches.

---

[288] www.mod.uk, Defence Acquisition Change Programme, 24 September 2008.

- DE&S's Performance, Agility, Confidence, Efficiency (PACE) programme.
- Commercial transformation.

These thrusts are supported by two cross-cutting workstreams:
- People, skills and behaviours.
- Knowledge management.

The key to the work is TLCM. The RUSI Acquisition Focus paper on TLCM is at Appendix 7–3.

The objectives of the refocused DACP are excellent – how could anyone not agree with them? This is, of course, what we should have been about for the last decade or more. But reading the bits after the first sentence of each rather knocks a hole in the euphoria. It's one thing to lay down the right objectives, quite another to meet them.

Take the admirable objective to reduce acquisition cycle times by 30% to 50%. It is not long ago that I was told that was impossible. Of course it's possible. But it doesn't depend on changes to process and procedures, systems architectures and technology insertion. Sure, these things help, but it is the culture that has to change – faster decision-making, sensible risk-taking, proper empowerment and all the rest. But looking at the four major thrusts of work, it is difficult to see how a 30%, let alone a 50%, reduction in time will be achieved. Will this be another worthy aim that fails?

Yes. It has already failed. The original requirement was for a 50% reduction, but this was then modified to a reduction of 30% to 50%. Guess what: that means 30%. But since September 2008, even these figures have disappeared and the MoD website has been amended to say that the requirement is for a 'significantly shorter' acquisition cycle time. What does that mean? 25%? 20%? 15%? 10%? Less?

I will tell you what it means. First of all it means any reduction that can be achieved without moving out of comfort zones will be called 'success'; and second, it means the whole exercise is doomed to failure because anything much less than a 50% reduction will not achieve the improvement in acquisition performance that we so desperately need.

> Another worthy initiative has failed before it has started

Another worthy initiative has failed before it has started.

Reducing Staff

On 23 October 2007, MoD announced that more resources would be released to the front line by streamlining the MoD's Head Office in London ensuring it is as efficient as possible.

The announcement went on to say that the Streamlining programme would simplify MoD's organisation and work, ensuring the Ministry is focused on strategic tasks and better able to respond to priorities; that other parts of Defence have been reformed along similar lines now being carried out by the Head Office; and that at least £50M of ongoing savings, which can be reinvested in operations, will be released per year by reducing the Head Office staff by 25%. This means the loss of around 1000 civilian jobs and 300 military posts. The number of military posts being reduced will not require redundancy.

The Streamlining programme is planned to be implemented over two to three years.

This streamlining of MoD Head Office is long overdue, but it will have little effect unless it is begun by assessing what work or responsibilities will no longer be done. Too often, a cut in staff numbers simply means the same work is done by fewer people so that those left have to work even harder, put in even longer hours and get no guidance on what the priorities are in their larger workload.

> Above all, let's not have any *Yes, Minister* shenanigans

Above all, let's not have any *Yes, Minister* shenanigans where posts cut from Head Office reappear in other organisations with no overall savings. This wouldn't happen, would it? Maybe, for we have seen such manoeuvres with acquisition cost 'savings'.

Defence Exports

Of course, the Defence Exports Support Organisation (DESO) decision had nothing to do with cutting MoD manpower. Did it? If it didn't, then it is difficult to see a reason why it was made.

The DIS acknowledged that the UK defence industry is the second largest defence exporter after the US and wins orders worth an average of £5Bn per year – indeed in 2007, it was the leading exporter with a 33% market share. Advantages include the support of defence diplomacy, enhanced interoperability, spreading of overheads, government income and help for maintenance of key sovereign capabilities, but DIS did suggest that there were disadvantages too:

> While exports will often sustain supply chains that would otherwise have been without business, this can be undermined by other nations' requirements for offset – i.e. that particular elements of work on UK programmes should be subcontracted offshore or new industrial capabilities established in their territory.[289]

It goes on to quote a York University study which concluded that *"the economic costs of reducing defence exports are a relatively small and largely one-off ... as a consequence the balance of argument about defence exports should depend mainly on non-economic considerations"*.

Whether as a consequence of this or not, Prime Minister Tony Blair announced on 25 July 2007 that:

> Trade promotion for defence exports should be more effectively integrated with the Government's general · trade support activities while recognising and accommodating the specific requirements of the defence sector.

The Defence Export Services Organisation was disbanded and its activities taken over by UK Trade and Investment

As a result, responsibility for defence trade promotion became the ministerial responsibility of the Minister of State for Trade and Investment, the Defence Export Services Organisation was disbanded and its activities taken over by UK Trade and Investment (UKTI) from 1 April 2008. Within UKTI, a separate business unit – Defence and Security Organisation (DSO) – took over DESO's responsibilities. About 200 military and civil staff were transferred on loan.

In theory, the pulling together of defence and civil trade promotion makes good sense, but how would it work in practice? Would defence and security become a low priority within UKTI? How would its links with MoD work? Many people were sceptical, if not downright hostile:

> From a government that brought us 'joined-up' departments it is striking that one of the first actions of its defence industrial policy is to abolish DESO and hide

---

[289] DIS, page 47.

> *the decision in the parliamentary background … The biggest loser will not be …*
> *any large prime. Instead, the SMEs for whom DESO acts as a key surrogate*
> *business development and conduit for opportunities will suffer.[290]*

No wonder SMEs do not believe that government really wants to help them. The same article alleges that industry wasn't consulted and that Lord Drayson was informed only on the day of announcement.

DESO has indeed been successful in securing export-driven revenues that have enabled reinvestment in new technological capabilities. Exports have enabled the defence industry to survive the low profit margins allowed by MoD in the teeth of the roughest competition weather. In effect, exports have kept prices down for MoD equipment.

The export performance has been all the more remarkable because the user has never paid much attention to export potential when setting down the equipment requirement – indeed there has always been much talk of 'gold plating'. For example, the Royal Navy wants dense, complex warships – even today when land operations and Maritime Security Operations seem to demand more, less complex units – and these lack the wider appeal of vessels such as the German MEKOs. As a result, exporting UK equipment has been made more difficult, for few nations wish to afford the sophistication that the UK offers, while many of those that do have their own defence industry.

Any significant reduction in defence exports is going to have two adverse effects for MoD. The first is that the cost of DIS will rise; the second is that MoD will have to invest more in R&T if DIS is to be successful. Neither is an enticing prospect.

> Any significant reduction in defence exports is going to have two adverse effects

Will the change be successful in maintaining the high level of defence exports? We will see, but the signs are not propitious.

> *There is now no involvement from any junior ministers at the MoD. The lack of*
> *adequate defence based ministerial support is hugely important and at least one*
> *country, if not two, that have in the past acquired significant amounts of UK*
> *defence equipment, have said that because they are only prepared to deal with UK*

---

[290] Adam Baddeley, 'DESO Destroyed', *Defence Director*, May 2007, Govnet Communications.

> *defence ministers when it comes to matters defence they will only see senior or even junior UK T&I ministers as a matter of courtesy – not to do business.*[291]

The new head of DSO, former BP Director Richard Paniguian, has no past experience of defence matters.

Strategic Partnering

The starting point of the DIS and much of the DIS White Paper was the need to maintain a strong onshore defence industry. Key to this, in the future environment where orders from MoD would be fewer and farther between, was strategic partnering with large defence primes, whether British companies or foreign ones with a major presence in the UK. I have discussed at length the difficulties in moving from the competitive, adversarial regime to partnering.

Is it happening?

Yes, it is – to an extent, although some partnering arrangements are taking longer to set up than others, and some partnering arrangements have been in place since well before the DIS: the Defence Fixed Telecommunications Service (DTFS) contract with BT is usually held up as a shining example of partnering.

> *That kind of partnering agreement was hard won – the first two years were very, very difficult – however we came out of that and the programme now shows all the very best characteristics of partnering. BT and ourselves were, and still are, both working towards driving costs down and increasing volume while introducing best quality services through innovation – a 'win-win' situation.*[292]

Successful partnering can reduce costs and improve quality

Another example is the transformation in the logistic support of fast jets, which made significant reductions in the cost of support.[293]

So, successful partnering can reduce costs and improve quality – provided the

---

[291] Howard Wheeldon, Senior Strategist, 'Record 2007 UK Defence Exports – Yet Another Slap in the Face for the Brown Government', BGC Partners, 17 June 2008.
[292] Rear Admiral Rees Ward, Interview, *RUSI Defence Systems* (Volume 10, No. 3, February 2008), page 9.
[293] National Audit Office, *Transforming Logistics Support for Fast Jets*, HC 825 Session 2006–2007, The Stationery Office, London, 17 July 2007.

partnering mentality is present on both sides of the MoD/industry divide.

Helicopters

Lord Drayson drove the partnering arrangement with AgustaWestland and this was signed in June 2006. MoD believes that it creates, for the first time, contractual commitments and incentivisation for performance improvements across the full spectrum of the business relationship between MoD and AgustaWestland. The agreement:

- Has targets for specific improvements in aircraft availability, schedule adherence, responsiveness, and acquisition and support cost reductions.
- Provides a balance of risk and reward, offering opportunities for industry to secure bonus payments if performance improvement targets are achieved, and default payments retained by MoD if these performance targets are not met.

MoD admits that the success of the agreement depends on transformation in both MoD and industry.

Armoured Vehicles

The arrangements with BAE Systems on armoured vehicles and munitions were likewise agreed early. However, little progress on strategic partnering on armoured vehicles appears to have been made. The reason may well be that there is little commonality of interests between MoD and BAE Systems.

Team Complex Weapons

One area where Europe competes equally with the US is 'complex weapons' – those strategic and tactical weapons reliant upon guidance systems to achieve precision effects. The problem in this sector is that MoD investment has peaked, and will now decline, leaving the truly world-class European expertise to fight for survival. The answer was to establish a multi-disciplinary team to sustain the technologies and capabilities.

The formation of 'Team CW', which represents a partnering arrangement of national 'CW' companies to be led by MBDA UK and including QinetiQ, Thales Air Defence, Thales Missile Electronics, Roxel and other suppliers, was announced by Lord Drayson at the Farnborough Air Show in July 2006. Team CW now faces a more certain future within the unfolding world of UCAVs, Directed Energy Weapons (DEW) and NEC.[294]

Alongside a Teaming Agreement with all of the Team CW members, two contracts have been placed with MBDA (UK) Ltd and Thales UK to develop six Complex Weapons projects within the Assessment Phase, at a value of around £74M for the first year:

- Indirect Fire Precision Attack Loitering Munition (MBDA-led with Team Loitering Munition).
- 100kg weapon family to meet first the Future Air to Surface Guided Weapon (heavyweight) requirement for Royal Navy helicopters (MBDA).
- Light weapon family to meet first the Future Air to Surface Guided Weapon (lightweight) requirement (Thales UK).
- 50kg weapon family to meet the Selected Precision Effects At Range (SPEAR) requirement for fast jets and helicopters (MBDA).
- The Common Anti-Air Modular Missile family to meet first the requirement for a Future Local Area Air Defence System (FLAADS) for the T23 Frigate and the Future Surface Combatant (MBDA).
- An upgrade programme for Storm Shadow currently used on the Tornado GR4 (MBDA).

So, real progress here?

There is still, however, some uncertainty.

The underlying problem could be that with these programmes finished, the design teams will break up due to the gap in new programmes coming on stream, thus the £74M is a sop to the CWS Teams to keep their teams in place. The MoD has been procuring a large number of missiles from Lockheed Martin and Raytheon outside CWST. The Admiral [MoD's Rear Admiral Amjad Hussein] could not promise anything beyond that progress will be made if the proposals submitted by industry meet with the requirements of the MoD. There was no detail of the technology or application of these systems or which missiles they would replace.

---

[294] Chris Conroy, 'Complex Weapons: Challenges for Industry', *RUSI Defence Systems* (Volume 9, No. 3, March 2007) – electronic version only www.rusi.org/defencesystems

One only has to look at the stalled Joint Common Missile Program in the USA to wonder what will come after the £74M? [295]

Success of the Team CW Assessment Phase might lead to the majority of current and future UK Complex Weapons being included within the scope of a long-term partnering arrangement and enable the optimum use of approximately £6Bn expenditure in this sector over the next 10 years. But with the DIS apparently being sidelined, it is not surprising if industry is nervous.

Maritime Industrial Strategy

It was the maritime industrial sector that was perhaps the most important catalyst for the DIS, because of the huge shipbuilding programme over the next decade and then a steady decline of orders that would make the retention of critical industrial skills very hard, if not impossible.

Current shipbuilding plans are for managed decline … Officials have no expectation [after CVF and Type 45s] and – in answer to direct questioning at the RUSI Maritime Conference in November 2006 – not merely no capability for surge production, but not even any recognition that this might be a requirement that should be considered. This is simply madness. If the CVF programme was delayed or cancelled, and FSC [Future Surface Combatant] not brought forward, there is a real risk that warship building capacity would disappear from the UK and that design and systems engineering will migrate. [296]

> Drayson made no secret of his determination to get a maritime strategic partnering arrangement in place

Of course, this is exactly the problem that DIS is trying to resolve. Drayson made no secret of his determination to get a maritime strategic partnering arrangement in place, but progress has been slow.

I have made little secret of my frustration around the maritime sector and my determination to make progress. I have made clear we will reward companies who respond positively to DIS, and the future aircraft carrier (CVF) Main Gate will be a key decision point. [297]

---

[295] Julian Nettlefold, 'Keeping the Missile Teams Together, Battlespace Update (Vol. 10, Issue 28), 17 July 2008.

[296] Sir Jeremy Blackham, 'The Royal Navy at the Brink', *RUSI Journal* (Vol. 152, No. 2, April 2007), page 15.

[297] Lord Drayson, 'Our Relationship with Industry', *RUSI Defence Systems* (Vol. 9, No. 2, October 2006), page 21.

MoD has since agreed a 'core workload' that it will underwrite equivalent to one complex warship, or a 5500 tonne frigate, once work on the aircraft carriers begins to tail off. This agreed workload also assumes a redesign every six or seven years.[298] The report goes on to say that *"this will enable industry to plan the necessary rationalisation and long-term transformation required to meet this future steady-state demand"*. But for how long will that remain the case?

The DIS made clear the need for industrial restructuring in the maritime sector. This has been taken forward slowly.

> *In the submarine sector, there was already in effect only one main supplier of build facilities and in June 2007 the Government used its Golden Share stake in DML Group to influence consolidation of the support services. Babcock International Group now has a controlling interest in both the Devonport and Faslane submarine bases.*[299]

This should bring benefits:

> *Consolidation of in-service support under Babcock Marine, which now supports the entire Royal Navy submarine flotilla, contributes beneficially in bringing together Britain's submarine support facilities at Devonport and Clyde and presenting opportunities for rationalisation and avoidance of duplication in capacity, capability and skills.*[300]

> *This partnering agreement addresses the position of three monopoly suppliers and meets the Defence Industrial Strategy's vision of a 'programme-level partnering agreement with a single industrial entity for the full life cycle of the submarine flotilla, while addressing key affordability issues'. It thus overcomes the traditional fragmentation of submarine manufacture and support, bringing the two under single programme management.*[301]

Progress in the surface ship sector has been slower

Progress in the surface ship sector has been slower. The same report states:

---

[298] National Audit Office, *Ministry of Defence: Major Projects Report 2007*, HC 98-1 2007/2008, Volume 1, Part 2, page 24, The Stationery Office, London, 26 November 2007.

[299] National Audit Office, *Ministry of Defence: Major Projects Report 2007*, HC 98-1 2007/2008, Volume 1, Part 2, page 25, The Stationery Office, London, 26 November 2007.

[300] Roger Hardy, MD Submarines Babcock Marine, *RUSI Defence Systems* (Volume 11, No. 2, October 2008).

[301] Ibid.

> *We found that the Department and industry have together been able to establish a suitable route to restructuring, although this has taken longer than was initially planned. On 25 July [2007] BAE Systems and VT Group announced that they were to form a Surface Ship Joint Venture, which will focus on construction and longer-term support.*

The Joint Venture company, BVT Surface Fleet Limited, officially started operations on 1 July 2008. MoD believes that a single national champion will be better placed to win export orders once the new generation of Royal Navy ships has been completed and there are few domestic contracts for a couple of decades.

In the longer term, MoD wants industry to consolidate further, with synergies between surface ship and submarine sectors.

Partnering and Competition

Strategic Partnering is, therefore, going ahead even if progress has been patchy and overall rather less than envisaged in DIS. Has it finally overcome the 'competition, competition, competition' approach? Well, not entirely and there seems to be a backlash. Consider this from a draft MoD document:

> *Fair and open competition remains fundamental to government procurement policy ... competition has been shown to reduce costs, increase productivity and stimulate innovation ... [in certain circumstances] partnering will be considered alongside other procurement approaches, and tested as to whether it offers improved value-for-money ....*

It then provides a list of factors which may be considered in arriving at a decision to partner. It must be emphasised that this comes from an unendorsed document, but it does show that there is still a strong school of thought that competition is the preferred option and that partnering will be considered if competition does not appear to offer an attractive approach.

Cost, Time and Performance

So, across the board there has been progress, although on the whole it has been slower than envisaged and is still very patchy. But what sort of progress and how much? Certainly, if activity equals progress, there has

been a lot. But has output been improved and, if so, to what extent? This
is a difficult question to answer after such a short time has elapsed since

> Has output been
> improved and, if so,
> to what extent?

DIS was published as changes in culture,
process and organisation take time to feed
through into output improvement.

However, we can assess output
performance – generally listed as cost, time
and performance – over the last several years and note improvement or
reduction in performance as a result of the various initiatives since Smart
Acquisition was launched.

Cost

The first thing that jumps out of the various reports on costs is the lack
of through-life costs.

> *It is notorious that for many projects the cost of operations and support during
> their service lives are larger (sometimes much larger) than their procurement
> costs, and the 1998 Smart Acquisition initiative properly included a commitment
> that the MoD would adopt a through-life approach to project management,
> basing decisions for each project on the effect of those decisions on its through-life
> cost. However, nearly a decade later and despite considerable resources expended
> within the Department and by its contractors, project through-life costs are not
> yet included in the annual Major Projects Report.[302]*

This omission of through-life costing may be obvious, but the
procurement costings that are produced are veiled in official obfuscation.
The movement of costs from procurement to support or other budget
lines and counting those as 'savings' has already been highlighted. This
'creative accounting' is designed to mislead. My dictionary defines 'lie' as
'convey a false impression'. If you are going to lie, you had better lie well.
Here MoD doesn't.

Delving into the Major Projects Reports for the last two years, it is
clear that costs of the top 19 projects (Typhoon costs are withheld) have
increased by nearly £2.7Bn or 11% – and that is the increase since Main
Gate approvals, **not for whole projects**. Moreover, the cost increase in
2006/07 was claimed as 'only' £43M, but this had been artificially

---

[302] Professor David Kirkpatrick, 'More Spurious Savings by the MoD', *Newsbrief*
(Volume 28, No. 1, January 2008), RUSI, page 3.

depressed by 'creative accounting' – £609M – and by reduction in capability – this last is difficult to calculate without more detail than is available, but could be £81M.[303] This suggests that the in-year cost increase is not £43M but £733M.

The in-year cost increase for the top 19 projects in 2005/06 was, when creative accounting and reduction in capability are taken into account, of a similar size. Many of these projects have recently passed Main Gate and have not yet had time for some cost increases to become apparent. It does not seem that MoD has programme costs under control. As the size of in-year cost increases have been growing steadily since 1998, it doesn't seem as if Smart Acquisition, DIS and other acquisition initiatives have made much difference.

> It doesn't seem as if Smart Acquisition, DIS and other acquisition initiatives have made much difference.

Some may say that many of the projects included were suffering ills from the past. That may be true, but most are what MoD has termed 'Smart' projects – that is, they were launched after 1998. Nevertheless, it is worth looking at those at an earlier stage to see if there are any pointers to future improvement. Unfortunately, reported costs of pre-Main Gate projects are sketchy indeed as only Assessment Phase costs are detailed. Of the ten pre-Main Gate projects reported on in the Major Projects Report,

> *It is disturbing to note that the scope of assessment work on three projects (FRES, IFPA and SAR–H) has been drastically expanded since Initial Gate approval, and on another three projects (CVF, UKCEC and FSTA) the cost of the planned assessment work has more than doubled … it is regrettable that the MoD still appears to be unable to plan and budget such assessment work realistically.*[304]

There are many examples of Assessment Phases not delivering project maturity at Main Gate over the decade since the CADMID cycle was adopted (and before that as well). Examples from the NAO Major Projects Reports 2005 include the following statements:

---

[303] Includes reduction of PAAMS missiles for Type 45, deletion of a communications system for A400M, and capability trade-offs for BVRAAM.

[304] Professor David Kirkpatrick, 'More Spurious Savings by the MoD', *Newsbrief* (Volume 28, No. 1, January 2008), RUSI, page 3.

- ASTOR: Problems emerged with the radar technology after Main Gate ... The activities prior to the main investment decision were driven hard against a target of zero or minimal cost growth, and this increased pressure on the project team to get to Main Gate on budget and to time.

- BVRAAM: The nature of the Assessment Phase made discrimination between the candidate systems difficult ... Ultimately the Main Gate submission did not make a firm recommendation ... Down-selection during the Assessment Phase and continued development with a preferred contractor before Main Gate may have delivered a more mature project before the main investment decision was made.

- Watchkeeper: The Assessment Phase was extended in order to ensure greater project maturity at Main Gate ... The extended Assessment Phase gave the military customer a greater level of confidence that the equipment and other lines of development were deliverable ... This additional work and overall programme affordability dictated a later in-service date.

In contrast, these reports give examples of Assessment Phases where there was little or no cost increase:

- IFPA: Early dialogue with industry indicated that the procurement of the IFPA capability was not going to be met through a traditional competitive Assessment Phase structure and it was decided to contract an industry partner to undertake the assessment ... A consortium led by BAE Systems won the competition and a Joint Integrated Project Team partnership structure was formed with the Project Team and other Departmental stakeholders.[305]

- LFATGW: Candidate systems were demonstrably mature ... the customer was fully involved in assessment.

Of course, the last two were largely buys off-the-shelf and it was therefore much simpler to identify the scope of work. Nevertheless, the three points made above – maturity of the systems, dialogue with

---

[305] The cost for the Assessment Phase was shown as a decrease in the MoD Major Project Report 2006, but the 2007 report showed that the Assessment Phase cost had nearly trebled. This was because the second phase was now included. It is impossible from these figures to see what the cost increase of the first phase might be, if any.

industry and involvement of the customer in assessment are surely important enough to pull through into most Assessment Phases.

If the huge increases in the cost of the Assessment Phases of FRES (446%), SAR–H (1100%), CVF (153%) and FSTA (185%) are the result of learning from the results of previous projects, then we should see better maturity at Main Gate with less slippage and cost overrun after the main investment decision – and that would be welcome progress. But if not, then we must conclude that MoD still appears "to be unable to plan and budget such assessment work realistically".

> MoD still appears "to be unable to plan and budget such assessment work realistically"

Is that because of conspiracy or cock-up? Usually the answer, at about 99–1, would be cock-up. We have discussed the Conspiracy of Optimism, and that could be a factor. However, cock-up is the more likely. Recently, the House of Commons Select Committee on Defence had this to say about MoD costings:

> *MoD admitted that this [underestimate] was down to a failure to report fully the indirect cost of operations in 2006–07 ... We find it hard to believe that a failure properly to cost the use of Hellfire missiles and the damage to, and loss of, equipment in theatre could lead to such a considerable underestimate of cost.*[306]

This was not a trivial underestimate: the indirect resource costs rose from £69M in 2006–07 to a projected cost of £424M in 2007–08. The report went on:

> *It has to be asked whether MoD is doing enough to provide robust cost forecasts to the House, robust not just in terms of stating as accurately as possible expected costs, but doing so in a timely fashion, using information that is up-to-date.*

The report also stated that no proper relation seems to exist between operational decisions, political announcements and financial scrutiny.

Time

When considering time, we should consider both overall procurement cycle time and delay to that planned cycle time.

---

[306] House of Commons Defence Committee, *Ministry of Defence Main Estimates 2008–09*, HC 885 2007–08, 7 July 2008, The Stationery Office, London.

The first is not easy to identify clearly as the newer projects, particularly the Smart projects, have yet to enter service, while those that have are accepted with large numbers of caveats.

> *Bowman CIP was accepted into service in March 2004 with 27 major provisos that reduce the operational capability of the system. An increase in funding of £121M has been required to enable this phase to be completed. Furthermore, several important capabilities have also been removed from the system to enable the remainder to be delivered in 2007/08; deletions include key requirements such as the ability to communicate data directly to allies' systems, which, again, should have helped reduce the risk of friendly fire incidents.*[307]

So, how do we identify the overall cycle time and the programme delay?

Some claim that cycle time for major programmes may have reduced a little from around 20 years to about 16. Figures in MoD suggest that Category A projects (>£400M) take on average 18 years, while Category B projects (£100M–£400M) take 12 and Category C (<£100M) about 8. Whether this is correct or not is debateable and unlikely to be proved on the data available. But assuming it has reduced, has this improvement been achieved by rushing more equipment into service with major provisos and important capabilities deleted?

> MoD is now looking to reduce cycle time but how it is going to do that is not yet clear

Whether or not it has reduced, 16 years is still far too long. MoD, under the refocused DACP, is now looking to reduce cycle time – a most important, if belated, recognition of the importance of time – but how it is going to do that is not yet clear.

There are, however, some encouraging signs. My reading of the situation in October 2008 is that key individuals in MoD recognise that we must:

- Find a new way of doing business, not refine the old way.
- Move to an approach focused on delivery.
- Ensure that lower level decisions are taken more quickly by skilled people.
- Engage with industry much earlier.

---

[307] House of Commons Committee of Public Accounts, *Ministry of Defence: Delivering Digital Tactical Communications through the Bowman CIP Programme*, Fourteenth Report Session 2006/07, 27 February 2007, page 3, The Stationery Office, London.

But I also believe that even the most enlightened people are less clear on how to implement this. This is proved by the erosion of the reduction in acquisition cycle times sought by the refocused DACP – from the original 50%, to between 30% and 50%, to the latest (October 2008) of 'significantly shorter', which means anything you want it to.

But anything much less than a halving of cycle time is unlikely to achieve all the good things you need – major financial savings, less delay giving greater commitment in the programme, overcoming obsolescence on fielding, boosting exports, increased operational agility and dealing with the pace of technological change. It is also essential in delivering DIS.

So, MoD has to swallow its pride, do a U-turn and go back to the original aim of 50% reduction. It won't, of course, because it has already placed it in the 'too difficult' tray. Of course it is difficult. If it was easy it would have been done years ago. The great men must earn their pay. By backing away from difficulties, they don't.

If cycle times are to be halved, then a number of actions are needed:

- More investment upfront to reduce technical and process risks.
- Less tinkering with the requirement during development stages.
- No delay imposed for financial or political reasons.

The last, of course, is ubiquitous. Could it be eliminated? I doubt it, but I am sure it could be reduced greatly if we were to cost the delay properly. If the costs of delay were measured and tracked and MoD managers were assessed against these measures, delays would be reduced. But of course this would mean that moving programmes or elements of programmes to the right every year or so to fit the equipment programme to the budget would be more difficult, so politicians would have to face up to the fact of cancellation rather than delay.

But without changing the culture, little is likely to be achieved. The seven bullets above are very important, but it is the cultural aspects which are key.

> Without changing the culture, little is likely to be achieved

What is required above all is real empowerment of individual IPT Leaders, and others at similar levels, to make 'tactical' decisions without achieving consensus all round; an environment in which mistakes can be made without the immediate addition of yet more procedural constraints; and elimination of almost all mandated processes for the bigger projects allowing leaders to lead, take sensible risks, improvise and be proactive.

All this will not be possible without buy-in at the top – from politicians, top MoD officials, the Treasury and Number 10. Will this happen? They may all say the right words, but when it comes to the crunch, will they really back this up when a project goes pear-shaped because sensible risk-taking leads to an outcome less good than it should be? Will they really remain hands-off when industry complains to a Minister about the way MoD's tactical decisions were made?

Perhaps the only way those at the top will buy in to new ways is if delays, or long schedules, are properly costed and laid at the door of an accountable official, and if a reduced procurement cycle is shown clearly to be cheaper than a longer, apparently less risky one, favoured by an accountable official. Only then will we make the real progress we need to reduce cycle times by the desired 50%.

No doubt much effort will be put in, but will the figures in ten or a dozen years show the necessary achievement? I hope they will but it is a big ask, especially as there is so little sign of change for the better at the 'top-of-the-shop'. Will Lord Drayson's emphasis on learning from motorsport speed things up, or will the emphasis be placed solely on exploiting motorsport technology?

An interesting study by John Dowdy of McKinsey's looked at delay as a percentage of the planned cycle time. In 2003 he predicted the time variation four years later for nine of the twenty projects in the 2003 Major Projects Review[308] against the MoD's planned schedule at that time.

Then, at the end of 2007, he compared his 2003 prediction against the actual delay reported in the Major Projects Report 2007 (see Figure 10–1).

> So, how did we do? Results were even worse than anticipated. Predicted schedule performance … was an average delay of 20% against plan, versus reported performance of 25% schedule slippage. Project-by-project predictions were, on average, within 5% of the actual result … There have been many changes to UK equipment acquisition in terms of strategy, structure, process, approach and tools

---

[308] Dowdy did not consider the remaining eleven for a variety of reasons, including project discontinuity, those that completed well within the period and those that are still stuck pre-Main Gate.

since 2003. But have the root causes of delay really been addressed? This analysis suggests that despite all of the effort to improve UK acquisition performance over the years, there is still much to be done.[309]

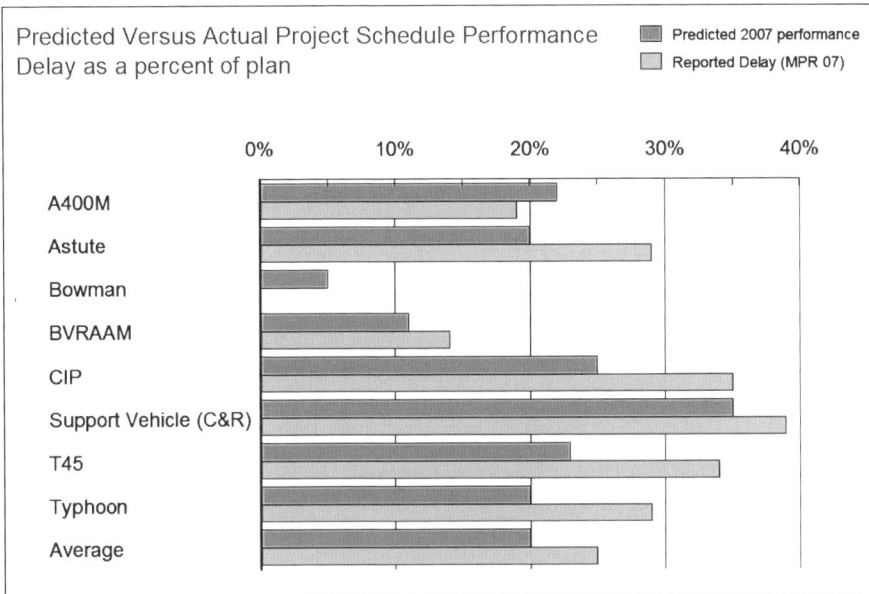

Figure 10–1: Predicted v. Actual Project Delay

Source: John Dowdy, McKinsey's, RUSI Defence Systems, Volume 10 No. 3, February 2008, page 105.

Comparison with US

Dowdy also examined UK performance on cost and time and compared it with that of the US (see Figure 10–2). He found that the UK has consistently outperformed the US in overall cost with average cost growth of 22% against the US increase of 37%.

However, the UK has consistently underperformed the US on programme delay over the last 13 years, being at least 40% behind schedule in every year since 1994, against the US average since 2002 (no systematic reporting before this) of 23%. Furthermore, both UK and US schedule performances have deteriorated over the past five years.

Over the past few years, UK performance has taken a turn for the worse. Costs, once under control, have drifted, as the UK has finally resorted to reducing unit production to stay within its overall budget, causing unit cost growth matching

---

[309] John Dowdy, 'Root Causes of Delay: Have They Still Not Been Identified?', *RUSI Defence Systems*, (Volume 10, No. 3, February 2008), page 105.

addition of yet more procedural constraints; and elimination of almost all mandated processes for the bigger projects allowing leaders to lead, take sensible risks, improvise and be proactive.

All this will not be possible without buy-in at the top – from politicians, top MoD officials, the Treasury and Number 10. Will this happen? They may all say the right words, but when it comes to the crunch, will they really back this up when a project goes pear-shaped because sensible risk-taking leads to an outcome less good than it should be? Will they really remain hands-off when industry complains to a Minister about the way MoD's tactical decisions were made?

Perhaps the only way those at the top will buy in to new ways is if delays, or long schedules, are properly costed and laid at the door of an accountable official, and if a reduced procurement cycle is shown clearly to be cheaper than a longer, apparently less risky one, favoured by an accountable official. Only then will we make the real progress we need to reduce cycle times by the desired 50%.

No doubt much effort will be put in, but will the figures in ten or a dozen years show the necessary achievement? I hope they will but it is a big ask, especially as there is so little sign of change for the better at the 'top-of-the-shop'. Will Lord Drayson's emphasis on learning from motorsport speed things up, or will the emphasis be placed solely on exploiting motorsport technology ?

An interesting study by John Dowdy of McKinsey's looked at delay as a percentage of the planned cycle time. In 2003 he predicted the time variation four years later for nine of the twenty projects in the 2003 Major Projects Review[308] against the MoD's planned schedule at that time.

Then, at the end of 2007, he compared his 2003 prediction against the actual delay reported in the Major Projects Report 2007 (see Figure 10–1).

So, how did we do? Results were even worse than anticipated. Predicted schedule performance ... was an average delay of 20% against plan, versus reported performance of 25% schedule slippage. Project-by-project predictions were, on average, within 5% of the actual result ... There have been many changes to UK equipment acquisition in terms of strategy, structure, process, approach and tools

---

[308] Dowdy did not consider the remaining eleven for a variety of reasons, including project discontinuity, those that completed well within the period and those that are still stuck pre-Main Gate.

Equipment Performance

Time performance is reasonably easy to assess, despite MoD attempts to rewrite history. Cost performance is more difficult and in some cases, where the latest cost figures are withheld for reasons of 'commercial sensitivity', near impossible. But equipment performance is impossible to assess by outsiders and, I suspect, by insiders too because many of the spurious cost savings remove capabilities within a programme based solely on the financial profile ('accountants' logic') without any clear idea of what the output effect will be. Even if that is modelled, it will take much time, the assumptions may be dubious and the findings may be bad news for the accountants. This is nothing new – it was happening when I was in the MoD in the 1980s and early 1990s.

How do you quickly assess the final operational detriment of reducing numbers by, say, 5%? Or the output power of a radar by 10%? Or fitting for, but not with, a subsystem in a major proportion of the fleet? Of course it can be done, but only with time and effort. Is the necessary time and effort available in a hurry during the annual cuts exercise?

I would hazard a guess that a majority of the 'savings' in which capability is reduced are not clearly assessed for performance degradation within MoD.

In addition, the key user requirements (as defined in the NAO reports) are open to interpretation. For example, how do you interpret the following?

- The User shall be provided with an **engagement** capability for targets at a maximum range of 2500m.
- Ease of use.
- Make effective, robust use of the electromagnetic spectrum without degrading other systems.
- And many more.

Even if they are defined more minutely than in the MoD Major Project Reports, it is difficult to see how some of them can be definitively classed as met; moreover, it is easy to see how some of them can apparently continue to be met even when performance parameters are reduced.

It is, therefore, hard to see whether the original requirement is met. It is still harder to see that performance is not an Aunt Sally to be hit by overruns in cost and time.

Acquisition Performance

What is not clear is why costs rise and schedules increase by such a large percentage, and why, with all the initiatives and effort expended over the last decade, things have not improved. We know some of the reasons – the 'conspiracy of optimism', poor cost estimation, the overheated defence programme, Whitehall's 'delay mentality', lack of leadership, use of immature technology and so on. But is this the whole story? What is or are the root cause(s)? We simply do not know.

> What is or are the root cause(s)? We simply do not know

Despite the overwhelming criticism that is directed at MoD's acquisition performance, there are many successful projects, many of them smaller than those reported on in the Major Projects Report.

> *The relationship with industry needs working on, but is stronger than in the past. Together we have generated some genuinely innovative approaches to the acquisition of through-life capability. The NAO report[311] cited armoured engineer vehicles and aircraft carrier refit as two projects which performed particularly well against their 'gold standard', and the support strategies for Merlin, Skynet 5 and Future Lynx are other good examples.[312]*

No doubt there are many others, but if there are, why isn't MoD shouting about them? Does it not know about them, or are they so few? What about the other side of the coin?

In 1995, MoD ordered 14 Chinook Mk2a helicopters from Boeing, of which eight were to be upgraded to a Mk3 standard with specialist equipment and larger fuel tanks. MoD took delivery of the helicopters from Boeing in December 2001.

> *The Chinook Mk3 helicopters have not flown on operations because the Department refused to grant the helicopters an airworthiness certificate. Although Boeing met its contractual obligations the avionics software could not be shown to meet United Kingdom standards. The helicopters can fly but are restricted to flying on cloudless days above 500 feet where the pilot can navigate by landmarks. In 2004, the Committee of Public Accounts' report described the*

---

[311] National Audit Office, *Driving the Successful Delivery of Major Defence Projects*, HC 30 2005/6, The Stationery Office, London, 20 May 2005

[312] Bill Jeffrey, 'Implementing the Defence Industrial Strategy', *RUSI Defence Systems* (Volume 9, No. 2, October 2006), page 22.

procurement of the Chinook Mk3 helicopter as 'one of the worst examples of equipment procurement' that it had seen.[313]

Since the 2004 report, MoD first developed a 'fix-to-field' solution, then cancelled it. Instead, it pursued the Chinook Mk3 Reversion to Mk2/2a standard which involves removing the existing Mk3 hybrid digital/analogue cockpit and replacing it with the analogue cockpit fitted to the Mk2/2a, and fitting a health and usage monitoring system, UK specific communications and defensive systems. However, there are risks which could further delay the current operational readiness date of 2009/2010 and these are laid out in the referenced report.

Overall, the project is estimated as now costing £422M rather than the original £259M.

The 2004 report concluded that major changes had been incorporated into MoD's procedures to ensure that these problems would not recur, and these include:

- A more rigorous prioritisation of the requirement.
- Clear guidelines on responsibilities.
- Improved Military Aircraft Release procedures.
- A rigorous project review and assurance process.
- A single point of accountability for projects – the SRO.

But are the changes above (if properly implemented) going to stop similar recurrences? With the lack of clarity within MoD on responsibilities, authority and accountability, this is very unlikely. According to the original 2004 report, the Committee found that the Department was unable to say who was responsible for the flawed procurement of the Chinook Mk3. It would be a brave man who said now that, should such a procurement event recur, MoD would be able to say who was responsible.

> But are the changes going to stop similar recurrences?

An NAO report on the Landing Ship Dock (Auxiliary) – LSD(A) – published in late 2007 considered that:

> *Initially this project did not apply the principles of Smart Acquisition, did not manage risks effectively and grossly underestimated both project cost and*

---

[313] National Audit Office, *Chinook Mk3 Helicopters*, HC 512 Session 2007-2008, 2 June 2008, The Stationery Office, London.

*timescale. Since the 2003 crisis, remedial measures by the MoD and its
contractors have delivered a satisfactory outcome ... MoD claims confidently that
lessons have been learned so that such problems should not recur.*[314]

MoD has identified lessons from both the Chinook Mk3 and the LSD(A)
procurements but, although lessons are so often identified by MoD, it is
rare that the right corrective action is taken. In any case, I suspect that the
root cause will not be eliminated by taking such procedural actions.
Instead, I suspect that the root cause of poor performance lies primarily
in culture and behaviours, particularly at
the top. This is why improvement will
amount to nothing much without a
change of culture. But as I have indicated,
culture change does not seem to be a
priority.

> The root cause of
> poor performance lies
> primarily in culture and
> behaviours, particularly
> at the top

Where Are We Now?

So, nearly three years downstream from the publication of the DIS, but
rather less than that from the publication of the EAC, DTS and the
launch of the DACP, how is implementation faring? Although this is too
short a time for a proper assessment of progress, there are pointers.

The procurement and support organisations have been brought
together to form DE&S, enabling a much more effective through-life
approach. There are strong signs of a closer link between DE&S and the
front line, and the formation of the 2-star IPT clusters gives hope that the
problem of stovepiping and consequent loss of coherence in
procurement may be largely overcome. However, against this, the
empowerment of the 2-star cluster managers could undermine the
empowerment of the IPT leaders, which is currently lacking bite.

Another change for the worse is the disbandment of DESO. There
is no doubt that UK will now have to work harder for export contracts
which, in the cut-throat world of defence exports, is potentially
damaging.

Strategic partnering has made some progress. Partnering
agreements have been signed with AgustaWestland and BAE Systems,

---

[314] Professor Kirkpatrick, 'More Spurious Savings by the MoD', *Newsbrief* (Volume 28,
No. 1, January 2008), RUSI, page 4.

while Team CW has been formed to include several leading companies. Progress has also been made in the maritime sector, but is less advanced. Overall, less has been achieved than was originally envisaged. This progress, important though it is, will be undermined, however, if either MoD or industry fails to identify and adopt the right partnering mentality. But a greater threat lies in the turbulence of the equipment funding plan, which we know is badly overheated. Will the major savings that will have to be found in the near future overturn agreements such as the maritime core workload that MoD is to underwrite?

> But a greater threat lies in the turbulence of the equipment funding plan

In terms of time and cost performance, things seem to get no better with escalating cost overruns and delays. This suggests that Smart Procurement has achieved nothing in terms of output and, although it is too early to make judgements on whether or not DIS has improved output performance, there is no clear evidence that it will do so in the near future. Indeed, the desperate attempts recently to conceal the true cost and schedule increases by claiming 'savings' through moving costs to other budget lines without any reduction to defence costs overall, together with the policy which now reports cost and schedule overruns from the last decision point, rather than over the whole project, suggest that things are really not getting better.

But the main reason for taking a gloomy view of progress is that the main change effort has gone, and still is going, on reorganisation and process change. This puts in place many enablers – very worthy in their way – but unlikely to make major impact on output. What is desperately needed is for a strong assault on ingrained, negative culture – and not just at the working level, but all the way up to the top. This must be done and continued under strong, consistent leadership for several years. But it isn't being done and the emasculation of the excellent DACP objective of reducing cycle time by 50% to the present 'significantly shorter' is proof of this.

How will we measure success or otherwise of DIS at some stage in the future? Is it the improvement in the effectiveness of our Armed Forces or the cost-efficiency of our acquisition system? Is it the preservation of a strong onshore defence industry and the jobs that go with it? Or is it an amalgamation of the process and organisational changes that will have been effected. I fear it might be the last, but I hope it's the combination of the first and the second.

Whatever it is, how do we measure it? Does anyone know?

> *I would highlight the development of more relevant metrics and measures of success. At the moment we concentrate on the key indicators of cost and timeliness up to the point when equipment is brought into service. We must continue to do so; but we are also working on a set of performance metrics which will better capture the through-life capability dimension, and enable us to judge how we are doing against that wider criterion.*[315]

Whether the development of such metrics will enable us to measure success objectively is debateable – it is more likely that they will be used by politicians and officials to declare success than as an analytical tool.

> *I am not sure whether it is a purely MoD disease – indeed in my experience it is actually a British disease – to seek to use data to declare a programme a success, rather than to use it as an analytical tool to determine what improvements are required, beyond the initiatives taken, to deliver a successful result. It is undoubtedly true when looking back over the initiatives designed to improve procurement in MoD, that the claimed level of success is significantly higher than can be supported by any analytical measurement, and indeed for many of those involved, little improvement in performance can be detected despite a succession of change efforts. Rather than a fresh round of initiatives with every significant senior management change, analysis of the effects of initiatives, and comparison of the shortfalls against expectations, followed by further modifications and improvements to correct the deficiencies, would provide more productive outcomes.*[316]

> **MoD has the propensity for puncturing its own wheel of improvement**

What price analytical measurement of success against the still wider criterion of the improved effectiveness of our Armed Forces?

Frustration

There is no doubt that some progress has been made, but not necessarily on the most important subjects. MoD has the propensity for puncturing its own wheel of improvement.

---

[315] Bill Jeffrey, 'Implementing the Defence Industrial Strategy', *RUSI Defence Systems* (Volume 9, No. 2, October 2006), page 23.
[316] John Weston, email to the author, 11 September 2008.

*Last week [January 2008] I chaired a very well attended conference on partnering and alliances. There was considerable interest as evinced by the fact that virtually the entire audience remained until the end of a long two-day conference – a somewhat rare occurrence. There was a number of speakers from both sides of the MoD/industry partnering arrangements ... What was very striking was that views were absolutely shared; there was unanimous agreement that 'one size does not fit all'. I have rarely seen such harmony between MoD and industry speakers. You will then imagine the shock and dismay caused by two MoD HQ Policy speakers who, stating that they had an important new initiative to disclose, announced that MoD was on the point of producing a partnering handbook which would **mandate** partnering procedures and contracts. From the reaction in the room, there appeared to have been very little consultation either internally or externally. This appeared to be the antithesis of partnering, since it would clearly elevate one partner above the other, and would place MoD in its old place of trying to dictate to industry, rather than to partner with them. Both MoD and industry attendees were vociferous in their disapproval and dismay.[317]*

No doubt this partnering handbook is being produced for the best of reasons, and no doubt those who have beavered away in producing the handbook have the best of intentions. But whose idea was it in the first place, what instructions were given to those doing the donkey work, and why has there apparently been little or no consultation with industry on the subject of partnering? How can you partner in this way?

This appears to be just plain boneheaded. However, it is much more likely to be a case of left hand not understanding what the right is doing and is akin to the way in which stovepiping has arisen in IPTs: "I will do this to meet my objective but the wider effect is not my concern".

This may be a minor matter in terms of process, but it is a major indication of a failure to make the necessary culture change. And, to reiterate the point, without culture change, nothing will change.

> Without culture change, nothing will change

Perhaps the brightest chance of culture change comes from the overworked UOR process and culture. There the culture is clearly very different and much closer to what we want throughout the acquisition organisation. There is little sign that UOR culture is being pulled through into 'normal' procurement, although we will have to wait and see. But will the numbers of middle-ranking military officers and officials who

---

[317] Sir Jeremy Blackham, email to the author and others on chairing a conference.

have been immersed in that culture make a difference as they ascend the ladder? Let us hope so.

So, has the progress over the first two years of DIS implementation been a case of one step forward, one step back?

Unfortunately there was worse to come.

SUMMARY: PROGRESS AND STAGNATION

Reorganisation
- Defence Equipment and Support (DE&S) formed from amalgamation of the Defence Procurement Organisation (DPA) and the Defence Logistics Organisation (DLO).
- 2-star clusters may solve stovepiping and loss of procurement coherence.
- Integrated Project Team (IPT) leaders are not empowered.
- Abolishing the Defence Exports Support Organisation (DESO) brings risk to export earnings.

Strategic Partnering
- Agreements signed with AgustaWestland and BAE Systems.
- Team Complex Weapons formed.
- Less progress than envisaged.
- Partnering mentality not understood in many parts of MoD, particularly in the centre and at the top.

Time and Cost Performance
- Time and costs continue to overrun badly.
- Figures are massaged to present false picture.

Overall Progress
- Main effort placed on reorganisation and process change.
- Little sign of major culture change; no clear culture change strategy.
- Outlook 'gloomy'.

Measuring 'Success'
- No clear metrics in place.

"Don't worry lad, we'll send body armour and trousers out to join you in Afghanistan… as soon as we get some"

Chapter Eleven

Crisis in Defence Spending

Defence aspirations have for decades outstripped defence funding, even during the 3% growth in real terms at the height of the Cold War, with the result that the defence programme has become increasingly overheated since the fall of Communism in Eastern Europe. Every year it has become worse and, as the new millennium began, the size of the threatening bow wave was perceived more and more clearly. The days of 'salami slicing' and fiddling with ISDs – the traditional method of control – were, it seems, clearly numbered.

The Tory governments of the 1990s took the massive 'Peace Dividend' and saw few votes in defence. After Labour came to power in 1997, Prime Minister Blair was happy to use the Armed Forces, but his governments failed to fund them adequately. Blair used them anyway. The result is that men and equipment are being stretched ever more tightly as Defence Planning Assumptions (DPAs) and 'Harmony Guidelines' (intervals between operational tours) are repeatedly overtaken by political commitments. The former Chancellor, now the Prime Minister, continues the starvation rations.[318]

Do Defence Chiefs fight hard enough for their men? The previous Chief of the General Staff, General Sir Mike Jackson, found the MoD very frustrating.

> I didn't always find the MoD wholehearted about the interests of soldiers. I was constantly battling the civil servants, and it was often very frustrating. I'd come back from a visit and say, 'We've got to do something about the state of those barracks', but it was like trying to fight your way through cotton wool.[319]

He was criticised by some who thought he should have made his frustrations public while he was in post. However, he made his frustrations clear in the Richard Dimbleby lecture shortly after retiring. The morning after the lecture on the *Today* programme, he answered the

---

[318] The RUSI Acquisition Focus paper, 'The Underfunded Equipment Programme – Where Now?' is at Appendix 11–1.
[319] General Sir Mike Jackson, *Soldier: The Autobiography* (London, Transworld, 2007), p. 358.

criticism by insisting that he had spoken very bluntly behind closed doors while he was serving. His successor, General Sir Richard Dannatt, did speak out and was criticised for doing so – and not just by politicians and civil servants.

Rumours that the Chief of the General Staff, General Sir Richard Dannatt, will not be the next Chief of the Defence Staff because of his outspokenness may prove premature, but they are dismaying nevertheless.[320]

> New Labour politicians have tried to muzzle them. This is a sign of great weakness

New Labour politicians have ignored the problems of the Armed Forces and have tried to muzzle them. This is a sign of great weakness. In contrast, Churchill selected and stuck with Sir Alan Brooke as Chief of the Imperial General Staff through most of The Second World War because he admired his moral courage: *"I bang the table at him, and what does Brooke do? He bangs it even harder".*

No sign of that today. Politicians do not attempt to have proper dialogue with the military – they evade the issues.

Other Chiefs have also spoken out, despite ever tighter control by the politicians. Others have been less keen to do so.

Defence Funding and the Real World

Defence funding has been sharply reduced since 1991. It may have seemed to some then that, with the removal of the Soviet threat, the world would be a safer place and therefore defence funding could be cut sharply for a 'Peace Dividend'. But others thought this a remarkably naïve assumption. They have been proved right. Wars and operations in the Gulf, the Balkans, Sierra Leone, Iraq and Afghanistan have stretched the Armed Forces, but the large cuts made in the defence budget have not been restored, even in the years of plenty. There is even less chance in the gloomy economic forecast of today.

Will an election change anything? If Gordon Brown continues as Prime Minister it seems unlikely. And the Conservatives appear as hypocritical as Labour was in 1996 – criticising the low level of funding by the Government but refusing to promise any more money if they gain

[320] Allan Mallinson, *The Times*, 4 July 2008. Since confirmed.

power, although Liam Fox, the Shadow Defence Secretary, has said that he will find more money for defence from more efficient acquisition. This, of course, should be possible but, with the experience of the last decade, will he achieve this?

Seemingly it needs a major defence shock to change things – a major defeat in the field, perhaps, or the collapse of DIS with the demise of the onshore defence industry. Even then, these may not be important enough to impact sufficiently on politicians' and civil servants' attitudes to defence funding. No wonder that servicemen feel that the country is not supporting them properly.

> No wonder that servicemen feel that the country is not supporting them properly

> *I find it deeply shaming that Parliament feels able to commit the wonderful young men and women of our Armed Forces to battle – not on one, but on two fronts – while not guaranteeing them the resources they so desperately need to maintain the front-line strength of our forces, to ensure that they have the best and most modern equipment, that they don't have to live in shoddy, slum-like accommodation, while operating vehicles, helicopters, ships and aircraft that afford them inadequate protection.[321]*

Winston S. Churchill cites as an example the 40-year old Nimrods, which he describes as 'flying coffins', and lays the blame for the recent crash with the loss of 14 lives squarely on the shoulders of decision-makers in the MoD.

> *The Nimrod that crashed on September 6th, killing all 14 on board – the biggest single loss that we have suffered in recent years – had 26 known fuel leaks …These planes are still being flown despite the known fuel leaks.[322]*

> *Vital safety features were left out of the design specification for Nimrod surveillance aircraft despite being requested by the Royal Air Force, an enquiry has revealed. Fuel tank explosion protection and a ban on carrying fuel in the fuselage were both listed as 'air staff requirements' by the RAF. But they were among several items not included in the final design blueprint known as the 'design specification'. The RAF's comments about the design criteria were rejected by the Ministry of Defence when it drew up the specification for the aircraft.[323]*

[321] Winston S. Churchill, 'Demand for Action', *Defence Director*, March 2008, page 7.
[322] Ibid.
[323] Michael Evans, Defence Editor, 'MoD rejected safety fears over Nimrod design, *The Times*, 16 June 2008.

After the inquest into the deaths of the 14 servicemen, the assistant deputy coroner for Oxford called for the grounding of all 15 Nimrod MR2s. This was, not surprisingly, rejected by the Government both because the RAF believes that enough steps have been taken to remove the flaws in the design and for obvious operational reasons. It should be noted that the Nimrod MR2 is not due to be replaced by the MR4 until 2011, as its development has suffered more than 7 years' delay since Main Gate approval.

At another Oxford inquest, soldiers said that they were:

> ... *totally outgunned and lacked basic equipment, including Minimi machineguns, rifles with underslung grenades and night-vision kit.*[324]

> Soldiers were not being defeated by the Taleban, but by the lack of basic equipment

At another inquest, the Wiltshire coroner called for a review of government spending on the Armed Forces after two soldiers in a 'Snatch' landrover were killed by a roadside bomb because a Mastiff was not available. He said that soldiers were not being defeated by the Taleban, but by the lack of basic equipment.

In February 2008, *The Times* reported that the RAF is being forced to borrow American spy planes and paint roundels on them to replace its fleet of Nimrod R1 signals intelligence aircraft, due to the MoD cash crisis that rules out the money for a replacement aircraft. US personnel will be expected to take control on some missions.[325]

Helicopters have been, and still are, in very short supply, while Chinook helicopters have sat in hangars unable to fly. There are not enough transport aircraft. Armoured vehicles are very old and an interim buy has been necessary because of the repeated postponement of FRES, and a further buy has recently been announced. Nimrod MR2s have been labelled 'flying coffins'. We seem to have been taken by surprise by the deployment of IEDs by insurgents, despite the lessons of Northern Ireland. UAVs should have been available years ago but, except for Phoenix which entered service a decade late and largely obsolescent,

---

[324] Michael Evans, 'Coroners blame soldiers' deaths on an acute lack of equipment', *The Times*, 16 February 2008.
[325] *The Times*, www.timesonline.co.uk , 3 February 2008.

were not in the inventory from the start in Iraq or Afghanistan. Indirect fire precision attack was funded, then cancelled, then subject to a long acquisition programme. Lives have been lost because infantry is without the Minimi machine guns, underslung grenade launchers and night-vision kit that it needs – FIST has been repeatedly postponed. NEC has not made the progress either promised or necessary. Bowman was brought into service with 27 major provisos, which included high-capacity data radio and data management. Progress on Combat Identification has been inadequate.

> No part of the Army seems properly equipped to fight Counter-Insurgency campaigns

In view of the above, no part of the Army seems properly equipped to fight Counter-Insurgency campaigns. Why is this? Is it because:

- Acquisition management has been bad?
- There has been insufficient money to do any better?
- Industrial jobs in political party constituencies decree spending on big programmes rather than what the ground forces must have to fight on the ground?

The answer is, I believe, a combination of all three. Better acquisition management would reduce waste and release resources, but more money would still have to be found. Should the Government not spend enough to ensure that soldiers are properly equipped to do as they are bid by the Government? Should industrial jobs take precedence over servicemen's lives?

Prime Minister Gordon Brown has not shown any sign of giving any priority to defence, even though he is presiding over the UK's efforts to fight simultaneously two wars that have been described as the most demanding since the Korean War, and has recently increased the UK's commitment in Afghanistan. His decision to 'double hat' the post of Secretary of State for Defence Des Browne by giving him a second job as Secretary of State for Scotland borders on contempt for our servicemen.

This 'double-hatting' of defence and Scotland was clearly too much for Browne. In October, according to *The Times*, he told the Prime Minister that:

> *He didn't feel it right for the Defence Secretary to share his ministerial time with Scottish affairs. He told Mr Brown that he would prefer to keep defence and give*

up Scotland. The Prime Minister, however, offered him Scotland and Northern Ireland as a joint ministerial package. Mr Browne rejected the offer and his Cabinet career came to an end.[326]

The Times estimated, from freedom of information requests to the MoD, that the Defence Secretary was having to spend between 15% and 20% of his time on Scottish matters.

In late 2008, defence does seem to be making more of an impact on the general public. A poll by ComRes for the United Kingdom National Defence Association in September 2008 suggested that Defence is now an election issue for the majority of the British public:

> *More than three quarters of voters (78%) believe that Britain's Armed Forces are 'dangerously over-stretched'. 70% think that the Government is 'failing to give the Armed Forces the resources they need'. Only 32% feel that the Government 'treats our Armed Forces with the respect they deserve'. Over half of the electorate (57%) say that they will consider each party's policy on Defence when deciding how to vote in the next election. This figure rises to 63% among voters in vital seats in the South East.*[327]

But how seriously can we take these answers? Will the same people feel the same by next year or the next elections if the credit crunch and the global financial situation continue to bite? They may still think the same, but what will their priorities be? Or, more importantly, what will the politicians think they are?

Funding in Real Terms

The Government is keen on saying that they have increased defence expenditure 'in real terms' several times over the last decade. This is, of course, only partly true and is entirely misleading. Last year's **increase** of 1.5% a year for the next three years 'in real terms' is accurate in terms of the uplift over and above the national inflation figure. However, as we have seen, defence inflation is higher – about twice as high – so, taking that into account, the 'increase in real terms' is actually a **cut** of around 1.5% per year.

> The 'increase in real terms' is actually a cut of around 1.5% per year

---

[326] *The Times*, 4 October 2008.
[327] UK National Defence Association news release, 28 September 2008.

There are other factors. While the cost of operations is supposedly fully paid for by the Treasury, the mass of UOR equipment is only supported for a very limited period and if that equipment remains in service for longer, then its support has to be paid for by the defence vote. About half of the UORs procured for Iraq in 2003 have been retained (which suggests that we may be pursuing the wrong equipment programme). This UOR 'time bomb' represents a large hidden cost.

Cost growth is another funding factor. We have yet to get it under control – indeed it is not yet certain that we have identified the root cause. Cost growth can be reduced but unless we identify the root cause, and deal with it, we cannot reduce it by a great deal, much less eliminate it. And even if we do identify the root cause, we may still not be able to eliminate it.

> *It follows that the unit cost of new weapon systems may continue to rise over the coming decades because of the combined effects of: the improvement in the military capabilities of potentially hostile nations; advances in the technology available to the UK and its allies; and political/diplomatic imperatives to minimise the adverse effects of conventional warfare, even when victorious ... It would be equally unrealistic to expect that equipment cost growth will be entirely eliminated.*[328]

To which, of course, should be added the higher inflation rate in defence.

It is also worth asking how many of the assumptions that have been made during costing of programmes have been revisited so that the implications of changes in those assumptions are visible, particularly on running costs.

> *Recently, an unremarked but remarkable answer was given to a UK Parliamentary question about aircraft carriers. With the multi-site celebration of progress of the JV and the carriers, no action is likely. But there is certainly an underlying reality to ponder on. That reality is the oil price used when the decision was made on propulsion – $19 a barrel. Now it maybe either the grey matter isn't what it was, or incipient laziness which ruled out an Internet search, but this correspondent is hard put to remember how long ago it was that oil was at such levels. Apart from wondering if the original analysis was ever revisited during the extensive competition and design phases (if not, why not? Who's afraid of nukes in the Navy?), the big thought is – what else? What other*

---

[328] Professor David Kirkpatrick, 'Future Cost growth of Major Weapon Systems', *RUSI Defence Systems* (Volume 9, No. 2, October 2006), page 14.

programmes have been analysed and through-life costs estimated based on hopelessly unrealistic future energy cost forecasts?[329]

A good point. If future energy costs have not been taken into account, then the knock-on effect on future training and routine deployments could be devastating. This refers back to the discussion on decision-making in Chapter Eight and, in particular, to the RUSI Acquisition Focus paper (Appendix 8–1), about the difference between decision-making in industry and MoD. One of the key points was that in industry, plans will be revisited regularly and changed when necessary, as commercial organisations that don't adapt, don't survive; while in MoD, plans and projects once agreed are stuck to rigidly, often because the commercial and political implications of cancellation are too tough to confront.

> **Unless something drastic is done, the defence budget will buy less and less**

There is also the question of headroom in the defence programme. Headroom was for long a dirty word in the Treasury. Recently it has become acceptable as one way of bringing more stability into the programme. But to find headroom, savings will have to be found in the overheated programme with the result that increased turbulence will have to precede more stability.

All this means that, unless something drastic is done, the defence budget will buy less and less even if the Government provides the sort of 'increase in real terms' that it has thought fit to do so far. This in turn increases the programme turbulence and makes decisions on what to cut ever more difficult. And what about finding the extra funding, which may be large, to retain the required skills onshore to provide the appropriate sovereignty deemed essential by DIS? The current programme is unsustainable.

It is time to face facts, especially in relation to the equipment programme. There is no management fix for the present ills. These stem not from deficiencies of administration, numerous and evident though these are. Rather the fundamental cause is that current defence policy requires equipment whose costs are beyond the ability of the budget to sustain. Moreover, the inevitable rise of equipment unit costs, generation by generation, means that the present inability to sustain the

---

[329] UK Defence Forum, DEFENCEnet Daily Comment: Defence with Oil at $150 a Barrel, 8 July 2008.

equipment programme can only get worse, and quickly so. There is an urgent need to cut our coat according to our cloth.[330]

This was written two years ago. As he forecast, things have indeed got worse. So much so that last winter's planning round (PR 08) was widely seen as the last chance saloon to make agonising decisions. 'Salami-slicing' was generally thought to be dead. We had, indeed, to cut our coat according to our cloth. Eighteen months later, Pugh returned to the charge:

No nation, even a superpower, is armed as it would wish. Rather, all are armed as they can afford – and must adapt their foreign policy accordingly. The folly of the last decade has been to disconnect the commitments of an over-ambitious foreign policy from the military capabilities that can be afforded over the long term. In remedying this, awkward choices will have to be made. Cherished ambitions of vested interests will have to be given up.[331]

The RUSI Acquisition Focus, in its paper on the underfunded equipment programme (Appendix 11–1) called for[332] a new strategic defence review and an increase in the defence budget from around 2% of GDP to 2½% of GDP. A move from a specific sum to a percentage of GDP would at least compensate for the higher inflation rate or more in good economic times, although it would mean cuts in an economic recession – just the time when politicians might welcome some room for manoeuvre.

However, there will clearly be no defence review before the next general election at the earliest, and whether there would be one after an election and whether, if there is one then, it would be funded adequately are debateable.

We have a key strategic decision to make. In effect, do we go for war prevention and security management, or for high intensity warfighting because we have failed to manage security? I am certain that we can't do both, but it is a decision which has to be faced or we are on Lord Trenchard's famous road to absurdity ... i.e. the whole defence budget will eventually buy one ship. Until we face and answer this question, no one will take us seriously. It is simply absurd to suppose

---

[330] Philip Pugh, 'Time for Change', *RUSI Defence Systems* (Volume 9, No. 2, October 2006), page 12.
[331] Philip Pugh, 'Expensive Ineffectiveness', *RUSI Defence Systems* (Volume 10, No. 3, February 2008), page 22.
[332] RUSI Acquisition Focus, 'The Underfunded Equipment Programme – Where Now?', *RUSI Defence Systems* (Volume 9, No. 3, February 2007), page 25.

that we can afford whatever the Services might like. The failure is one of government as a whole, the failure to face this very tough question. It is not just a matter for the MoD.[333]

So, drastic action is required.

But what sort of action?

Capability v. Numbers

One of the pressing debates during the last few years has been the balance between quantity and quality – have we got it right or, if not, what rebalancing is needed? There is little agreement. Some believe that we have to retain a serious warfighting capability of world-class (i.e. US) quality or we would be outgunned in any future state-on-state war; others that Counter-Insurgency operations such as those in Iraq and Afghanistan, and Maritime Security Operations, require greater numbers than we can deploy, or intend to deploy in the future.

> You cannot divide a frigate in two if you need presence in more places

There is something of a vicious circle in this process. We have to design more capable aircraft to make up for declining numbers, which increases complexity and costs and thence to the inter-generational trade-off of quantity in favour of quality.[334]

Clearly we need the quality if we are to do any serious warfighting in the next couple of decades but, equally clearly, we need the numbers, not only to warfight, but to provide the 'boots on the ground' to operate in Counter-Insurgency situations, and the ships across the world's oceans to carry out Maritime Security Operations. You cannot divide a frigate in two if you need presence in more places.

By 1998, UK attack submarine force levels had been reduced to 12 from a Cold War force level target of 27. Despite SDR's background operational analysis recommending a force level of at least 14 SSNs, SDR reduced the number further to 10. The 2003 Defence White Paper sliced the number again to just eight boats. Then, in December 2007, the SSN force level issue was addressed again: Minister for the Armed Forces (MinAF) Bob Ainsworth stated that, while an eight-boat flotilla would be sufficient to meet predicted medium-term tasks, the new Astute-

---

[333] Sir Jeremy Blackham, email to the author, July 2008.

[334] Professor Keith Hayward, 'Quantity v. Quality: The Eternal Military Dilemma', *RUSI Defence Systems* (Volume 9, No. 3, February 2007), page 17.

*class SSN's improved design, build, capability and availability would enable a
further reduction to just seven boats by the time all Astute boats are in service by
2022.[335]*

Following this article by Lee Willett is one by Dr Andrew Davies of the
Australian Strategic Policy Institute. He describes the programme for the
replacement of Australia's submarine force.

> *Having six boats actually translates, at best, into three or four available at any
> given time. Given the transit times to distant operating areas, the entire fleet
> would be stretched to maintain operations in even two distant areas. More boats
> would mean more operational flexibility and the ability to seriously hamper the
> operations of adversary surface fleets over a wide area. Ten or twelve submarines
> are a better fit to Australia's strategic requirements and might also result in long-
> term reductions of cost and risk in build programmes.[336]*

Of course, affordability may force this number downwards, but this
statement of Australia's need reinforces the view that, operationally, any
nation which operates widely outside its own territorial waters needs
greater numbers than accountants will dictate. Does 'accountants' logic'
properly take into account the cost of operational risk? I doubt it, and
they will no doubt cite the great improvements in technology and overall
equipment capability as clear reasons for making do with fewer numbers.

Sir Jeremy Blackham and Professor Gwyn Prins state five fallacies which
point up the threat to the Royal Navy and its sister Services. The first is:

> *The fallacy that technological quality can substitute for the quality that numbers
> alone can give. This fallacy is a product of ignorance of history in general and of
> military history in particular. It is also a product of ignorance of the principles
> of strategy. If sufficient means are not given to permit force to be used in a way
> that the public likes, then harsher ways may have to be employed to leverage
> smaller means to achieve a specified end. It is also a misplaced confidence in the
> powers of technology.[337]*

In addition to the obvious reduction in operational capability, there is also
an important acquisition issue.

---

[335] Dr Lee Willett, 'Diving Down Below the Layer', *RUSI Defence Systems* (Volume 11,
No. 2, October 2008).
[336] Dr Andrew Davies, 'Australia's Future Submarine', *RUSI Defence Systems* (Volume 11,
No. 2, October 2008).
[337] Vice Admiral Sir Jeremy Blackham and Professor Gwyn Prins, 'The Royal Navy at
the Brink', *RUSI Journal* (Volume 152, No. 2, April 2007), page 12.

> *It is important to note that UK submarine force levels have, to many, reached the point of no return. From an industrial but, most importantly, from an operational perspective, to continue to reduce UK submarine force levels below four SSBNs and eight SSNs will reduce UK industrial and operational submarine capacity to the point that it may no longer be worthwhile for the UK to invest in nuclear-powered submarines. Such a decision will have critical – even catastrophic – consequences for UK defence and security policy.*[338]

To reduce numbers to such a degree that industrial investment in nuclear submarines may no longer be justified strikes a huge blow at the DIS. Does the left hand of Government not know – or more likely understand – what the right hand is doing? Maybe not, but more likely the explanation is that the accountants will do anything to balance the books whether their actions make sense or not. 'Accountant's logic' strikes yet again.

But give these hard-pressed accountants a little sympathy because the required quantity and quality cannot, it seems, be afforded within the defence budget, with the result that we are trying to do too much with too few men and too little equipment. This has been highlighted so many times recently in the words of coroners, chiefs of staff and the press, that the man in the street is surely beginning to wonder if the defence budget – taxpayers' money – is being spent to best effect and with greatest efficiency.

> *We are told that we are now engaged in a protracted war against terror, which threatens the very existence of our liberal democratic society. The more taxpayers are persuaded of this the more they will demand the defence budget be spent to proper ends. The taxpayer supports defence spending not to create employment either in ministerial constituencies or among the officer class. Neither is it to gain some politician a supposed place in history. First and last, it is the price that the taxpayers pay to keep themselves safe.*[339]

There are two strong arguments against cutting equipment numbers. One is the 'boots-on-the-ground' argument that I have mentioned; the other is that the fewer equipments that come off the production line, the more costly each of them is. As unit prices increase, further cuts are

---

[338] Dr Lee Willett, 'Diving Down Below the Layer', *RUSI Defence Systems* (Volume 11, No. 2, October 2008).

[339] Philip Pugh, 'Expensive Ineffectiveness', *RUSI Defence Systems* (Volume 10, No 3, February 2008), page 22/23.

made, which in turn drives unit prices still higher – this is known as a 'death spiral'.

If we don't cut numbers, can we man the higher numbers? Figures 11–1 and 11–2 suggest we can.

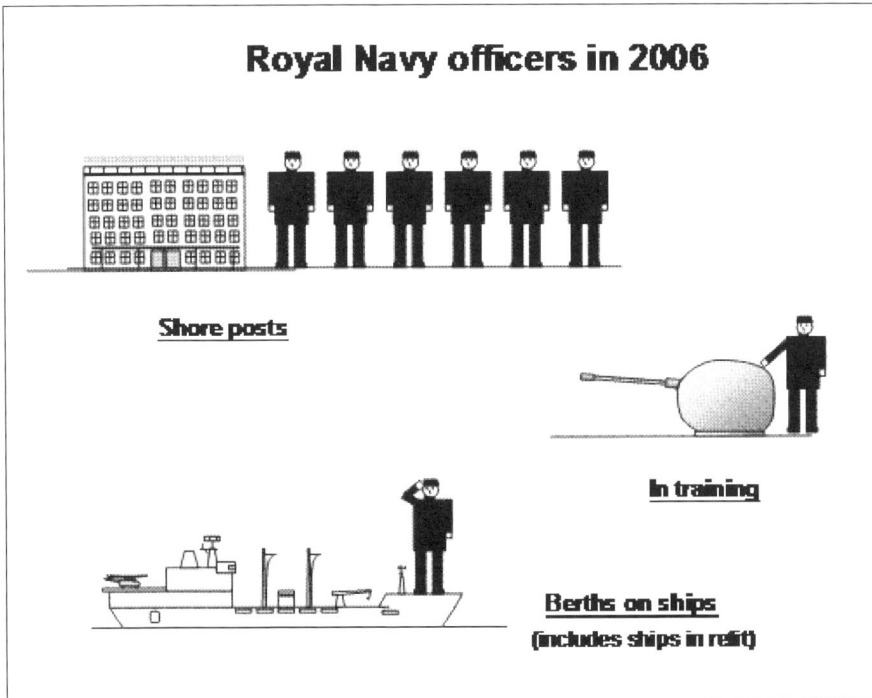

Figure 11–1: Deployment of Royal Navy Officers in 2006
Source: Philip Pugh, 'Expensive Ineffectiveness', *RUSI Defence Systems* (Volume 10, No. 3, February 2008), page 23.

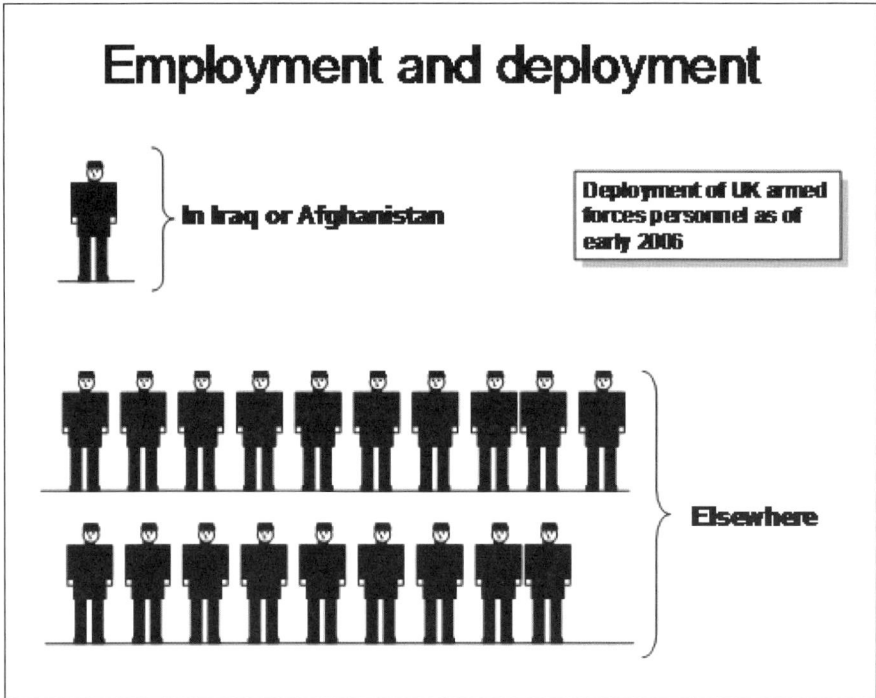

Figure 11–2: Employment and Deployment of UK Armed Forces
Source: Philip Pugh, 'Expensive Ineffectiveness', RUSI Defence Systems (Volume 10, No. 3, February 2008), page 23.

The figures show that we do not have a sensible balance between numbers on operational deployment and those elsewhere. This is not new: many people have drawn attention to the relative numbers of admirals and ships, of air marshals and aircraft squadrons, of generals and deployable battalions. All this is clearly out of balance. The current MoD Streamlining exercise is welcome but will only nibble at the problem. We need to grasp the whole issue firmly.

Some believe that quality will almost always defeat quantity:

> *Other things being equal, quality has almost always defeated quality, and that accumulated military experience should continue to guide defence equipment acquisition. It remains important to define quality appropriately, taking account of all lines of development, and to select equipment designs which maximise national military capability within a given budget.*[340]

---

[340] Professor David Kirkpatrick, 'Quality Rules, OK?', *RUSI Defence Systems* (Volume 9, No. 3, February 2007), page 19.

In contrast, Jeffrey Bradford suggests six reasons[341] why too few numbers of equipments and men are not good: a reluctance to put platforms in 'harm's way'; the impact on skills and experience of senior commanders; the impact on personnel of fewer platforms and higher operational tempo; a reluctance to innovate doctrine; effect on industrial skills of fewer platforms; lengthier acquisition cycles and less agility.

These and other views published in the 'Contention' section of the February 2008 edition of *RUSI Defence Systems* showed that there needs to be a balance between quantity and quality. But it also showed that if numbers are allowed to drop below a certain point, other considerations came into play – you cannot halve a frigate to maintain presence in two places distant from each other – as well as Bradford's points made above. Below that point numbers became more important than quality in some scenarios such as Counter-Insurgency and Maritime Security Operations.

The question is: have we reached that point as we watch numbers of Type 45 destroyers and Astute submarines increasingly reduced? It seems that we do not have the money to buy the quality we need in the numbers that make sense.

What Now?

If we cannot sensibly reduce quality or quantity any longer with the money available, what do we do? There are three possibilities.

The first is to deliver greater capability through our NEC.

> *The Armed Forces have accepted over a period of time a reduction in numbers, on the basis that we are going to deliver more effective capability by ensuring information flows through NEC. This leads me to the position that we had better take our NEC strategy to completion: I don't think that we are making sufficient progress.*[342]

The problem here is that whenever IT systems have been given the go-ahead on the basis of greater capability from fewer people, they have always failed to deliver on that promise. NEC has, as described in Chapter Nine, repeatedly failed by pursuing a gold-plated, 'big bang' approach.

---

[341] Dr Jeffrey Bradford, 'Stop Deliberating, Get Iterating', *RUSI Defence Systems* (Volume 9, No. 3, February 2007), page 19/20.
[342] Rear Admiral Rees Ward, Interview, *RUSI Defence Systems* (Volume 10, No. 3, February 2008), page 11.

Nevertheless, we must not give up and we need to drive NEC hard.

The second possibility of getting more for our money is to eliminate waste from the acquisition process. In the past I have calculated[343] that we could save between £1.5Bn and £3Bn a year in procurement – or £15Bn to £30Bn over the ten-year equipment programme – and I see no reason to change my mind. The savings would not reduce either quantity or quality, but would come from the sort of things that the DIS and DACP were attempting to do – but are now seen to be failing at – for example, the original aim of reducing cycle time by up to 50% being cut to 'significantly shorter'.

> The third possibility is a wholesale overhaul of our defence strategy. A defence review, in other words

The third possibility is a wholesale overhaul of our defence strategy. A defence review, in other words. That is not likely before the next General Election and, if Labour gets back in, it may not happen even then. Even if the Conservatives are victorious, they may not tie their findings to the reality of funding – as Labour didn't in 1997.

Dr Liam Fox, the Shadow Defence Secretary, has said he is unable to determine how much a Conservative government would spend on defence. He said it would be:

> Quite irresponsible to start making spending promises we couldn't fulfil. What we've said is that when we come to office we will have a proper strategic defence review, which is hugely overdue at the present time. When we've done that we can decide what we need in terms of defence and then we can look at what we can afford and how we balance those up.[344]

So, if NEC is not delivering greater capability for less money, and if more money for defence is unlikely over the next few years in the quantity required, and if DIS and its subsequent implementation does not deliver large savings, we must overhaul our defence strategy. Under pressure from the Chiefs of Staff in March 2008, Prime Minister Gordon Brown promised some sort of review within three months. It will be interesting to see what sort of review he had in mind and how it is conducted. It is unlikely to recommend an increase in the budget, and just as unlikely to

---

[343] Bill Kincaid, *Dancing with the Dinosaur*, page 185, UK Defence Forum, 1999.
[344] Dr Liam Fox, Shadow Defence Secretary, GMTV Sunday Programme, 6 April 2008.

recommend a major reduction in forces and equipment deployed on operations, and even more unlikely to cancel big equipment programmes in Labour constituencies and marginals. So, it will at best be an exercise in numbers and ISD slippage. It is not going to solve the funding crisis.

Operational Imperatives

Whether or not a full defence review takes place soon, MoD must take a long hard look at its operational imperatives. Should

> It will at best be an exercise in numbers and ISD slippage

we continue to aspire to a warfighting capability of US standard, or can we scale it down in either quantity or quality? Is Counter-Insurgency and Maritime Security Operations the name of the game for the foreseeable future? And, if it is, should we not sacrifice quality in some areas for quantity and perhaps fit for, and not with, for the shorter term? What is really essential?

> The latest version of Labour's interventionism, adumbrated by David Miliband, involves offering 'security guarantees' to unstable democratic regimes to protect them from insurgency. Such wars do not require carriers, nuclear submarines or jet fighters. They require the one thing the government puts lowest on its priority list, a well equipped and highly mobile army.
>
> That army, undermanned and ill equipped, is now engaged in the Government's service in Iraq and Afghanistan. When a British soldier deploys to the front, his or her family receives a letter from the defence secretary promising that he has taken 'all measures possible to ensure that the equipment issued to the UK armed forces is both right for the job and right for them'.
>
> This is simply not true. To take one example, a recent article in the Journal of the Royal Army Medical Corps pointed out that British troops were taking longer to get to a field hospital than it took the Americans in Vietnam. Two hours' delay in Iraq has become seven hours in Helmand.[345]

The RUSI Acquisition Focus tried to answer these questions – in its paper, which is reproduced at Appendix 11–1 – and suggested the following was essential:[346]

- Access to strategic intelligence systems.
- The nuclear deterrent.

---

[345] Simon Jenkins, 'Lovely new aircraft carrier, sir, but we're fighting in the desert', *The Sunday Times*, 24 February 2008.
[346] RUSI Acquisition Focus,' The Underfunded Equipment Programme: Where Now ?', *RUSI Defence Systems* (Volume 9, No. 3, February 2007), page 25.

- An expeditionary force capable of deploying and successfully conducting both high-intensity warfighting and Counter-Insurgency, with back-up in manpower and equipment to operate in the second of these roles over a long period of time.
- A maritime force capable of contributing to Maritime Security Operations worldwide in defence of UK interests.
- Ability to ensure the integrity of UK, and contribute to the integrity of European, airspace.
- The required NEC to achieve the above.

Against these essentials, the whole equipment programme needs to be scrutinised very carefully to weed out any programmes that do not contribute essentially to the above. Whether this will save a great deal is debateable, but it still needs to be done – and soon.

But the best hope of saving very substantial sums of money lies in the full implementation of DIS and DACP – with culture change the top priority.

Planning Round 2008

For many years, MoD had been solving the annual affordability problems by pushing programmes or parts of them into future years beyond Year Ten, creating an ever-growing bow wave. By 2007, this bow wave had become a tsunami which threatened to sink the equipment plan. Estimated as about £6Bn in 2002, it has got worse – perhaps £10Bn today. Much of it lies outside the ten-year plan, but each year this tsunami becomes more and more threatening. What could once be dealt with by 'salami-slicing' and movement 'to the right', cannot any longer be managed without major programme cancellations.

> By 2007, this bow wave had become a tsunami

Significant (i.e. several years) movement to the right of several major programmes would:

- Make those programmes more costly and introduce early obsolescence.
- Severely undermine DIS if the resulting industrial 'drum beat' drops below the minimum level, or if a hole appears in future orders.

It seems strange that, just as MoD has recognised that delay costs a lot of money, it tries to solve its budget problem by stretching procurement schedules of major programmes. All this does is inc. the bow wave that lies outside the ten-year EP, make those programmes more expensive overall and import turbulence and lack of commitment into its relationship with industry, thereby increasing costs yet further.

Last winter's planning round (PR 08) was seen as the last chance for long-delayed action, agonising decisions and blood on the floor. This dominated the winter months in MoD and eventually a package of measures was reluctantly agreed. However, this was not accepted by the politicians who decreed that cancellations of major equipment programmes were not to be made.

Coherence or Incoherence?

The problem with this sort of decision-making is that it is not based on military priorities, but on financial profiles and what is not firmly committed by contract. This undermines the coherence of the equipment programme in the medium to long term, without giving the troops the equipment they need in the short term.

> The problem with this sort of decision-making is that it is not based on military priorities

> There is much good work going on within both MoD and industry to improve capability planning, but currently it is set against a backdrop of an unprecedented mismatch between available funds and the future programme that MoD believes it has to deliver. There are two risks from this: first, decisions that are made to balance the books in the short term may run counter to the aims of TLCM. For example, investment in platforms which are receptive to hosting capabilities through-life could be cut, resulting in more costly upgrades to those platforms in future years. Secondly, TLCM could be deemed a failure because it has not sorted out the budget problem, although in itself it could never do that.[347]

It seems that the biennial (now returning to annual?) planning round cannot produce decisions that retain or produce a coherent equipment programme (or, indeed, a coherent defence programme). If that is so, then there is an urgent need for a defence review – the last one was a

---

[347] Ron Finlayson, industry co-chair of the NDIC subgroup on TLCM planning, 'The Role of Industry in MoD's Capability Planning', *RUSI Defence Systems* (Volume 11, No. 1, June 2008), page 35.

decade ago, was never properly funded and has been overtaken by major events such as 9/11, Iraq and Afghanistan. It is now apparent that MoD's review of the equipment programme is in train, although how this is to be carried out when there is unlikely to be any more cash and without reviewing defence planning and assumptions is less than clear.

There is mounting frustration within the defence industry about the paralysis in MoD decision-making, and any such review will prolong the period of paralysis. If the review is not wide or deep enough to come to clear conclusions about where cuts are to be made, we will increase paralysis, undercut many of the key DIS planks through increased turbulence in the programme and unrealistic industrial drumbeats, and achieve little. This period of paralysis will inevitably extend through the next planning round – PR 09 – which will have to integrate the review decisions.

> The room for manoeuvre has been restricted by Gordon Brown's commitment to two big new aircraft carriers and a replacement of the Trident nuclear deterrent. This has left the defence industry and workforces in a state of high uncertainty and has made the Government's defence industrial strategy ... unworkable, they say.[348]

While many would support Brown's commitment to the aircraft carriers and the Trident replacement, it does mean that any review of the equipment programme would be skewed by the ring-fencing of such large sums of money.

> The question now is how will PR 09 be conducted

The question now is how will PR 09 be conducted given the world economic turmoil, the fragility of both the Prime Minister and the Government, and the looming General Election which is likely to bring the Conservatives to power?

Defence Board

> After the summer political and bureaucratic recess in the United Kingdom, the Ministry of Defence, as other Government Departments, returns to normal to pick up where business left off in July. This season is somewhat different. The

---

[348] Stephen Fidler, 'Black Mood at Overwhelmed Ministry', *Financial Times*, 28 April 2008, page 3.

recent financial upheavals globally will likely leave UK plc needing to cut back unnecessary government expenditure, and the Ministry of Defence, being one of the biggest spenders on goods and services, will face significant budgetary pressures.

The mechanism of the Defence Board (DB), the most senior decision-making body in the Department, will likely rely on is the Equipment Plan (EP) – a spreadsheet containing 10-year costs for all on-going and planned programs in the UK defence establishment. Given the typical three-year term of service of Defence Board officials and a ten-year plan, making decisions can be compared to moving into a house in which there are several large pieces of immovable furniture – all you are left with are options to move the ornaments. Putting this into the context of current likely budgetary decisions, what is likely to happen next month of relevance to the Defence Industrial Base?[349]

The author then suggests programmes that might, in his words, go into limbo (read 're-scoping', 'further development', 'independent review' or 'further scrutiny') and these include FRES. This seems a good bet as it was recently announced that MoD would spend £500M on more armoured vehicles for current operations in Afghanistan. Also likely, he suggests, is a further cut in warship numbers.

> Whatever PR 09 does it is bound to undermine DIS still further

Whatever PR 09 does, whether cuts in numbers or delay to programmes, it is bound to undermine DIS still further. Once again, a good initiative is at risk of being thrown off course by the short-term financial bottom line. The reluctance to grip the ever-worsening financial problem may well torpedo the huge effort that MoD is making to improve capability delivery. 'Accountants' logic' rules in Whitehall to the detriment of both the short and long term.

---

[349] Dr Jeffrey Bradford, defensrindustrialbase.blogspot.com, 19 September 2008.

Chapter Twelve

Acquisition Now

By the second half of 2008, a great deal of activity had taken place in the wake of the DIS, but rather less progress had been made than originally planned, and progress on the most important issues – culture and behaviours – was very much less. This called into question whether MoD had the understanding and determination to implement DIS successfully – like so many previous initiatives over the last 40 years.

As already noted, reorganisation and process changes are largely enablers and on their own can only deliver a small amount of output change. Only a step change in culture will deliver the sort of improvement that the refocused DACP, in aiming to cut procurement cycle times, is trying to achieve. MoD needs to understand that culture change is not just about the way IPTs and industry work together on projects, but – perhaps more crucially – the behaviours of the men at the top in Whitehall.

A good example is the way the civil servants and politicians have handled last winter's planning round – PR 08. For narrow political reasons, it seems that they were happy to undo much of the good work that had gone on and to accept penalties to DIS, severe enough to risk serious subsidence. This is hardly the example they should be setting if they really want to implement DIS. It is easy to conclude that DIS is seen as a good thing as long as it doesn't interfere with traditional Whitehall behaviour.

It seems that we are fighting two wars with an early 20th-century peacetime mentality.

Exit Lord Drayson

DIS was the brain child of Lord Drayson and he was its driving spirit. With him in the ministerial chair, things moved and progress was made. He was a demanding minister and, no doubt, shook many people out of the traditional routine, but if he did it was with the wholly laudable intention of improving acquisition performance.

His was the approach of a 21st-century industrial CEO with a time-to-market mentality in marked contrast to the Whitehall 'delay mentality'. This was a clash of cultures and it was vital for the implementation of DIS and DACP that Drayson's culture carried the day.

> But there is a third stakeholder, and that key stakeholder is key to the implementation of the bold design of the DIS – the Civil Service. Just how will it react to Lord Drayson's managerial style, developed during years of successfully running high-tech businesses, where results matter more than 'process'? It is the civil servants who will have to implement the DIS and their reaction is far from clear.[350]

Would Drayson's results culture or the Whitehall culture of process carry the day? It didn't take long – less than two years – to get an answer. Drayson's sudden resignation in November 2007,

> Sent shock waves through the acquisition community and left it wondering whether his initiatives, in particular the changes laid out in DIS, will be carried forward by his successor or whether there will be a change of course.[351]

The reason given was that he was taking up a not-to-be-missed opportunity to take his motor racing career the next step. But many people felt there was more to it than that. Was he pushed, or did he get fed up fighting MoD inertia? What seems clear is that his battles on behalf of DIS, and the need to make sure that industry had a more stable and better planned workload, were running into stiff opposition in PR 08 over, inter alia, the proposals to delay FRES significantly.

> Drayson did not have the full support of the part time Secretary of State or of Number Ten

What is also clear is that Drayson did not have the full support of the part time Secretary of State or of Number Ten. If this is so, sacrificing Drayson to preserve the traditional way of doing things was short-sighted to say the least, and certainly counter-productive in pursuing the worthy objectives of DIS.

---

[350] Paul Beaver, 'Is the System ready for the Defence Industrial Strategy?', *RUSI Defence Systems* (Volume 9, No. 1, June 2006), page 16.
[351] RUSI Acquisition Focus, 'Defence Acquisition after Drayson', *RUSI Defence Systems* (Volume 10, No. 3, February 2008), page 24.

Lord Drayson brought strong direction and, with his background in industry, much expertise and commercial understanding to bear on defence acquisition. His expertise was unprecedented for a defence minister and we are sure that not only will it be much missed, but that we may not see his like again for many years.[352]

Within at least some parts of MoD, this view was shared.

Although Drayson said it wasn't down to one man, I beg to differ. The vision was down to one man. He was very ably supported by CDM and a number of other influential people, but it was Drayson who drove things. DIS 1 would not have come out in the timescale it did if it hadn't been for Drayson; it would not have been driven forward in the way it has if it hadn't been for Drayson. He understood the business piece of this and was a real breath of fresh air. I believe he was a watershed in the affairs of acquisition ...[353]

It is difficult to say who 'won', but it is not acquisition, nor is it the Armed Forces; not the defence budget and it is certainly not cost-efficiency in the equipment programme.

There is a glimmer of light. In an interview for *RUSI Defence Systems*,[354] Lord Drayson hinted that he would very much like to get back into defence. We should do everything we can to get him back.

Defence Industrial Strategy Part 2

The DIS was produced in a hurry and, not surprisingly, many things were only sketchily done. Drayson knew this and planned a second part. This he insisted was to be published in December 2007. He also insisted that it included full costings. In the middle of PR 08, these two dictates were impossible to meld, although in the chaotic aftermath of the planning round, costing DIS probably would not have mattered.

An MoD spokeswoman said the update was 'an essential review' intended to reflect progress in implementing the DIS. She said 'it will look to provide clarity and transparency, update policy and to develop themes that were less fully explored in the original document, for example, SME engagement, supply chain management. There are also proposed new sectors for space and IT.'[355]

---

[352] RUSI Acquisition Focus, 'Defence Acquisition after Drayson', *RUSI Defence Systems* (Volume 10, No. 3, February 2008), page 24.
[353] Rear Admiral Rees Ward, Interview, *RUSI Defence Systems* (Volume 10, No. 3, February 2008), page 10.
[354] Gavin Ireland, 'Accelerating Defence Acquisition: What Defence Can Learn from the World of Motorsport', *RUSI Defence Systems* (Volume 11, No. 1, June 2008), page 83.
[355] *Defense News*, 9 July 2007, page 6.

DIS 2 is essential, but the resignation of Drayson allowed the pressure to be eased on MoD. The timetable for DIS 2 was pushed back from December 2007 to March and then the Summer … or the Autumn … By then, many people believed that DIS 2 was dead.

If DIS 2 is dead, then the original DIS will almost certainly die. In the Foreword to DIS, the five co-signatories – John Reid (Defence Secretary), Alan Johnson (Trade and Industry Secretary), Des Browne (Chief Secretary to the Treasury), Lord Drayson (Minister Defence Procurement) and Alan Michael (Minister of State for Industry and the Regions) – stated that:

> **If DIS 2 is dead, then the original DIS will almost certainly die**

> The complex, technologically challenging and high-value systems which we are introducing – and which take many years to design and bring into service – will last for many years. This places increasing emphasis on an ability to support and upgrade them through life, as well as having implications for industrial capability and capacity that it is sensible or economic for industry to retain … Together, the defence industry and government have to change their relationship, working to ensure that our Armed Forces have the equipment they need. Doing this will help ensure the UK defence industry has a sustainable and bright future.[356]

So, if we don't produce a competent DIS 2 and if, thereby, DIS dies, does this mean that the onshore defence industry will not be sustainable? Unless DIS has been a mistaken initiative, that is what we must conclude. But perhaps DIS 2 is not dead, but just taking rather more time over its completion than DIS itself. If it is not dead, what must it do?

The RUSI Acquisition Focus believes that DIS 2 must address the following:

- An authoritative scheme for addressing the DIS aspirations of appropriate sovereignty and operational autonomy.
- The cost of this and how it will be paid for post-PR 08.
- Proper codification of strategic partnering, including underpinning structures and metrics, in the light of both progress and problems since December 2005.
- Increased agility to cater for the faster speed of both technology and operational change, which will require continued

---

[356] DIS, Foreword.

implementation of culture change. In particular it will need to embed in both MoD and industry a different culture in decision-making, in trust and transparency, and in the relationship between MoD and industry; and, in MoD, changes in commercial thinking and attitudes to 'time to market', risk-acceptance and accountability.

- A basis for the future Defence Industrial Plan.
- Increased R&D spend by both Government and industry.[357]

Focusing in a bit more, I believe that DIS 2 must cover how MoD is to achieve the following:

- More transparency in MoD's financial plans. This was promised in DIS, but in Autumn 2007 a MoD spokesman said that it had not been possible to pursue this yet, but it would be once PR 08 had achieved a stable and affordable equipment programme. It hasn't. So, it looks as if this fundamental aspect of strategic partnering is once more on the back burner. DIS 2 must drive this forward.
- MoD pressure on primes to place work with UK SMEs onshore as is done in the US and France. Until the DIS is taken the next step, the status quo will be maintained and there will be no change to the level of SME involvement.
- Greater national investment in developing sufficient resources, particularly systems, architects and engineers. Other nations are doing so and failure to take action in UK will inevitably lead to finding these capabilities overseas.
- Increased, and better-targeted, research funding that reaches the really innovative companies, not necessarily primes or large firms.
- Transformation of the very unsatisfactory situation on the range and levels of skills which MoD staffs require.
- Expert oversight of, and a framework of appropriate incentives and penalties for, strategic partnering arrangements.[358]

The actions above are all procedural. What has been the most disappointing aspect of DIS and the follow-on studies is the consideration of cultural and behavioural aspects, which are not only inadequately

---

[357] RUSI Acquisition Focus, 'Defence Acquisition After Drayson', *RUSI Defence Systems* (Volume 10, No. 3, February 2008), page 25.

[358] Professor David Kirkpatrick, 'DIS: The Next Steps', *RUSI Defence Systems* (Volume 11, No. 1, June 2008), page 108.

covered, but have been less determinedly implemented than the majority of the organisational and procedural recommendations.

So, DIS 2 must include a more detailed plan on how to change acquisition culture and how it is to be implemented. It must consider how MoD is to:

- Become less risk-averse.
- Become less innovation-averse.
- Become more knowledgeable about industry.
- Develop a true partnering mentality with industry.
- Instil trust both within MoD and between MoD and industry.
- Achieve both accountability and empowerment at all levels.
- Develop and foster leadership qualities.
- Improve decision-making.

Decision-making lies at the heart of the problem and much of that is cultural.

> We need to consider why it is that important decisions fail to be taken in a timely and effective way. The answer lies with individual performance. Many of the people who are in the decision-making loops come from backgrounds that focus more on the organisation than the individual. They may not feel that they own the decision or indeed the consequences. They are unlikely to have been trained to use their emotional intelligence, a crucial element of effective decision-making, but still a new concept ...[359]

The author goes on to say that we need to empower individuals to take decisions effectively. Leaders should stand back, allowing teams to find their own way to the solution. If they are not empowered, they will be taking the organisation's journey, not their own. This requires a major cultural change at all levels from the very top to the lowest. DIS 2 must seriously promote cultural change.

> Leaders should stand back, allowing teams to find their own way to the solution

What is not required is a new policy initiative labelled DIS 2. We have had enough initiatives. What is required is the continuing progress that has been set in train since DIS, as well as impetus given to those aspects of DIS which have not made progress. But most

---

[359] Stephanie Ayres, 'Coaching and the Defence Industrial Strategy', *RUSI Defence Systems* (Volume 11, No. 1, June 2008), page 110.

importantly, those issues which DIS did not set in train must be recognised, set in hand and become part of MoD core business. This applies particularly to culture change and costs.

But, whatever the form, the question remains – is DIS 2 dead? There is no mention of it in the DIS section of the MoD Defence Plan 2008–2012, so it must be assumed that, at the very least, it has been shelved *sine die*.

The Defence Plan 2008–2012

The MoD's Defence Plan for the period until 2012 was published in June 2008.[360] It is, necessarily, a short summary of the main points but, short as it is, it leaves unanswered many more questions than it answers clearly. No doubt much of it is flowed down in fuller detail within MoD, but it is neither a wholly persuasive nor a clear document to those outside.

The section on Single Service Transformation is one example. The sub-objective for the Army states:

> *In line with the Future Army Structures work, continue to rebalance the Army better* **to meet current concurrency and Harmony assumptions for planned operations** *[author's bolding] … and developing units with broader utility across the spectrum of operations.*

This seems to put the emphasis on current operations. The sub-objectives for the other two Services are also seemingly embedded in the near future. So, how does the signing a month later of the contract for two *large* aircraft carriers help to meet these sub-objectives? Would smaller aircraft carriers be any less useful for Afghanistan-type operations or Maritime Security Operations? And what about Type 45 Destroyers and Astute submarines which, like the carriers, seem predicated upon future high-capability warfare? And large numbers of high-performance jet aircraft? Wouldn't less capability allow the greater numbers that are needed in Counter-Insurgency and Maritime Security Operations? This Defence Plan therefore does nothing to resolve one of today's major issues – the problem of capability, numbers and affordability.

> This Defence Plan therefore does nothing to resolve one of today's major issues

---

[360] MoD, *Defence Plan 2008–2012*, Cm 7385, The Stationery Office, London, June 2008.

Nor does it tackle the key science, innovation and technology issue – that of inadequate funding.

The Defence Plan makes strange reading in many places as it sets aims and objectives some of which seem divorced from reality. For example, it states as a key aim for change: deliver DIS. Yet, this is surely impossible without DIS 2 (not mentioned and therefore assumed shelved) and, more importantly, without any attempt by MoD to quantify the overall cost of the initiative, which will be large if we are to retain onshore expertise when orders are falling.

Another statement appears little more than hopeful: "NEC will deliver benefit by enabling decision superiority across both the battlespace and the business space". While this is undoubtedly the case if NEC is implemented, we have made so little progress over the last two decades that it seems unlikely by 2012. A good aim, but will it be delivered in four years' time?

Targets for time, cost and performance delivery, too, are questionable as user requirements are reduced (usually to reduce costs or delay), cost increases are artificially reduced by 'creative accounting' (which magically change huge cost overruns to overall savings), and cost overruns and delays are measured only from Main Gate.

The Plan, like so many MoD initiatives, strategies and plans, is full of really good intentions, aims and objectives. Deliver them and we will be a long way down the road towards major improvements. But, like so many MoD initiatives, implementation is so full of question marks that many will not be confident that enough will be achieved to lift acquisition out of the slough of mediocrity it has occupied for too long. Achievement, not aims, will be the only way to meet the laid down sub-objectives on 'reputation' – particularly the 50% target for positive opinion of MoD by the public and the 75% target of positive opinion of MoD by MoD staff: there's a long way to go.

The problem, of course, is that the Plan is divorced from funding reality. What PR 08 proved yet again is that there are insufficient funds to achieve political commitments and no doubt, after the failure of PR 08 to achieve programme reality, PR 09 will reconfirm. So, what is the point of this Defence Plan, other than window dressing?

The Concerns in 2008

By late 2008, we should have seen greater progress in the implementation of DIS, especially in terms of the work on culture change and achievement of a balanced and affordable defence programme. While other work has achieved considerable progress in implementing reorganisation and process change (though not all to the good), culture change has been neglected and work towards a stable programme has been short-sightedly torpedoed.

This needs to be remedied immediately but, despite the Prime Minister's promise of a defence capability review, this is unlikely to happen. The resignation of Drayson has seen to that.

So, what are the main concerns in 2008? These are tabulated in Figure 12–1.

Key Problems in 2008
An unaffordable, and increasingly incoherent, defence programme
The procurement time cycle is far too long
A culture, particularly at the top, which is: risk aversive; innovation aversive; 'Do-as-I-say' not 'Do-as-I-do'; ignorant of, and antipathetic to, industry; lacking in accountability
Particular cultural problems: • Poor leadership. • Official encouragement of caution, emphasis on detail and avoidance of risk. • Whitehall's delay mentality. • A fear/blame culture. • Concentration on the minimisation of the downside rather than the maximisation of the upside. • Pre-occupation with cost and a refusal to see the overall financial picture. • A refusal to learn from experience.
Other Major Problems in 2008
The 'one size fits all' approach
Accountability is vague and authority and responsibility are not matched
The inability, or unwillingness, of officials to make difficult decisions
Little empowerment of individual managers and leaders
Poor MoD skills in technical costing, expertise in technologies and systems, industrial knowledge and understanding
Lack of motivation of staff
The tendency to slide back into comfort zones
MoD performance is input-centred, not output-driven
Under-resourcing of early procurement stages

Innovation, agility and flexibility still poorly supported
Large cost growth and delay still import turbulence and undermine commitment
Technical risk reduction achieved too late
Lack of support for SMEs and their innovative approach
Difficulties in collaboration
Slow progress towards a strategic partnering mentality in MoD and industry
Lack of trust and transparency, both within MoD and between MoD and industry
Unknown, and likely high, cost of DIS
Lack of a Defence Industrial Plan
Level of R&T investment so low that it threatens to undermine DIS in the future
Lack of a Defence Technology Plan
Other S&T issues: • Poor pull-through into procurement programmes of MoD-funded research. • The 'Valley of Death'. • Difficulties in transferring technology to, and between, commercial companies. • Maturity of technology available before Main Gate. • Integration of hi-tech equipment.
Exports threatened by abolishing DESO

Figure 12–1: The Problems in 2008

Comparison with 1997

How do these problems compare with those in 1997, 1999 and 2002? These were listed at length in my earlier books,[361] but the progress on solving the key problems are shown in Figure 12–2.

Problems in 1997	Progress by 1999	Progress by 2002	Progress by 2008
Lack of Accountability and Empowerment	Some	Regression	Little
Lack of professionalism, skills, experience and expertise	None	None	Small
Weak decision-making (except UORs)	None	None	None
Ineffective process	Little	Little	Some
Convoluted procedures	Little	Little	Regression
Stifling but ineffective scrutiny	Little	Little	Little
Early stages of procurement cycle ineffective and under-resourced	None	Little	Some
Too much reliance on competition	None	None	Some
Tenures too short	None	None	Some
Carrots and sticks too small	None	Small	Small
MoD Organisation	Significant	Significant	More significant
Adversarial relationship with industry	None	None	Significant, but patchy
Inadequate R&T spend	Regression	Regression	Regression
Unbalanced and unaffordable programme	None	None	Regression
Process-centred, not output focused	None	None	None

Figure 12–2: Progress since 1997

---

[361] Bill Kincaid, *A Dinosaur in Whitehall* (Brassey's, London, 1997); *Dancing with the Dinosaur*, UK Defence Forum, 1999; *Dinosaur in Permafrost* (TheSauras Ltd, 2002).

Overall progress has been, to say the least, disappointing since 1997 when Labour came to power and said that the Strategic Defence Review was to include:

> *A ruthless examination of how value-for-money for defence procurement, one of the most important aspects of the review, can be improved.*[362]

The fault can hardly be laid at the door of those who wrote either the Smart Procurement Initiative or the DIS, for both acknowledged the problems and recommended solutions. The fault lies in the failure to implement them successfully. This may seem to be a hasty judgement on implementation of DIS after less than three years, but pointers are much in evidence.

Settling Back into the Comfort Zone

In implementing both Smart Procurement and DIS, we have seen an initial burst of effort under strong ministerial leadership that has achieved significant progress in reorganisation (Operational Requirements (OR) to Equipment Capability (EC), joining up the three Service logistics organisations to form DLO and amalgamation of DPA and DLO), many changes in procedures and, more recently, the relationship with industry. Then, with the departure of those ministerial leaders, we've seen a slow relaxing of the drive for change with unfortunate regression to the *status quo ante*, particularly in those areas where either progress was difficult to drive (culture, behaviours, accountability, decision-making and the focus on output), or where money is a significant factor (R&T, cost of DIS, affordable programme, funding of early programme stages).

Formulating initiatives is one thing – implementing them is far harder. Major change demands a move out of the comfort zone for everyone. Unless this is driven hard from the top, most people, whether at the top or the bottom of an organisation will, consciously or subconsciously, slide back into their own comfort zones. Many MoD staff prefer to live in a vacuum, isolated from the real world, ignoring political and industrial realities until these can no longer be ignored late in the day, often causing major upsets to plans. This is not entirely the fault of DECs

---

[362] House of Commons Defence Committee, Eighth Report 1997/98, *The Strategic Defence Review*, Volume 1, paragraph 333.

and IPTLs because, if they seek guidance early, so often they get no useful pointers from Ministers' outer offices. And as for industrial realities, these are not well understood in MoD and, in many cases, deliberately ignored. The same might be said of the Treasury and the Department for Business, Enterprise and Regulatory Reform (BERR). This is one reason why the move to a partnering mindset is so hard to achieve in MoD and other government departments.

This sliding back into comfort zones is what happened in 2001, and that is what is happening now. Given this, is it surprising that decision-making in MoD does not deliver realistic decisions within the wider perspective?

Of course there are excuses. But that's what they are. Culture change must not be left while reorganisation and process changes are pushed through; PR 08 should never have been the mess it has become for political reasons. Hard decisions have to be made whenever the next election might occur. Ducking the issues only stores up more problems.

> Ducking the issues only stores up more problems

Unless hard decisions are taken, DIS will have failed in terms of significantly improving output. And the price of failure is too high.

Appendix 12–1

RUSI ACQUISITION PAPER[363]

DEFENCE ACQUISITION AFTER DRAYSON

The members of the RUSI Acquisition Focus are: John Weston (Chairman), Tim Banfield (NAO), Bob Barton (co-chair of the MoD/Industry Equipment Capability Group), Vice Admiral (retd) Jeremy Blackham (recently EADS UK President), John Dowdy (Director, McKinsey), Professor Christopher Elliott (GD UK), Graham Jordan (formerly S&T Director, MoD), Gerry Paulus (Managing Director, SVGC Ltd), Major General (retd) Bill Robins (formerly DGICS, MoD), Professor Trevor Taylor (Head of Defence Management and Security Analysis, Cranfield University), Bill Kincaid (Editor RUSI Defence Systems)[364]

Summary
The recent resignation of Lord Drayson, Minister for Defence Equipment and Support, has raised concerns that full implementation of the Defence Industrial Strategy (DIS) and the Defence Acquisition Change Programme (DACP) may founder under less expert political leadership.

DIS provided for the first time a clear vision of the future position of the defence industry in the UK and importantly gave a modern vision of the desired relationship between the MoD and industry. It has much to say about things of great importance to the UK defence community – appropriate sovereignty, strategic partnering, MoD's commercial approach, trust and transparency, together with many changes that are required to improve agility in acquisition.

Since DIS was published, much work has been done on amplifying its recommendations through the Enabling Acquisition Change (EAC) report and subsequently the DACP. While good progress has been made in changing acquisition processes and MoD organisation, work on cultural change seems to be lagging. The Defence Technology Strategy (DTS) has laid down priorities for

---

[363] RUSI Acquisition Focus, 'Defence Acquisition after Drayson', *RUSI Defence Systems*, (Volume 10, No. 3, February 2008), page 24.
[364] Names and posts of the members have in some case changed but were correct when this paper was published.

advancing science and technology, but neither the DIS nor the DTS has been properly costed, nor the origin of the required resources identified.

A revision of DIS (DIS 2) was due to be published in December 2007, but has been delayed. We find this regrettable. It raises profound questions about the direction that the MoD acquisition programme will now take, since we regard DIS 2 as essential for clarification and consolidation of the original strategy. Publication should not be delayed beyond the resolution of this planning round (PR08).

DIS 2 must address the following:

- An authoritative scheme for addressing the DIS aspirations of appropriate sovereignty and operational autonomy.
- The cost of this and how it will be paid for post-PR08.
- Proper codification of strategic partnering, including underpinning structures and metrics, in the light of both progress and problems since December 2005.
- Increased agility to cater for the faster speed of both technology and operational change, which will require continued implementation of culture change. In particular it will need to embed in both MoD and industry a different culture in decision-making, in trust and transparency, and in the relationship between MoD and industry; and, in MoD, changes in commercial thinking and attitudes to 'time to market', risk-acceptance and accountability.
- A basis for the future Defence Industrial Plan.
- Increased research and development (R&D) spend by both Government and the defence industry.

We believe that Lord Drayson clearly understood the industrial dynamics and the MoD environment: he brought leadership that was unique, determined and unconstrained by past inertia. Post-Drayson, the future of defence acquisition looks bleak. If DIS 2 is further delayed or is weaker than is needed, or above all is not fully costed and the cost not planned for, it will signal that the Government is not fully committed to the major changes in DIS 1 endorsed by four Departments of State.

We look to the leadership of MoD to prove us wrong.

The sudden resignation last November of Lord Drayson, the Minister (Defence Equipment and Support), sent a shock wave through the acquisition community and left it wondering whether his initiatives, in particular the changes laid out in the Defence Industrial Strategy (DIS), will be carried forward by his successor or whether there will be a change of course.

Lord Drayson brought strong direction and, with his background in industry, much expertise and commercial understanding to bear on defence acquisition. His expertise was unprecedented for a defence minister and we are sure that not only will it be much missed, but that we may not see the like for many years. However, as Bill Jeffrey, the MoD's Permanent Under Secretary, said in answer to an earlier RUSI Acquisition Focus paper:[365] *"... when it comes to internal change, I am in no doubt that it is up to the permanent leadership of the Department to make this stick. I appointed myself Senior Responsible Owner of the programme to implement the changes recommended by Tom McKane, and regard it as at the very top of my own agenda, and this is just as true of other senior colleagues too"*.

This suggests that there will be no significant change of direction or emphasis with the departure of Lord Drayson. But, as always, this is conditional on the political will and direction remaining in place to support the permanent staff and keep the right pressure on them. If the direction remains the same then this of course would be very good news, for there is much good in what Drayson has started. But will it? To provide a yardstick to measure what the MoD does next, we examine the key aspects of the Drayson legacy.

The Defence Industrial Strategy

The Defence Industrial Strategy (DIS), published in December 2005, produced for the first time a reasonably clear vision of the way MoD and the defence industry will have to operate together in the future to deliver mutual benefit. It contained several essential features that needed to be fully implemented, and we believe that the key ones are as follows.

The DIS is to promote 'a sustainable industrial base that retains in the UK those industrial capabilities (including infrastructure, skills, tacit knowledge, intellectual property (IP) and capacity) needed to ensure **appropriate sovereignty**'. It goes on to say that 'we must

---

[365] Bill Jeffrey, 'Implementing the Defence Industrial Strategy', *RUSI Defence Systems* (Volume 9, No. 2, Autumn 2006), page 23.

maintain the appropriate degree of sovereignty over industrial skills, capacities, capabilities and technology to ensure **operational independence** against the range of operations that we wish to be able to conduct … not only being assured of the delivery of ongoing contracts, but also the ability to respond to Urgent Operational Requirements (UORs) …'

The second key feature is the aim to introduce a **more commercial approach** within MoD. It has long been recognised that it is in commercial skills that MoD appears to be at its weakest and where the permafrost lies deepest. Amyas Morse was brought in specifically to instil a better commercial approach, but without Lord Drayson this is going to be much more difficult.

The next key feature is the move away from a policy of 'competition, competition, competition' to a more flexible policy including **strategic partnering**. DIS considers each industrial capability area and derives a policy for each. Strategic partnering features in several, notably in maritime, armoured vehicles, aircraft and helicopters, and since the publication of DIS some progress has been made, notably the long-term partnering arrangement (LTPA) with AgustaWestland.

Compared with competition, strategic partnering is not an easy option: to be successful, both MoD and industry will have to develop a strategic partnering mentality – not simple when the whole of middle and senior management have built their careers in an adversarial relationship. If they are to do so, **trust and transparency** have to be developed. This is a two-way requirement, and industry needs to change too. However, partnering is client-led and the MoD has only scratched the surface of what might be possible by following civil sector comparators of deeper partnering. It is questionable whether the MoD will have the confidence to do this without the inspiration and leadership that Lord Drayson so evidently provided.

The DIS endorses Defence Values for Acquisition. These not only include trust and transparency, but also many of the principles laid down by Smart Acquisition, which were never implemented under that initiative. One of these is to 'understand that time matters' and, although it doesn't say so in so many words, these Values for Acquisition all go towards improving **agility**. This need for greater agility in acquisition has, in the time since DIS was published, been underlined time and again by operations in Iraq and, particularly, Afghanistan. It is indeed a clear operational necessity.

DIS was produced in remarkably short time and could not have been expected to be totally comprehensive. Indeed, much further work, including both the DACP and the DTS, has followed its publication.

The Defence Acquisition Change Programme

The DIS stated that, 'We will place real effort and priority on driving forward the programme of cultural, behavioural, procedural and where necessary organisational change.' This was the subject of the Enabling Acquisition Change (EAC) report, which focused on structures, organisation and processes, but qualified this by stating that: 'This is not to understate the paramount importance of skills, training, culture and behaviour.'

The driving changes recommended by EAC were, firstly, the **implementation of Through-Life Capability Management (TLCM)** and, secondly, the merger of the Defence Procurement Agency (DPA) and the Defence Logistics Organisation (DLO) to form **Defence Equipment and Support (DE&S)**. The combination of the acquisition and sustainment areas into a single budget, with visibility of both parts out to a full ten years, is a step change and will probably prove the greatest driver towards making TLCM work. However, while the two organisations have now been co-located, it is not clear to us that the two elements are as yet working as one. In particular, the attitude to the reduction of competition and the move to strategic partnering has been embraced by the former DLO elements, but is still foreign to the ex-DPA mentality.

TLCM represents a completely different way of working – with an emphasis on long-term capability management. If the DE&S change is a 'simple' organisational move it is the profound cultural shift of TLCM, which the formation of DE&S underpins, that will shape future acquisition practice.

Not surprisingly, given the way the recommendations of the EAC report were worded, implementation of acquisition change – the DACP – is centred on organisation and process rather than **culture** and **behaviour**. The latter, of course, is more difficult to change than the former, so this is where strong Ministerial pressure needs to be brought to bear and that pressure then maintained. In particular, accountability must be central to change, so that the responsible individuals are given the requisite authority and, publicly named, are seen to be accountable for decisions. Meshing accountability with proper oversight is difficult, especially where public funds are concerned, but not impossible. Further, required in-service dates (ISDs) should once again be publicly stated at the start of programmes.

The Defence Technology Strategy

DIS was relatively weak on R&D, but it did direct that the Defence Technology Strategy (DTS) would be updated and this has subsequently been done. It lays down priorities in advancing science and technology and identifies areas for setting up communities of practice and university centres of excellence. However, it is a disappointing document in that, while it states the need for more investment from both industry and MoD, it does not say how this extra investment is to be produced. Without it, little improvement will be possible.

Clearly, the DTS needed to be taken further and, since Lord Drayson's departure, it has been announced that a Defence Technology Plan will be produced by the end of 2008. This is a welcome announcement, but it will have little impact if it does not include a realistic plan for **increasing R&D investment**.

The Need for Further Change

Lord Drayson's changes have been embraced with great enthusiasm in many areas of the MoD – they were seen as having clarity and based on common sense – but it is clear that Drayson's approach overloaded some parts of the MoD with too many initiatives that required much change. Undoubtedly, managing change is hard work, and against resistance particularly so; but equally it is clearly needed and must be effected as soon as possible. 'Slow change' will suggest to those outside the MoD, particularly to industry, that DIS and the change programme is not a high priority and, therefore, may be shunted into a siding. The changes called for in DIS 1, DTS and DACP need buy-in from everyone, MoD and industry alike. So far, the key changes required have only been partially implemented. Several years of consistent and strong political leadership, with clear direction by Ministers, will be needed if the post-DIS work is not to be largely wasted.

DIS 2

DIS 2 must do four things:
- Endorse those elements of DIS 1 that require further work for full implementation.
- Revalidate the DIS 1 implementation plan.
- Re-examine any elements of DIS 1 that now need refocusing after post-DIS work, set out a new path and plan its implementation. This implementation should then become the basis of the future Defence Industrial Plan.
- Fully cost DIS.

We believe that an overwhelming proportion of the elements of DIS 1 must be endorsed and its implementation plan refocused and made more detailed. For example, while MoD has finalised a LTPA with AgustaWestland, how should the difficulties in other capability areas be carried forward? How will design expertise be retained in those capability areas where new platforms are not likely to be procured for decades? Indeed, just what does 'design expertise' in such cases mean and what is required? Do they vary from sector to sector – is there a difference between what is required in the maritime sector and that needed in the complex weapons area? Is some expertise vital and some only desirable and, if so, what can be sacrificed if we cannot afford it across the board?

DIS 1 was produced in remarkably short time and further clarity over many of its elements is required. This clarity is needed not only to amplify the DIS 1 implementation plan and set out the basis for the future Defence Industrial Plan, but also to cost the whole strategy. This lack of costing, although understandable, was perhaps the single greatest weakness of DIS 1 and needs to be remedied in DIS 2 if industry and others are going to be convinced that MoD is not only serious about implementing it, but also capable of doing so.

PR 08

The costs that were implicit in DIS but never properly addressed bring inevitable conflict with this year's extremely difficult planning round, PR08. Not least, because they drove out into the open latent costs that were previously hidden in many programmes. It is well known that the significant 'bow wave' of unfunded commitment that has been building up in the defence programme for some years is now compromising the whole financial structure of the equipment plan. Difficult decisions are needed now: salami-slicing and moving programmes to the right will no longer suffice. We have already heard that the FRES schedule is one of the likely victims, but if several major projects are similarly delayed, this will undermine the whole DIS structure. For the DIS vision to work, there must be confidence that MoD will stick to its schedule of enough new platforms ordered at a realistic production rate, as well as maintain ISDs so that partnering agreements for their support can be conceived and adhered to.

Very hard choices will have to be made. Decision-makers, particularly the Defence Management Board (DMB), will not want the added difficulty of a large DIS cost being identified, but unless DIS as a whole is costed in step with PR08, the credibility of DIS will be undermined, perhaps fatally.

The Defence Acquisition Change Programme (DACP)

The DACP has now been divided into five primary Workstreams: DE&S; R&D; approvals & scrutiny; TLCM; and the commercial interface with industry. Arguably, one of these addresses process (approvals and scrutiny), one is about organisation (DE&S), one is about innovation (R&D) and one is about relations with industry. Just one is about changing culture in MoD (and industry) – TLCM – and even this emphasises improving skills rather than changing culture.

It is both quicker and more straightforward to change process and organisation than it is to alter culture, so it is hardly surprising if those who want 'quick wins' concentrate on process and organisation. Yet without culture change, the benefits brought about by changes to process and organisation will not yield more than a fraction of the potential benefits. MoD has started to shift culture and much effort is in hand to continue that. So far that change has been weak and patchy: indeed in some areas it is negligible. Successful culture change usually depends on a committed leader (e.g. the CEO in industry). Drayson, although not a CEO in the industrial sense, was committed. Can the same be said of others? If so, how would we know?

DIS made it clear that change in culture is essential, as did Smart Acquisition before it. We believe that DIS 2 must reinforce the need for, and methods of, implementing culture change. The Pathfinder pilots showed that such a change is possible in a short timescale, and it is expected that the Joint MoD–industry helicopter project team, located at Yeovil, will underscore this. The conclusions from these experiences, where positive, together with UOR culture, must be effected across acquisition as a whole and become acquisition practice and policy.

It is vital that DIS 2 dictates that several aspects of MoD culture be changed irreversibly and quickly:

- Lack of accountability.
- Slow and diffuse decision-making.
- The adversarial relationship with industry.
- Skills inadequacy.
- Focus on input rather than output.
- Lack of 'time-to-market' consideration.

These changes are vital to speed up the procurement cycle and introduce the necessary agility into defence acquisition; they are also vital if we are to successfully introduce TLCM. Without implementing changes in these areas, DIS 2 will have failed. Reinforcing this, the converse holds true: that implementing these changes will be impossible without DIS 2.

DTP

The DTP will not report until late this year. No doubt it will expand on the DTS and lay down a clear implementation path. However, the real issue is the woeful lack of funding for research and technology, and without a clear plan for increased funding from both MoD and industry, the DTP can only be a damp squib.

Conclusions

We believe that DIS 2 is essential and must not be postponed beyond the resolution of PR 08, or it will signal to industry that, with the resignation of Lord Drayson, MoD sees DIS 1 as just a cosmetic exercise.

Ideally, DIS 2 should become the Defence Industrial Plan. However, if DIS 1 cannot do everything an industrial plan should, it must at least point the way to the production of such a Plan.

The main areas that DIS 2 needs to cover are as follows:

- An authoritative scheme for addressing the DIS aspirations of appropriate sovereignty and operational autonomy.
- The cost of this and how it will be paid for post-PR08.
- Proper codification of strategic partnering, including underpinning structures and metrics, in the light of both progress and problems since December 2005. At present, the concept is much too poorly defined.
- The agility to cater for the increased speed of both technology and operational change, which will require continued implementation of culture change – to embed in both MoD and industry a different culture in decision-making, in trust and transparency, and in the relationship between MoD and industry; and, in MoD, changes in commercial thinking and attitudes to 'time to market', risk acceptance and accountability.
- A basis for the future Defence Industrial Plan.
- Increased R&D expenditure by both Government and the defence industry.

Ideally, the area of metrication should also be covered. As Lord Kelvin put it: 'If you cannot measure it, you cannot improve it'. Open, output-based metrics that are published are a vital element in driving change: in the MoD they are critical to breaking the Departmental sub-optimisation that destroys real value.

Unless DIS 2 does all of this, it will be stillborn, and the MoD's immune system will have won yet another battle.

We think the outlook is bleak. We will be delighted if the MoD's top management reinvigorates their commitment and proves us wrong.

"I don't see what all the fuss is about... if we get it wrong it isn't as though anyone's going to die..."

Chapter Thirteen

The Price of Failure

DIS, EAC, DTS and DACP together constitute a start to improving acquisition performance, but only a start. Just like Smart Procurement. As I wrote in 2002,[366] but substituting DIS for Smart procurement, we could say:

> *[DIS] is a start. However, its implementation is patchy and there is major stagnation in many important areas, to say nothing of several significant problems which were not foreseen and which have been generated during implementation, and others which were never part of [DIS] but should have been. Some of the stagnation and emerging problems may well be tackled successfully in the future, although it seems that they will continue to be brushed under the carpet for the moment.*

Let us look back a little further – to the Strategic Defence Review of 1998. To many, this was an excellent review torpedoed by insufficient funding to carry it out. But even at the time, there was some serious concern about how it was to be carried forward:

> *The SDR has faults, and many people would disagree with many things in it. It does begin to open things up. That is very welcome. Whether that window, which has been opened, is kept open is going to depend very much on people like us. If not, we are going to lose an extraordinary opportunity to do the kind of rethinking that is needed for the next quarter-century.*[367]

Has that 'extraordinary opportunity' for rethinking been seized? Has that window been kept open? No. Although there has been some new thinking – not least in the need to retain a strong onshore defence industry – there are still huge gaps between current operations (which are expected to last for a generation) and the forward equipment programme; between the political commitment of the military and the actual defence budget; between the concept of joined-up government and the actuality of separate Departments of State pursuing their own

---

[366] Bill Kincaid, *Dinosaur in Permafrost* (TheSauras Ltd, 2002), page 141.
[367] Professor Paul Rogers, Bradford University, 'The Outcome of the Strategic Defence Review', *RUSI Whitehall Paper Series 44*, 10 September 1998.

la. The opportunity for radical rethinking has been missed it won't recur for some time.

piece of really fresh thinking – DIS – like Smart Procurement and like so many earlier initiatives, appears to be losing steam and implementation, and, although being pursued with much activity, it does not seem to be setting a course for a coherent future. This is a tragedy for the Armed Forces, for industry and for the taxpayer, if not for many of those involved in the acquisition business in MoD.

> ..e opportunity for radical rethinking has been missed and looks as if it won't recur for some time

A tragedy? Some would call it a farce, and indeed if it were found in the pages of a novel or on the stage, it might be considered most amusing – the television programme, *Yes, Minister*, which portrayed the farcical side of government most brilliantly, leaps to mind. But defence is not a black comedy nor a stage farce – defence is far more important than that. The failure to improve acquisition is not for want of identifying the problems that exist, nor for efforts and activity in trying to do things better, but is the result of a failure to understand implementation.

The real tragedy is that heroic activity by so many people has made so little difference to acquisition output and, therefore, has resulted in failure. Does it matter? Yes. How much does it matter? A great deal. It matters in terms of:

- Lower operational readiness.
- Waste of a significant proportion of the defence budget.
- Weakening of the defence industrial base with the adverse effect on appropriate sovereignty, operational autonomy and UOR development and fielding.
- Above all, greater loss of servicemen's lives.

Failure, therefore, matters.

Cost and Waste

I have estimated that we waste between £1.5Bn and £3Bn per year,[368] or between £15Bn and £30Bn over the ten-year equipment plan. This is serious money – another whole defence budget over a decade or enough

---

[368] Bill Kincaid, *Dancing with the Dinosaur* (TheSauras Ltd, 1999), pages 183–185.

to dissipate the great bow wave that we have built up over the last decade or so (I choose to ignore the very real possibility that eliminating this waste would be seen as 'efficiency savings' by the Treasury and grabbed).

> *Not that waste is confined to information systems. Much more arises from the addiction of Smart Acquisition to extended studies. Especially notable are those on the Future Offensive Air System (FOAS) ... After ten years, and having spent more than £39M, this all ended with a whimper. It was decided not to decide.*[369]

Pugh also mentions waste in IT projects, in the Future Rapid Effect System (FRES) and Chinook helicopters. These are relatively small examples of waste, but there are plenty more and, when aggregated, they add up to very large sums indeed. Look at the **in-year** cost rises over the last two years of the largest 19 projects as reported in the NAO Major Projects Report. These add up to about £1.4Bn. The overall cost increase of these 19 projects comes to about £2.8Bn since their different Main Gate approvals – some of which were not long before. And this figure does not include Typhoon cost increases which were running at £2.3Bn in 2005 (the last year that Typhoon costs were given), nor does it include the cost increases before Main Gate approval.

How much of these very large cost increases is due to the 'conspiracy of optimism' is not known, but even if we allowed a large proportion, the remaining cost growth would still be a large figure – not least because it introduces programme turbulence leading to the undermining of commitment and consequent delays and cost increases.

But even that is small compared with what is wasted because of the overall culture of MoD – risk-averse, innovation-shy, anti-industry and devoted to delay. It is largely because of this culture that huge sums are wasted. This is where the bulk of the DACP effort should be concentrated – not on process and organisation.

What would be the outcome of eliminating the waste? We would be able to afford to do one or more of the following:
- Increase the size of the Armed Forces to eliminate 'over stretch' while still able to 'punch above our weight' as politicians require us to.

---

[369] Philip Pugh, 'Smart Acquisition: A Record of Failure', *RUSI Defence Systems* (Vol. 10, No. 1, June 2007), page 29.

- Pay servicemen a reasonable salary for what they are doing.
- Buy greater numbers of equipments to ensure there is always enough for all operational deployments.
- Invest much more in R&T to strengthen our industrial and research bases.
- Buy new capability much earlier (e.g. precision, UAVs and robotics).
- Replace ageing equipment earlier before they become coffins (e.g. the 40-year-old Nimrods and armoured vehicles).
- Provide adequate servicemen's accommodation before the need for a public outcry.

All these are serious needs, and the continued failure to meet them is harming our forces and the public perception of them. There is substantial waste and, until it is eliminated, it is difficult to make a strong case to the Treasury and politicians that the Defence Budget needs a serious increase.

> More importantly, it translates directly into a greater loss of servicemen's lives

More importantly, it translates directly into a greater loss of servicemen's lives.

Time

Time is cost. It was heartening to see that the refocused DACP had, as one of its objectives, the reduction of cycle time by 30%–50%. We really need to reduce it by at least 50%, but even cutting it by 30% in the near-ish future would have been a very real gain, and might have persuaded the authorities to build on it further. Reducing time would contribute greatly to reducing waste. But it will be difficult and that is presumably why even the 30% target has now been jettisoned, with the result that no useful reduction in cycle time will be achieved.

And if we fail to reduce time significantly? We will continue to get further and further behind the pace of technological and operational change, so becoming even less agile in our equipment programme. We will continue to schedule very long and costly procurement programmes with cost escalation, delay and obsolescence on fielding. We will continue to remain over-dependent on UORs. We will find exporting equipment more difficult as we get relatively less agile and produce increasingly obsolescent equipment at high prices. This will undermine onshore industrial capability and thence industrial jobs, particularly in the SME sector.

All this adds up to equipment arriving in operational theatres many months, if not years, after front-line forces need it – a good example is the continued delay of replacement armoured vehicles over the last 30 years.

All this, too, translates directly into the greater loss of servicemen's lives.

A Strong Onshore Industrial Base

This potential increase in obsolescence, loss of agility, reduction of exports and loss of onshore capability will inevitably mean a loss of jobs in industry. This may not matter too much as far as the overall health of the country's economy is concerned but, more importantly, it will weaken the industrial base. We are very dependent on UORs and to keep the UOR process as effective as it is, we need to retain a strong onshore defence industry – a key objective of DIS. Without this strong onshore industrial base, many UORs would not be delivered in the very short timescales that are demanded. Not only that but, without such a base, we would have to buy abroad – particularly from the US with the inevitable concerns over technology transfer and operational autonomy.

Many saw the DIS as an essential initiative to halt – or at least slow – the shrinking defence industry. Many SMEs were going out of business or migrating entirely to the civil sector, while primes were increasing their business in the US where the money is. BAE Systems has stated that it will transfer its corporate presence to the US once its business there is predominant. Other primes are also looking to invest more heavily in the US.

> If the implementation of DIS fails we will possibly lose appropriate sovereignty and operational autonomy

If the implementation of DIS fails to halt the reduction of the defence base in this country, we will possibly lose appropriate sovereignty and operational autonomy. We will certainly lose the ability to produce much UOR equipment as quickly as the front line demands.

To repeat, this will inevitably translate into greater loss of servicemen's lives.

The Loss of Lives

What usually gets forgotten in many parts of Whitehall and Abbey Wood is that lives are at risk.

> *Delays to delivery of new equipment may result in the military having to expose personnel to additional risk in the operational theatre ... The MoD's procurement system must take into account the risks that the military user is exposed to and factor them into any risk management and general programme decision-making. Moreover, with the military currently operating in an environment where the threat can change rapidly, it is even more important that the risks of a delay to a programme are weighed against the risk to military operations.*[370]

'Accountants' logic' too often takes precedent over military logic and the financial bottom line is the overriding factor. Even if this may 'save' a relatively small sum of money, or decrease the very short-term risk, the potential increase in casualties is considered as a minor factor or not considered at all – I don't ever remember seeing the cost of lives included in 'impact' statements when delays or cuts to programmes are proposed.

> 'Accountants' logic' too often takes precedent over military logic

Does this fulfil the Duty of Care? How does this achieve the Government's side of the Military Covenant? The answer is that it doesn't.

That is why improving acquisition is so important. That is why it is so important to fully implement the DIS. Activity does not necessarily equal improved output.

Another failure to improve acquisition should be unthinkable. Is it?

---

[370] Rick Hussey, 'Are Programme Delays and Overruns Caused by the MoD's Approach to Risk Management?', *RUSI Defence Systems* (Volume 10, No. 1, June 2007), page 22.

The Price of Failure

- Continuing waste of between £1.5Bn and £3Bn per year.
- Decreasing acquisition agility as the pace of technological and operational change continues to increase.
- Proliferation of obsolescent equipment.
- Loss of up to 300,000 industrial jobs.
- A weakened, or non-existent, industrial base.
- Decreasing ability to produce UOR equipment as quickly as required
- Decreasing operational readiness.

ALL LEADING TO A GREATER LOSS OF SERVICEMEN'S LIVES

Chapter Fourteen

Action This Day

This has been a tale of huge effort, relatively little progress and mounting frustration. The key to this has been the reluctance in MoD to force through culture change – without it, all the effort that has gone into changing organisation, processes and procedures is so much effort largely wasted.

Much of what was recommended in the Smart Procurement Initiative and in the Defence Industrial Strategy has been, or is being, implemented with much effort. But although this might represent, say, 80% of the recommendations, it may improve overall delivery by only a small amount. It is the other 20%, which is so much harder to implement, that will deliver the major improvement.

Let us look at what action needs to be taken now.

Referring back to the table at Figure 12–1, we can match the required actions to the problems.

Key Problems in 2008

An unaffordable, and increasingly incoherent, defence programme

Action Required: Strategy and commitments must be more closely linked to resources.

The Government must hold a Defence Review, cost its findings and match resources to commitments.

It must then update this every year, and take account of the higher rate of defence inflation (3% above GDP deflator, 6% above in equipment). During planning rounds, the MoD must come up with courageous decisions and politicians and Treasury must endorse them.

(Ch. 11)

The procurement time cycle is far too long

Action Required: Reduce the cycle time by 50% as the DACP was originally trying to do.

Determine what aspects of the UOR process can be imported into 'normal' procurement.

Fully cost delay (including cost of lives) so that it is clear how speed in decision-making will save money and reduce obsolescence.

All this will require a major change of culture and motivation. But so much flows from this.

(Ch. 7, 10)

A culture, particularly at the top, which is: risk averse; innovation averse; 'Do-as-I-say' not 'Do-as-I-do'; ignorant of, and antipathetic to, industry; and lacking in accountability

Action Required: This is the key. The culture must change from the top.

A culture change supremo must be appointed with ministerial backing to force it through over five years.

Risks and delays must be financially and operationally quantified.

Accountability must be introduced, particularly at the top.

A Mission Command approach must be adopted. Lessons must be learned from the UOR culture and applied.

Without a major culture change, little improvement will be made.

(Ch. 8, 10)

Particular cultural problems:
- Poor leadership
- Official encouragement of caution, emphasis on detail and avoidance of risk.
- Whitehall's delay mentality
- A fear/blame culture
- Concentration on the minimisation of the downside, rather than the maximisation of the upside
- Preoccupation with cost and a refusal to see the overall financial picture
- A refusal to learn from experience

Action Required: Encourage sensible risk-taking.

Get rid of the fear/blame culture.

Cost all aspects of delay (including loss of lives). Emphasise maximisation of the upside rather than minimisation of the downside.

Learn from experience (good or bad) and make those lessons easily accessible for all.
(Ch. 8)

Other Major Problems in 2008

The 'one size fits all' approach

Action Required: All projects are different.
Large projects need outstanding leaders with experience and expertise who must not be constrained with extensive procedures.
(Ch. 7, 8)

Accountability is vague and authority and responsibility are not matched

Action Required: Clear accountability must be introduced at all levels (including at the very top) and must be matched with responsibility and authority.
This is a very difficult exercise, but needs to be tackled quickly and authoritatively.
(Ch. 8)

The inability, or unwillingness, of officials to make difficult decisions

Action Required: Increase the number of staff from civil sector industry and other decision-making walks of life – at all levels.
Uncomfortable decisions must not be postponed and must be properly costed and accounted for.
(Ch. 8)

Little empowerment of individual managers and leaders

Action Required: There is a difficult balance between empowerment of individuals and the need for sensitive oversight to avoid the problems of 'stovepiping'.
Experienced leaders should be unfettered by process – one size does not fit all.
Mission command should be imposed.

Accountability must apply to those who say 'no' as well as to those who have to take action.

Clarify SRO authority over non-equipment DLoDs.

(Ch. 8, 10)

Poor MoD skills in technical costing, expertise in technologies and systems, industrial knowledge and understanding

Action Required: Education and training must improve further, but this is only part of the solution.

The quality of individuals must be improved and this can only be done with a significant increase in pay and rewards.

To offset the cost, more drastic cuts in staff must be imposed: the higher quality staff will work more quickly and effectively.

MoD/industrial exchanges (short and long) must become more frequent.

(Ch. 8)

Lack of motivation of staff

Action Required: Increased pay and rewards will help, but recognition of achievement is the greater motivator.

UORs provide such motivation, so a reduction in the time cycle of 'normal' procurement is important as is less turbulence in the equipment programme.

(Ch. 8)

The tendency to slide back into comfort zones

Action Required: The 'top of the shop' must get out of their comfort zones and drive everyone else out of their comfort zones and keep them out.

But they will only be able to do this if they set a clear example and embrace all of the above, including major culture change.

(Ch. 11)

MoD performance is input-centred not output-driven

Action Required: Output must be the target across the board.
UOR culture is the culture to be adopted (even though UOR processes are not entirely suitable for 'normal' procurement).
Delivering 'stuff' to theatre within time, cost and performance must be the aim and targets must be set to reflect that.
(Ch. 7)

Under-resourcing of early procurement stages

Action Required: Early procurement stages must be adequately resourced. 15% is only a guideline and every project will have different financial requirements.
Increasing upfront expenditure will be difficult, so projects without an urgent ISD must be slipped (not just allowed to slip in due course).
(Ch. 3)

Innovation, agility and flexibility still poorly supported

Action Required: DACP work on reducing cycle time by 50% must be accorded the very highest priority and hard decisions on implementing recommendations must not be side-stepped.
Processes inimical to innovation must be replaced by those that encourage innovation, particularly through SMEs.
(Ch. 7)

Large cost growth and delay still import turbulence and undermine commitment

Action Required: Root out the 'Conspiracy of Optimism'.
Improve cost estimating and management skills. Use independent cost experts.
Cease 'spinning' MoD figures.
(Ch. 7)

Technical risk reduction achieved too late

Action Required: Technical risks must be satisfactorily reduced before Main Gate. This requires greater investment in the early stages (as above), but also the greater use of proven technology.

Delays late in the CADMID cycle may introduce greater obsolescence and the implications of this must be taken into consideration when considering the imposition of delay.

(Ch. 9)

Lack of support for SMEs and their innovative approach

Action Required: MoD support for SMEs must be moved from warm words to positive action. In particular MoD must:

• Determine the circumstances in which SMEs should be helped.
• Provide sensible and more frequent stage payments.
• Provide IPR safeguards. Place more emphasis on innovation.
• Reduce long bidding schedules.
• Consider mandating SMEs in contracts, a mentor-protégé programme and 'brigading' of SMEs to bid for larger contracts.

(Ch. 5)

Difficulties in collaboration

Action Required: Collaborative projects should be the exception and must not be entered into for political reasons. Collaborative projects, where possible, should be led by industry (cf. Storm Shadow). Interoperability should be met with a pragmatic, bespoke approach, rather than through commonality of equipment and an overall big-bang policy.

(Ch. 7)

Slow progress towards a strategic partnering mentality in MoD and industry

Action Required: Strategic partnering is a hard and demanding arrangement but must be pursued by both MoD and industry.

Both industry and MoD must share pain as well as gain.

Achieving trust and transparency will enable a strategic partnering mentality to grow in MoD and industry.

Competition dogma is impeding its growth and must be used much more flexibly

(Ch. 3, 4, 5, 10)

Lack of trust and transparency, both within MoD and between MoD and industry

Action Required: Although progress has been made, there is still a long way to go.

Within MoD, the constraints imposed by suffocating 'process' shows the absence of trust, as does the DE&S attempts to keep others from talking to industry.

Between MoD and industry, trust and transparency must become central to every project with a 'one team ethos' and full disclosure of future programme and financial plans.

Trust and transparency must not be jettisoned when difficulties occur.

(Ch. 8)

Unknown, and likely high, cost of DIS

Action Required: The DIS is a non-event without its costs being determined and funds earmarked. This must be done as soon as possible.

(Ch. 4)

Lack of DIS 2 and a Defence Industrial Plan

Action Required: DIS 2 must be published in the near future to flesh out those parts of DIS which were sketchily done or not done at all.

It must then be followed by a Defence Industrial Plan with adequate and earmarked funding.

(Ch. 12)

Level of R&T investment so low that it threatens to undermine DIS in the future

Action Required: The Defence Technology Plan must identify and earmark significantly greater funding for R&T and recommend how to spend it more effectively.

There must be greater linkage with industry. Competition must be reviewed as it spreads the money and expertise more thinly.
(Ch. 9)

Lack of a Defence Technology Plan

Action Required: The Defence Technology Strategy must be turned into a Defence Technology Plan with adequate and earmarked funding.
(Ch. 9)

Other S&T issues:
- Poor pull-through into procurement programmes of MoD-funded research
- The 'Valley of Death'
- Difficulties in transferring technology to, and between, commercial companies
- Maturity of technology available before Main Gate
- Integration of hi-tech equipment

Action Required: Pull through more MoD-funded technology into programmes by mandating it where appropriate and avoiding competition.

Inject more R&T funds (see above) to remove the 'Valley of Death'.

Examine ways to overcome difficulties in transferring technology between commercial companies – perhaps looking at the way the Pathfinder Projects worked, or how 'brigaded' SMEs do it.

Mature technology much earlier in the CADMID cycle – or use existing technology.

Place greater emphasis on integration and experimentation.
(Ch. 9)

Exports threatened by abolishing DESO

Action Required: Reinstate DESO.
(Ch. 6)

The action recommended above is extensive and much of it will be difficult to implement. But it must be done. Our Servicemen and women deserve no less. Hard graft in life-threatening environments must be matched by similar hard graft on the home front. The home front was tough in both World Wars and we are now fighting a global war on terrorism. We need to take tough action – not least on defence acquisition. Unless we do, our Armed Forces will be fighting in a wartime environment, and we will be supporting them with a peacetime mentality.

That's not good enough.

Action this day.

ABBREVIATIONS AND ACRONYMS

ACDS (Log Ops)	Assistant Chief of the Defence Staff (Logistic Operations)
ADCIS	Air Defence Command and Information System
AIA	Advanced Information Architecture
ALDS	Acquisition Leadership Development Scheme
AFV	Armoured Fighting Vehicle
A400M	The collaborative European military transport aircraft
ARL	Army Research Laboratory (US)
ASTOR	Airborne Stand-off Radar
BAe	British Aerospace (forerunner of BAE Systems)
BP	British Petroleum
BT	British Telecommunications
BVRAAM	Beyond Visual Range Air-to-Air Missile
CADMID	Concept, Assessment, Demonstration, Manufacture, In-service, Disposal (acquisition cycle introduced by Smart Procurement)
CASOM	Conventionally Armed Stand-Off Missile
CBI	Confederation of British Industry
CBRN	Chemical, Biological, Radiological and Nuclear
CDL	Chief of Defence Logistics
CDM	Chief of Defence Materiel
CDP	Chief of Defence Procurement
CDS	Chief of the Defence Staff
CEDRIC	Centre for Experimentation, De-risking and Integration of C4I Capability
CEO	Chief Executive Officer
CIP	Combat Infrastructure Platform (capability used with Bowman)
CIS	Command and Information Systems
CofM	Chief of Materiel
COTS	Commercial Off-The-Shelf
C3	Command, Control and Communications
CVF	The UK's future aircraft carrier
CW	Complex Weapons
DACP	Defence Acquisition Change Programme
DAM	Defence Acquisition Management
DAMEP	Defence Acquisition Management Education Programme
DARPA	US Defense Advanced Research Projects Agency
DCDS(EC)	Deputy Chief of the Defence Staff (Equipment Capability)
DB	Defence Board
DE&S	Defence Equipment and Support
DERA	Defence Evaluation and Research Agency
DESO	Defence Exports Services Organisation
DEW	Directed Energy Weapons
DFTS	Defence Fixed Telecommunications Service
DG	Director General
DII	Defence Information Infrastructure

DIS	Defence Industrial Strategy
DIS 2	Defence Industrial Strategy Part 2
DLO	Defence Logistics Organisation
DLoD	Defence Lines of Development
DMB	Defence Management Board
DPA	Defence Procurement Agency
DSDA	Defence Storage and Distribution Agency
DSO	Defence and Security Organisation
DSTL	Defence Science and Technology Laboratory
DTC	Defence Technology Centre
DTI	Department of Trade and Industry
DTS	Defence Technology Strategy
DVA	Defence Values for Acquisition
EAC	Equipment Approvals Committee
ECC	Equipment Capability Customer
EDA	European Defence Agency
EFA	European Fighter Aircraft
EP	Equipment Plan
EW	Electronic Warfare
FS	Field Standard
FCS	Future Combat System (US)
FIST	Future Infantry Soldier Technology
FPA	Framework Partnering Agreement
FRES	Future Rapid Effect System
FSC	Future Surface Combatant
FSTA	Future Strategic Tanker Aircraft
GDP	Gross Domestic Product
HCDC	House of Commons Defence Committee
HMG	Her Majesty's Government
IA	Incremental Acquisition
IAB	Investment Appraisal Board
IED	Improvised Explosive Device
IFPA	Indirect Fire Precision Attack
IPR	Intellectual Property Rights
IPT	Integrated Project Team
IPTL	Integrated Project Team Leader
ISD	In-Service Date
ISTAR	Intelligence, Surveillance, Target Acquisition and Reconnaissance
IT	Information Technology
ITA	International Technology Alliance (UK/US)
ITAR	International Traffic in Arms Regulations
ITT	Invitation to Tender
JC2CIF	Joint Command and Control Integration Facility
JC2SP	Joint Command and Control Support Programme
JOCS	Joint Operational Command System
JSF	Joint Strike Fighter

LFATGW	Land Forces Anti-Tank Guided Weapon
LIMAWS	Lightweight Mobile Artillery Weapon System
LM	Loitering Munition
LoI	Letter of Intent
LSRC	Land Systems Reference Centre
LRSOM	Long-Range Stand-Off Missile
LSD(A)	Landing Ship Dock (Auxiliary)
LTPA	Long-Term Partnering Agreement
MA	Military Assistant
MARS	Military Afloat Reach and Sustainability
MASS	Munitions Acquisition – the Supply Solution
MLRS	Multiple Launch Rocket System
MOTS	Military Off-The-Shelf
MOU	Memorandum of Understanding
MRAV	Multi-Role Armoured Vehicle
MTDS	Military Training through Distributed Simulation
MTI	Moving Target Indication
NAO	National Audit Office
NATO	North Atlantic Treaty Organisation
NCW	Network Centric Warfare
NEC	Network Enabled Capability
NIH	Not Invented Here
NLAW	Next Generation Light Anti-Armour Weapon
OR	Operational Requirement
OST	Office of Science and Technology
PACE	Performance, Agility, Confidence, Efficiency (a DE&S programme)
PFI	Private Finance Initiative
PJHQ	Permanent Joint Headquarters
PPP	Public-Private Partnership
PR 08, PR 09	Planning Round 2008, 2009
PUS	Permanent Under Secretary
R&D	Research and Development
R&T	Research and Technology
RFP	Request for Proposals
RUSI	Royal United Services Institute
2nd PUS	Second Permanent Under Secretary
S&T	Science and Technology
SAR	Synthetic Aperture Radar
SAR–H	Search and Rescue Helicopter
SDR	Strategic Defence Review
SIB	Submarine Industrial Base
SIT	Science, Innovation and Technology
SME	Small- and Medium-sized Enterprises
SRO	Senior Responsible Owner
SSBN	Ship Submersible Ballistic Nuclear
SSN	Ship Submersible Nuclear

STANAG	NATO Standardisation Agreement
T&I	Trade and Investment
TCIS	Tactical Communications and Information System
TDP	Technology Demonstrator Programme
TI	Technology Insertion
TLB	Top Level Budget
TLCM	Through-Life Capability Management
TRIGAT	European Trilateral Anti-Tank programme
TRL	Technology Readiness Levels
UAV	Unmanned Air Vehicle
UCAV	Unmanned Combat Air Vehicle
UGV	Unmanned Ground Vehicle
UKCEC	UK Cooperative Engagement Capability
UKTI	UK Trade and Investment
UOR	Urgent Operational Requirement
USAF	United States Air Force
VCDS	Vice Chief of the Defence Staff
VFM	Value-for-Money
WLC	Whole Life Costs

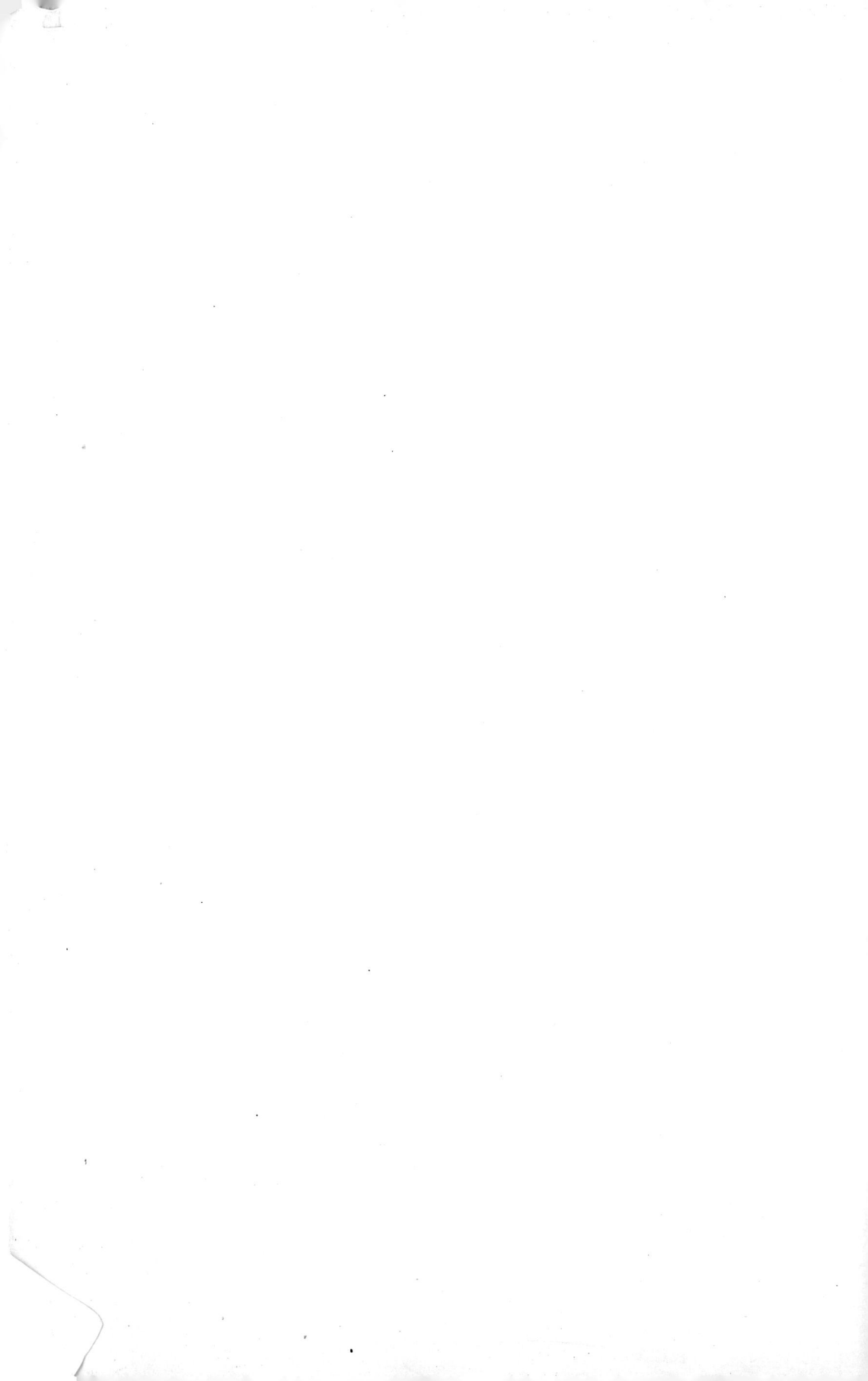